From Patriarchy to
Empowerment

Gender and Globalization
Susan S. Wadley, *Series Editor*

SYRACUSE UNIVERSITY PRESS is pleased to announce the inauguration of a new series, Gender and Globalization, with Susan S. Wadley, Ford Maxwell Professor of South Asian Studies, Maxwell School of Citizenship and Public Affairs, Syracuse University, as its editor. This series aims to create a greater awareness of the gendered nature of economic, political, social, and cultural processes associated with globalization, in particular the increasing flow of capital, labor, and information across national boundaries. Books in Gender and Globalization will examine not only formal, state-based mechanisms such as law where injustices associated with globalization processes have been addressed but also the informal, everyday means deployed by men and women to cope with, accommodate, redress, and resist the changed lifestyles and injustices associated with globalization.

All persons interested in submitting manuscripts-in-progress, book proposals for monographs, edited volumes, or text-oriented manuscripts for this series should contact Professor Wadley at sswadley@maxwell.syr.edu or Mary Selden Evans, Executive Editor, Syracuse University Press, Syracuse, N.Y. 13244 msevans@syr.edu.

From Patriarchy to
Empowerment

Women's Participation, Movements,
and Rights in the Middle East,
North Africa, and South Asia

Edited by

Valentine M. Moghadam

 SYRACUSE UNIVERSITY PRESS

To the memory of Deborah "Misty" Gerner

Copyright © 2007 by Syracuse University Press
Syracuse, New York 13244–5160

All Rights Reserved

First Edition 2007

   08 09 10 11 12   6 5 4 3 2

The paper used in this publication meets the minimum requirements
of American National Standard for Information Sciences—Permanence
of Paper for Printed Library Materials, ANSI Z39.48–1984.∞™

For a listing of books published and distributed by Syracuse University Press,
visit our Web site at syracuseuniversitypress.syr.edu.

ISBN-13: 978-0-8156-3111-8   ISBN-10: 0-8156-3111-1

Library of Congress Cataloging-in-Publication Data

From patriarchy to empowerment : women's participation, movements, and rights in the Middle East, North
Africa, and South Asia / edited by Valentine M. Moghadam. — 1st ed.
p. cm. — (Gender and globalization)
Includes bibliographical references and index.
ISBN 978-0-8156-3111-8 (pbk. : alk. paper)
1. Women—Social conditions—Middle East. 2. Women—Social conditions—Africa, North. 3. Women—
Social conditions—South Asia. 4. Women's rights—Middle East. 5. Women's rights—Africa, North. 6.
Women's rights—South Asia. 7. Women in politics—Middle East. 8. Women in politics—Africa. 9. Women in
politics—South Asia. I. Moghadam, Valentine M., 1952–
HQ1726.5.F76 2007
305.4209172'4—dc22   2007003003

Manufactured in the United States of America

Contents

vi • **Contents**

Contents • vii

PART THREE

Violence, Peace, and Women's Human Rights

Tables and Map

Preface

THIS BOOK HAS ITS ORIGINS in a stimulating and enjoyable conference in Istanbul, hosted by the Fulbright Commission, in September 2002. "Women in the Global Community" brought together a large number of Fulbright grantees and other participants to discuss a broad range of issues pertaining to women's lives. When I was asked after the conference to review the papers for possible publication, it became clear that not all papers could be included, if only because of space restrictions. What also emerged from my reading of the disparate papers was a common theme—that of women's empowerment—which I decided to make the focus of the volume. Most of the papers in the present volume were initially prepared for the Istanbul conference, although two were commissioned afterward. Many thanks go to Renee Taft, now retired from the Fulbright Commission, whose dedication to women's rights saw through a successful conference and plans for an edited volume. I am also grateful to the two anonymous reviewers for their very helpful comments, and to Mary Selden Evans of Syracuse University Press for her consistent support.

This book has been several years in the making, and much has transpired since then, not least war and devastation in Iraq and Lebanon, democratic elections in Palestine that brought Hamas to power, and India's emergence as a technological center. The theme of the book remains as pertinent as ever, and I trust that readers will agree that each chapter stands on its own while also being well integrated and tied to the theme of women's empowerment in the Middle East, North Africa, and South Asia. But one change pertains to the author of the second chapter, a well-known political scientist of the Middle East and a wonderful human being. It is to the memory of Deborah "Misty" Gerner that this book is dedicated.

Contributors

Evelyne Accad was born in Beirut, Lebanon, and is a writer, singer and composer, poet, and professor of comparative literature, Francophone and Arabophone literature, African studies, and feminist studies at the University of Illinois and at the Lebanese American University in Beirut. The author of many studies and novels in both French and English, she has received several prizes.

Abla Amawi is the Capacity 2015 regional coordinator for Arab states and the Capacity development adviser at the United Nations Development Programme in Beirut. Her doctoral research at Georgetown University focused on state and class formation in Jordan. She has served as a visiting assistant professor at the Center for Contemporary Arab Studies at Georgetown University, Randolph-Macon College, and the Applied Science University in Jordan. She has published several books and articles on issues of gender, democratization, civil society, and political economy.

M. Laetitia Cairoli is an adjunct professor of anthropology at Montclair State University.

Ziva Flamhaft teaches in the Department of Political Science of Queens College, City University of New York. Her work focuses on the effects of war and its aftermath on women and on the connection between personal narratives and political activism.

Deborah J. Gerner was associate professor of political science at the University of Kansas at Lawrence and the author of many studies on the Middle East.

Sarah E. Gilman obtained her M.A. in international studies from the University of Oregon in 2000. At present, she is a doctoral candidate in the Department of Sociology at the University of California at Berkeley, where she is researching American

Christianity in relation to Israel and U.S. foreign policy in the Middle East as it informs contemporary questions of nation, state, and religion.

Ayşe Gündüz-Hoşgör is an associate professor in the Department of Sociology at the Middle East Technical University in Ankara, Turkey. She has worked in the areas of social change, sociology of development, and social stratification by gender and ethnicity. She has conducted research on rural development, women's education and employment, ethnic women's position in society, and child labor.

Dana Crowley Jack is a professor of interdisciplinary studies at Fairhaven College, Western Washington University, teaching and conducting studies in women's psychology, specifically on depression, anger, and aggression. Her many publications include *Moral Vision and Professional Decisions* (1989), *Silencing the Self: Women and Depression* (1992), and *Behind the Mask: Destruction and Creativity in Women's Aggression* (1999). In 2001, as a Fulbright Senior Scholar, she taught in Nepal at Tribhuvan University's women's studies graduate program and conducted research on gender and depression at psychiatric outpatient clinics.

Lilia Labidi teaches psychology and women's studies at the University of Tunis. In 2001–2002 she was a public policy fellow in the Middle East Program at the Woodrow Wilson International Center for Scholars in Washington, D.C.

Carol Malt, Ph.D., is an independent scholar. A former museum director and curator, she is the recipient of two Senior Scholar Fulbrights and the author of the historical biography *The Free Woman* (2002), *Museums of Jordan* (2002), *Women's Voices in Middle East Museums: Case Studies in Jordan* (2005), and many journal articles and papers. She teaches a course on women in the Muslim world at the University of West Florida.

Ibrahim al-Marashi completed his Ph.D. at the University of Oxford, and his thesis dealt with the Iraqi invasion of Kuwait. He lectures at the International Relations Department at Koç University in Istanbul, Turkey, and is also a visiting fellow in the Program for Global Communication Studies at the University of Pennsylvania's Annenberg School of Communication, conducting research on new Iraqi news and entertainment media.

Valentine M. Moghadam is a professor of sociology and women's studies and director of the women's studies program at Purdue University. During 2004–2006 she was heading research on women and gender in the Social and Human Sciences Sector of UNESCO. She is the author of *Women, Work, and Economic Reform in the Middle East and North Africa* (1998), *Modernizing Women: Gender and Social Change in the Middle East* (2nd ed., 2003), and *Globalizing Women: Transnational Feminist Networks* (2005). This book is her seventh edited volume.

Nilufer Narli is a professor of political sociology and the dean in the Faculty of Communications at Kadir Has University in Istanbul. Her books and articles on Islamist movements and women include *Unveiling the Fundamentalist Woman: A Case Study of Malay Undergraduates* (1991) and "The Rise of the Islamist Movement in Turkey," *MERIA Journal* (Sept. 1999).

Senzil Nawid is an independent scholar and research associate at the University of Arizona. She is the author of *Religious Response to Social Change in Afghanistan: King Aman-Allah and the Afghan Ulama, 1919–1929* (1999).

Sarab Abu-Rabia Queder, the first Bedouin woman from the Negev region to receive a Ph.D., obtained her doctorate in education from Ben Gurion University in 2006. A mother of two boys, she is currently a postdoctoral fellow at the Lafer Center for Gender Studies at Hebrew University in Jerusalem. Her fields of research are Palestinian women's feminism and activism in Israel, identity, higher education, narrative study, and minority relations in Israel.

Poonam Saxena is a professor in the Faculty of Law at the University of Delhi in India. A specialist in women and law, clinical legal education, family law, and succession, she is the author of five books: three volumes on Halsbury's laws of India, *Trusts and Charities* (2000); *Property and Easements* (2002); *Family Law Lectures: Family Law II* (2004); *Property Law* (2006); and *Family Law* (in press). She has written some fifty articles that have been published in legal journals and books. She is the recipient of a Senior Fulbright Fellowship and a Shastri Indo Canadian Fellowship.

Lucie Senftova is a research associate at the International Institute for Management Development in Lausanne, Switzerland, where she undertakes research on gender differences and similarities in management and leadership. Previously, she worked on gender equality and development issues at UNESCO, OECD, and the World Bank.

Ahmad Shamshad is a senior researcher at the Department of Political Science at Aligarh Muslim University in Aligarh, Uttar Pradesh, India. He is the author of many articles on development, nongovernmental organizations, and governance that have appeared in the *Indian Journal of Public Administration, Kurukshetra,* and the *Indian Journal of Politics.*

Loubna H. Skalli teaches in the School of International Service at American University in Washington, D.C. She is the coauthor of *Vulture Culture: The Politics and Pedagogy of Talk Shows* (2005) and the author of *Through a Local Prism: Gender, Globalization and Identity in Moroccan Women's Magazines* (2006). Her fields of research are gender, communications, and development.

Jeroen Smits is a senior researcher in the Department of Economics of Radboud University at Nijmegen in the Netherlands. His major research interests are inequality, development, social cohesion, and data enrichment. He has published works on intermarriage, gender and language issues, health inequality, the relationship between social and geographic mobility, labor market issues, and educational participation.

Mark van Ommeren worked from 1996 to 2002 for the Transcultural Psychosocial Organization on culture-informed research and training for survivors of violence. His doctorate from Vrije Universiteit in Amsterdam covered psychiatric epidemiology among Bhutanese refugees in Nepal. At present, he works for the Department of Mental Health and Substance Abuse at the World Health Organization in Geneva, where he is the focal point for mental health in emergencies.

From Patriarchy to
Empowerment

1 Women's Empowerment

An Introduction and Overview

VALENTINE M. MOGHADAM

THE MIDDLE EAST, North Africa, and South Asia are home to a huge proportion of the world's population, are part of what has been called the "patriarchal belt," and are also sites of political conflicts, cultural battles, and social change. The overlong Israeli-Palestinian conflict, tensions along the India-Pakistan border and in Sri Lanka, the continuing influence of Islamist movements, and conflict and reconstruction in Afghanistan and Iraq are but some of the political and military challenges facing the regions. And for at least a generation, the regions have been immersed in cultural conflicts between modernizers and traditionalists, feminists and fundamentalists, and those individuals who speak the language of citizenship, equality, and rights versus those who engage in the politics of identity, difference, and "authenticity." These issues have been the subject of several bodies of scholarly literature, numerous policy reports, and large numbers of international conferences.[1]

At the same time, the Middle East, North Africa, and South Asia have seen the emergence of vibrant women's movements that—along with human rights organizations—are boldly confronting the political sclerosis, cultural rigidities, and patriarchal gender relations found in many of the countries. They are questioning the status quo, forming alliances, calling for democratization, and insisting on women's full participation in economic development, the political process, and conflict resolution. The 1995 Beijing Conference launched the global call for women's empowerment at the economic, political, cultural, and personal levels, but even before then,

---

1. The demographer John Caldwell (1982) refers to the Middle East, North Africa, South Asia, and East Asia as "the patriarchal belt." See also Kandiyoti 1988, 1992. On South Asia, see Agarwal 1988. On gender and change processes, see Moghadam 2003. On feminisms, fundamentalisms, and communalisms, see Moghadam 1994.

women in the Middle East, North Africa, and South Asia had formed their own organizations, joined transnational networks, lobbied their governments, and worked with other civil society groups.[2] It is true that, as in most countries around the world, activist women come largely from the educated middle class or from elite families. But their activities and approaches have positive ramifications for peace, democratization, and equality. If the Middle East, North Africa, and South Asia are known for cultural conservatism and—apart from India—authoritarian polities, the women's movements and the feminist research that they have engendered hold the promise of unprejudiced analysis, nonviolent practice, bridge building, cultural innovation, and a democratic politics. For women, this is a time of transition from patriarchy to empowerment. For the broader societies, women's empowerment accelerates the transition to modernity, democracy, and social justice.

Empowering Women in an Era of Globalization

In the Middle East, North Africa, and South Asia, women find themselves at the nexus of patriarchy and globalization. Patriarchal social structures and gender relations have long characterized the regions, with dire implications for women's status and life chances, but globalization seems to be offering new constraints as well as enormous opportunities. Globalization is a complex economic, political, cultural, and geographic process in which the mobility of capital, organizations, ideas, discourses, and peoples has taken on an increasingly global or transnational form. Much has been written about globalization from different disciplinary and political vantage points, but it can be argued that among its defining features are the expansion of neoliberal economic policies, the power of institutions of global governance, the emergence of various resistance movements such as fundamentalism and communalism, and the growing influence of nongovernmental civil society organizations such as women's organizations. As such, globalization has given rise to contradictory tendencies and trends, including hegemonic discourses of neoliberal capitalism, backlash discourses of fundamentalists and communalists, and counterhegemonic discourses of women's rights. The latter have been promoted by women's movements, the UN Decade for Women, and feminist research and are inscribed in such international conventions as the UN's 1979 Convention on the Elimination of All Forms of Discrimination Against Women; the Cairo Declaration of 1994, which produced an agenda for women's reproductive health and rights; and

2. See Basu 1995; Moghadam 2005.

the Beijing Declaration and Platform for Action of 1995, which presented a broad agenda for women's rights and participation.

The Beijing Platform for Action is a call for action to realize women's human rights and to empower women economically, politically, and culturally.[3] Many of the issues covered in this book—political participation, educational attainment, health, employment and economic resources, conflict and peace, women and the media—fall within the purview of the Platform for Action's twelve critical areas of concern. Around the world, activists and advocates are lobbying governments, building consensus within civil society, and enlisting international support for the realization of the Platform for Action's call for women's empowerment. The 1995 conference and the platform gave rise to research programs, new policies, and instruments to measure women's empowerment, such as the UNDP's Gender and Development Index (GDI) and the Gender Empowerment Measure (GEM).[4] Appropriate measures include women's share of parliamentary seats and governmental positions; access to economic decision making via the female share of managerial, administrative, and professional positions; and women's share of earned income or per capita gross domestic product. The United Nations produced a widely cited report, *The World's Women, 1995: Trends and Statistics*, which was placed on the Internet after its second (2000) edition, and is updated every two years. More recently, progress toward the UN's Millennium Development Goals—a series of eight goals agreed to by the international community in 2000, one of which aims to promote gender equality and bring about women's empowerment—is being assessed through elaborate quantitative measures.[5]

Another framework for the measurement of women's empowerment has been developed at UNESCO. Here, women's empowerment is defined as a multidimensional process of achieving basic capabilities, legal rights, and participation in key social, economic, political, and cultural domains, and the authors offer a set of

---

3. See United Nations 1996.

4. The GDI corrects the Human Development Index for gender inequalities and measures life expectancy; literacy; combined enrollments at the first, second, and tertiary levels; and earned income. The GEM is even more specific and ranks countries by women's access to political power and economic resources through measures such as the female share of parliamentary seats, women's share of managerial and administrative jobs, the female share of professional and technical workers, and women's per capita gross domestic product. See various issues of the UNDP's *Human Development Report* since 1995.

5. See http://www.un.org/millenniumgoals/.

forty-four indicators for its measurement.[6] This framework and the other gender indicators discussed above allow researchers to obtain a useful picture of women's economic and political empowerment at the country level and comparatively. At the same time, more qualitative measures provide a deeper and more comprehensive portrayal. In this respect, a framework developed by sociologist Janet Giele in the 1970s remains pertinent, with some minor adjustments (1977).[7] Women's empowerment may be captured by addressing the following questions:

• Political expression: What rights do women possess, formally and otherwise? Can they own property in their own right? Can they form independent organizations? Can they express any dissatisfaction within their own political and social movements? *How are they involved in the political process?*

• Work and mobility: How do women fare in the formal labor force? How mobile are they, how well are they paid, how are their jobs ranked, and what leisure do they get? *What policies exist to enable women to balance work and family?*

• Family—formation, duration, and size: What is the age of marriage? Do women choose their own partners? Can they divorce them? What is the status of single women and widows? Do women have freedom of movement? *Do family laws empower or disempower women?*

• Education: What access do women have, how much can they attain, and is the curriculum the same for them as for men? *Are separate girls' schools adequately resourced?*

• Health and sexual control: What is women's mortality, to what particular illnesses and stresses (physical and mental) are they exposed, and what control do they have over their own fertility? *What laws exist to prevent or punish violence against women?*

• Cultural expression: What images of women and their "place" are prevalent, and how far do these reflect or determine reality? *What can women do in the cultural field?*

These questions are a useful way of specifying and delineating changes and trends in women's social roles in the economy, the polity, and the cultural sphere and of assessing the strengths and weaknesses of women's positions and actions. It

6. See Moghadam and Senftova 2005. See the Appendix for data on women's participation and rights across domains in the countries covered in this book.

7. This framework was used by Moghadam in the first and second editions (1993, 2003) of her book *Modernizing Women: Gender and Social Change in the Middle East.* The sentences in italics are Moghadam's additions to Giele's framework.

provides universal measures of women's status and empowerment that may be applied across cultures, religions, and political systems. And it draws attention to women as actors.

The chapters in this book address some of the key issues taken up at the Beijing conference from different disciplinary perspectives, with a focus on women's participation and rights in the domains of politics, economics, and culture. At the normative level, this book is oriented toward the achievement of women's empowerment and women's enjoyment of human rights.

Overview of the Book

This book examines the ways that women are situated in and responding to various economic, political, and cultural processes in the Middle East, North Africa, and South Asia. It considers the contributions that women and feminist movements are making to cultural and political change, including the call for women's empowerment. Chapters provide historical and contemporary perspectives on women's engagement with state building, nationalist movements, and political processes; their involvement in economic activities and strategies to empower women economically; the ways that women are interrogating and redefining cultural landscapes through literature, filmmaking, and the use of new computer technologies; the problems and prospects of women's human rights to health, education, and violence-free home life; and women's responses to war, occupation, and conflict.

Following this Introduction, Part One consists of chapters examining women's political expression, participation, and rights in Palestine, Jordan, Afghanistan, and Turkey. Deborah Gerner offers an in-depth look at Palestinian women's consistent involvement in the national liberation struggle, as mothers, teachers, social workers, political activists—especially in the first Intifada. But Gerner also describes their exclusion from positions of political power and decision making, and their vulnerability after the weakening of the Left and rise of Islamist forces afterward, as in the *hijab* campaign of 1988–1989. In the face of Islamist reaction and tokenism or sheer indifference by the Palestine Authority, there were valiant attempts by activist women to assert themselves, including the formation of new women's organizations calling for political emancipation and formal equality of women in employment and education. As noted by Palestinian feminist Eileen Kuttab, the women's organizations of the 1970s and 1980s "did not necessarily address deeper social and cultural issues explicitly," but "the groups did structure themselves in ways that emphasized democracy, gender, and class concerns" (1993, 69, 85). In the 1990s, women's organizations assumed a more feminist stance—as they did elsewhere—and issues of women's rights were approached directly and audaciously. More recently, however, the violence of the second Intifada and Israeli military actions compelled Palestinian feminists to put a brake on their activities.

In the context of liberalization in Jordan, women began to mobilize themselves politically, and by the 1997 elections they emerged as important candidates, voters, and constituents. Only the Communist Party list included women; other women candidates ran as independents, and none of the women candidates won. But Abla Amawi examines the 1997 elections as a turning point in women's political expression, as well as an opportunity to explore the serious obstacles to women's candidacy and their political participation, which she notes are rooted in Jordan's social structure: the primacy of the tribe or clan, the patriarchal family, and the patriarchal state, along with Jordan's legal frames that confer second-class citizenship on women. In such a context, women compete in a male-dominated political culture that has long excluded them from the political process.

The salience of patriarchal structures is likewise discussed in the case of Afghanistan, where Senzil Nawid shows how women were long excluded from any meaningful decision making, including personal choices, in the male-dominated Afghan culture. Beginning in the early part of the twentieth century, reforms were attempted to improve the status of women, but they largely failed in the face of resistance on the part of the entrenched rural, religious, and landowning forces. The most audacious reforms—and the only instance of progress made in women's political participation—came about during the Democratic Republic of Afghanistan (1979–1992). In her analysis of this period, Nawid argues that the reforms were too bold and culturally audacious, while the ruling party's association with the Soviet Union compromised its legitimacy. When the political experiment failed, it was women who suffered more than any other social group, first under the Mujahideen and later under the Taliban.

Since the Kemalist reforms of the 1920s, Turkey has been a secular republic, with political parties and regular elections punctuated by military coups, the most recent of which occurred in 1980. Turkish women were given the right to vote in 1934 and almost immediately found themselves elected to parliament, but over the decades their political participation and representation declined. Feminism, however, expanded in Turkey during the 1980s, and by the 1990s women had become important political actors. A new development was political activity on the part of believing women who questioned strict secularism (Islamic women) and of Islamist women who were associated with the emerging Islamic political parties. Nilufer

Narli's careful examination of the political participation of Muslim women shows that class continues to be salient, that party ideology determines women's participation, and that parties are responsive to external and global pressures—such as Turkey's desire to join the European Union—as well as pressures from women.

How do women, especially feminists and women political actors, relate to the state when it is patriarchal or authoritarian? Many feminists accept the state and the parameters that it sets, engaging with state agencies and seeking to influence the direction of change through participation in the political process. Others prefer to maintain a distance in order not to compromise their autonomy and critical perspectives, while also applauding legal reforms. An example of such a stance is that of Tunisia's Association des Femmes Démocrates, described by Sarah Gilman as among the country's "autonomous women's groups." Like other independent civil society groups, Femmes Démocrates have faced harassment from the authorities, and this interference may have strengthened their resolve to maintain a critical distance. Gilman shows, however, that while avoiding co-optation, they have also sought to avoid the other pitfall of irrelevance. Hence, they have joined state initiatives that aim to improve women's legal status or their working conditions. Gilman also shows how Femmes Démocrates and other Tunisian feminist groups link up to regional and transnational women's networks.

Moroccan and Tunisian feminists—along with Algerian feminists—have long cooperated in building their movements and in pushing for reform of family laws, but a difference seen in recent years has been the feminist-state alliance in Morocco. The focus of Loubna Skalli's chapter on Morocco is how women use the new communication technologies to network across borders, raise awareness, and empower themselves. In the context of political liberalization in Morocco, feminist organizations began to use the Internet strategically for lobbying, advocacy, and research on women's empowerment and to further the cause of democratization. This strategy—which was combined with coalition building and an effective discursive campaign—proved successful when, following a ten-year campaign, the country's family law was reformed in 2003–2004.

We then turn to women's participation and rights across economic, social, and cultural domains. Women and work issues have been the subject of cultural debates in many parts of the Middle East, North Africa, and South Asia, but feminists have long argued that economic independence is a sine qua non for women's empowerment. Hence, they have promoted employment opportunities for women and changes in laws that restrict women's property ownership. This theme is the subject of Ahmad Shamshad's chapter on women's empowerment in India. In describing the evolution of government policy on women and development in India, he draws attention to the discursive shift from welfare to empowerment but also highlights the gap between government rhetoric and the realities that so many women face. The focus of his chapter is the need for women's economic empowerment, whether through paid employment or entrepreneurship, but he stresses the connection with political will as well as women's own political empowerment.

Notwithstanding consensus on the importance of employment opportunities for women, research has shown that women's positions are almost universally subordinate in formal labor markets, inasmuch as they face discrimination, harassment, and concentration in low-wage and low-status work. The much vaunted "feminization of labor" is as much a function of "flexibilization" in an era of globalization as it is of women's aspirations and their economic empowerment.[8] In the Middle East and North Africa, where the female labor supply has been limited compared to other regions, some governments have sought to promote women's employment, especially in the new export-oriented manufacturing enterprises. Such is the background to Laetitia Cairoli's chapter on women workers in Fez, Morocco. In addition to describing working conditions, she offers a fascinating perspective on the sociodemographics and cultural politics of the female labor force in Fez. The different meanings attached to "working daughters" and "working wives," the relative autonomy of unmarried women workers versus married women workers, and control over the income earned are among the issues analyzed.

If factory work in Fez does not offer much by way of autonomy or empowerment, other types of employment offer status and meaning, as well as better wages and conditions. Carol Malt's study of women's employment in the museum sector in Jordan elucidates the connections between employment and empowerment for middle-class women. Malt was surprised to discover that throughout the Middle East, museums tend to be staffed in large numbers by women, although not necessarily at the highest levels of management. She concludes that in conservative societies like Jordan, working in a museum is considered culturally appropriate employment for professional women with families. Some of the women she interviewed shared this conservative view, whereas others regarded their time in the museums as a springboard for more ambitious business projects.

Both Cairoli and Malt note that women's power tends to correlate with age. In patriarchal societies, younger women are often under more constraints than are

8. See Standing 1989.

older married women and especially women who are past their reproductive years. The question of the sexual control of young women and their lack of mobility has been the subject of much discussion in several bodies of literature, including feminist and anthropological. Some authors have also argued that rural migration to urban areas does not necessarily result in rural women's empowerment, as it could result in "housewife-ization," or imposed domesticity, as well as tighter controls over girls' dress and behavior. But in their chapter on regional differences in the status of rural women in Turkey, Ayse Gündüz-Hosgör and Jeroen Smits argue that although living in a town may result in more restrictions on younger women, it may also be an advantage because of the educational facilities available in towns and the opportunities to become economically independent through employment.

Along with women's employment, education is regarded as the key to women's empowerment. Though it is a right of citizenship, education is not always extended to all women. In many parts of the Middle East, North Africa, and South Asia, women's illiteracy rates have been very high, and the literacy and educational attainment gaps between men and women have been very wide. It has been a problem not only for adult women but also for young girls, especially in the poorer countries of the regions. Girls have been denied education partly owing to lack of schools or transportation for girls in poorer areas and partly owing to family controls over daughters. Where marriage is seen as the destiny of girls, schooling is not encouraged or girls' dropout rates are high. Dropout rates may also be a function of cultural contradictions, which Sarab Abu-Rabia Queder highlights in her chapter on the factors behind the very high dropout rates of Bedouin girls in Israel. Caught between the aggressive modernization of the Israeli state and the patriarchal controls of their own community, Bedouin girls rarely complete high school. How can girls be helped to escape this untenable situation and raise educational attainment rates, thereby improving Bedouin girls' chances of autonomous and empowered lives? Abu-Rabia Queder criticizes what she sees as colonialist and patronizing approaches to the problem and calls for programs that draw on the cultural resources of the Bedouin while also increasing financial resources to the community.

Cultural change—and women's contributions to it—is addressed in a number of the chapters, including those by Skalli and Malt. Another contribution, by Ibrahim al-Marashi, shows how Iranian women participate in a key cultural sector: the movie industry. In the second half of the 1990s, Iranian cinema began to receive international acclaim. Censorship was always a feature of Iranian cultural production, and in prerevolutionary days writers, filmmakers, and others in the arts faced imprisonment or worse for approaching sensitive political matters. After the revolution, censorship remained in force, although now it extended to sensitive issues pertaining to culture, religion, morality, and sexual interaction. Filmmakers had to make do with prohibitions against close-ups of women's faces, scenes of unveiled women (even in their homes, where normally Iranian women do not cover), or scenes of male-female interaction, not to mention intimacy. Once again, society's capacity for creativity and cultural innovation revealed itself, in terms of both subject matter and cinematography. After a period of filmmaking in which small children and universal themes prevailed, films began to focus on the status of women in Iranian society and in this way mirrored the broader societal debates in Iran concerning the legal status and social position of women in the Islamic republic and before its laws. In the new Iranian cinema, women also began to take their place behind the camera, and a generation of feminist filmmaking has emerged, which is the topic of al-Marashi's chapter. The "question of women"—of their subordinate status and of the need for expanded rights, participation, and empowerment—remains a matter of public debate in parliament, the popular press, the feminist press, and the new Iranian cinema.

Human rights in the family, the elimination of violence, and women's contributions to peace are the foci of Part Three. The chapters show how patriarchy operates in the family, in public institutions, and at the level of macropolitics. Patriarchal gender relations are at the center of the chapters on women's depression in Nepal, the problem of dowry deaths in India, and Muslim family laws in Egypt and Tunisia. Dana Jack and Mark van Ommeren discuss the serious physical and health problems, including domestic violence and depression, experienced by many Nepalese women, the result of patriarchal gender relations, extreme poverty, and limited state interventions. Socialization patterns are such that women engage in "silencing the self," as Jack calls the internalization of gender subordination. But her and van Ommeren's study, facilitated by Nepalese physicians and social workers, offered women an opportunity for self-expression. Given the government's preoccupation with fighting an insurgency, Nepalese women's health and well-being seem to be addressed only by nongovernmental organizations and women's empowerment programs.

In India, the state is nominally committed to women's rights and, in that connection, has formally banned the dowry. But the practice continues throughout the country and across castes and social classes; dowry demands are made with impunity, and young wives are made to suffer the consequences of what in-laws consider to be insufficient dowries. Legal advocate and scholar Poonam Saxena casts a highly critical perspective on "the menace of dowry" and highlights inadequate and at time outrageous approaches by parliamentarians and the courts. She argues that raising public awareness and tight enforcement of antidowry laws, including stricter punishments for those individuals who carry out harassment, blackmail, and physical harm in connection with dowry demands, will serve to empower young wives and guarantee women's human rights.

Legal reform toward women's human rights is addressed in Lilia Labidi's chapter. As seen in Janet Giele's framework, women's status within the family is a critical indicator of empowerment. Around the world, many women still cannot choose their own partners or divorce them or leave the home without permission. In a patriarchal context, a woman moves from the control of her father to the control of her husband, and family laws often codify such forms of guardianship. Women also lack equal rights of child custody and of inheritance. Western countries have seen the transformation of family laws from patriarchal to egalitarian, and the reform of family law is the focus of feminist activism in the Middle East and North Africa.[9] Labidi examines three Islamic practices with implications for marriage and the family and for the status of women: *al-ijbar* (the father's capacity to oblige his daughter to marry and thus to attain adult status), *mahr* (the sum given to the bride by the groom, which becomes her personal property), and *diya* (compensation for murder as a substitute for the law of private vengeance). These practices are defended by some and criticized by others; in her analysis of debates and reformulations surrounding these practices in Egypt and Tunisia, Labidi shows the capacity of these societies for cultural innovation and social change.

Although patriarchy may persist, it has a formidable opponent in feminist literature. Evelyne Accad shows how women, gender, and sexuality have been prominent themes in Lebanese literature, especially the genre known as war novels, produced during and after the long Lebanese civil war (1975–1990). Feminist scholarship has drawn attention to the highly gendered nature of conflict, to the way that the language and conduct of war are infused with what R. W. Connell (1987, 1995) has called "hegemonic masculinity," and to the association of vulnerability with femininity. The conflicts in Afghanistan in the 1980s and 1990s, where women were pawns in masculine power struggles, are examples.[10] Comparing and contrasting the themes in women's war novels and men's war novels, Accad counterposes the nonviolence of feminism to the violence of patriarchy and of male-directed wars.

9. See Glendon 1977, 1989. For an examination of Muslim family laws, see An-Naim 2002. On women's citizenship rights, see contributions in Joseph 2000.

10. See Moghadam 2002.

Feminism is at its core a nonviolent movement for women's rights and for broader transformations, and modern history has been replete with examples of women's peace movements, organizations, and initiatives. We know that not all women are nonviolent or even espouse nonviolent alternatives, but women have been almost invariably key actors in peace movements. Context, of course, matters, and Ziva Flamhaft's chapter on war and women's bereavement among Israelis and Palestinians is sensitive to the ways that many women can become mired in untenable circumstances and find solidarity across conflict zones a luxury. As Flamhaft notes, "It is not their nurturing nature that motivates women to seek peace but their rejection of their social conditioning, on the one hand, and, on the other, their demand for accountability and justice." And as Carol Gilligan has maintained, women speak "in a different voice."[11] In many conflict situations, women are given no voice at all, let alone representation during mediation, negotiations, and postconflict reconstruction and governance. These are the reasons that UN Security Council Resolution (SCR) 1325 of October 2000 is so important: it seeks to provide women with voice and representation, as well as protection from violence during conflict. The following are the key points of SCR 1325:

- ensuring protection of and respect for human rights of women and girls
- protecting women and girls from gender-based violence
- supporting women's grassroots organizations in their peace initiatives
- integrating a gender perspective into peacekeeping missions
- appointing more women as special representatives and envoys of the secretary-general
- involving women as participants in peace negotiations and agreements
- integrating a gender perspective into disarmament, demobilization, and reintegration of former combatants
- increasing the representation of women at all decision-making levels.[12]

As I argue in my chapter on Afghanistan, Iraq, and Palestine, this resolution is yet to be implemented in all conflict situations. But if women are to be empowered,

11. See Gilligan 1982.

12. See http://www.un.org/docs/scres/2000/sc2000/htm. Though SCR 1325 has not been implemented in all conflict situations, it has much potential as international law. Women's organizations have devoted many seminars and working papers to issues of its implementation, efficacy, and so on. Likewise, the European Parliament passed a resolution that no peace negotiations should be held without the presence of a minimum of 40 percent (critical mass) of the underrepresented sex.

and the world transformed, the resolution will have to be taken seriously by governments and international organizations. And in the Middle East, North Africa, and South Asia, empowering women to speak, to act, and to participate is the surest way out of patriarchy and conflict and toward equality and peace.

PART ONE

Political Processes and Women's Participation

2 Mobilizing Women for Nationalist Agendas

Palestinian Women, Civil Society, and the State-Building Process

DEBORAH J. GERNER

PALESTINIAN WOMEN have a long history of participation in the struggle for national liberation, both in the "traditional" female arenas and on the front lines. More recently, they have been deeply involved in the vibrant Palestinian civil society, promoting democracy and a respect for diverse views, and in nongovernmental organizations concerned with the state-building process.[1] Yet women have not been included in formal power structures to any significant extent. Neither the "inner circle" of the Palestinian Authority (PA) nor the core of the various opposition movements has included women. Women hold few high positions within government, and, with several notable exceptions, they appear not to have significant influence on political decision making, either in general or with respect to issues of gender specifically. There are a number of explanations for this situation. Here I mention just three interrelated factors, each of which is important in the analysis that follows.

---

1. My use of the term *civil society* follows the sense of Egyptian sociologist Saad Eddin Ibrahim: "While there are a variety of ways of defining [the concept of civil society], they all revolve around maximizing volitional, organized, collective participation in the public space between individuals and the state. In its institutional form, 'civil society' is composed of non-state actors or nongovernmental organizations (NGOs), including political parties, trade unions, professional associations, community development associations, and other interest groups. Normatively, 'civil society' implies values and behavioral codes of tolerating—if not accepting—others and a tacit or explicit commitment to the peaceful management of differences among individuals and collectivities sharing the same 'public space'—that is, the polity" (1998, 29).

First, despite the wide array of institutions of civil society that developed during the years of occupation and a significant amount of freely expressed opposition opinion, there is little in the way of *institutionalized* government responsiveness to those critical perspectives. Indeed, in the decade after the 1993 Oslo Agreements, Palestinian Authority governance became more rather than less authoritarian, leading Ziad Abu Amr to describe the Palestinians as having a "fragmented" democratic system that combines sociopolitical pluralism with "underdeveloped patterns of democratic thought and practice" (1994, cited in Brynen 1998). This situation restricts the ability of women (and men) to affect choices made by the top leadership.

A second issue is the often complex relationship between nationalism and feminism. The shared ideology that underlies nationalism serves as the glue holding otherwise disparate peoples together and can be an extremely powerful and positive influence for change. It can also, however, be used to promote a particularistic conception of what issues are considered significant for the nation to address (for example, state power or sovereignty), which items are defined as subordinate and thus lower on the agenda (such as discrimination against women), who gets to make these judgments, and what roles men and women are expected to play. In the Palestinian context, political life is severely constrained by the legacy and present reality of the Israeli occupation. In this environment, gender concerns and other potentially transformative issues have consistently been shunted to the side as less critical than the nationalist agenda, with its emphasis on territory, self-government, and state building. (For male progressives, gender is also often ranked as less important than the class struggle.)

Although this phenomenon has been seen in other national movements as well, it is by no means inevitable.[2] Throughout the third world, there have been occasions when nationalism and feminism had common objectives and reinforced each other so that the national struggle also served as an opportunity for societal reforms (Jayawardena 1986; see also Berkovitch and Moghadam 1999). In the discourse of nationalism presented by male narrators, women are frequently identified as society's "maintainers and reproducers of 'national soldiers, national heroes and manpower.'" Clearly, as Nahla Abdo points out, nationalism is "a double-edged weapon: [it can serve either] as a mechanism of domination and oppression . . . [or] as a potential force for gender-social liberation" (1994, 150). Thus, in the

2. See, for example, Augustin 1993; Kandiyoti 1991; Moghadam 2003; Ranchod-Nilsson and Tétreault 2000; Rubenberg 2001; Sabbagh 1998; Sharoni 1995.

discussion that follows, it is worth keeping in mind that positive social change with respect to gender and the Palestinian nationalist struggle may not go hand in hand.

Religious beliefs provide a further complication. The Palestinian national movement has long pursued a secular ideology, yet in the past decade it has come under strong pressure from those endorsing forms of political Islam that preclude significant female engagement in the formal political life of the state. There is widespread debate about what, exactly, Islam has to say about female participation in political activity, with the mainstream view generally supportive of such involvement, albeit for a variety of reasons, not all of which indicate acceptance of women actually *influencing* political agendas rather than simply acting in support of "the state." For instance, Mary Elaine Hegland points out that "all recent Islamist movements have called upon women to play crucial roles" and that "women are central to the Islamic agenda" (1999, 183). At the same time, some Islamists attempt to control women's activities so that they will fulfill *only* the roles designed for them. It is not clear that this balancing act (women as involved yet politically constrained and lacking full emancipation) can be sustained indefinitely.

This chapter has several goals. I first review briefly the evolution of Palestinian women's involvement in the national struggle in order to make three points. First, although their activities received little attention, at least in Western academic circles, Palestinian women were politically engaged long before the first intifada. Second, at least until the 1980s, the Palestinian women's movement was predominantly secular, upper class in its leaders and membership, and clearly linked with the national struggle. Third, the historic emphasis on resisting the Israeli occupation, combined with a reluctance to address patriarchal structures directly, reinforced existing gender constraints in ways that continue to influence women's political roles today. I then describe the formal and informal political participation of Palestinian women in the 1990s and the beginning of the twenty-first century to understand how, if at all, the nascent state structures have attempted to incorporate or co-opt women into the state-building process and what structural and practical impediments hinder greater involvement of women. In short, I want to explore what Tami Amanda Jacoby describes as "the distinct constraints and opportunities of feminisms that are implicated in national liberation struggle, religious contestation, and conditions of acute international conflict" (1999, 511). Throughout the chapter, my concern is primarily with women in the Occupied Territories rather than with Palestinian women living in Israel or in exile.

Women's Early Political Activity

As is true in many societies that have not yet gained independence, Palestinian women mobilized initially as part of the broader national struggle, with women often acting on behalf of this cause in ways that were consonant with their traditional responsibilities as wives, mothers, daughters, and sisters. At the same time, some women challenged these roles and took on tasks that were quite similar to those performed by male activists.

Responses to Zionism and al-Nakba

Most official histories marginalize the activities of women during the years prior to the first intifada (1987–1993). It seems likely that the pressures of the occupation and the desire for a set of unifying nationalist stories led to the construction of a single dominant historical narrative, an official version of Palestinian political and military resistance in which women's grassroots activities were virtually ignored. Yet if one looks at the historical record, there are abundant references to women's engagement in the national struggle.[3]

For instance, few authors mention Palestinian women's opposition to the earliest Zionist settlement activities. There is evidence, however, that some rural women—acting individually rather than as part of a group—responded violently to the increasing presence of the settlers as early as the 1880s, that urban women joined in demonstrations against the 1917 Balfour Declaration, and that in 1920 a group of women met with the British high commissioner to argue against British policy in Palestine. The development of women's charitable organizations began early in the twentieth century, with the establishment in 1910 of the Orthodox Ladies Society in Jaffa and the Arab Ladies Society in Jerusalem in 1919. In contrast, the Palestinian Women's Union, founded in Jerusalem in 1921, was more political. Throughout the 1920s and 1930s, women—mostly urban, upper class, well educated, and from activist families—opposed both increased immigration by European Zionists and the British military presence, while also maintaining a focus on social welfare concerns. Most significantly, on October 26, 1929, several hundred individuals representing a variety of religious and secular women's organizations gathered in Jerusalem for the first Palestine Arab Women's Conference.

3. This discussion draws on Dajani 1994; Fleischmann 1995, 1996; Gluck 1995; Peteet 1991, chap. 2.

By the mid-1930s, several women's associations engaged in "demonstrations; fundraising for prisoners and their families; smuggling and providing arms for the 1936–39 [Arab] Revolt; garnering regional and international support through propaganda and the press for the Palestinian national cause; offering services such as medial care and education within a nationalist framework; and participating in regional, pan-Arab, 'Oriental,' and international women's conferences" (Fleischmann 1999, 146). The range of activities reflects both the accepted female attribute of caregiver (supporting prisoners' families and providing education and medical aid) and a more explicitly political and activist role (the solicitation of international support for Palestinian aspirations and involvement in conferences and weapons smuggling). These women were strongly nationalistic; they were also quite willing to make use of gender stereotypes to support their subversive activities when necessary. Whether there was an explicit ideology in support of changing gender roles or not, the simple fact of their participation in the public arena meant a subtle shift in their position in society (Peteet 1991, chap. 2, 45).

The Arab Revolt exacerbated existing political differences within the Palestinian community regarding the direction of the national struggle. In 1937–1938 the Jerusalem-based Arab Women's Association, founded some years earlier, split into two organizations, although they continued to work together on occasion. The Arab Women's (Ladies) Association (allied with the Nashashibi group) and the Arab Women's Society (associated with the Husseini family) mirrored the divisions that existed in male political bodies at the same time, although this fact was rarely discussed explicitly and illustrates the way these groups were fundamentally embedded in the larger nationalist project. It also presaged a pattern that persisted throughout the twentieth century in which women's groups were affiliated with male-dominated political movements, making it more difficult to transcend partisan divisions and articulate a distinct and autonomous agenda.

Britain's successful suppression of the Arab Revolt and the subsequent establishment of the State of Israel in 1948 led to a period of greatly diminished political activity by both women and men. The Palestinian *Nakba* (catastrophe), with its massive dislocation, dispossession, and economic deprivation, shocked Palestinians and created an immediate and profound societal crisis, both within the borders of the newly created State of Israel and in the West Bank and Gaza Strip. Demoralized, concerned with immediate issues of economic and cultural survival, and pressured by Jordan and Egypt not to engage in acts of resistance against Israel, Palestinian women, whether in the West Bank and Gaza Strip or in exile, returned their attention and energy to the social welfare activities typical of their public work during much of the first half of the century. Hind al-Husseini established a home in Jerusalem for children orphaned by the Deir Yassin massacre, for instance, and Samiha el-Khalil established a women's self-help association, In'ash el-Usra (Family Rejuvenation Society), in el-Bireh in 1965. The operation of such organizations—numbering at least sixty-eight within the Occupied Territories in 1967 (Jad 1990, 128)—did much to educate women and helped sustain a distinct and coherent Palestinian community in the 1960s and 1970s; however, their activities were quite different from the overtly political responsibilities women had undertaken in the 1920s and 1930s. "Women," wrote Rita Giacaman in 1989, "were being trained in jobs that serve as a backup for men's work: to be good housekeepers and mothers; and to have as many children as possible because this is their *wajib watani* (or national duty). The women's lives were not considered important" (quoted in Hiltermann 1991, 130).

Another change in the post-1948 period was an increased social conservatism regarding the public behavior of women. Looking back, one woman who had been involved in the Arab Revolt commented, "The Palestinian [man] used to be much more advanced in his own country and women were more independent and freer . . . but after 1948 this changed: in the camps the Palestinian [male] became ultra-strict, even fanatic about the 'honor' of his women. Perhaps this was because he had lost everything that gave his life meaning and 'honor' was the only possession remaining to him" (Antonius 1983, 72). In other words, men understood their status and honor to be contingent on the behavior of "their" women. With the loss of Palestinian autonomy came new restrictions in activities that were "acceptable" for women, since this area was one of the only dimensions of life that men could control.

Activism after the June 1967 War

The relative political quietude among women did not last, either within mandatory Palestine or outside it. In 1965, individuals involved with various Palestinian women's organizations came together to form the General Union of Palestinian Women (GUPW). Although formally independent when first established, the GUPW quickly came to function as part of the Palestine Liberation Organization (PLO) created the previous year; indeed, one of the founders (and later the president) of the GUPW, 'Issam 'Abd al-Hadi, was also a delegate to the first meeting of the Palestine National Council (PNC) and remained in the PNC for her entire political life (Talhami 1990, 22). Thus, the quasi-political activities of this group were strongly molded by the male-dominated PLO leadership, hindering the ability of the diaspora-based GUPW to act as an autonomous feminist voice.

As a consequence of the June 1967 war, Israel gained control of the remaining parts of mandatory Palestine. In Gaza, women and men responded with an insurrection that began in 1968 and lasted for three years (until Israeli military leader and later prime minister Ariel Sharon crushed it). In the West Bank, the existing charitable organizations provided an organizational structure through which women could undertake resistance activities, especially as arrests and deportations led to a vacuum in male leadership. In addition, individuals associated with progressive political factions based within the Occupied Territories began to build trade unions, grassroots committees, and other agents of civil society targeted at the recruitment of women as part of a larger mobilization strategy pursued by the various political organizations. With a commitment to working with villagers and women in refugee camps and poor urban neighborhoods, many of whom found themselves in the paid labor force when the males in their families were jailed or deported, these activists focused on developing local political leadership and empowering women to think and act independently.

The first of the new broad-based political action groups was the Union of Women's Work Committees, whose founders were educated, nationalistic, socially progressive, and politically active. According to Amal Kawar:

> The Women's Committees' Movement began at an afternoon meeting on March 8, 1978 [International Women's Day], in the old library in Ramallah in the West Bank. Some thirty women, all from the urban middle class in the Jerusalem and Ramallah areas, came to discuss how women could be organized to support the steadfastness effort. Steadfastness was the Palestinian buzzword for peaceful resistance against the Israeli occupation, and by the early '70s it had replaced the collapsed armed struggle movement in the West Bank and Gaza Strip. . . . To an outsider, the library meeting would have been innocuous; the idea of women doing volunteer work was as old as their great grandmothers. . . . A closer look would have revealed the nucleus of the Occupied Territories' incoming second and third generations of women's leadership. . . . [At] the meeting were women from all the major PLO factions and several independents. The Ramallah library meeting concluded by setting up the first Women's Volunteer Work committee. It was a modest step that no one at the time could have predicted would lead to a women's political movement. (1996, 100; see also Kamal 1998)

Eventually, the organization founded in Ramallah by Zahira Kamal and others came to be identified primarily with the Democratic Front for the Liberation of Palestine (DFLP) and changed its name to the Federation of Palestinian Women's Action Committees (FPWAC).[4] In rapid succession, additional women's committees were formed, each affiliated with one of the main political tendencies, which saw them as a valuable recruitment tool (Kamal 1998, 83; see also Hiltermann 1991, chap. 5). The Union of Palestinian Working Women's Society (PWWS) was formed in 1981 and was associated with the Palestine Communist Party (now the Palestine People's Party); the Union of Palestinian Women's Committees, also established in 1981, was linked to the Popular Front for the Liberation of Palestine; and the Union of Women's Committees for Social Work, created in June 1982, was affiliated with Fateh.[5] Each organization included the political emancipation and formal equality of Palestinian women in employment and education as part of its official mandate, although the extent to which the activities actually reflected this directive varied. At least initially, none addressed deeper social and cultural issues explicitly. Eileen Kuttab argues that the groups' structures nonetheless emphasized democracy, gender, and class concerns (1993).

International developments also influenced the focus of activity. In the mid-1970s, the United Nations declared the "Women's Decade" and sponsored a series of international conferences (Mexico City in 1975, Copenhagen in 1980, and Nairobi in 1985) to address gendered social and political concerns. Although Palestinian women had attended international conferences in the past, these high-visibility events provided new opportunities for elite Palestinian women activists to articulate the goals of the Palestinian national movement to a broader audience. It also exposed them to the strategies and ideologies of feminist and nationalist activists from India, Cuba, South Africa, and elsewhere (Israel clearly viewed such participation as important, since it denied some delegates permission to leave the Occupied Territories to attend the conferences; author interview with Samiha Khalil, July 1985).

Taking part in these women's conferences did not, however, translate into in-

---

4. For a detailed discussion of the relationship between the FPWAC and the DFLP, see Hasso 1998.

5. According to the PWWS Web site, "In 1993, the Society was registered as a non-governmental organization. Due to the rich experience both in the national struggle and in the community intervention, we had realized that we should perform a kind of balance between the national and the social struggle . . . to achieve our goals as women and as a nation. . . . Since then, the philosophy of the organization has thus been developed to widen women's involvement in building Palestinian democratic civil society" (http://www.pal-pwws.org/).

creased involvement of Palestinian women in other international forums. Interviewed in the early 1990s, Fateh activist Khadijeh Abu Ali reported expressing her frustration to the men in charge of picking delegates for various international missions, saying to them, "Your delegation has about fifteen or sixteen persons. Why didn't you think to include one of us? You will go and find out that the delegations from the other movements or the delegations from the states that are coming no doubt they will include women. And also we share with you the political work, the *tanzim* (cadre) work, the intellectual work. When there is decision making we are not [included]." The men's response was typically something like "No problem. . . . We didn't think." But, Abu Ali remarks, "Sometimes they remember and sometimes they forget. If they forget with one delegation, they will remember with the next one. Then they will forget again" (quoted in A. Kawar 1996, 62–63). These experiences convinced many women that they needed to concentrate on the local level, rather than focusing on the high-level, publicly visible activities that were still controlled by the male leadership.

Women and the Intifada

With the first intifada came a much larger-scale mobilization of the entire Palestinian community than had been seen previously, involving not just urban activists but village and refugee women as well.[6] All were affected by the massive Israeli arrests of Palestinians (more than one hundred thousand by the end of 1993, several thousand of whom were female), the "administration detention" of more than eighteen thousand suspected activists for periods of six months to several years, deportations, curfews and closures, the sealing or destruction of hundreds of homes, and the killing of more than nine hundred Palestinians (11 percent of whom were female) in the first four years of the uprising.[7]

Passionately engaged women joined demonstrations against the occupation and directly confronted Israeli soldiers in the streets, claiming a public space more often reserved for men. Drawing on the extensive organizational networks created over the previous decade, women also became the backbone of the neighborhood

6. There is prodigious literature on the first intifada. See, for example, Gerner 1990, 1991; Lockman and Beinin 1989; Nassar and Heacock 1990; Schiff and Ya'ari 1990.

7. These data come from the East Jerusalem-based Palestine Human Rights Information Center (PHRIC), whose efforts to monitor systematically the human rights situation in the West Bank and Gaza Strip began prior to the intifada and continued through 1993.

popular committees that were responsible for everything from garbage pickup in the refugee camps to increasing Palestinian economic self-sufficiency. After Israel declared the popular committees illegal on August 18, 1988, their activities moved underground. This maneuver required closer coordination and led to the creation in December 1988 of the Higher Women's Committee, which served as an umbrella organization uniting the four national women's committees. Although this consolidation had a number of positive aspects, it also served to reestablish firmly the dominance of the nationalist struggle above gender-based concerns.

Another role for women was more subtle and related to the politicization of traditional female identities of mother, daughter, sister, and wife. In frequent communiqués from the Unified National Leadership of the Uprising (UNLU), women were reminded of their responsibility for reproduction (birthing a new generation of Palestinian fighters). They were also called upon to remain steadfast, visit those individuals in jail, and treat all children as their own, protecting them from the soldiers and educating them in the political realities of the uprising. For many women, these seemingly ordinary activities came to be imbued with revolutionary meanings:

> As they prevent Israeli soldiers from running after graffiti writers, Palestinian flag raisers, or even stone throwers, Palestinian women give the idea nationalized resonance: "this is my duty as a mother to protect the children from the hands of the soldiers, from the enemy." . . . Palestinian mothers have also become important symbols of nationalism, sacrifice and strength in their greatest moments of grief: during and after the funerals of children. Many of these mothers who used to be apolitical have become politicized with the death of a child. (Mayer 1994, 78)

This period was an exciting time, especially for those Palestinians who saw the intifada as both a way to end the Israeli occupation and a vehicle for the transformation of traditional social and gender relations. Yet in a prescient article published in 1989, Rita Giacaman warned:

> Active participation by women in public life—be it in political leadership or in economic or social life—does not necessarily guarantee the continued radical transformation in the condition of women and their status in society in the period after liberation. We must draw on, and learn from, the experience of our Algerian sisters, who ironically signaled the beginning of their own downfall after liberation by calling for conformity to Arab-Islamic culture in the process of protecting the family unit. (144)

The *hijab* campaign of 1988–1989, and the delayed response of the UNLU, gave a taste of what was to come. Almost immediately after the outbreak of the intifada, the Islamic Hamas movement in Gaza attempted to define wearing the *hijab* as an essential dimension of the national struggle, even though it was not historically part of Palestinian attire. Women must wear the *hijab,* Hamas said, as a sign of respect for the martyrs, as a way to promote cultural pride, and as proof of their nationalist sympathies. Implicitly, the claim was that Israeli political and military dominance was a result of the Palestinians turning their backs on Islam. Women who rejected this demand were criticized, then attacked verbally and even physically, first in Gaza, then in Hebron and in the Old City of Jerusalem. Reflecting on the *hijab* campaign, one secular activist argued that the intent of the campaign was "to make women feel ashamed" (Boulatta 2001, n.p.).

It took some eighteen months before the UNLU explicitly condemned the *hijab* campaign, writing in a communiqué: "Nobody has the right to accost women and girls in the streets on the basis of their dress or absence of a veil." Once the UNLU did so, the harassment of women without the head scarf declined dramatically (although there was a resurgence in violence against unveiled women the following year that was not addressed by the UNLU). As Rema Hammami pointed out at the time, "The inability (or reluctance) of activist men to deal with the *hijab* campaign represents both the weakness of the left and of feminist agendas in the West Bank and Gaza" (1990, 28).

With the increasing strength of reactionary religious groups, the weakening of progressive elements within the PLO after the collapse of the Soviet Union, the militarization of the intifada (particularly in the third year and beyond), and the parallel decline of the role of the popular committees, gender issues were increasingly ignored, and the distinctive role of women in the uprising began to fade. Women worried that if gender issues remained on the side during the uprising, "We won't be able to push them later on, and we'll be abused by the national movement. We are struggling for independence but we don't want to compromise our role as women. The issue has come up now because we have realized through our work in the *intifada* how important our role really is. This has given us confidence" (unnamed activist, quoted in Hiltermann 1990, 35).

The Women's Studies Committee of the Bisan Center for Research and Development responded to these concerns by organizing a conference in Jerusalem in December 1990 called "The *Intifada* and Women's Social Issues." The original idea was to focus discussions on the question of veiling; however, conference organizers concluded this subject was too politically sensitive and opted for a broader considera-

tion of the intifada's impact on Palestinian social structures, the increasing marginalization of women in the political structures of the uprising, and the return to more
traditional social patterns such as early marriage (A. Kawar 1996, 123; Sharoni 1995,
79). This broader focus allowed organizers to address the *hijab* campaign indirectly
as a phenomenon that reflected larger gendered issues. Between five hundred and
seven hundred people attended the presentations and workshops. Had it occurred
at a different time, the high-visibility conference, with its effort to discuss gender-
based issues without subordinating them to the national struggle, might have had a
significant impact on the male Palestinian leadership. However, the Iraqi invasion of
Kuwait the previous August and the subsequent U.S.-led war against Iraq focused
attention in other directions, and the critical gender concerns raised were again
ignored.

The Post-Oslo Period

The 1991 Madrid multilateral peace conference that followed the end of the war
against Iraq opened a new phase in the Palestinian national movement. During the
intifada, significant power had flowed to the Palestinians on the ground: those
women and men living under Israeli occupation and actively confronting that occupation on a daily basis. With the Madrid conference, the balance shifted away from
the mass mobilization of the intifada and back toward the centralized diaspora leadership. To be sure, the delegates to Madrid were all Palestinians from "inside," owing
to the continued Israeli refusal to meet with official representatives of the PLO. It
was widely understood, however, that at least in their public statements, those delegates reflected the views of Arafat and the Tunis-based administration. The central
difficulty, from the perspective of female activists, was that

> while the emergent national leadership in the prefigurative state . . . had begun to
> incorporate women's interests into their political discourse [notwithstanding
> counterpressures from Islamists and the weakness of the progressive movement],
> the PLO leadership in Tunis had remained untouched by the women's movement.
> As a result, when the reins of authority were transferred from the activists on the
> ground to the overwhelmingly male politicians and bureaucrats, women began to
> see their gains threatened. When only four women were appointed to the more
> than three hundred slots on the technical committees formed after the Madrid
> conference, the "loyalist" leadership of the women's movement who supported the

peace process mobilized to form a Women's Affairs Technical Committee [WATC] to demand the appointment of more women. (Gluck 1995, 11)

The problem became more acute once the 1993 Oslo Agreement was signed and hundreds of Palestinian "returnees" left the diaspora for the Occupied Territories to become part of the new Palestinian Authority based in Gaza and Jericho. As Arafat consolidated his control, patterns of patriarchy reasserted themselves, and women were further marginalized (N. Abdo 1999, 40). There seemed to be an attitude among many in the diaspora leadership that it was not important to incorporate women into the political structures once the Palestinian movement moved into a state-building phase. Women were well aware of the danger to their hard-won gains. One told a reporter, "To my sorrow, after women had contributed so much to the struggle and helped bring us to where we are today, they risk being dropped with no major part to play in shaping this new era. . . . We have to start on the right foot. Otherwise ten years from now we're going to look back and say: 'Too bad we weren't there, we weren't involved when the whole structure was built' " (Lana Abu-Hijleh, quoted in Kessel 1993).

Echoing concerns raised since the early months of the intifada, another woman, a former political prisoner and trade union activist, worried: "[Women] should not be shunted back into the kitchen. I am afraid that the PLO will let our revolution go the way of Algeria where women played a central role until freedom was won, only to be sidelined completely thereafter" (Amneh Rimawi, quoted in Kessel 1993). A further complication was that the women's movement was deeply divided between the women who supported Oslo and others who viewed it as a complete sellout. This political split made joint work all but impossible in the years immediately following Oslo. Still, there were some collaborative projects, particularly around the drafting of the Palestinian Basic Law.

The Basic Law

For both practical and symbolic reasons, one of the first tasks facing the Palestinian Authority and the Palestinian Legislative Council (PLC) was the construction of rules of law to govern Palestinian society. The original draft of the Basic Law, created by a group of male lawyers appointed by Arafat, made no mention of women's rights. The outcry from women was immediate. Representatives from virtually all the West Bank women's groups joined together in a press conference in Jerusalem on August 3, 1994, to present the "Draft Document of Principles of Women's Rights," also known as the Palestinian Women's Charter. The three-page charter, which drew from the 1988 Palestinian Declaration of Independence and various UN conventions, demanded that the future Palestinian state and the National Authority "be committed [to] . . . all international declarations and conventions pertaining to human rights, particularly the 1979 Convention on the Elimination of All Forms of Discrimination against Women; and must enhance the principle of equality between women and men in all spheres of life and declare this, clearly and unequivocally, in the constitution as well as in the legislation of the national authority." In terms of citizenship and nationality, the document emphasized that a woman should have the right "to acquire, preserve, or change her nationality" independent of her husband's citizenship and should also have "the right to give citizenship to her husband and children." It also called for women's economic, social, and cultural rights, ending, "The efforts of women as well as all democratic forces in Palestinian society must unite to remove all obstacles hindering the equality of women with men. We must work hand in hand toward a democratic society based on comprehensive national independence, social justice, and equality" (General Union of Palestinian Women, Jerusalem-Palestine, "Declaration of Principles on Palestinian Women's Rights, Third Draft," quoted in Sabbagh 1998, 251–54).

By the time the fourth version of the Basic Law was completed, there were three articles that referred directly to the rights of women. Article 10 states, "Women and men shall have equal fundamental rights and freedoms without any discrimination." Article 38 reads: "All persons shall be equal before the courts and the law, and are entitled to the equal protection of the law without discrimination on any ground such as race, colour, sex, language, religion, political or other opinion, national or social origin, birth or other status." In contrast, Article 22 refers specifically to women in their role as mothers: "Motherhood, childhood, the family, the young and the youth have the right to protection and to the availability of proper opportunities for the development of their talents. Such protection is a duty on society to be discharged by the Palestinian authorities within the limits stipulated by law" (*Draft Basic Law for the National Authority in the Transitional Period* 1996).

One crucial issue not fully articulated in the draft Basic Law is "how current and future Palestinian political and community leaders can begin to think about modifying customary and Islamic norms to meet a declared national goal in the 1988 PNC Declaration of Independence of improving the legal status of women" (Wing 1994, 55). Instead, the framers of the Basic Law attempted to sidestep this critical task to avoid the anticipated political battles between secularists and Islamists. The content of the Basic Law is significant for what it reveals about debates within the Palestinian polity. As a practical matter, however, it has been virtually irrelevant. For years, the Basic Law languished on Arafat's desk, leaving numerous legal issues in limbo. In 2002, Arafat finally signed the Basic Law, but Israel reasserted military control over much of the (limited) territory it had turned over to Palestinian authority as part of the Oslo process, leaving the still not fully ratified Basic Law a document without a country.

Women and the 1996 Elections

The 1996 Palestinian presidential and legislative elections present a mixed picture for women's participation in the state-building process. On the positive side, a 1994 public opinion poll by the Center for Palestine Research and Studies found that a large majority of Palestinians supported suffrage for women; further, only 10.7 percent of those individuals polled indicated they were not prepared to vote for a qualified Palestinian woman because "I do not support women running for election." (Another 21 percent indicated they would not vote for a woman because "a man is probably more qualified.")[8] Given the embedded patriarchy of much of Palestinian society, these numbers are encouraging. On the other hand, the electoral "rules of the game" were determined by Israel and a male-dominated PA without significant internal debate rather than emerging out of grassroots discussions over an extended period of time (as occurred, for instance, in South Africa). The specific type of electoral system chosen was problematic in a number of ways and, unsurprisingly, was designed to strengthen the likelihood that the PLC would be supportive of Arafat's agenda.[9] Out of frustration with the heavy-handedness of decision making about the electoral system (as well as an awareness of their weak political position at the time), the major secular opposition groups as well as Hamas called for a boycott of the election and declined to run candidates.

Despite serious structural flaws, the 1996 elections, with a turnout of nearly 80 percent of registered voters who clearly rejected the opposition boycott, represented a potentially significant step in the direction of increased political accountability

8. http://www.pcpsr.org/survey/cprspolls/94/poll8.html. The center is now called the Palestinian Center for Policy and Survey Research.

9. A summary of some of the issues, which were widely discussed at the time, can be found in Amr 1996.

within the Palestinian polity as well as an indication that Palestinian women were indeed serious political figures. A number of Fateh politicians, including some PA officials, lost to independent candidates; some Fateh activists who were not chosen as part of the official slate ran anyway and were elected, and Samiha Khalil (the female head of In'ash el-Usra) won 9 percent of the vote in her quixotic presidential challenge to Arafat.[10]

Although meaningful elections are only one piece of political liberalization (and do not by themselves provide a guarantee that it will continue and strengthen), they are an essential element, in part because they "both initiate and sustain democratic process" (Abu Amr 1997, 90). Furthermore, political liberalization has a tendency to take on a powerful forward momentum unless explicitly constrained by the ruling elites, and female activists have been among the most outspoken advocates of movement in this direction. Women have used the contemporary rhetoric of *dimuqratiyya* (democracy) at both elite and mass levels to strengthen their claims for improvement of women's civil, political, and legal position.

Of the more than 550 individuals who stood for election to the 88-seat council, some 28—about 5 percent—were women. A perceived lack of family or societal support, financial constraints, the reluctance of the political parties that were participating in the election (Fateh, Fida, and the Palestine People's Party) to nominate women, and the boycott by opposition parties that might have included women on their slate all served to minimize the number of women on the ballot. "During the Palestinian revolution," Zahira Kamal remarked, "women were treated as equal partners. But it is true, just like in any Western country, when it comes to the more prestigious and higher-ranking positions, the men want to keep them. The discrimination comes at that level" (Brenoff 1998). Prior to the elections there was discussion spearheaded by the WATC about establishing a 30 percent electoral quota to ensure female representation, similar to the quota for Christians. Arguments against the gender quota won out, however, at least in part because many (although not all) female political activists themselves opposed the idea as nondemocratic (Barron 2002, 81). (Interestingly, a majority of the Palestinian public—60 percent, according to one poll—favored a quota for women [Kawar 1996, 238].) When the vote count was complete, two women from the West Bank and three from Gaza had

10. Khalil died in February 1999.

been elected, meaning women held just under 6 percent of the seats.[11] The biographies of the five women—plus a sixth who came very close to winning—reveal some of the similarities and differences in their backgrounds.[12]

Hanan Mikhail Ashrawi, representing Jerusalem as an independent, is the best-known Palestinian female in international circles, largely because of her highly visible role as Palestinian spokesperson during the 1991 Madrid conference and subsequent negotiations in Washington, D.C. An articulate advocate for Palestinian national aspirations and for women's political rights, she became a favorite of the Western media after her participation in a special three-hour *Nightline* debate between Israelis and Palestinians in April 1988. With a Ph.D. in medieval and comparative literature, Ashrawi was formerly a professor of English literature at Birzeit University. Ashrawi was born in Nablus into a Christian family and is married, with two adult daughters. Ashrawi served briefly as the minister of higher education for the Palestinian Authority.

Dalal Abdul Hafiz Mahmoud Salameh, a Fateh political activist from Nablus, is a Muslim who wears the head scarf and lives in a Balata refugee camp, where she was born. She has a B.A. in biology, has served as a Fateh higher committee member, and was an early member of the WATC. Salameh considers gender issues and building a democratic society, including a separation of powers, as two of her key priorities as a member of the legislature and has called on the PNC to "reinforce the role of Palestinian women, equalize chances of work, [and] support the participation of women in decision-making" (JMCC, *The Palestinian Council*, 90). She supports an electoral quota for women to ensure their representation in the public arena.

Gaza journalist Rawya Rashad Said As-Shawa was elected as an independent. In her late fifties, the mother of four comes from a politically active Muslim family and was a member of the Higher Education Council and the Gaza Cultural Group. She has said that she does not view herself as a women's political activist, although the issues in which she involves herself, particularly those matters addressing economic concerns of women, have clear political overtones. "I am active on issues of society. . . . In Gaza, women suffer because of the economic situation. . . . We need to work

11. In comparison, there were thirty-seven women in the Palestine National Council, which is about 12 percent of the total (Sabbagh 1998, 15).

12. Descriptive information about each woman comes from the Jerusalem Media and Communication Centre, the Palestinian Council (Jerusalem, October 1996), and from author interview with Terry Boulatta, Aug. 8, 2003.

on raising the level of social awareness so that women will not shy away from work" (D. Kuttab 1999). In addition, As-Shawa was involved in the campaign to ensure that a woman could obtain a passport without the written permission of her husband or another male guardian.

Longtime Fateh activist Jamileh Ahmad Seidam (Umm Sabri) is a widow with two adult children whose husband was killed in the 1970–1971 Jordanian civil war. She is a returnee, originally from Deir al-Balah, and represents the Khan Yunis constituency. With a B.A. in history, the Muslim Seidam has been a supporter of increased civil society in Palestine and has called for the development of cultural centers for youth and women. Most of her political interests revolve around economic concerns and the problems of refugees. She serves on the Executive Committee of the General Union of Palestinian Women, with particular responsibility for internal relations, and has been a member of the PNC. Looking toward the second Palestinian parliamentary elections, she hopes to see "a modern electoral law that secures [female] participation, . . .puts an end to tribal law and grants women their rights" (quoted in Saoud 2002).

Intisar Mustafa Mahmoud al-Wazir (Umm Jihad) is the widow of high-ranking PLO figure Khalil al-Wazir (Abu-Jihad) who was assassinated by Israel in 1988 in Tunis. Umm Jihad is a returnee who received a B.A. in history. In her sixties, Umm Jihad has been politically active for many years as head of the Families of the Martyrs foundation, the PLO's social welfare institution, and also served on the PLO's Executive Committee. Unlike the other female legislators, when questioned by the Jerusalem Media and Communication Centre she did not list any gender-related issues as among her top five legislative priorities, focusing instead solely on the national liberation agenda. Al-Wazir was the minister of social affairs in Arafat's government.

A sixth candidate, Fida's Zahira Kamal, lost by only 104 votes out of 32,316 votes cast in the Jerusalem constituency. Kamal, who has a B.A. in physics, played a key role in the 1978 establishment of the Women's Committees' Movement, then spent six years (1980–1986) under town arrest for her political activism (ironic, given that one of those activities was promoting Palestinian-Israeli dialogue) (Najjar, "Zahira Kemal," *Portraits of Palestinian Women*, 133–48). She was a member of the Palestinian delegation to the Madrid conference and later traveled to Tunis with other prominent West Bank and Gaza Palestinians to meet with Arafat in violation of an Israeli ban on contacts with the PLO. Kamal's main political focus has been on grassroots women's issues, from education and health to participation in electoral politics. She was the general director of gender planning and development in the

Ministry of Planning and International Cooperation for the Palestinian Authority and in 2002 was named minister of the first Ministry of Women's Affairs.[13]

Women's Nongovernmental Organizations

Reflecting the professionalization of the women's movement, another arena in which women have articulated their political and societal aspirations during the state-building phase of the Palestinian movement is through the numerous nongovernmental organizations (NGOs) that have sprung up in the past decade, often funded by foreign donors. Some of them are truly autonomous; others are more or less closely associated with the government (not unlike the situation elsewhere in the world). Four stand out: the Women's Studies Center (WSC), the Women's Center for Legal Aid and Counseling (WCLAC), the WATC, and the Women's Studies Program at Birzeit University.[14]

The WSC is significant in part because it was the first of these new professionally oriented groups. Founded in 1989, the WSC describes itself as an independent, progressive NGO "that strives for the realization of the principle of equality between women and men." Its work is fundamentally grounded in "international human rights covenants as well as local customs and values which conform to the principle of gender equality." The WSC holds training workshops, often in cooperation with other institutions; produces a variety of media materials; is one of the founding members of the Arab Women's Forum (AISHA), for which it serves as the central coordinator; and is home to the first Palestinian library specializing in women and gender (see Women's Studies Center Vision, http://www.wameed.org).

Two years after the creation of the WSC, a group of women established the Jerusalem-based WCLAC. According to its mission statement, the WCLAC attempts "to contribute to the rectification of the long-standing neglect of women's human rights in Palestinian society, . . .to provide support and guidance to Palestinian women whose human rights and rights under the law have been violated, . . .[to] defend women's rights as human rights and work to promote the development of a

---

13. When elections were held again in January 2006 and the Islamist party Hamas gained the majority of seats to form a new government, Zahira Kamal relinquished her position as minister and became interim director of the newly formed Palestinian Women's Research and Documentation Center, established in collaboration with UNESCO [editor's note].

14. Rubenberg 2001, table 7.2, summarizes basic information on nearly two dozen Palestinian women's organizations, many of which are NGOs.

social, political and legal order in which human rights are well respected and women's rights are well protected" (mission statement, http://www.wclac.org). In support of these goals, the WCLAC provides legal aid services, promotes the rule of law, encourages the PLC and the PA to adopt international human rights conventions, lobbies the government regarding legislation that discriminates against women, encourages research on human rights violations, and promotes legal literacy. In December 2002, *Ms.* honored the director of WCLAC, Mahla Abu-Dayyah Shamas, as one of two *Ms.* "Women of the Year."

The Women's Affairs Technical Committee, which began in the early 1990s as a way to get women involved in the technical committees that were established after the Madrid conference, has become one of the most visible and inclusive women's nongovernmental organizations. Its activities involve women affiliated with each of the six main political tendencies as well as independents and representatives of human rights organizations and women's centers. As a networking, lobbying, and training institution, the WATC emphasizes programs to increase mass awareness of women's rights and strives to mainstream gender issues so they are part of all discussions about the future development of Palestinian society. The WATC actively promoted the Women's Charter in 1994, and in 1995 and 1996 they lobbied heavily against proposed laws that discriminated against women (including laws dealing with driving tests and passports). Prior to the 1996 elections, the WATC's Women's Election Program encouraged political parties to include women in their official list of candidates, conducted door-to-door campaigns to increase female voter turnout, held a number of meetings with candidates, and worked with the media to promote the empowerment of women. The organization also created an election guide, with sections on democracy, the electoral law, the criteria for candidacy, and information on the mechanics of registration and voting. More recently, they have established women-only Internet centers in remote areas of the West Bank and Gaza Strip and continue to promote a quota to ensure significant and genuine representation of women in the PLC and in municipal councils (see http://www.palwatc.org).

Finally, the Institute of Women's Studies at Birzeit University, founded in 1994, combines teaching and training, systemic research on gender relations in Palestinian society, and community outreach to pursue its goal of gender equality in the social, cultural, political, and economic arenas (see http://www.birzeit.edu/centers/iws.html; and E. Kuttab 1997). With the involvement of some of the preeminent gender studies scholars in the region, the institute has had a notable impact on knowledge about and action regarding women and development, law, social policy, and the family. The institute engages in networking activities and tries to influence government policy; it also maintains a specialized gender studies library and directly publishes research results.[15]

Model Parliament Project

In 1998, the WCLAC, with the involvement of the WATC, the Birzeit Women's Studies Center, and other women's organizations, sponsored a major undertaking, "The Palestinian Model Parliament: Women and Legislation."[16] The intent of the project was to promote information about the current legal status of Palestinian women and to inform Palestinians about international norms and standards regarding women's rights. In addition, organizers hoped "to change long-term attitudes that women aren't strong enough to decide anything, and that only their brothers or father can decide. We need to start somewhere" (Murwa Kassem, the coordinator of the Gaza Parliament, quoted in Scheindlin 1998, n.p.). Preparation for the project began in 1995 as the WCLAC reviewed current laws that discriminate against women to determine how they needed to be modified to be consistent with international norms. They then began to raise awareness of their findings and build support for recommendations, through workshops on the status of women held throughout Gaza and the West Bank.

The original conception called for a single parliament of 88 delegates, equally divided between women and men, that would meet to discuss legislation with relevance to women. However, the project eventually grew to include five Model Parliament sessions in four different locations: Gaza City, Hebron, Nablus, and Ramallah. As a result, "hundreds of participants, men and women, members of the Palestinian Legislative Council and religious leaders debated and discussed issues like inheritance; custody of children; divorce and separation; polygamy; rape, adultery; crimes of domestic violence; legal competence of women; the right to equal job opportunities; the right to freedom of movement; the right to sue and go to court; the right to participate in public life; and many other related issues" (Duaibis 1999, n.p.). Each Model Parliament had its own character. For instance, the Gaza Parliament dealt solely with personal-status issues (marriage, divorce, inheritance, health, and so on)

---

15. For instance, one project in the mid-1990s resulted in papers on gender and society by Nahla Abdo, Rita Giacaman, Rema Hammami, Suha Hindiyyeh, Islah Jad, Sa'ed Jasir, Penny Johnson, Deniz Kandiyoti, Eileen Kuttab, Majdi Malki, Valentine M. Moghadam, and Lisa Taraki.

16. For an excellent discussion of the Model Parliament, among other issues, see Hammami and Johnson 1999.

rather than also addressing gender-based economic and political inequalities. Among the Gaza Parliament's most controversial decisions was a vote to ban polygamy. The delegates also called for raising the minimum age of marriage to eighteen years for both women and men (under Egyptian law, girls can marry at age nine) and abolishing the requirement that women must receive permission from a male relative in order to marry. The Ramallah Parliament focused its attention in part on the sensitive topics of honor killings and abortion (Barron 2002, 84). The actions of both the West Bank and Gaza Parliaments came under severe criticism by some conservative Islamic clerics, including Bassam Jarrar, who argued that the ideas promoted were "devilish" because in his view they failed to respect Islamic rules, and more than 170 Muslim religious leaders publicly condemned the Model Parliament as "an assault on family values" (Antonelli 1998; Barron 2002, 88).

Conclusions

In reviewing the political participation of Palestinian women, it is clear that their historic focus on resisting the Israeli occupation has provided them with both opportunities and constraints. During periods of active rebellion, such as in the second half of the 1930s and in the initial years of the first intifada, the nationalist struggle opened social spaces for women and provided them with opportunities to develop a political voice. At the same time, Palestinian women clearly recognize that, despite their decades-long political activism, the future achievement of national liberation does not guarantee women will gain social, economic, and political emancipation. Focusing on the positives, Birzeit sociologist Rita Giacaman commented in 1995, "We don't think the clock can be turned back on Palestinian women, because we are much more powerful now. We have built . . . women's organizations here during the struggles of the 1980s that can't be dismantled" (quoted in D. Connell 1995). There is much truth to that assessment. Yet by situating gender-specific issues within—and to a large extent secondary to—the nationalist struggle for so many years, Palestinian women may have undercut their ability to now articulate the need for social change within Palestinian society and the body politic.

There are further complications that women activists face today. First, life in Palestine is extremely tough. The economic damage since the second intifada has been severe, and the financial security net provided during the first intifada by Palestinian workers in the Gulf no longer exists. In an economically marginal situation, impediments to successful political mobilization can be as simple as not having sufficient funds to print leaflets or as transparently manipulative as the government co-opting opposition leaders through the promise of jobs for themselves or their relatives.

In addition, because of the long tradition of collective protest against the occupation, there is a strong societal norm against "submitting" to *any* government entity.[17] Thus, Palestinian women (and men) face an additional challenge: how to best express opposition to their *own* government. Conventional political participation is one option; however, the lack of legitimate democratic institutions and the shallowness of democratic experience make this difficult in the short run. Alternatively, Palestinian women can draw on their recent history with unconventional political action to develop new strategies of expression. This idea is an intriguing possibility that deserves further consideration. Either way, some women may feel constrained or be unwilling to confront nascent state structures because of uncertainty over the level of protest that can be directed against the current government without undermining the (extremely limited) gains in legitimacy attained thus far.

The widespread discontent with the Palestinian leadership and disappointment in the failed Oslo process, which did not provide tangible long-term benefits, may have been factors in the election of the Islamist party, Hamas, in January 2006. How will women respond? Clearly, the challenges of nationalism, democratization, citizenship, and state building in the Palestinian community are intimately connected to the ways women are understood within the society. Whether the mobilization of Palestinian women throughout all levels of society and their efforts to integrate gender concerns and legal rights into the mainstream public debate can be maintained and strengthened remains to be seen.

17. This problem is not unique to the Palestinians. One of the first challenges that confronted the government of Nelson Mandela in South Africa was persuading blacks who had for years refused to pay taxes, or even utility bills, to the white-dominated apartheid government that they should pay for the services provided by a democratically elected regime. Further back in time, the government of George Washington faced similar revolts against taxation in the early U.S. republic.

3 Against All Odds

Women Candidates in Jordan's 1997 Elections

ABLA AMAWI

THE 1997 PARLIAMENTARY ELECTIONS are widely considered to be a watershed in women's political participation in Jordan. The seventeen women candidates who ran in the elections did not differ much from their male counterparts in terms of their basic characteristics and academic and professional qualifications. Most of their campaign programs were well structured and revolved around the major issues facing their constituencies. However, their programs reflected a deeper understanding of the challenges facing both their own constituencies and the electorate at large. Although they employed campaign tactics and strategies similar to the approach used by the male candidates, their struggle was more arduous and the outcome of their candidacies less fortunate.

What was the impact of the electoral system, gender-based discrimination, and the tribal and patriarchal sociopolitical system on the female candidates, and to what extent did these issues determine their fate? Did they have what it takes to win in the elections, or was the reality in which they operated structured in ways that inevitably circumscribed their efforts? This chapter addresses these and other relevant questions.

The 1997 Elections

Prior to 1989 and the start of the democratization process, women's political participation in Jordan was limited. Between 1978 and 1992, only 9 women were appointed to the 190-member National Consultative Council. The percentage of women in municipal councils never exceeded 2 percent of the total, and only 10 women were ever elected to these councils (Al-Urdun al-Jadid Research Center 1997, 36). In unions, especially professional unions, women have always enjoyed high membership levels because of the obligatory nature of membership but have not held top decision-making positions. This condition is true also for most political parties and other institutions of civil society. In the 1989 parliamentary elections, 12 female candidates ran, but none of them won seats; in the 1993 elections, however, 3 of the 534 candidates (0.056 percent) were women, and only one—Toujan Faisal—was able to make it as the first elected female parliamentarian (Amawi 1994, 15–16).

Encouraged by Toujan Faisal's success in the 1993 parliamentary elections and the appointment of other women in political positions, 17 women nominated themselves for the elections to the Thirteenth Chamber of Deputies held on November 4, 1997. Registered voters comprised about 1.8 million persons, out of a population size of 4.2 million. A total of 1,479,968 voted, making up 54 percent of all registered voters and 42 percent of those individuals who were eligible to vote. Proestablishment politicians and tribal leaders won 62 seats, while Islamists and pan-Arab nationalists who opposed the peace treaty and tough International Monetary Fund economic reforms won the rest. Unlike the previous one, this parliament had no woman deputy.[1]

The candidates were middle-aged, between thirty-five and sixty-nine years old, with the average age somewhere in the fifties. Their educational mean was very similar to that of the male candidates, of whom 17.5 percent had a secondary education and 63.8 percent held bachelor of arts or college degrees (Hourani 1997, 12). In addition, many of the women had extensive professional experience, representing a broad range of occupations, with many holding leadership positions. Candidate profiles showed that they were very active within nongovernmental organizations (NGOs) and other civil society institutions.[2] Only two, however, were active political party members. This aggregate of educational and professional experience and the level of their participation in voluntary work help explain the candidates' active involvement at the local, national, and international levels, as well as their high level of awareness of the critical issues affecting their communities and the country as a whole.

In their campaigning strategies, they followed more or less the same methods as

1. Information and data from *Al-Hayat,* Nov. 5, 1997; *Al-Ra'y,* Nov. 3, 4, 5, 1997; *Jordan Times,* Nov. 29, 1997. Other sources put the voting percentage at 54.4 percent of those individuals registered (*Al-Aswaq,* Nov. 5, 1997) and 54.63 percent (*Jordan Times,* Oct. 11, 1997).

2. See the Candidates' Electoral Program distributed prior to and during the campaign. See also Hourani 1997, 22.

their male counterparts: securing the approval and support of their immediate and extended families as well as their clan and tribe. This reliance on familial and tribal links serves many purposes. It works to guarantee a wider network of support and provides candidates with natural allies who eventually act as campaign managers and support-team staff. Moreover, they had to depend on their families and tribes for campaign financing. This reliance was important for the women candidates, most of whom owned fewer assets in terms of property and capital than the male candidates. Women in Jordan own less property and earn less than males and suffer from higher unemployment rates.

For the most part, the campaign slogans of both male and female candidates were moderate and realistic, focusing on general public services and less bent on attacking the government's record on issues such as corruption and nepotism (*Star* (Beirut), Oct. 16–22, 1997).

What was interesting in the elections was the strong emphasis, by all candidates from both sexes and from all political affiliations, on women and their role in society. The Islamists emphasized the notion that women were the "sisters of men," while others called for amending certain laws in favor of women and vowed to work on getting women to Parliament and gender equality at all levels.

This heightened focus on women's issues was mainly aimed at attracting female voters and could be attributed to the presence of the female candidates, which made competition for votes even tighter. However, this enthusiasm never actually reached the level of endorsing the participation of women in the political process on equal footing, as evidenced by the fact that all parties and tribes, with the exception of the Communist Party, refrained from fielding female candidates. Thus, all women candidates ran as independents, representing themselves without tribal backing, financial clout, or party endorsement.

What was particular to the women's candidacy was that they all shared one common goal, which was their desire to improve women's status in society. They all agreed on the need to urgently achieve legal equality, integrate women in the decision-making process, and improve the socioeconomic conditions of women. Furthermore, they all agreed that the election of women to Parliament would be the best way to serve these objectives.

It must be noted that most of these women had not run for election before. Not only were they competing in a male-dominated political culture that had long excluded women from the political process, but they were also competing against a general lack of confidence among voters in women's abilities to deliver on their electoral promises. Sadly, all of the women candidates failed to win seats. This inability of the women candidates to gain seats made the issue of female marginalization in the sphere of political representation glaringly apparent and created an urgent need for analysis.

Analyzing the Results

Analyzing the female candidates' election results has to be done on two levels. The first level examines the electoral environment in general through a systematic approach that considers political and economic factors, which affected both male and female candidates. These issues pertain to the electoral setup, divisions of electoral constituencies, the nature of the election law, processes of voter registration, voting card acquisition, vote counting, and finally the socioeconomic and political variables characterizing the period in which the elections took place. The second level examines the specificity of the females' candidacy and focuses on the gender-based discrimination ingrained in society at all levels, which has made women's candidacy a much more arduous endeavor. The prevalence of tribalism, the gender-based discrimination inherent in the patriarchal structure of society, and legal frameworks as well as traditions and norms have all worked to weaken the female candidates' chances for success.

Much like their male counterparts, the female candidates had to face an inhospitable election environment. During the 1997 elections there was a deep sense of despair over local, regional, and global developments that negatively affected the atmosphere of the elections. Economic conditions did not improve much after the peace treaty concluded in 1994 between Jordan and Israel, contrary to speculations of high economic dividends following "peace." The increase in the percentage of families living in abject poverty rose from 1.5 percent in 1989 to 5.3 percent in 1993, with the percentage of families living below the absolute poverty line reaching 18.3 percent in 1993 and even higher in 1997. There were also widening inequalities between the rich and the poor as well as intensified regional disparities. Despite the announced "economic growth" figures, peace has not translated into increasing job opportunities for the population or into improvement of its productive sectors (Amawi 1996a). Politically, there was a sense of disenchantment over the uncertainty of the peace process, escalating to an outright rejection by some groups in society of the peace treaty itself and of normalization with Israel (Human Rights Watch 1997).

Women candidates, like their male counterparts, also suffered from the application of the "one-person, one-vote" electoral formula and from all the manifestations of various electoral irregularities (Amawi 1994, 15–16). The Electoral Law that was applied in the 1993 elections was also in effect in the 1997 elections. The introduction of single-vote polling as opposed to multiple votes (reaching up to five votes per person in some electoral districts) as in the 1989 elections affected the manner in which election campaigns were conducted and the way voters cast their ballots. Within the "one-person, one-vote" electoral formula and the electoral system of proportional representation in which the number of seats per district is defined, women did not have a very good chance of success. Parties and competing tribes could win, at most, one seat in each district. In this zero-sum game, women candidates were forced to compete directly against their fellow tribesmen and more organized groups for the one vote that each voter was allowed to cast. Believing that women's chances for success were slender within the Jordanian context, both parties and tribes refrained from backing women candidates for fear of losing their representation in Parliament.

The application of the Electoral Law, seen in the context of the social composition of Jordanian society, affected not only the way independent candidates ran their campaigns but also the level of involvement of political parties. Capitulating to the significance of tribal power in winning votes, many political parties fielded candidates who enjoyed strong tribal backing. Moreover, many parties did not even endorse their own candidates; rather, they allowed them to run as independents. In doing so, they were attempting to distance themselves from lingering public fears about political affiliations.[3] The need to win the nonpoliticized tribal votes in an election where tribalism was paramount forced these parties to play it safe, which also meant that they would not endorse female candidates. The notable exceptions were the Communist Party and the National Constitutional Party. Thus, the Electoral Law represented a death knell for women's chances of gaining broad support in an environment that favored the chances of tribally based candidates and the ones with financial clout.

The elections were also marred by the elections' boycott. The Muslim Brotherhood and its political arm, the Islamic Action Front, spearheaded a boycott of the elections (Duclos 1998). Prominent independent political figures and activists, the Union of Professional Associations, and eight secular opposition parties joined

3. The memories of what took place in 1931, 1951, and 1957, when parliaments were dismissed, political parties were banned, and extreme measures were taken against political activists, remain alive today. See Jaber 1969, 220–50.

the boycott.[4] In general, those individuals who boycotted called for constitutional reforms, the separation of powers, amendment of the Electoral Law, progressive amendments to the Press Law, an end to the normalization of relations with Israel, constructive solutions to economic challenges facing the country, and increased autonomy for civil society's institutions (Human Rights Watch 1997).

The boycotters who formed the National Reform Front stated that "fraud in the 1997 elections was rampant in the government's lists, which deprived some 400,000 citizens of their right to vote; in the abuse of voting cards, which in most cases were duplicated; in allowing certain candidates to retrieve voter cards, which enabled them to use them in a manner that served their own purpose; and in providing the public with incorrect and conflicting figures and information on voter lists and voting cards" (*Jordan Times* 1997c).

The women candidates had to operate within this atmosphere of disenchantment with the electoral process and a less than ideal socioeconomic and political situation in general. For them, the boycott meant losing the margin of support they would have gained from the boycotting "liberal" constituency, who might have endorsed the women candidates' agenda for change. It also meant losing some of the tribal support, which could have been theirs—if only minimally—had some of the tribes not joined the boycott. Finally, they had to face a confused, apathetic public who had witnessed their leaders' disengagement from politics.

Since the Election Law and the election irregularities deriving from it affected both male and female candidates, why were some men able to circumvent the various obstacles? The answer lies in the gender-based discrimination that is equally embedded in spheres other than politics, including education, economic participation, legislation, and cultural variables—all of which continue to diminish women's chances of success.

The Broader Context: The Patriarchal Social Structure

An understanding of women's status in Jordanian society is not possible without considering the historical conjuncture, political phenomena, cultural traditions, and family praxis, among other relevant variables. To examine the political phe-

4. The eight secular parties were Al-Hashd, Al-Ansar, Democratic Party of Popular Unity, Al-Mustaqbal, Arab and Jordanian Constitutional Front, Freedom Party, Islamic Democratic Movement, and Nationalist Jordanian Democratic Party.

nomena requires an analysis of the various underlying concepts such as gender, patriarchy, tribalism, and familial structures that have shaped and affected the nature of women's political participation in Jordan. It will also help us to examine the factors that influenced society's perception of women and women's perception of themselves. This evaluation will, in its turn, help clarify the reasons for the results of women's candidacy in the 1997 parliamentary elections.

A natural element of Jordanian society has been the tribal structure. The tribe, as defined by Richard Nyrop, is a "pyramidal and segmentary relationship aggregating extended families into higher orders of organization based upon an accepted myth that all living members of the tribe [are] descended patrilineally from a remote common ancestor" (1994, 70–71). Thus, the tribe entails affiliation based on blood ties, superseding every other kind of relation.

The tribal structure is a complex one that rests on vertical and horizontal relationships. As Peter Gubser indicates in his study of Jordanian tribes, "The significance of the pyramidal pattern is that there is an overall vertical organization of the tribe, not just a series of horizontal units with the same general identity. Thus, each unit at a structurally higher level automatically contains all those groups below it" (1983, 24).

There are a number of distinguishing features of a tribally dominated structure that will help us analyze the inner dynamics of tribalism. According to Hisham Sharabi, the most important characteristics of a tribally dominated social structure are: (1) factionalism, where one makes a distinction between kin and nonkin, clan and opposing clan, "self" and "others," and so on; (2) affiliation based on blood ties surpassing any other kind of affiliations; (3) well-defined social obligations, whether within the same tribe or through contractual obligations with other tribes—those who fall outside of these obligation networks can be considered enemies; and (4) mutually reciprocal tribal collective responsibility over individual actions strengthening kinship and tribal allegiance and amplifying the individual identification with the tribe as the essence of this loyalty (1988, 28–29, 31).

Tribalism has been transformed over the years with the weakening of traditional economic structures and with increased urbanization. This situation has led to the emergence of nuclear family formations *(usrah)* and extended families *('ailah)* as distinct from the clan family *(hamulah),* the subtribe *('ashirah)* or the tribe *(qabilah).* "The tribe's activities are mainly political, consisting of the management of relations with other tribes and the governments" (Barakat 1993, 51). However, the foundations of tribalism remained the same. As noted, several observers of Jordanian society have pointed out that in urban contexts, the population tends to reproduce the tribal structure and its social organizational patterns. Thus, it is possible to argue that the tendency to continue basic patterns of localization and the importance of family relations dominating modern processes remains prevalent, despite modernization's tendency to break up and change traditional ways of living (Layne 1987, 135).

Why have these relationship patterns continued despite socioeconomic transformations and the emergence of nuclear families? What has stood in the way of a radical transformation of tribal and familial relations? Tribal allegiance and loyalty, kinship, and religious affiliations remain supreme because they continue to fulfill basic needs embodied in material interests, security and safety, feeling of belonging, and fulfillment of identity that no other structure, even the state, has been able to fulfill (Sharabi 1988, 28).

The emerging bureaucracy of the modern state could not substitute for these affiliations. Red tape, personalized power structures, and the mechanism of *wasta* (mediation), predominant in Jordanian society, inhibited the transcending of these tribal and familial allegiances. The *wasta* system is based on the ability of a powerful individual in terms of social status, economic power, or political influence to use these power or status sources to fulfill the needs of the recipient (Cunningham and Sarayrah 1993). The recipient's vulnerability in transcending these obstacles can be overcome by the provider; thus, the recipient of these privileges develops loyalty. Moreover, despite the appearance of ideological parties and groups, the individual's basic affiliation remains to the family, the clan, and the ethnic or religious group.

This type of behavior is reinforced in individuals through patterns of upbringing, socialization within society, and interaction in society at large. The impact of this prevalence of the *wasta* and tribal system on women and participation in the elections is dramatic. In order to bypass it, the female candidates would have to possess their own *wasta* connections and linkages. They would have to be able to grant favors, facilitate job finding, procure acceptance in the universities to those individuals unable to acquire a placement, provide services to the community, and so on. In return, they would get the privileges that possessing *wasta* connections endows.

Tribal ascendance in these elections as well as in previous elections caused some to refer to the tribes as miniparties.[5] Tribalism, with its rigid and paternalistic structure, tremendously affected the female candidates' chances for success. Tribal social

---

5. One observer went as far as describing tribalism in the elections as a new kind of democracy, "tribalocracy," or *al-'asha'irocratiyya,* invented in the Arab world to refer to "rule, by the tribe, for the tribe" as opposed to "rule by the people, for the people" (Malhas 1997).

structures marginalized women's role in the decision-making process, since, more often than not, they do not take part in the special gatherings and primary elections that their tribe holds in order to select its candidate. No wonder then that many women were discouraged from running as candidates in the elections. The results of the various parliamentary elections held so far in Jordan have demonstrated the extent to which tribal allegiance has impacted the voters' choices of candidate, compared to allegiance to political parties and programs. The ascendancy of tribalism and political Islam became major factors weakening women's chances of winning the elections. Tribalism meant that blood ties, family networks, allegiances, and hierarchy took precedence over individual qualifications. Female candidates had to either transcend these systems of allegiance or secure tribal support for themselves. With political Islam, women candidates had to compete against what had become the country's best-organized political grouping enjoying broad popular support (Amawi 1992, 26–29).

The change in the Election Law from a multiple-vote to a "one-person, one-vote" formula much like in the 1993 elections altered the way the electorate voted and the way the candidates conducted their campaigns. It centered voters' attention on their respective clan, tribe, and source of origin rather than on ideologies and issues. The chances of any of the female candidates winning under these circumstances were not high. As one observer noted, "With all my respect to women, I do not think they have a chance of winning, especially in the Fifth District, which is characterized by Bedouinism and tribalism" (*Jordan Times* 1997b).

Moreover, many women candidates had to confront various societal perceptions stemming from the tribal patriarchal mind-sets against women's participation in politics as well as the resulting accusations leveled at them for transgressing established tribal hierarchy and religious norms. These gender-biased notions, however, were not confined to the tribal domain. Many candidates had to respond to questions from their constituencies about their abilities as females to meet the demands of public office. These questions focused on matters such as whether they would be able to work at night and travel and coordinate their duties as housewives and parliamentarians. In addition, they had to contend with the often-repeated question of "Was the world so short of males that women had to run for office in their stead?" Some voters, exhibiting disenchantment with Parliament in general, asked, "If men could not achieve anything, what could women do?" (*Jordan Times* 1997a).

The women candidates had to compete with male counterparts who, with the exception of a few leftists and liberals, were actively nurturing their allegiance to their tribe or clan in an attempt to strengthen regional identification at the expense of a coherent ideology and a concrete agenda.

It must be highlighted that parliamentary elections provide the tribes with the opportunity to partake in a significant event that allows them to prove their identity as a tribe and their significance in the political structure. Within this tribal composition, women's public role can be extremely circumscribed. Individualism is subsumed under identification with the tribe. The tribe has the collective responsibility over the individual's actions and behavior and in return he or she ascribes to tribal solidarity. In this context, the authority of the father and the tribal leader defines the direction and object of the individual's allegiance. What this type of relationship engenders is mutual loyalty, dependence, patronage, and protection (Layne 1987, 125).

This tribal structure is patriarchal. A patriarchal society for the most part does not acknowledge a role for women except within socially accepted conditions and within the limits of certain confines that they should not violate. Within this structure, relationships are organized in a vertical manner, where the paternal will of the father is absolute and further strengthened by tradition or coercion or both (Sharabi 1975, 112).

Traditionally, patriarchy privileges males and elders, stressing men's domination over women, since the latter are viewed as the weaker sex in need of protection. Females are generally taught to respect and defer to their father, brothers, grandparents, uncles, and, at times, male cousins. A woman's accepted role in society is that of a mother, consort, and housewife. As Halim Barakat notes, "In the traditional Arab family, the father has authority and the responsibility. The wife joins his kin group (patrilocal kinship) and the children take his surname (patrilineal descent). The father expects respect and unquestioning compliance with his instructions. His position at the top of the pyramid of authority is based on the traditional division of labour, which has assigned him the role of breadwinner or provider" (1993, 100–101).

The nucleus of this patriarchal system is the family. An understanding of the family helps us understand relationships within society, since the family is linked to other social institutions in a "relationship often simultaneously complementary and contradictory . . . [within] the complex network of interconnections between family and social class, family and religion, and family and politics" (Barakat 1993, 116). Political socialization takes place in the home, resulting in the congruency of political orientations among members of the family (117). The family thus constitutes an economic and social unit, where all members cooperate to secure its livelihood and improve its standing in the community, since "the success or failure of an individual member becomes that of the family as a whole" (23).

The impact of the family on women can be seen in various aspects, including the patterns of marriage, the concept of honor, the status within the marriage, and more. Aspects of the family can also be seen in the relationship between husband and wife. The centrality of the family's impact on women is magnified such that, as Hisham Sharabi notes, "family patriarchy provides the ground for a dual domination—of the father over the family household, and of the male over the female" (1988, 32).

Of course, these family relations, much like gender and tribal relations, are not static. With the transformation Jordan has witnessed, these familial patterns have been changing through progress in the educational, economic, and social realms; women acquired more freedoms in terms of public participation and professional roles. This evolution has led to the weakening of vertical relations and patterns of subordination-domination and the disintegration of the extended clan family.

The Department of Statistics/FAFO survey indicated that the majority of Jordanian women above the age of fifteen (83 percent) could nowadays visit their neighbors without being accompanied. Furthermore, six in ten adult women can travel alone within the borders of the town or village where they live; 27 percent are able to move around very freely or quite freely as opposed to 12 percent that can never go alone. Mobility, as the survey indicates, has a strong correlation with participation in voluntary organizations and with voting and the political process in general. Those women who are more mobile tend also to be the ones who participate more broadly within society (Hanssen-Bauer, Pedersen, and Tiltnes 1998, 310–11).

Yet it is important to highlight the fact that despite this loosening of the patriarchal system, the family remains patriarchal and hierarchical in structure on the basis of sex and age, where "the young are subordinate to the old and females to males" (Barakat 1993, 102). Traditional values, family structures, kinship bonds, gender roles and relations within the family, male leadership over women, and perceptions of women's diminished capacities in comparison to men were maintained despite the recent transformations.

What we witness in Jordan even in the twenty-first century is that within urban centers, relations for the most part are still dominated by the same kinship ties characterizing villages and tribes. In this context, tribalism is not to be identified with the "Bedouins." Villages and, to some extent, towns have been largely an outgrowth of tribal substructures. Despite the fundamental social division distinguishing between the settled as opposed to the nomadic community, urban society has been based on kinship ties. Both the *fellahin* (villagers) and the Bedouins have maintained their tribally based structures (Jureidini and McLaurin 1984, 46). This "closeness" "carries multiple layers of meaning, ranging from asserted and recognized ties of kinship to participation in factional alliances, ties of patronage and clientship, and common bonds developed through neighbourliness" (Eickelman 1989, 156, cited in Hanssen-Bauer, Pedersen, and Tiltnes 1998, 261). These residential patterns result in several consequences, including the strengthening of social networks, the increased control over female behavior, and the supremacy of group identity over individual privacy. In the elections, these closely knit relations have affected the patterns of voting where these networks and relations heavily influenced votes by tribal and family members.

Gendered Citizenship

Tribalism, patriarchy, and family structures reflect notions of gender discrimination and reinforce them. In the context of analyzing the results of the elections, gender analysis is crucial. Understanding it allows us to go deeper than the surface of merely examining the elections. The results must be explained not only by statistical data of winners and losers but also by looking at what has shaped those results within the specific Jordanian context, such as the structure of gender relations in Jordan. A gender analysis examines the relationship between men and women in society and the roles that women and men acquire through complex societal processes. These processes include the roles that society predefines for females and males, that is, acceptable behavior patterns, modes of interaction between the sexes that reflect societal traditions, and society's perception of women's role in terms of division of responsibilities whether in the private or public domains. What is clear is that these roles and responsibilities, though based on biological differences, have ultimately become flagrant discriminatory practices and are found not only within the family domain but also within the economic, social, cultural, and political domains.

Why has the transformation that Jordan experienced over four decades in education, the economy, and political participation not altered the long-held perceptions regarding women's capabilities and role? The primary reason is that the state itself perceives women differently from men and deals with them accordingly. Men are seen as full-fledged citizens authorized to enjoy all the accompanying rights and entitlements, whereas women have a diminished value as citizens. The manifestations of this condition, including the negative attitudes, inferior treatment, and restricted entitlements women face, are all sanctioned by and enshrined in the state's legal structure and framework. The various factors limiting women could not have operated as effectively without the support of existing laws.

Although notions of equality are enshrined in the Jordanian Constitution, the laws and regulations governing the lives of citizens fall short of actualizing that equality by allowing discriminatory practices. For instance, laws relating to marriage; nationality, passports, and citizenship; and taxation and social pension all exhibit gender bias and discrimination between women and men. In the Social Security Law, for example, a woman employee's rights and entitlements are unequal to a man's. Upon her death, her family does not receive her social security benefits unless they can prove that she was the sole provider for her family. Old-age benefits accrue only to the husband, again on the assumption that he is the sole provider. A female cannot receive both her retirement benefits and her salary; rather, she must choose one or the other (Government of Jordan 1959, 960). Similar restrictions are found in the Health Insurance Law, which prevents a woman from being included in her husband's health insurance policy if she is employed and excludes her family from her own health insurance benefits (Government of Jordan 1983, 202).

If citizenship is defined as the guarantee of equal civil, legal, political, and social rights, entitlements, and responsibilities for all citizens, then it can be emphatically argued that Jordanian women possess a "diminished" form of citizenship. Citizens are granted rights, but their access to various entitlements must be facilitated and mediated by the state, with which they should share a direct relationship. Although the Jordanian state grants women rights as citizens, these rights can be actualized only through intermediaries, namely, the males in the family, who have control over women's actions and conduct.[6]

The entitlements that citizenship bestows on individuals must be equal, according to Article 6 of the Jordanian Constitution. Yet Jordanian citizenship has been grounded on assumptions of male superiority and female inferiority and subordination. This fact can be clearly seen in the Jordanian Nationality Law of 1954 and its amendment of 1987, which essentially identifies men as "true" citizens. Specifically, men alone can pass citizenship on to their offspring. Anyone born to a father holding Jordanian nationality is automatically considered a Jordanian citizen. Consequently, the children of a Jordanian mother married to a non-Jordanian are not considered citizens of the mother's country. Moreover, since the Nationality Law is

6. This section draws on the author's article, Amawi 2000.

not territorially based, the children of a Jordanian male are, according to Article 9, Jordanians wherever they are born (Government of Jordan 1954/1987).

The "masculinity" of the Nationality Law resounds in other laws as well. Fundamentally, it reflects the underpinnings of a paternally based citizenship, the main function of which is to build a nation made up of "full" sons. Only through the "superior male" citizen can the "subordinate female" citizen conduct her relationship with the state. The *Daftar al-'ai'la* (Family registration book) and the Qanoon al-Ahwal al-Shakhsiyya (Personal Status Law) are relevant examples (Government of Jordan 1976).

The *Family Registration Book* exemplifies the limitations placed on women's control over their own lives and the imposition of a mediator between them and the state. Issued in the name of the head of the household (father, brother, or husband) and including all female family members and children, the *Family Registration Book* has been increasingly used in place of the passport as a source of identification and is required to facilitate all administrative transactions. It rests on the assumption that the household head is the male, and only he can access all entitlements from the state, including obtaining voting cards, registering children in schools, renewing passports, and registering land, to name just a few.

These citizenship, passport, and residency provisions provide a basis for looking at the relationship between gender and citizenship in terms of inclusionary and exclusionary criteria. Women's status in the public domain, as defined by the state, is merely a reflection of the way relationships are constructed in the private domain, namely, relationships within marriage and within the family. This public-private dichotomy is culturally specific and inevitably leads to a discussion of the Personal Status Law.

The state, through its laws, reproduces the patriarchal structure within the family. The head of the family, the patriarch, enjoys the prerogative of demanding obedience, dissolving the marriage, and regulating the behavior of family members, especially women; most important, he constitutes his wife's "direct" link to the state. The Personal Status Law regulates marriage contracts and their dissolution, the custody of children, and entitlements within the marriage. In accordance with the provisions of the law, a woman cannot conclude her own marriage arrangements (Government of Jordan 1976). Moreover, the Penal Code also stipulates this gender-based discrimination. Under the provisions of Articles 326–32 of the code, capital punishment is to be applied in cases of premeditated murder. However, the law does not define the crime as premeditated murder but treats it as a special case that warrants reduced punishment. The justification for reducing the sentence relates to the perpetrator's temporary loss of reasoning—the "fit of fury" he experiences as a result of the "defamation" of the family's honor (Government of Jordan 1960).

"Honor crimes" are instances where the father, brother, or first cousin murders a female relative to "cleanse the family honor." These crimes have averaged between 1990 and 1995 about 150 cases, or 30.3 percent of all murder cases in Jordan. In 1995 alone there were 19 cases, or 24.3 percent of all murder cases (Al-Multqa al-Insani Li-Hoqoq al-Mara'a 1997, 22). Most of these crimes are committed based on the suspicion of an illicit relationship or other behavior perceived to have dishonored the family. What accounts for these hideous crimes? They are linked to a broader trend among males who are resistant to changing patterns of social behavior owing to women's increasing exposure to and involvement in public life and the changing power relationships between the genders. Before women are granted equal citizenship status before the law, they have to be perceived as equal human beings in terms of capabilities. Thus, under the Penal Code, including punishment for a particular crime must be equally applied to both males and females.

It can be argued that the progress Jordan has witnessed has not been translated into improvement in the lives of women and their empowerment. There remains a significant gender inequality in wages, as one example among many. Comparing the average wage for males and females who have the same educational level reveals that a female receives about one-third of a male wage at the illiterate level, one-half at the elementary level, two-thirds at the basic education level, 82 percent at the secondary level and about the same for the intermediate diploma, and 71 percent of men's wages at the university level (Government of Jordan 1997). Moreover, women's unemployment has steadily increased over the years. In 1987, male unemployment was 13 percent compared to 27 percent among women. By 1991, male unemployment had increased to 14.7 percent compared to a high of 34.4 percent for women (M. Kawar 2000, 59).

How are women to believe in themselves and in other women when their membership in a patriarchal society shapes their reality—a reality in which authority, domination, and dependence characterize social relations between sexes within the family, clan, and tribe? How do women break free from these restrictions when they legally have a lower status as citizens? These negative forces affect not only society's perception of women but also women's perception of themselves, converging to diminish women's enthusiasm for political participation.

These domination and dependence patterns become deeply internalized through the process of socialization. This process includes the upbringing of children, the provision of education, and various societal patterns and forms of interaction. It shapes one's perception of oneself and one's capacities and the abilities of others, and it affects the consciousness of individuals and groups.

Men's views, society's perceptions, and women's perceptions of themselves combine to diminish women's political aspirations. Evidence is provided in the dominance men exert over women's votes. The fact that they can successfully do so derives from women's low level of political awareness and society's attitudes toward them. In the Department of Statistics/FAFO *1996 Survey on Living Conditions in Jordan,* a question was asked of six thousand people regarding their views on women's participation in politics. Among the men surveyed, 57 percent of those between the ages of twenty and twenty-four were against having a woman minister or member of Parliament, as opposed to 39 percent of those between the ages of fifty and fifty-nine. The study also revealed that the rise in unemployment had negatively affected attitudes toward women's professional and political activities (Hanssen-Bauer, Pedersen, and Tiltnes 1998, 307).

Conclusions

Analyzing the experience of women candidates in the 1997 parliamentary elections is not an easy undertaking. As Fatimah 'Obeidat, running in the Bani Kananah district, noted of her knowledge of the obstacles she was going to face if she ran, "We must challenge everyone and face difficulties if we wish to succeed" *(Jordan Times* 1997a). She attributed her failure to the difficulty of convincing tribe members to alter their traditional voting habits, including women who, despite her effort to improve their overall legal and social situation, did not vote for her. She concluded that there is a general lack of awareness among women about their rights and of the power that their vote carries.[7]

There are two ways of looking at the situation: one could be pessimistic as a result of the election's outcome or optimistic on the basis of what was achieved through women's participation. Much of what occurred during the elections was unfair, which could generate a good amount of general pessimism. The women had to overcome many difficulties and hurdles to win the limited acceptance by and support of their families, tribes, and communities. Some women candidates had all the

---

7. For a comprehensive analysis of the 1997 elections focusing on female candidates' participation and based on three workshops conducted with the candidates and extensive interviews and questionnaires, see Amawi 2001.

requisites to become thorough politicians. Yet the mere fact that they were women created uncertainties about their legitimacy as candidates, and for that reason alone, in many cases, people simply did not vote for them.

It must be affirmed here that the picture is not bleak. It is possible to maintain a sense of optimism stemming from an objective look at the realities and seeing the glass as half full rather than half empty. One must remember the 13,086 votes that the women received and how the women candidates who ran in tribal strongholds and refugee camps fought with determination against historically skewed odds. And finally, women should draw courage from the many volunteers who worked on these campaigns, tirelessly and without any ulterior motive, in the simple hope of seeing real change occur.

This belief in the power and possibility of change is what should motivate us to continue the struggle. Change, in the Jordanian case, is inevitable; to some degree, it has already begun. Seeing the mobility of Jordanian women, their achievements in the educational and other professional fields, and their support for human rights and democratic practices should motivate us to push forward. Only three decades ago our mothers lived under much stricter conditions. Our daughters will chart their own paths, characterized by greater freedom and more equality. We have to look at history to plan our future.

What women need to strive for is attaining legal equality in the public and private domain, enshrining equality as a virtuous societal attribute, actualizing equality in socialization patterns, empowering the self-perception of women, influencing decision-making institutions, increasing participation in civil society and participation at all political levels, influencing agendas of research centers and cultural associations, enhancing involvement in NGOs and creating an effective women's movement, increasing effective interaction with the media, and, finally, working for a more democratic system with a quota built in.

The path of the future has been partially charted by the women candidates who took part in the 1993 and 1997 parliamentary elections. The inability of the women candidates to win any seats ushered in a period of extensive debates over gender political empowerment. As a result, a quota of six seats for women was introduced into the parliamentary elections held on June 17, 2003. Yet the road ahead does not seem to be less arduous. Indeed, observing the decisions of the 2003 parliament—which rejected a law that gave Jordanian women the right to file for divorce and temporary legislation to tighten the penalties for crimes of "honor"—does not give us much hope. What is even more ominous is that the elected women candidates joined forces with those individuals opposed to the progressive laws. They seemed to have agreed with member of Parliament Mahmoud Kharbasheh who noted during the session, "If it was up to me, women would be at home raising their children" (Associated Press 2003).

4 Afghan Women under Marxism

SENZIL NAWID

RELATIVELY LITTLE is known about how Afghan citizens experienced the opportunities and challenges of the Marxist era (1978–92) in Afghanistan, and virtually nothing is known about what the period meant to Afghan women. With the passing of the socialist experiment in Afghanistan, historical assessments of its achievements tend toward the negative. In the words of Fred Halliday, "it was in this 14-year period that the society and politics of the country were brutally transformed, from above and below, leading to the chaos of the 1990s in which another radical authoritarian faction, the Taliban, came to power" (1998, 1).

This chapter examines the policies of the Soviet-backed Afghan Marxist regimes, their early impact on women, and their longer-term ramifications for women in Afghanistan.

Background

Afghanistan is a predominantly rural-tribal society, dominated by patriarchal attitudes and practices. Concepts of honor and shame proscribe the behavior of men and women. The honor of family, clan, and to a certain extent the nation is centered on women. Women are viewed as family possessions and symbols of family honor. This point of view is particularly true in the Pashtun tribal regions, where a widow is customarily claimed by her deceased husband's family and forced to marry his closest surviving male relative. Tribal and subtribal disputes are often settled by giving one or several women in marriage to the family of the aggrieved party without requiring customary bridal payments. This particular practice severely negates family honor and is only prescribed in the case of grave crime.

Initial efforts to change the status of women coincided with the nationalist liberal movement led by King Amanullah (1919–29) following the achievement of Afghan independence from Great Britain in 1919. Among other social reforms,

King Amanullah introduced public education for girls and promulgated the family law in 1921 that discouraged polygamy, abolished child marriages and forced marriages, and outlawed the Pashtun tribal practices of giving women in marriage as retribution for crime and forcing a widow to marry the closest male relative of her deceased husband. The custom requiring that money be given to the father of the bride was also prohibited by the family law of 1921. These matters were very sensitive issues in the patriarchal, kinship-based society of early-twentieth-century Afghanistan, where customary law granted fewer rights to women than were accorded them by Islamic law.

Led by Queen Soraya, Amanullah's wife, and upper-class urban women, the early women's movement in Afghanistan flourished in an era that increasingly looked with favor upon secular education and access to education for girls. Until 1921, education for women was restricted to reading the Qur'an and did not include writing, except for a few upper-class women. In 1928, Amanullah also started a campaign to unveil women.

King Amanullah's attempt to impose Western-style reforms was immediately challenged by traditional groups. As I have shown elsewhere, his attempt to improve the status of women was one of the major causes of the widespread clergy-backed revolts that eventually led to his abdication in January 1929 (Nawid 1999).

With the departure of King Amanullah, the pace of change benefiting women slowed drastically. In 1920, Habibullah Klakani, one of the leaders of the opposition, established his authority in Kabul and enforced a strict policy of veiling and secluding women, a policy reimposed in the 1990s by the Taliban government. All girls' schools were closed, and women were forced back into the home.

The rise to power of Nadir Shah (1930–33) and his son, Zahir Shah (1933–73), opened a new phase in the status of women in Afghanistan. Alerted by the disastrous consequences of Amanullah's measures, the new regime adopted a cautious policy of expanding schools for girls in urban centers. Issues relating to the liberation of women resurfaced in the late 1950s when Prime Minister Mohammad Daoud (1956–64) initiated new reforms to modernize the state and encourage economic development. Dimensions of economic development and modernization required changes in the status of women. Again in 1958, the government began to encourage the unveiling of women and their entry into the workplace and public life. While committing itself unofficially to supporting women who wished to abandon the veil and pursue higher education, the government supported only voluntary change in hopes of minimizing opposition.

The mid-1960s marked a turning point for women. During this period, women's emancipation was closely linked to broader issues of economic and social development. In 1964, a new constitution granted women the franchise and equal employment opportunity. Family law, however, remained unchanged. The status of women improved in urban centers with only limited legal changes. Leaders within the Zahir Shah government presumed that the role of women in the family would improve with the expansion of educational and employment opportunities for women.

Following the coup d'état of 1973 and the establishment of republican government under Mohammad Daoud (1973–78), a comprehensive family law deemed compatible with Islamic law was enacted in 1976 under the new civil code. Similar in content to measures introduced during the 1920s by King Amanullah, the new family law fixed the minimum age of marriage for boys at eighteen and for girls at sixteen, imposed restrictions on the practice of polygamy, and outlawed forced marriage and the payment of bridal money. Article 133 granted women the right to initiate divorce in certain conditions (Government of Afghanistan 1355/1976, no. 19, 19–75). The family law also provided in detail provisions on child support and alimony. In these matters, the marriage code of 1976 was more progressive than the marriage law of the 1920s.

By the time of the establishment of the Democratic Republic of Afghanistan (DRA) in 1978, popular attitudes toward women had changed in urban areas. It had become acceptable for women to seek higher education, work outside the home, and take part in the broader life of the community. Although old patterns of behavior were not completely uprooted and disparities between urban and rural life were increasing, government policies increased educational and employment opportunities for women in urban areas and slowly increased popular acceptance of women in the public arena. Women occupied judicial and ministerial positions in the government, had been elected to both houses of the Afghan parliament, and held academic positions at Kabul University. So when new political parties were organized in 1965, they were able to enlist in their ranks a number of female high school and university students in major Afghan cities.

The Marxist Era

In 1965, two communist political parties emerged, the pro-Soviet Hizb-i Demokratik-i Khalq-i Afghanistan (People's Democratic Party of Afghanistan [PDPA]), which was composed of Khalq (Masses) and Parcham (Banner) factions, and the pro-China Sazman-i-Demokratik-i Navin-i Afghanistan (New Democratic

Organization of Afghanistan [NDOA]), also known as Shola-i-Jawid (Eternal Flame). Both of these parties attracted female high school and university students in major cities. In 1966, the Parcham faction of PDPA formed the Sazman-i Demokratik-i Zanan-i Afghanistan (Democratic Organization of Afghan Women [DOAW]) as one of its main organs under the leadership of Dr. Anahita Ratibzad. The DOAW's main function was to expand the base of the PDPA among women. Whereas the Khalqis drew their support from the provinces (mostly sons of provincial landowners), the Parchamis were primarily urban based. Although dominated by middle-class, educated families of Kabul, the Parchamis also included many young men and women from Kandahar, Herat, Kunduz, and Baghlan. The NDOA stressed class struggle and revolutionary armed uprising as means to end class oppression. Women of working-class families tended to support the NDOA.

While the government-sponsored Mirmono-Tolena (Women's Association) organized itself around charitable activities and pursued projects to improve the status of women, political parties endeavored to raise political consciousness among female students. In the 1960s and early 1970s many female students were recruited to the party and were taught the skills of political organization. Newly politicized women became actively involved in social and political controversies of this period.

The Sawr (April) Revolution and the Establishment of the Marxist Regime

The People's Democratic Party of Afghanistan gained power in a coup led by insurgents in the armed forces on April 27, 1978. The coup came to be known as the Sawr (April) Revolution. Shortly thereafter, the Democratic Republic of Afghanistan was established under Nur Mohammad Taraki, the leader of the Khalq branch of the PDPA. The DRA went further than any previous regime in the effort to liberate women by pushing for radical changes in the structure of Afghan society. To understand the political dynamics of the Marxist era with regard to women in Afghanistan, it is necessary to understand certain aspects of Marxist-Leninist theory to which the leaders of the People's Democratic Party of Afghanistan adhered.

Marxist-Leninist feminist theory connects the oppression of women with the broader issues of class struggle, labor, and economy. Double standards for men and women, according to the Marxists, are created in a class society and are innate in the patriarchal family system that determines sex roles and protracts the oppression of women. "Oppressions are rooted in the social organizations through which one class (owner of productive means) exploits the labour of others (those who must work to live), and until the means of production are held in common, no oppression, whether class, national, race, or sex, will be eradicated from our society" (Guettel 1989, 2). Women will achieve equal status with men, according to the Marxists, when the functions of the family are replaced with superior institutions run by the state. Lenin went even further by identifying imperialism as the main enemy of oppressed people (Moghissi 1994, 97). Leninist theorists then defined women in nonindustrial societies as the proletariat and argued that women would secure full control over their lives and reshape their destinies only as an integral force in the world socialist revolution.[1] Guided by Marxist-Leninist ideology, the PDPA leaders linked Afghanistan's backwardness to feudalism, traditional taboos, and widespread female illiteracy. To move forward, they attacked the structure of tribal feudalism and championed women's liberation as central tenets in the fight against feudalism, capitalism, and Western imperialism. In so doing, the PDPA pushed the issue of women's emancipation to its radical extreme in Afghanistan.

In Decree No. 7, issued by the Revolutionary Council in October 1978, the DOAW declared its goal: "to free the toiling women of Afghanistan from humiliating feudalistic relations and provide opportunities for their advancement at all levels." As leader of the DOAW, Dr. Ratibzad hailed the April Revolution as a great historical event opening wide horizons for women's progress. "This is the first time," she wrote, "that the issue of the protection of women's rights as mothers and toiling citizens of Afghanistan is an agenda item for political discussion at a high official level and is included in an official platform" (Nelofer 1981, 3).

Meanwhile, the Democratic Organization of Women expanded its activities to include four new committees: (1) Committee to Fight Against Illiteracy, (2) Financial Aid Committee, (3) Fine Arts Committee, and (4) Committee for the Promotion of Cottage Industry. These committees were set up to support the illiterate working class and prepare its members for jobs outside the home. Their main purpose was to strengthen women's position by making women less vulnerable to economic exploitation and less dependent upon their husbands.

The Revolutionary Women's Emancipation Movement

The primary concern of the women's emancipation movement under the PDPA was to create consciousness of the political importance of gender and make women vis-

1. The theory of the female proletarian was developed by Vemadskay and Thachev (see Stites 1978, 59). The application of this theory to women in central Asia has been analyzed in Massel 1972.

ible in the public arena. Women's emancipation was connected with the DRA's revolutionary program that challenged the existing traditional social order in Afghanistan. The DRA government targeted first the structure of tribal feudalism. Decree No. 7 abolished forced marriage; the customary exchange of women in marriage for cash, known as *shir-baha;* and extravagant wedding expenses. It limited the amount of bridal money *(mahr)* and set the minimum age of engagement and marriage at sixteen for women and eighteen for men. A special postal stamp was issued to commemorate the decree as the first sign of the dismantling of feudal practices in Afghanistan.

The DRA linked Afghanistan's backwardness to widespread female illiteracy and traditional taboos blocking women's progress. To remedy the situation and strengthen its base of support among the masses, the regime launched an aggressive literacy campaign. Adult literacy courses were offered in every district in the cities and in the countryside. The main target of the literacy campaign was women, the largest sector of the illiterate population.

In 1979, an inner power struggle between the two factions of the PDPA resulted in the expulsion of Anahita Ratibzad, Babrak Karmal, and several other leading members of the Parcham branch of the PDPA from Afghanistan. Nur Mohammad Taraki and his prime minister, Hafizullah Amin, who succeeded him a few months later, attempted to consolidate the power under the banner of the Khalq Party. They endorsed the regime's prior commitment to liberate women and at the same time changed the name of the DOAW to the Khalq Organization of Afghan Women and appointed Delara Mahak, a member of the Khalq faction of the PDPA, as its president.

In 1980, following the Soviet military intervention in Afghanistan, Ratibzad returned to Kabul and resumed her position as the president of the DOAW. Her appointment as minister of education under the Karmal regime and as a member of the Presidium of the Revolutionary Council and the PDPA Central Committee Politburo also boosted the importance of the DOAW as a government organ. As resistance against the DRA assumed broader dimensions after the Soviet military intervention, the DOAW intensified its political activities under Ratibzad's leadership, who now also presided over the DRA Afghan-Soviet Friendship Organization. Issues concerning women became increasingly overshadowed by the PDPA's broader political concerns and its fight against the reactionary forces, which had gained strength as a result of military and financial support from outside foreign powers. During her inaugural speech at the All Afghan Women Conference held in Kabul in November 1980, Anahita Ratibzad asserted that the most important objective of the

DOAW was the protection of the achievements of the April Revolution against imperialism.[2] In this effort, the regime attempted to recruit students to act as agents of change. It also intensified the activities of the Pishahangan (Pioneers' Organization), whose members were recruited from male and female high school students. They were required to take military training after school. Armed and dressed in special uniforms, they worked as revolutionary agents against feudalism and Western imperialism in Afghanistan. Their emblem, a shield and dagger that symbolized defense and attack, was a modified version of the KGB insignia. The activities of Pishahangan as well as the endeavors of the Youth Organization, which was also composed of high school students, were periodically examined by the Soviet advisers. Every year a group of students belonging to these organizations was selected for higher training in the Soviet Union.

The regime encouraged female party members and the female members of the youth student organizations to fight along with men to counter feudalism and take part in the PDPA's four-front struggle policy: (1) the fight against imperialism *(mojadela bar zedd-i isti'mar)*; (2) the fight against black reaction, that is, religious and feudal power *(mojadela bar zedd-i irtija'-i-siyah)*; (3) the struggle against regional reaction, that is, Iran and Pakistan *(mojadela bar zedd-i irtija'-i mantaqawi)*; and (4) the struggle against patriarchy *(mojadela bar zedd-i padar-salari)*.

Mobilization of women became a multifaceted process. Women were moved to mobilize other women and attract them to the party agenda. This campaign was done through a network of clubs, workshops, private meetings at homes, and social work organizations. Politically active women were assigned to go to villages and urban neighborhoods to mobilize the community and promote political awareness in support of revolution among women. In 1984, the DOAW maintained that the organization had succeeded in uniting approximately 30,000 women in 669 primary organizations and had mobilized more than 80,000 rural women in social production. According to official reports, by 1990 the organization had attracted more than 160,000 members, with 1,405 women of working class, 7,309 farming women, 62,810 housewives, and 33,764 female students. It had 30 provincial and 33 subprovincial committees and 29 branches in the rural areas and had forged affiliation with 152 national, regional, and international organizations, including the In-

2. The All Afghan Women Conference was the first international women's seminar to be held in Kabul. It was attended by delegations from foreign countries and a number of international women's organizations. Ratibzad's speech has been printed in *Matn-i-Awalin Canfrans-i-Sartasari-i-Zanan-i-Afghanistan* [The Manual of the First All Women's Conference] (1980, 11–35).

ternational Democratic Women's Federation, National Organization of African Women, Committee of the Women of the Soviet Union, as well as the women associations of India, Vietnam, Cuba, Bangladesh, Iran, Pakistan, and Turkey (Government of Afghanistan 1369/1990b, 56:69).

Nancy Dupree has argued that women were attracted to the party either through pressure or because of unhappy male-female relations at home. "The young were particularly attracted by loosening parental control. Most had no ideological reasons for joining. They joined for the sheer excitement of doing something different, of defying elders. . . . Moreover, party meetings provided an alternative to cloistered, family-chaperoned outings" (1984, 319).

The regime also intensified its efforts to expand the literacy programs. In an interview with *Soviet Women* (issue no. 5, 1980) Ratibzad maintained that 500,000 had completed literacy courses in 27,000 courses throughout the country (Dupree 1984, 331). An important aspect of the literacy campaign was *tajdid-i-tarbiyyat*: introducing the masses to the Marxist-Leninist ideology.

Drawbacks of the Women's Emancipation Movement under the DRA

No doubt, these policies enhanced political awareness and self-confidence among women and gave them a sense of involvement in the civic life of the country and a sense of responsibility for its future. The other great impact of PDPA policies was to make education accessible to women of all ages and classes. When the Marxist regime collapsed in 1992, 50 percent of the students and 60 percent of the teachers at Kabul University were women. In addition, 70 percent of all schoolteachers, 50 percent of civilian government workers, and 40 percent of the doctors in Kabul were women. However, the DRA's gender policies had several drawbacks.

Despite their declared policy to uproot oppressive family conditions in Afghanistan, the PDPA leadership did not pursue in earnest the issue of gender equality or for that matter any issue directly related to the condition of women. This lack was partly because Marxism-Leninism does not treat feminism as a separate agenda but also because the Afghan Marxist leaders could not quite separate themselves from the deeply entrenched patriarchal values of their own culture. Women remained as secondary figures throughout the Marxist revolutionary movement. During the fourteen-year PDPA rule, Anahita Ratibzad was the only woman to ever rise to a high position in the party and be included in the Presidium of the Revolutionary Council. Until 1990, Ratibzad was the only woman to receive a position in the cabinet. While applauding the emancipation of women and encouraging the mixing of the opposite sexes in the workplace, in private life most Marxist leaders held on to their superior position at home and their tight control over the female members of the family, and these practices were followed more strictly as the threats to the capital from opposition groups increased.

Family law remained basically unchanged. Unlike the policies of King Amanullah and President Mohammad Daoud that attempted to change the structure of the family in Afghanistan, the PDPA family law was vague in areas regarding polygamy and child support, and the divorce law was not officially announced. The only provision of the family that was pursued rigorously by the PDPA was in the matter of dowry. Without changing the provision of the Islamic law related to bridal money *(mahr)*, Decree No. 7 abolished the dower proper *(shir-baha)* that was customarily paid to the father of the bride. The introduction of family courts presided over by women judges did provide a hearing for discontented wives and protected their rights to divorce, alimony, child custody, and child support. However, as Dupree points out, "principles crucial to true emancipation, such as equal right of women to demand divorce, work opportunities, and inheritance—all guaranteed by Daoud's Civil Law—were not considered. Hopes that the DRA would effect a meaningful direction for the women's rights program were dimmed by the lack of guarantees in Decree no. 7" (1984, 324).

Despite the DRA's great achievements in the area of education, the educational program had several downsides. The policy of engaging students in the party agenda provided grounds for discrimination within the educational system. The majority of the Afghan women refugees I interviewed in Peshawar, Pakistan, complained about the constant pressure they were under during the Karmal government to join the party and take part in exhausting street demonstrations. The students who were willing to adapt received leadership positions and special favors from their teachers, and those women who did not comply were discriminated against and spied on by party-affiliated peers.[3]

In 1985, the content of textbooks was changed to include the concept of dialectical materialism, and education became the means for the dissemination of socialist doctrine. Attempts by the government to enforce the Leninist dogma through schools prompted the first wave of mass exodus in the 1980s. Many urban, educated families chose exile over complying with the new indoctrination programs in schools.

---

3. These interviews were carried out with educated Afghan women refugees in Peshawar, Pakistan, in the spring of 2000 under the auspices of the American Institute of Pakistan Studies.

Reaction to the Mobilization of Women

The campaign to engage women as a revolutionary force for change in Afghanistan, a traditional Islamic society with deeply seated tribal and patriarchal values, was bound to ignite a strong reaction among traditional forces. Dramas depicting women in feudal bondage on television and a Flag Day parade in which female students were televised dancing and chanting Marxist slogans and waving red flags infuriated many. Most of the female students participating in the parade were from Kandahar. Many of them had turned to the PDPA prior to the April Revolution in reaction to the antifeminist attitudes of male Akhwani students.[4] As it turned out, many Kandahari fathers who had pleaded to get their daughters admitted to Kabul University before the April Revolution were deeply offended by the participation of their daughters in the Flag Day parade. Many of these Kandahari men turned against education for women altogether.

The literacy campaign seemed promising at the beginning. Reportedly, the citizens initially welcomed this initiative and were happy for women to join literacy classes. The regime succeeded in recruiting women in remote villages as far away as Badakhshan, in northern Afghanistan, to join midwifery and literacy courses. However, public opinion turned against the new regime when partisans of the government began using offensive anti-Islamic rhetoric. Although the official policy of the regime claimed loyalty to Islam, zealous young cadets and officials traveling in the countryside propounded revolutionary messages with negative references to Islam (Nawid 1993, 24). In response, opposition mounted to the literacy campaign, land reforms, and women's emancipation, and religious leaders declared jihad, denouncing the regime as a puppet government intent on replacing Islam with communism. By emphasizing what many citizens perceived as an alien, non-Islamic ideology in support of the emancipation initiative, the PDPA leaders turned the majority of the general population against female education. For many Afghans, women's liberation was associated with atheism, and the disastrous times that had befallen their country were frequently attributed to promiscuity associated with the emancipation of women.

The free mixing of politically active women with politically active men also generated malicious gossip. Anahita Ratibzad, the head of the DOAW, was accused of having improper relations with Babrak Karmal and was seen as condoning im-

---

4. Members of the Islamic Party of Afghanistan were dubbed Ikhwanis because of their alleged association with the Akhwan al-Muslimin (Egyptian Muslim Brotherhood).

morality among party-affiliated women. The following lines reflect the perception of many citizens regarding women's emancipation under the Marxists:

> The Khalqis and the Parchamis were both morally corrupt. The only difference between the two was in the way the male party members treated women. The Khalqis, who came from a conservative social background, were still under the influence of their ancestral cultural milieu and were restrictive with their own female family members. They were, however, impertinent in seeking promiscuous relations with other women. During the celebration of Taraki's birthday, hundreds of women were forced at gun point to sexually gratify party members.
>
> The Parchamis, on the other hand, encouraged communal relations between men and women and generously shared their women with each other and with Russian soldiers. Anahita Ratibzad's relations with Babrak Karmal were the source of debauchery. The Women's Organization [DOAW], a frequent participant in the Soviet-Afghan Friendship programs, actively encouraged this trend. In the name of "service to the international proletariat" [party-affiliated] women were coerced to espionage and prostitution and were thrown in the arms of Russian soldiers. (Tanweer 2000, 240)

Negative views about party-affiliated women were fueled further by the DRA's practice of recruiting female singers and dancers who could sing and dance to new music composed to propagandize the regime. The state promoted these stage performers and introduced them as the revolutionary women of Afghanistan. Tanweer opined that the communist regime "denigrated performing arts by promoting debauchery in the name of 'art in the service of the proletariat.' Young schoolgirls were driven out of their schools to dance at galas held for the entertainment of party members" (2000, 239).

As a central tenet of the political agenda of the Marxist regime, the mobilization of women became a threatening symbol of an atheistic ideology. A growing discontent with the Khalq and Parcham government focused primarily on their policies regarding women. Outrage against the radical emancipation of women was one of the causes of violent uprising in Herat in the fall of 1978, which resulted in the killing of two prominent female party members.

To counter the PDPA women's liberation movement, Burhanuddin Rabbani and Gulbuddin Hikmatyar, leaders of the resistance movement who had established their base of operation in Peshawar, Pakistan, established their own organizations for women, the Islamic Association of Afghan Women and the Um al-Muslima Organization, to preserve traditional practices with regards to women. Many refugee women joined these two organizations in order to obtain support for themselves and for their families; in the process, some were indoctrinated in the ideology of fundamentalist groups. In response to the declarations of Decree No. 7, Rabbani, Hikmatyar, and Mawlawi Khalis, three leaders of resistance, issued a joint fatwa, or religious verdict, to raise the amount of bridal money to Afs170,000 as opposed to the Afs300 determined by the DRA. At the same time, a group of Afghan women activists in the border city of Quetta, in Pakistan, came under attack from both sides. As a result of their opposition to the fundamentalist resistance leaders as well as the Soviet-backed Marxist regime, these women activists were disliked by both groups and were dubbed Maoists. In 1987, Mina Kishwar Kamal, the leader of the Quetta-based women activists and the founder of the Revolutionary Afghan Women Association, was assassinated along with two of her close associates in Quetta, allegedly at the instigation of Gulbuddin Hikmatyar, leader of the radical Islamic Party of Afghanistan.

The fight against Western-style female education and women's emancipation became a precept of Afghan fundamentalists, who gained strength during the war by allying with fundamentalist Islamic groups outside Afghanistan. They associated the feminist policies of the DRA with atheism, promiscuity, and immorality. Women who supported the policies of the DRA were regarded as symbols of social and moral decay and Sovietism. Not surprisingly, when the Mujahideen took over Jalalabad, a city in eastern Afghanistan, they immediately banned women from the University of Nangarhar.

In 1986, a change in the leadership of the PDPA brought Dr. Najibullah, the former head of the KHAD, the DRA's central intelligence service, to power. Babrak Karmal, Anahita Ratibzad, and several other members of the old guard were forced to step down. To minimize the growing armed resistance to the Marxist rule, Najibullah initiated a policy of "National Reconciliation," softening the PDPA's assault on capitalism in an effort to sustain economic growth. To increase the regime's support among the masses, he merged the Khalq and Parcham factions of the PDPA under a new banner, Padarwatan (Fatherland). In the matter of government policy toward women, he expanded the DOAW to include eleven pilot branches in Kabul and one similar branch in every provincial center. The main objective of these pilot organizations was to reach women of the working class by means of propaganda *(tablighat)* and literacy courses *(sawad amuzi)* and accelerate the process of the proletarianization of the women's movement *(tudai-sakhtan-i-jonbish-i-zanan)* (Government of Afghanistan 1345/1966, 52:737–39). The appointment of an illiterate working-class woman, Firuza Fidayi Wardak, to replace Dr. Anahita Ratibzad as president of the DOAW in 1986 symbolized the importance the regime attributed to the "toiling women of Afghanistan" and the equal role it assigned women in defending the objectives of the April Revolution. Firuza reportedly worked for the KHAD under Najibullah and was chosen as the president of the DOAW in recognition of the leadership she had demonstrated in a military clash between government forces and a resistance group in a village in the vicinity of Kabul (Nawid 1993, 22). However, greater propaganda activities among the masses produced the opposite result. Feminist rhetoric used by the Kabul government to further its political goals, in effect, reinforced suspicions of its intentions and strengthened the adherence of the fundamentalists to traditional patriarchal perceptions and attitudes toward women.

With the withdrawal of the Soviet troops from Afghanistan in 1988 and the growing strength of the resistance forces, Najibullah felt compelled to reverse some of the offensive measures, including efforts to engage women actively in support of Marxist revolution. In 1990, he abolished the DOAW and replaced it with the Shura-i-Sarasari-i-Zanan-i-Afghanistan (All Afghan Women's Council), whose main objective was announced to be the promotion of women's position in the family as mothers and as rightful members of Afghan society (Government of Afghanistan 1369/1990a, vol. 56) and reinstated the celebration of Mother's Day, which was dismissed in 1979 as a frivolous bourgeois initiative. The appointment of Saleha Farouq Etemadi and Masuma Esmati, prominent women figures in the pre-Marxist era, as the ministers of education and national security in 1990 marked the shift from sponsorship of revolutionary women's emancipation to support of the moderate women's movement of the pre-Marxist era. During interviews with the authorities in Kabul, Valentine Moghadam was informed that "the Afghan Women's Council was less political and more social and service-oriented than it had been in the past, especially when it was under the direction of Anahita Ratibzad." She was also reminded that "reforms initiated by Taraki and the PDPA in 1978 had been ill-conceived, badly implemented, and too dramatic and hasty for the rural Afghan population" (2003, 250).

However, efforts to abrogate extreme measures had little effect in changing the attitude of the opposition groups. It was obvious that the PDPA's highly politicized women's liberation movement had unleashed fundamentalist Islamic attitudes regarding women that were now harder to reverse. The general reaction against the feminist movement launched by the Marxists was so strong that many PDPA members, including Najibullah himself, prevented their wives from participating in public affairs for fear of terrorist acts against them by opposition groups.

Women were the primary victims of years of chaos, lawlessness, and factional wars that ensued the fall of the Marxist regime. With the Mujahideen takeover of Kabul in February 1992, progressive changes that had taken place in the status of women since the beginning of the twentieth century were reversed. Hundreds of women in Kabul were tortured, raped, and brutally murdered by factions of resistance forces as atheist communists. Although the Taliban treatment of women received global attention during the late 1990s and the first years of the twenty-first century, few of the horrendous crimes committed by these groups against the women of Kabul were ever reported in the Western press. The Western powers, especially the United States, which had actively supported the resistance forces against the Marxist regime, lost interest in Afghanistan after the disintegration of the Soviet Union.

The campaign of the Marxists to promote revolutionary women's emancipation provided an ample pretext for the conservative elements to mount concentrated resistance to women's emancipation. Resentment against the women's movement was articulated in a religious edict signed by sixteen members of the Judiciary Council following the Mujahideen takeover. The verdict reads in part:

> The Muslim people of Afghanistan launched a jihad, fought for fourteen years, and lost numerous lives in order to reestablish the Divine Ordinances in the Country. Now that this objective has been fulfilled by the Grace of the Almighty and our Islamic country is free from the bondage of the atheist rule, we urge that God's ordinances be carried out immediately, particularly those pertaining to the veiling of women. Women should be banned from working in offices and radio and television stations, and schools for women, that are in effect the hub of debauchery and adulterous practices, must be closed down.

The ordinances required women to cover their faces outside the home and not to leave their homes without a compelling reason and first obtaining their husbands' permission. The wearing of noisy shoes, anklets, perfume, or any other embellishment that might attract a man's attention was prohibited.[5] These ordinances were precursors to similar decrees issued later by the Taliban.

---

5. *Fatawa-i-shara'i dar mawrid-i-hijab* [The shari'a ordinances on veiling] was issued in 1994 by the Stera Mahkama (Afghan Supreme Court) during the Islamic government of Burhanuddin Rabbani (1993–96). The ordinances were published in pamphlet form and signed by sixteen members of the Riyasat-i-Ifta wa al-Mutali'at (Bureau of Jurisdiction and Deliberation) of the Supreme Court.

Conclusion

Barnett Rubin (1995) has referred to the period of Marxist rule in Afghanistan as a case of failed revolution from above. Although the PDPA leaders themselves blamed the failure of socialism in Afghanistan on the interference of foreign powers, many internal as well as external factors were responsible for the collapse of Marxist revolution in Afghanistan. Analysis of those factors is beyond the scope of this chapter. I have dealt only with the impact of Marxist policies on women. I have shown that the women's emancipation campaign under the Marxists, notwithstanding some positive effects, had long-term negative consequences for women. The positive aspect of the initiative of the Marxist era was to make education available to women of all ages and classes. The PDPA's literacy campaign, if successful, could have made a big difference in the status of Afghan women. Also significant was the regime's efforts to teach women organizational skills, to become involved in Afghan politics, and to become active members of Afghan society.

The Khalq-Parcham politics of gender, however, concentrated heavily on women as agents of struggle against the forces of tradition. The PDPA leadership attributed the depressed condition of women to the evils of feudalism and the pervasive oppression of class society in Afghanistan. The question of oppression of women in the sphere of reproduction and the patriarchal structure of the institution of the family was scarcely a subject of concern for either Khalq or Parcham leaders. Their policy of using women as a revolutionary force against tradition and their highly politicized women's emancipation movement based on class struggle pushed women into the forefront of the ideological conflict between the Marxists and the traditional Muslim indigenous society. In the absence of a viable secular political force and progressive counterculture, the force of Islamic discourse against feminism gained strength and sought support around the reconstruction of rural tribal life. The ultimate result was a serious setback in the liberation of women in Afghanistan.

5 Women in Political Parties in Turkey

Emerging Spaces for Islamic Women

NILUFER NARLI

SINCE THE LATE 1980S, an increasing number of Turkish women from the middle and lower-middle classes have been mobilized by Islamist, center-right, and pro-Kurdish political parties to be active in party politics. However, women's participation in institutionalized party politics and their numbers in the decision-making organs are lower than for men, and they form a smaller proportion of total membership than men. This situation especially applies to Islamist and ultranationalist parties that resisted female representation in the parliament and in the decision-making organs of political parties until the 1999 elections.[1] Across the political

1. The proportion of women parliamentarians rose from 1.8 percent in 1991 to 2.6 percent following the 1995 general elections that elected 13 women out of 550 members of the parliament. Following the 1994 local elections, the female representation in the municipality assemblies was 1.28 percent, but only 0.47 percent of the mayors were women. The 1999 general and local elections held on the same day (April 18) led to the increase in female representation both in the parliament and in the local governments. Their number in the parliament rose to 23 (4.18 percent), and their representation in the local governments also increased and reached 0.55 percent. But none of the women were mayors of cities; they were mayors of only districts and subdistricts. There was a further increase in female parliamentary representation after the November 3, 2002, general elections, and it reached 4.4 percent. Out of a total number of 550 seats in the parliament, 24 (13 from the Justice and Development Party and 11 from the People's Republican Party) are occupied by women. There are differences in the level of female representation across the political parties. Until the 1999 elections, none of the Islamist parties (including the Welfare Party and the Greater Unity Party) and the Turkish nationalist National Action Party had female representation in the parliament, nor did they list female candidates for local elections. However, the center-right parties, center-left parties, and Kurdish nationalist parties have always listed female candidates in general and local elections, and they have had female parliamentary representation and even women cabinet members. In the 2002 general elections, almost all the Is-

spectrum, the gender policies of parties differ. Studies also show that the women members of the Islamist-ultranationalist parties, the leftist-social democratic parties, and the center-right parties differ significantly in the political socialization and recruitment channels, in the worldviews adopted, and in the political functions carried out (Veri Arastirma 2000).

The main question that this chapter addresses is: What variations exist in the forms of political participation of Islamic and Islamist women in Turkey, and what political and social factors explain the differences?[2] Through the use of a number of research methods—interviews, participant observation, and a reading of the literature of the relevant political parties carried out in 1998 and 2002—I describe the differences in the gender policies of the parties studied, the types of activities undertaken by the Islamic women members of the political parties, the channels of their recruitment, and the factors that motivated them to join a political party. I also establish a relation between variations in the forms of Islamic women's political participation, on the one hand, and their socioeconomic background, their political socialization, and their party's gender approach and its ideology (whether it is a liberal-democratic party, an authoritarian party, or a party with Islamist tendencies or Islamist roots). I end with some information on the meaning of feminism and Islamic feminism to the Turkish Islamic women interviewed.

---

lamist, pro-Islamic, and nationalist parties listed female candidates. However, the data on the location of the female candidates in the lists prepared by the political parties for the November 2002 general elections show that social democratic parties, the Left, and the center-right more frequently gave the top-three places to them. The Justice and Development Party and Saadet Party did not include female candidates in the top-three places in these lists. These data are provided by the KADER Association, which lobbies for increased female parliamentary representation.

2. I distinguish between Islam as a religion and Islamism as a political ideology and between a Muslim, an Islamist, and an Islamic woman. A Muslim woman may be pious and practice religion or may be a believer who does not observe all rituals regularly. For an Islamic woman, not only piety but also strong religious identification and conducting life in accordance with Islamic values are important. Islamism, on the other hand, indicates a political consciousness rather than a religious one and is a conscious attempt to transform Islam from religion into ideology. An Islamist is not only a pious Muslim who follows religious observances as part of religion and folk culture; she or he also politicizes Islam and, therefore, rejects the idea of religion being limited to belief, prayer, ritual worship, and private consciousness. The Islamist rejects the separation of state and religion on the grounds that Islam is both state and religion (din wa dawla). The Islamist is very likely to consider the necessity of gradual progress toward the ideal Islamic state and may be willing to undertake any type of action that is justified in terms of "Islamic" morals.

Research Strategy and Conceptual Framework

Interview and documentary data were collected from three sources in Istanbul and Ankara in 1998 and 2002. First, I conducted interviews with the women members of the Islamist parties, and the Muslim women members of the Far Right Turkish nationalist parties, the leftist Kurdish nationalist party, and two center-right parties. In 1998, respondents were members of six political parties that I have grouped according to their overall ideology: (1) Islamist parties that included the now defunct Virtue Party (Fazilet Partisi [FP]) that replaced the Welfare Party (Refah Partisi [RP]) and the Greater Unity Party (Buyuk Birlik Partisi [BBP]); (2) the ultranationalist National Action Party (MHP); (3) the leftist, pro-Kurdish People's Democracy Party (HADEP); and (4) two center-right parties, namely, the Motherland Party (ANAP) and the True Path Party (DYP). I interviewed five women from each party, along with the heads of the women's commissions and the non-Islamic women members. A 2002 follow-up study entailed interviews with women members of the Justice and Development Party (Adelet ve Kalkinma Partisi [AKP]) and the Saadet (Happiness) Party (SP), both founded after the closure of the Virtue Party. Second, I attended and observed meetings and congresses of the political parties covered in the study. Observations focused on the treatment of women members by the women in the position of authority and by the male members and on the level of sexual segregation practiced. Third, I examined the party programs and other relevant documents with respect to gender equality in the public and private domains.

A number of hypotheses guided my research. First, I hypothesized that the roles undertaken by the Islamist women were more likely to vary from one political party to another depending on the political philosophy of the political party and the level of ideological orientation. The more ideologically oriented the party, the more secondary and auxiliary the roles given to women. (I assumed that the ultranationalist National Action Party and the Islamist Virtue Party and the Greater Unity Party were ideologically oriented and that their female members would be more likely to assume gender-biased roles.) Second, center-right parties, which are pragmatic-broker parties lacking a strong commitment to an ideology, are more likely to adopt gender equality compared to the parties with ultranationalist and Islamist tendencies. My third hypothesis was that individual differences in the level of accepting secondary and gender-specific roles would depend on the level of education and occupational position of the Islamic woman member of a political party. The higher the level of education and occupational position, the lower the degree of accepting secondary roles and positions. Finally, I hypothesized that changes in state policy toward Islamists would be more likely to cause adjustments in political discourse and the methods of the Islamists. This modification, in turn, is more likely to bring about changes in the party's gender policy.

Conceptually, the study is framed by two analytical categories adapted from Vicky Randall that define the major forms of political participation: "conventional" and "less conventional" forms of political participation (1987, 50–60). Conventional formal institutionalized forms of political participation and action include voting; activity in electoral campaigns; being a member of a political party or interest group; working in organs of political parties; performing institutionalized political action by becoming a deputy; and involvement in "communal activity," meaning citizen contact with government officials on matters of general interest and "particularized contacts" or citizen contacts with government officials on matters of concern to a specific individual or group (55). They are all types of constitutional political activities that are organized by the political parties or legitimate interest organizations. Not all political systems and social groups provide the avenues of political participation within the context of formal institutionalized politics. The less conventional forms of participation thus include ad hoc participation, or forms of "participation in political campaigns that are short-lived, throwing up makeshift organizations and tending to rely on direct tactics such as pickets, squats and self-help projects" (58). Such forms are not necessarily always constitutional. The less conventional forms of political participation also include political actions within the context of an underground political movement: an urban guerrilla movement, revolutionary movements, all types of antiregime activities organized outside the constitutional framework, and even "terrorist" politics. More informal modes of political influence exercised by women in traditional societies could also be categorized as less conventional forms of political participation.

Islamic and Islamist Women's Political Participation in Turkey

In Turkey, there is a tradition of female participation in less conventional politics including taking part in urban guerrilla movements, student protests, and clandestine leftist activities in the 1970s. Ad hoc political activity has included community actions and self-help projects targeting the welfare of people living in slums and raising their political consciousness. The legal arrangements made after the 1980 coup aimed to suppress less conventional political activities and to prevent the participation of women and youths in conventional party politics. The military government outlawed the formerly organized youth and women sections of political parties that had been active in both institutionalized party politics and in ad hoc politics. The parties' women's commissions are still informally organized under the current Law of Political Parties.[3]

There are various examples of less conventional forms of political activities undertaken by the Islamist women. Women's participation in the Islamist movement, which is organized through associations, foundations, political parties, informal groupings, and clandestine groups, began in the form of informal political participation in the early 1970s. Often, the wives and daughters of the male Islamists became involved in the Islamist political activities as auxiliaries to men. Yet there were a few activists, including public figures preaching to groups of women to raise their Islamic awareness.

Until the mid-1980s, Islamist women did not hold formal memberships in associations or in political parties. Neither did they work in campaigns as actively as they do today. Nevertheless, they were able to mobilize their kinship groups and neighborhood networks each time the Islamist men asked them to poll support for the party. Since the late 1980s, women's involvement in the Islamist movement has grown and taken many forms. with increased participation in public life and in conventional party politics. They mobilize people by their effective educational and propaganda activities and by fund-raising. They also conduct self-help projects with the aim of reaching the disadvantaged and the "oppressed" people. Furthering their activities beyond institutionalized party politics, many actively march and demonstrate in the streets to protest perceived injustices, and some collect and disseminate news or leaflets. Street activism included organizing nationwide demonstrations, sit-in protests, and the nationwide hand-in-hand campaign to resist the head-scarf ban in the late 1980s and later in 1997–99.[4]

3. Women's participation in interest-group politics was still limited in the late 1990s owing to the restricted associational rights in Turkey (the legacy of the post-1980 coup period) and women's socioeconomic disadvantages that limited their activities beyond the household. See Bianchi 1984; Kalaycioglu 1983.

4. In the late 1980s, veiling became a contentious issue in Turkey. Muslim dress had been prohibited in public since the early days of the republic, but in the 1990s more women began to don the head scarf and long coat. The 1997–99 resistance by university students against the head-scarf ban mobilized a large number of supporters who took part in numerous demonstrations that continued until the victory of the AKP in the November 2003 elections. Tarhan Erdem's nationwide survey shows that

From the early 1990s onward, women's participation in ad hoc political action (such as short-lived self-help projects and community actions) and conventional party politics increased with the rise of the Islamist movement and women's increasing participation in the Islamist and pro-Islamist parties, associations, and foundations. This process was parallel to the growth of civil society with an increased number of voluntary associations, foundations, and informal groupings since the late 1980s.[5] They have mobilized an increasing number of women to take part in associational activities. The large number of civil society organizations are led either by Islamists or by the groups that are organized on the basis of primordial identity, sentiments, and ties, such as ethnic, sectarian, regional, religious identities, and sentiments.[6]

The Islamist, ultranationalist, and center-right parties seem to welcome Islamic women's political activism, particularly in grassroots politics. The fieldwork data revealed a number of patterns in the political preferences of religious women. A pious woman with a low level of Islamist tendencies is prone to join a center-right party. A religiously conservative Sunni woman upholding strong nationalist ideas will tend to support the National Action Party or the Greater Unity Party. She chooses the latter if the Islamic component of her ideology has a higher leverage. On the other hand, a Kurdish-nationalist Islamic or a religiously conservative woman from the eastern and southeastern provinces who adheres to Kurdish nationalist ideas is more likely to prefer the pro-Kurdish HADEP. (See table 5.1 for a listing of the parties examined in this chapter.)

Islamist and Islamic women's activism is vital in gaining the support of the various segments of the urban and rural electorate. They reach the newly urbanized social classes residing in the periphery of Istanbul and in Ankara, where the majority of the population are religiously conservative and share Islamist tendencies. They are active in grassroots politics all over Turkey, and especially in the East and Southeast, the Black Sea region, and central Anatolia.

---

almost 70 percent of women in Turkey cover their heads (see "Turban Dosyasi" 2003). The question retains its symbolic functions in the power struggle between the Islamists and those individuals holding a secular worldview.

5. For the increase in the number of nongovernmental organizations in the 1990s, see Türkiye Ekonomik ve Toplumsal Tarih Vakfi 1996, 12–14.

6. For the role of primordial ties in Islamist associations and other organizantions, see Narli and Nari 1999.

Table 5.1
Political Parties by Type and Dates of Existence

Islamist Parties	Nationalist Parties	Center-right Parties	Center-left Parties
Welfare Party (RP, or Refah) (1980–98)	National Action Party (MHP) (1983-present)	Motherland Party (ANAP) (1983-present)	People's Republican Party (CHP) (1923–81)[a]
Virtue Party (Fazilet) (January 1997- June 2001)	Kurdish People's Democracy Party (HADEP) (1993-March 2003)	True Path Party (DYP) (1983-present)	Socialist People's Party (SHP) (1985-present)
Greater Unity Party (BBP) (1993-present)			
Happiness Party (SP, or Saadet Party) (July 2001-present)			
Pro-Islamic Justice and Development Party (AKP)[b] (August 2001-present)			

Note: The Kurdish Worker's Party (PKK) is a separatist party that is banned in Turkey and does not fit
the above classification.
[a] The CHP was closed in 1981 and reopened in 1992.
[b] The AKP defines itself as a conservative center-right party.

The Trajectory of Women's Conventional
and Less Conventional Forms of Participation

Women in Islamist Parties

The mid-1980s marked the beginning of female involvement in Islamist political activities; subsequently, growing numbers of women were recruited into the Welfare
Party and became active in its women's commission. Although the party excluded
women from decision-making organs and from parliamentary representation,
women's participation grew in grassroots party politics, ad hoc actions, clandestine
activities, and Islamist student organizations.

Under the Virtue Party (1997–2001), which moderated the Welfare Party's
more radical Islamist ideology, not only Islamist women but also non-Islamist
women (who were distinguished by their non-Islamic clothing, rhetoric, and polit-

ical objectives) took part in the party's decision-making organs and gained parliamentary representation following the 1999 general elections. Women in the higher
ranks were not selected from among the Islamist women who started their political
careers in the informally organized women's commission and played vital roles in
grassroots party politics. The same was also true of the Islamist Greater Unity Party.

With the foundation in 2001 of the Justice and Development Party—which further moderated its Islamist politics and adopted a liberal party program—Islamic
women's participation in grassroots party politics was accompanied by an increase
in the number of Islamic and even non-Islamic women in the party's decision-
making organs. Yet only non-Islamic women gained parliamentary representation.
Meanwhile, in the Saadet Party, the level of female activism and participation in
grassroots party politics declined, and there was a decrease in the number of women
in the party's decision-making organs.

Islamic Women in Nationalist Parties

In the 1990s, the National Action Party increased religiously conservative and Islamic women's participation in constitutional grassroots party politics through
their activities in the party's women's commission and ad hoc actions that were constitutional. Yet both the Islamic and non-Islamic members excluded women from
decision-making organs and parliamentary representation until the late 1990s. The
Kurdish nationalist party HADEP, which had included women in the decision-
making organs since its foundation, also initiated many Islamic women in its grassroots activities as a response to the increased influence of the Islamist movement in
Turkey in the 1990s. Many of those women participated in ad hoc, extraconstitu-
tional actions.

The Center-Right Parties: The Motherland Party (ANAP)
and the True Path Party (DYP)

A larger female participation in grassroots party politics and increasing women's
role in decision-making organs characterize the female participation patterns in
both the Motherland Party and the True Path Party. Both parties recruited Islamic
women to be active in grassroots politics in response to the increased influence of
the Islamist movement in Turkey in the late 1990s.

Variations in Gender Approaches of the Political Parties

Islamist Parties: The Welfare Party (RP) and the Virtue Party (FP)

After the Islamist Welfare (Refah) Party was closed down in February 1998 and its leader, Necmettin Erbakan, banned from politics for five years, the Islamists regrouped to form the Virtue (Fazilet) Party under the leadership of Recai Kutan, but the new party lost popular support after a change in that leadership. The party program also changed when the FP "liberalized" the program and altered its rhetoric by shifting the focus from religion to human rights.[7] The new program also improved its gender policy by creating avenues for women's elevation to the decision-making positions rather than confining their activities solely to the domain of women's commissions, as was done by the RP. This significant change was motivated by three factors: the growing emphasis on democracy that required the party to adopt a policy of gender equality, the criticism of the RP's former gender-biased policy coming from the secular feminist circles and from within the party,[8] and the desire to create a new image, one of a modern, democratic party.

In 1998–99, there were attempts to increase the number of women in the party's decision-making organs. The number of women in the province and district commissions rose from "a few" to four hundred, as reported by Oya Akgönenc in December 1998. The Virtue Party listed several female candidates for the 1999 general elections, and its electorate elected three women to the parliament: Oya Akgönenc, Nazli Ilicak, and Merve Kavakci. The first two "modern" women had no Islamist political socialization and did not don head scarves. But Kavakci, who had been active in Milli Görüs (a youth Islamist organization that had organic ties with the Welfare Party and the Virtue Party), did cover her hair. She is an upper-middle-class woman with a university degree from the United States. She may have been selected to give a message to the radicals that Islamist principles and symbols were just as important as the new approaches adopted by the party.

---

7. In addition to the party literature, an interview with Oya Akgönenc, a member of the Central Decision-Making Board, shed light on party policies. In an interview in September 1997, she explained the five main fundamentals of the party's new policy: democracy, human rights, personal liberties, the rule of law, and sustainable development.

8. For example, two former female members of the RP interviewed by the author were unhappy about the conviction shared by both the RP and the FP that there was a lack of "qualified" women members to be listed as candidates for parliamentary representation.

Women in decision-making organs were not selected from among a group of female activists who were engaged in grassroots politics during the time of the RP. Neither were leading Islamist women writers, like Cihan Aktas, invited to join the party's decision-making organ. Instead, the women chosen came from the class of highly educated urban, modern, and professional women. The exception was one religiously conservative upper-middle-class woman with no political experience but with close ties to the party leader. Many of the economically underprivileged women were excluded, revealing the existence of social class discrimination.

The Justice and Development Party (AKP)

After the Virtue Party was banned by the Constitutional Court in June 2001 "for activities contrary to the principle of the secular republic," the party members split into two groupings. The Recai Kutan-led Happiness Party comprised the conservative old guard. The younger and the more moderate members formed the Justice and Development Party under the leadership of Recep Tayyip Erdogan. The party won the November 2002 general elections by obtaining 35 percent of the total votes and went on to form a government.

Compared to the defunct Virtue Party, the AKP has taken more radical steps in distancing its rhetoric from the Islamist view. In the course of moderation, democratic principles and gender equality have gained priority in the AKP's program that includes a specific section on women calling for an end to discrimination and violence against women.[9] Consistent with its new policy, the AKP sought larger female representation in the parliament and in the decision-making organs. Among the AKP's seventy-four founders, ten are women; however, there are no women among the founding members. In 2003, out of fifty-two members on the Central Decision-Making Board (Merkez Karar Yönetin Kurulu), four were women. On the Central Executive Board (Merkez Yürütme Kurulu), there were no female members. The third major decision-making organ, the Board of Discipline (Disiplin Kurulu), included two women. In Parliament, there were fifteen AKP representatives, all highly educated professionals from urban middle-class families. None, however, occupied a strategically important cabinet post. The female representation in local government was low, too, with only one female mayor. There were no female heads of provincial branches.

There is a larger place for women in the AKP's women's commissions that have

9. See http://www.akparti.org, "Party Program" section.

played an important role in increasing the popularity of the party. Their role and identity vary from province to province with the characteristics of the targeted population and sociocultural identity of the city. In religiously conservative cities such as Konya, a covered lady is preferred, but in metropolitan cities like Istanbul, the head of the women's commission can be unveiled.

The Saadet Party (SP)

The Saadet Party, founded in July 2001, welcomed Erbakan as its leader after he was allowed to return to party politics in May 2003. The SP largely represents the traditional Islamists and the religiously conservative older generation. Its party program does not have a section for women but does have one for the family, as the empowerment of families is its main concern. In the November 2002 elections, Oya Akgönenc was reelected, but women came to be underrepresented in the decision-making organs. Among the party's founders and its Central Decision-Making Board (Genel Idare Kurulu), there is only one woman, Oya Akgönenc, and there are no women in the High Discipline Board (Yuksek Disiplin Kurulu).[10] The party's women's commissions were not functioning effectively, according to one of its members, and research showed that women's political activities did not go beyond doing the paperwork in the offices.[11] Other activities included organizing seminars to explain the party's plans, to discuss women's health, or to explore other subjects that might attract women to the party. Visiting homes and organizing ad hoc self-help projects were less frequent compared to the time of the Virtue Party.

The Greater Unity Party (BBP)

The Greater Unity Party, right-wing and nationalist, formed in January 1993 after Islamist members broke away from the National Action Party. Its leader, Muhsin Yazicioglu, the former leader of "Idealist Hearths" (Ulku Ocaklari) in the 1970s, injected more Islamist elements in the political discourse and included ideas of freedom defined within an Islamic framework. Anti-individualism, unity and cooperation, discipline, and joint effort for the realization of collective purpose under a Turkish-Islamic state are the pillars of the BBP. The party's policy on women

10. See http://www.saadetistanbul.org/gik.html#2.

11. Interview with Nevin Hanim, who was in charge of political affairs in the Istanbul Saadet Party Provincial Office in August 2002.

is defined on the basis of the BBP's pillars and communitarianism, that is, sacrific-ing individual freedom and aspirations for the general social interest defined by the party. Woman, the family, and the Turkish-Islamic community are one and the same. The role of women is to be the mother and wife. Empowering "the Turkish-Islamic family," rather than women per se, is the goal. As the program stated, one of the major duties of the state was to take all possible measures to protect the strength of "the Turkish-Islamic family." [12] In 2002, the program had no section on women and no concern for solving the problems of women. The party seemed not to know how to handle the gender issues and to respond to the growing political demands of women from all social classes and political groups, but it motivated women to join the party and to be active in grassroots politics for instrumental purposes.

The women's commission members interviewed in 1998 were discontented with the weakness and limited resources of the women's network in the party, with the party program, and with the underrepresentation of the women in the ranks of the party. In response to women members' demands for parliamentary representa-tion and involvement in decision-making organs, the BBP listed female candidates for the 1999 general elections, but female representation remained low. In 2002, the BBP General Administration Board comprised only two women, and there were no women in the local governments controlled by the BBP.[13]

Non-Islamist Nationalist Parties: The National Action Party (MPH)
and the People's Democracy Party (HADEP).

The MHP represents the Turkish ultranationalist movement that drew its inspira-tion from a century-old ideology of pan-Turkism, or pan-Turanism, that emerged as a response to the anxiety over the decline of the Ottoman state at the end of the nineteenth century. With its solidarist, corporatist, nationalist ideology that recog-nized the significance of national and religious values, the movement mobilized a large number of youths in the 1970s. The founder of the MHP, Alpaslan Turkes (1917–1997), founded the "Idealist Hearths" (Ulku Ocaklari) at universities and elsewhere across the country, which were youth organizations providing political indoctrination and produced Far Right youth. The party obtained the support of many college students of rural and provincial origin and mobilized marginal social

12. Quoted in the party program; see Büyük Birlik Partisi 1998, 10. See also http://www.bbp .org.tr/partiprogram.htm.

13. See http://www.bbp.org.tr/yerelyonetim.htm.

classes and rural elements by constructing an anticapitalist rhetoric that used anti-communist themes for "national" purposes in the 1970s. The National Action Party also needed active female participation in its *ulku*. In the 1970s, the small number of MHP women started their careers by working in the *ulku*. Female activism in grass-roots politics did not bring female representation in the decision-making organs of the party in the 1970s mainly because of the unquestioning loyalty to the leader and the highly hierarchic and almost quasi-military structure of the party organization.

The role of MHP women in rejuvenating the movement and increasing the popularity of the party by mobilizing many new members became more vital in the 1980s and the early 1990s. However, the young MHP women did not find a place in the decision-making organs, and their activities did not go beyond the boundaries of the party's women's commission. This situation changed during the late 1990s, partly as a response to the vocal political demands of the secular liberal women who appealed to all the political parties and urged them to increase female representation in the parliament and local governments. Consequently, there were changes in the party's policy on women in that the party supported the elimination of gender inequality by means of educating women and raising their social status, as specified in its publications. The program gave priority to women's education mainly because of their role as the main socializer of Turkish children. The party program contained a section on the family, but not on women.[14]

In addition to a modification of the party's gender policy, there was a change in the position of women in the party ranks. The party included a number of women in the decision-making organs, but the number was still low in the late 1990s. For example, there was just one woman in the central decision-making board.[15] It ran female candidates in the 1999 general and local elections.[16] A few women were elected to the parliament and to local governments, but there were only 3 women MHP mayors out of a total number of 486 MHP mayors ruling provinces, districts, and subdistricts.[17]

14. See Party Program Section, "9.4 Aile, Kadin ve Çocuk" (Family, Women and Children), http://www.mhp.org.tr/tanitim/Prog&Tzk/Program.htm#_Toc5115642247. See also Bahçeli 1988.

15. See http://www.mhp.org.tr/tanitim/myk.htm.

16. Of the MHP-listed female candidates in the 1999 general elections, three were elected to the parliament, one of whom wore a head cover in daily life but not at the office. The head-scarf issue became a source of conflict between Islamist and secularist members, but the MHP's list of female candidates for the November 2002 general elections included three women who wore head scarves. See *Radikal,* Aug. 18, 2002.

17. See http://www.mhp.org.tr/tanitim/, section "Belediyeler" (Municipalities).

Women accepted the lower level of female representation in the decision-making organs partly out of adherence to the party's ideological orientation and highly hierarchical structure, which put women under the party's male authority. Another reason had to do with the social class background of the MHP women. The majority of them originated from provincial conservative social classes, and they internalized the values of the gender-specific division of labor that is justified by making references to Islam and ancient Turkish customs. In 2002, observations showed that active MHP women members also tended to deny personal aspirations for a political career. They believed they were "idealist" Turkish-Muslim women serving the family and the nation's social goals, and saw feminist demands as detrimental to the nationalist cause and to the unity of the Turkish family and its moral values.

Compared to the MHP women interviewed, the level of BBP women's communitarianism was lower. They also were less ideological in that they had room for a variety of ideas including Islamic values and universal concepts that could coexist with their nationalist ideas without creating deep contradictions.

The pro-Kurdish People's Democracy Party was formed in 1994 to replace the Democracy Party (DEP), itself an outgrowth of the People's Labor Party (HEP). The HEP, the first legal and openly Kurdish party, had been formed in June 1990. The HEP made an alliance with the Socialist People's Party (SHP, a social-democratic party that was the Republican People's Party's predecessor in the 1991 elections) and won parliamentary representation. Just before the HEP was banned in 1993, its Kurdish deputies resigned from that party and formed the DEP. When the DEP was banned in turn in June 1994, the deputies re-formed as the People's Democracy Party. The HADEP represented Kurdish nationalism until it was closed down by the Constitutional Court in March 2003 on the grounds that it supported the outlawed separatist Kurdish Workers' Party (PKK) and therefore posed a threat to the unity of the nation and its territorial integrity.[18]

Despite their Marxist ideology, both HADEP and the PKK mobilized women to conduct "Islamic" politics in line with their "Kurdish agenda" when the separatist Kurdish nationalists discovered the instrumental value of effective "Islamic" propaganda in motivating people to take political action, legal or illegal. Religion was a driving force, as many religious Kurds were observed to be looking at the Islamist movement to rise above the nationalist discourse, though the unresolved tension between Islam and Kurdish nationalism remained. HADEP women were able to

18. See Turkish dailies of Mar. 14, 2003, for information on the closure of HADEP; for example, *Aksam*, Mar. 14, 2003.

reach the religiously conservative Shaafi Kurds via the slogan "Revolt against an op-pressive state in the name of Islam." Such an antistate stance was consistent with HADEP's general discourse and the party program that criticized the Turkish state for pursuing "incorrect policies towards the Kurdish Question," meaning the de-ployment of antidemocratic practices in the region. At the same time, it criticized the feudal structure and patriarchal order of the Southeast. As a solution, it advo-cated the liberation of children, workers, and women and in particular pledged women's liberation from the shackles of tradition and the constraints of the feudal and male-dominated social order. HADEP encouraged greater women's participa-tion in the party because it supported women's liberation as an extension of its lib-eration doctrine and because women's activism outside the home was important as a mobilizing mechanism toward electoral victory, as stated by many HADEP women who were interviewed.

The party's support of women was made visible through the representation of women in the decision-making organs of the party.[19] In order to increase female parliamentary representation, HADEP listed female candidates for the general and local elections in 1999. It did not pass the national threshold of 10 percent, but it ob-tained a larger proportion of the votes in the southeastern provinces and gained control of municipal governments in the eastern and southeastern provinces. In 2002, out of a total number of thirty-six HADEP mayors, three were women, whereas the total number of women mayors in Turkey was eighteen.[20]

The Center-Right Parties: The Motherland Party (ANAP)
and the True Path Party (DYP)

In the aftermath of the 1980 coup, the Motherland Party was founded in May 1983 under the leadership of Turgut Ozal and obtained 45 percent of the popular vote in the November 1983 elections. Successfully combining liberal, conservative, and na-tionalist trends, the ANAP program promised to bring peace and security to the country, strengthen the middle class, eliminate unemployment, designate priority

19. Of the fifty members of the party's Istanbul Province Executive Board in 1998, eleven were women. Of the twenty-eight district party chiefs, three in Istanbul were women. The Central Executive Committee and the Party Assembly had female representation of 20 percent, whereas 18 percent of the city and town administrations were made up of women. See http://www.sinirsizhost.net/users/hadep/kadin/English.htm.

20. For details, see http://www.hadep.org.tr/belediyeler.

areas of development and undertake necessary projects for developing the country, and rearrange the working of the bureaucracy. ANAP succeeded in implementing the program, institutionalizing a market economy, and integrating the leaders and networks of "hostile" groups into elite networks.

The Motherland Party has always listed female candidates to run for elections and has included women in its cabinets. When it was in office in the mid-1980s, the Ozal government executed several reforms to improve gender equality. First, in 1985 Turkey ratified the UN's Convention on the Elimination of All Forms of Discrimination Against Women. Second, the government established special units, such as the General Directorate on the Status and Problems of Women in April 1990. Third, it took steps to increase female representation in the executive branch and at the top level of bureaucracies, appointing a woman governor to Mugla in 1990. Fourth, a Motherland government, the Yilmaz-led coalition government, made changes in the law to protect women against violence and in 1998 passed a bill of protective orders against domestic violence.

The party program and the leadership gave importance to improving the situation of women through social reforms. Yet the ANAP Congress of November 1998 elected only one woman to its Central Executive Board. However, the level of female representation varied from province to province in 1998–99. In the large cities, female representation in the decision-making organs of the party was higher (for example, about 11 percent female in Istanbul) than in the disadvantaged provinces, many of which are located in the East, southeastern Anatolia, and the Black Sea region.[21] This pattern continued in 2003.

The True Path Party is the successor of the Justice Party that was banned following the 1980 coup. As the heir of both the Democrat Party and the Justice Party of earlier decades, the DYP has always portrayed itself as a "mass party" representing the interest of every social group and seeking to reconcile them through higher national interests, despite largely representing conservative rural and urban interests. Having ignored women in its 1983 party program, the True Path Party became prowomen in the early 1990s in order to change its image to a modern urban party and go beyond its rural electorate to obtain more support from the urban middle class and upper-middle-class electorate that had voted for ANAP in the late 1980s. As part of the plan, Süleyman Demirel, then chair of the party, invited a modern urban woman, Tansu Çiller, to join the party and take part in its higher ranks in

21. In the party's Istanbul Province and district commissions, there were 719 men and 81 women in the decision-making organs. This information came from the party's Istanbul office, Aug. 1998.

1990. After the electoral victory in the 1991 general elections, Çiller was given a ministerial position. This move was a significant step in the inclusion of women in the key decision mechanisms. Following Demirel's election as president, Çiller became the leader of the party and prime minister. Turkey had elected a female prime minister for the first time in the history of the republic.

During her rule (1993–95), Çiller did not show much sensitivity to the gender issue, unless it had instrumental value. For example, just before the December 1995 general elections, Çiller targeted secular urban middle-class and upper-middle-class women, and her rhetoric focused on empowering the "contemporary" women of Turkey. Empowering women through social and legal reforms was discussed in a special section on women in the party's 1998 and 2001 "Democracy Programs."[22] Second, the party adopted a 10 percent quota for female representation in its party organs. Moreover, Çiller promised to increase the number of female deputies; the party listed several women candidates in the 1995 general elections, and six were elected in addition to Çiller herself. This victory pleased a large number of the urban middle-class female electorate that had overwhelmingly voted for Çiller, but the same social group boycotted Çiller when she formed a coalition with the Welfare Party in 1997.

The Islamist women members of the ANAP and DYP were content with their party's programs and policies that were flexible and increasingly sensitive to women's rights and gender equality.

Variations in the Patters of Political Participation of Islamic Women

The field data revealed the differences in the recruitment channels of Islamic women and the importance of the family, kinship, and neighborhood networks that provided the channels of communication with the party and recruitment in its ranks. Ethnic, sectarian, or regional ties and networks were functional in the recruitment of the majority of the Islamist and Islamic women interviewed from the Virtue Party, Greater Unity Party, Justice and Development Party, Saadet Party, and center-right parties. The women members often came from provincial lower and middle social classes with a lower level of formal education that often did not go beyond the middle section of high school and limited access to networks in the city. Neighbors, kinsmen, and husbands provided the first contact with the party and

22. For these "Democracy Programs," see http://www.belgenet.com/parti/program/dyp1998-2.html and http://www.belgenet.com/parti/program/dyp2001-3.html.

initiated them in party politics. Not only traditional patriarchal ties but also patriarchal structures shaped the political recruitment of women who were initiated by their fathers or husbands who had already taken part in party politics.

Women's recruitment by the National Action Party and the pro-Kurdish People's Democracy Party differed from the women's initiation in party politics by the pro-Islamist Virtue Party, Greater Unity Party, Justice and Development Party, and center-right parties. The women's first contact with the MHP was frequently made in their teens at the institutions of secondary education, a formal institution rather than an informal group. Family members, mostly males, still played a catalyzing role in connecting them to the party or to its youth organizations. The HADEP women interviewed were often recruited as party members out of their own will soon after their contact with party members, rather being initiated by a male relative.

After joining a political party and becoming a member of the party's women's commission, Islamist women undertake many activities ranging from campaigning, educating the electorate, contesting for elections, and joining rallies and sit-in protests to taking part in clandestine activities. The type of political participation and the types of political roles assumed by the Islamist women interviewed varied from party to party. In the context of the conventional institutionalized party politics, there was not much difference in the political activities the Islamist women undertake. Almost all the Islamist women members of the political parties studied performed the following institutionalized political activities: organizing ward and district meetings, arranging education and propaganda activities, and organizing seminars, forums, concourses, and door-to-door campaigning.

Islamist women members of the Virtue Party, who were often from the newly urbanized lower-middle classes, were highly active in grassroots politics. They worked in the electoral campaigns by visiting thousands of homes with flowers and food baskets, explaining what the party was planning to do to protect Muslims, restore justice, and restructure Islamic values in Turkey. This work was not much different from the political function of the Welfare Party's female members who were often from the lower-income families and frequently the first or second generation in the city. Yet unlike the members of the Virtue Party who had limited access to decision-making process, the Welfare Party women were excluded from the party's decision-making organs.

The Justice and Development Party's Islamic women members' activism was high and diverse. During the election campaigns in the summer of 2002, they visited thousands of homes to explain the promises of the party, organized ward and district meetings, and did secretarial work in the party offices. The majority of the AKP's Islamic and pro-Islamist women, who originated from newly urbanized lower social classes, often kept a low profile, while the non-Islamist, highly educated, professional women from the urban middle classes were more visible in public. A new division of tasks and positions had emerged in the AKP: religiously conservative lower-middle-class women were in the grassroots politics, whereas the non-Islamist educationally and professionally qualified women were in the higher ranks, despite their lack of experience in party politics.

The level of activism of the Islamic women in institutionalized party politics was lower in the center-right Motherland and True Path Parties compared to their counterparts in the Virtue Party and the Justice and Development Party, as well as in the ultranationalist National Action Party and the Kurdish People's Democracy Party. Second, the center-right's Islamic women's activism was limited to socially disadvantaged sections of the big cities where religious values were an integral part of social and political life, whereas the Islamist and Islamic women members of the pro-Islamist and ultranationalist parties were visible in the party's grassroots activities all over Turkey.

The major difference between the parties was in the Islamic and Islamist women members' level of participation in the less conventional forms of political activity. Compared to their level of participation in institutionalized party politics that was largely confined to the activities of the women's commission, the Islamist women's activism in less conventional politics was high and diverse. They engaged in ad hoc political activities and short-lived political campaigns (for example, street demonstrations protesting the compulsory eight-year schooling policy in 1998 and the ban on the use of a head cover in public institutions in 1998–2002, sit-in protests, and "Support Palestine" rallies in April-May 2002). HADEP's Islamic women did not hesitate to participate in the activities aimed at creating public awareness of the political issues, which ranged from peaceful seminars and concerts to sit-in protests and even violent street protests. But the Islamic women members of the more ideological Greater Unity Party and the National Action Party seldom took part in such activities. Another type of activity was implementing self-help projects. In line with the party's policy to meet the needs of the underprivileged, the women of the Virtue Party, Justice and Development Party, and pro-Kurdish People's Democracy Party conducted several self-help or social welfare projects, such as recycling, child and elder care, and reaching needy women, children, slum dwellers, and those living in remote areas. They carried out these projects by involving themselves in neighborhood associations and community-action councils in the economically disadvantaged districts of the big cities and in many Anatolian towns.

The fieldwork confirmed the hypothesis regarding factors affecting the varia-tions in the type of political participation and the types of political roles assumed as well as in the level of representation in the decision-making organs. Salient factors were, first, the type of political party (whether it was an ideological party or a prag-matic-broker mass party) and, second, the party member's level of formal educa-tion, occupational position, and social background. The party's ideology and program were found to be significant in defining the role of women in the party, in creating awareness of gender issues, and in shaping gender relations in the ranks of the political party. HADEP's Marxist political ideology made it imperative to elimi-nate gender discrimination, and it stressed the liberation of women from the shack-les of feudalism and tradition. Accordingly, its party program was gender sensitive and embodied the principle of giving women an equal chance to be included in the decision-making organs. The fair distribution of gender roles in the party ranks is consistent with the principle of equality. On the other hand, the party programs of the ultranationalist National Action Party, Islamist Virtue Party, Greater Unity Party, and Saadet Party treated women as an extension of the family rather than considering them individuals having roles in public and private domains. They often defined the political roles on the basis of gender, in that women were assigned secondary roles and largely excluded from the decision-making positions.

Nevertheless, the MHP, FP, and BBP gradually responded to the feminist de-mands and began to deviate from a gender-based division of tasks and positions within the party ranks. In 2002, the AKP was ahead of the MHP, BBP, and SP in lib-eralizing its gender policy in the party program, which is against gender discrimina-tion. This change is partly the result of the AKP defining itself as a center-right party, rather than being an ideological party like its predecessors RP and FP, and conse-quently moderating its discourse and reconciling democratic principles. This fact confirms the first, second, and fourth hypotheses.

The field data describing the variations of the roles in the ranks of the party from party to party confirm the first hypothesis: the political philosophy of a politi-cal party and the level of being ideologically oriented are likely factors that affect the type of political role undertaken by the female members. Ideologically oriented Far Right and Islamist parties were found to be adopting a gender-based division of labor and decision-making and assigning more secondary and auxiliary roles to the women members. The data revealed that the Islamist women members of ideologi-cally oriented Far Right and Islamist parties, who often internalized their party's gender-biased ideology, were more frequently given secondary roles and largely excluded from the key decision-making positions. Yet the level of internalizing the gender-biased role ideology varied from individual to individual depending on the level of formal education and socioeconomic background. For example, the more urban women of the Greater Unity Party who were interviewed, who had obtained high school diplomas, were less willing to accept secondary roles and to subordinate individual women's rights to the Turkish-Islamist cause represented by the party. Likewise, Dr. Oya Akgönenc joined the Virtue Party not to assume a secondary role but to have a political career and position in the higher ranks of the party. A university graduate and businesswoman, Canan Kalsim joined the Justice and Development Party for similar reasons and not to forever assume a role in the party's women's commissions. The woman writer Cihan Aktas, who contributed to the expansion of the Islamist movement's influence on society, was less willing to accept the gender-specific division of labor within the Welfare Party and Virtue Party. This rejection confirms the third hypothesis: the higher the level of education and occupational position, the lower the degree of accepting secondary roles and positions.

Not only the level of accepting a gender-based division of political roles but also the level of former education obtained by a woman and her occupational position is important in gaining mobility and participation in the decision-making process of party politics. Educationally disadvantaged Islamist women from rural, provincial, and newly urbanized lower and middle social classes often join women's commissions and play an active role in grassroots politics, in ad hoc political action, and in less conventional political activities. On the other hand, urban upper-middle-class Islamist, Islamic, and non-Islamist women with a higher level of formal education frequently take part in the parties' decision-making organs. They gain mobility, in the Islamist and non-Islamist political parties, regardless of their previous contribution to the parties.

The reasons explaining the higher mobility of urban educated woman in the party ranks of the Islamist parties are related to the changes in the support base of the Islamists. The Islamist movement has outgrown its rural and provincial origins, and its appeal now extends to the newly urbanized middle and upper classes. As such, the need for the participation of non-Islamist modern upper-class women has increased, and they have been given places in the decision-making organs. As Islamist supporters moved from provincial towns and villages to urban centers, they gained upward social mobility and needed to associate themselves with the upper-middle-class professionals and businesspeople. Women members of the upper middle classes are accepted in the positions of authority, but the rural and provincial lower-class women are given active roles merely in grassroots politics.

There are differences in the factors that mobilized the Islamist women interviewed to participate in institutionalized party politics. They varied from political party to party depending on the party's ideology. They also varied from individual to individual with the differences in the social class background, in the level of formal education received, and in the type of occupational position. For the female members of the more ideologically oriented Virtue Party, Saadet Party, National Action Party, Greater Unity Party, and pro-Kurdish People's Democracy Party, accomplishing any tasks to serve the cause (for instance, spreading Turkish civilization worldwide, creating an Islamic Turkey, or gaining recognition of Kurdish identity) was the most significant motivating factor. The field data confirm my hypothesis that the Islamist women in the Islamist and ultranationalist political parties are more likely to be motivated by a religious or nationalist fervor. However, it was less important for the highly educated non-Islamist women members coming from the urban middle classes.

The perceived illegitimacy and the urge to fight against it and redress the perceived imbalances also motivated the Islamist women interviewed to participate in institutionalized party politics. Such an urge was more frequently observed among the Virtue Party and People's Democracy Party members who were occasionally driven to take part in the semiformal and even illegal political activities. This motivation is partly related to their level of discontent with the system; the level of protest potential was particularly high among the Islamist Welfare and Virtue Parties and the People's Democracy Party women who came from the provincial and rural lower social classes.

Liberation of women and improving the situation of women in Turkey were important motives for some of the center-right Islamist women members interviewed. They were particularly significant in motivating the HADEP respondents who believed that women's liberation was associated with the independence of their community. They also motivated some Islamist members of the center-right parties, who brought the women's issues, including the problems of divorced women, the high rate of female unemployment, and domestic violence, before the male decision makers.

Personal interest was not totally insignificant in the Islamist women's involvement in the women's commissions. The disfranchised women realized the significance of relying on a political network built on religious or ethnic solidarity and cause in a country where economic security is hard to reach, the fall in real wages and income disparity hit the larger segment of the society, and the social welfare system does not function effectively and cover all the citizens.

How did the women interviewed approach "feminism" and "Islamic feminism"? The research data showed that a party's political philosophy shapes an Islamist woman member's consideration of Islamic feminism in solving women's problems. The female members of the Virtue Party and the Greater Unity Party, whose parties took Islam as a fundamental pillar, more often considered Islamic feminism as an option. They supported the idea of making references to Islamic concepts to frame a new paradigm and rhetoric to discuss the liberation of women and to improve their socioeconomic position in 1998. They advocated a new reading of the Qur'an with the aim of eradicating the narrowly interpreted understanding of Islam that has been used to oppress women. The National Action Party women, who took Islam as an integral part of Turkish cultural identity rather than a fundamental pillar, were against considering Islamic feminism in reflecting on women issues. In interviews, female Muslim members of the pro-Kurdish People's Democracy Party were likewise reluctant to initiate a discussion of women's rights within an Islamic framework because of a concern that orthodox Islamic values might sustain patriarchal values. They believed that Islamic teachings, which are often interpreted in orthodox terms, could restrict women's mobility and encourage male or communal control over women. The Islamic women members of the two center-right parties gave ambiguous messages with regard to Islamic feminism. They often believed that Islam respects women and provides them with rights. At the same time, they expressed their suspicion of the likely use of Islamic teachings to reinforce patriarchal values and to suppress female mobility.

Conclusions

The level of formal education and socioeconomic background are important factors in shaping a woman's political attitude, her political expectations, and her political roles in a party. Socioeconomic discrepancies seem to lead to discrimination against the disfranchised Islamist women at the level of decision making, and contradictory demands are made on women by the Islamist male party members. Nonetheless, there are indications of powerful new demands coming from the Islamic women that could undermine the male-dominated party politics if they are well articulated and allied with the feminist demands from various circles. They suggest new moral imperatives and values that the political parties may no longer be able to satisfy unless they change their attitudes toward women. Such a likely development is a key for grassroots women to challenge the male-dominated party leadership and discrimination against disadvantaged women. In articulating and justifying their new demands, they may very well adopt a combination of Islamic and universal concepts.

What is clear is that Islamic and Islamist women, as well as secular women, are demanding more political participation in Turkey. They are engaging in both conventional and less conventional forms of political participation. They are eager to join political parties and associations for female political input and to increase women's voices in the decision-making process. And they take part in various political activities ranging from petition drives and sit-in protests against the war in Iraq to street rallies in protest over low wages.

6 Feminist Organizing in Tunisia

Negotiating Transnational Linkages and the State

SARAH E. GILMAN

THE ADVENT OF FORMAL women's organizations in Tunisia is typically traced back to the era of anticolonial struggle prior to independence from France in 1956.[1] However, Tunisia's nationalist leader and first president, Habib Bourguiba, consolidated and appropriated preindependence women's organizations much as he successfully broke down the kinship ties that threatened to interfere with his state-building efforts. Bourguiba declared himself the "father" of independent Tunisia as well as the "father" of Tunisian women's liberation and was so successful in his paternal mission that in 1975 he was named president for life.

Less than six months after independence, even before the constitution itself was drafted, Bourguiba created Tunisia's Personal Status Code, a document that broke with Islamic law without completely abandoning it, thereby radically reforming Muslim family law while stopping short of completely secularizing it (Charrad 2001, 222). Thus, instead of telling women to wait for their postindependence "liberation," he transformed their advancement into the capstone of his entire nationalist project, "liberating" women even before basic constitutional rights for either sex had been established. Rather than bubbling up from below, Tunisia's "nationalist project" lacked direct participation of Tunisian women or anyone else outside Bourguiba's circle of political elites; instead, rights were "handed down." Although women's organizations may have existed prior to independence, Tunisian women played no role in the promulgation of the family law legislation that ultimately propelled them, rather ironically, into the spotlight as symbols of the "emancipated" Arab woman (219).

With the liberation of women effectively subsumed within Bourguiba's nation-

1. This chapter is based on research conducted in Tunisia from August 1998 to July 1999 with the support of a Fulbright grant. The master's thesis from which the chapter is drawn is titled "Feminist Organizing in Tunisia: Resisting Appropriation While Maintaining Autonomy" (2000).

alist project, activists from a variety of preindependence women's organizations were brought into line and joined Bourguiba's newly created Union Nationale des Femmes Tunisiennes (UNFT), thus securing centralized state control of formal women's organizing in independent Tunisia. Bourguiba's monolithic state feminism reigned supreme until the 1970s, when he briefly loosened his hold on civic activity. This decade witnessed the brief flourishing of the labor movement, human rights activism, and opposition political parties. The women's movement was rejuvenated during this decade as well, with the emergence of the autonomous feminist movement.

The women who came together in the late 1970s to form the Club Tahar Haddad were challenging the refusal of men from the Tunisian leftist ranks to recognize the validity of women's oppression. However, this group of women was also intentionally organizing outside the sphere of state control. Thus, the activists established their "autonomy" in relation to two fields of power: the male-dominated political left and the homogenizing, authoritarian state. As the political left in Tunisia lost relevance over the following decades, the autonomous women's movement situated itself more and more against the hegemonic power of the state that worked tirelessly to form all of civil society into its desired image.

In 1989, what had begun as the Club d'Études de la Condition des Femmes, popularly referred to as the Club Tahar Haddad, was legally recognized as a formal women's organization, the Association Tunisienne des Femmes Démocrates (ATFD), popularly known as Femmes Démocrates.[2] This transition to official status was facilitated by a second phase of political liberalization in Tunisia, ushered in by the bloodless coup in 1987 that replaced Bourguiba with Zine al-Abidine Ben Ali, a former military general who has since managed to maintain control over the nation even after abolishing the position of "president for life." Today, ATFD has acquired a unique status in Tunisia: it is the only *autonomous* women's organization in Tunisia, the only women's group in the country that can be classified as a "protest" group, and the only organization that ventures to use the "feminist" descriptor in informal conversation, publications, and interviews.[3] It should be clarified that Femmes Dé-

2. I refer to Femmes Démocrates interchangeably with the "autonomous women's movement," although the latter also includes several individual feminist activists who are not official members of ATFD.

3. ATFD has an autonomous sister organization, the Association des Femmes Tunisiennes pour la Recherche et le Développement (known as AFTURD), but in 1999 this research-oriented group was only marginally active.

mocrates describes itself as "feminist," hence my use of the phrase "autonomous feminist movement" to distinguish ATFD from the broader, generally state-controlled, women's movement in Tunisia.

This chapter explores the relationship among the autonomous feminist movement in Tunisia, transnational linkages, and the state. Women in the Middle East and North Africa are typically excluded from the literature on the transnational women's movement, and the region as a whole is largely excluded from the more general literature on transnational social movements (Moghadam 2005). Although intraregional transnational organizing within North Africa and the Middle East might lack the dynamism of what is occurring in Latin America, for example, and though organizations within the region might participate less frequently in interregional transnational networks, taking a close look at the transnational linkages that *do* exist is a crucial part of the project of attempting to understand why these linkages are not more dynamic.

Tunisia happens to be a particularly interesting case in this endeavor because the state promotes a paradoxical vision of a vibrant yet controlled civil society. The government lists more than seven thousand groups on its list of officially recognized Tunisian civic organizations. However, all but a small handful of these organizations have received their legal status because of close ties to Ben Ali's ruling political party.[4] Thanks to the tight state control exercised through the Tunisian laws of association, most nongovernmental organizations (NGOs) in Tunisia function as examples of that interesting breed of "governmental non-governmental organizations."[5] Such state control over civic organizations likely spills over into the realm of transnational linkages. Indeed, the nature of the Tunisian state and the civil society it attempts to control impacts the ability of NGOs to maneuver across borders.

Autonomous feminist activists in Tunisia have been pursuing various forms of transnational organizing or collaboration since the early 1980s. The earliest linkages were regional, occurring within the Maghreb, the "geocultural entity" that includes Morocco, Algeria, and Tunisia (Charrad 1990). More recently, Femmes Démocrates

---

4. ATFD is one of a handful of groups without party ties.

5. Persons wishing to form an association must submit an application to the Ministry of Interior and then wait three months. If the ministry does not respond during this time, the group becomes a legally recognized association and receives its "visa"; if the ministry does respond, it is usually to deny the group legal status. The ministry must by law provide a reason for the denial, and appeals can be made to the administrative tribunal. For more information on these laws, see République Tunisienne 1992. See also Laghmani 1996; Chekir 1998a.

has pursued international linkages, either independently or in conjunction with state-affiliated women's groups, evidenced by their participation in the Fourth UN Conference on Women in 1995 and other international conferences. Another type of transnational linkage is the flow of funding from foreign foundations to ATFD. A handful of European—mostly German—foundations supply the great majority of the funds that keep Femmes Démocrates operating from day to day. Such heavy reliance on funds from abroad has not escaped the critical analysis of the autonomous activists. Scholars of the transnational women's movement have also begun to pay attention to the power differentials implicit in foreign funding. For Femmes Démocrates, its relationship to European funders has become a third arena of autonomy that it needs to negotiate and debate—in addition to those other two arenas of autonomy, from the Left and from the state.

Two broad constellations of power thus emerge as analytical "grids" in this discussion of the autonomous feminist movement, transnational linkages, and the Tunisian state. North-South power asymmetries constitute the first constellation. Transnational linkages increasingly cross the North-South divide and must thereby grapple with power imbalances informed by imperial and colonial residues and the ever evolving (and arguably intensifying) inequalities of the global neoliberal regime. Tensions between the state and civil society make up the second constellation of power. This constellation draws attention to the potential of individual nation-states to wield influence over nongovernmental involvement in transnational movements. Attributing analytical weight to the state-civil society power constellation also challenges the assumption within much of the literature on transnational movements that all nongovernmental participants maneuver within liberal democratic nation-states.

The blurry boundary between the state and civil society in Tunisia, which in the case of the women's movement is illustrated by the preponderance of state-affiliated women's organizations in the country, is likewise highlighted by this second constellation of power. Indeed, the relationship between autonomous feminist organizing and state-affiliated women's organizing is a key component of the relationship between the autonomous feminist movement and the Tunisian state. The varying degrees of animosity and mutual respect that exist across time between Femmes Démocrates and state-affiliated women's groups thus factor into an analysis of the autonomous feminist movement and transnational linkages. A primary divergence between the two camps of women's activism is, not surprisingly, their choice of strategy in dealing with the state. While state-affiliated organizations adopt collaborative "party-line" stances in relation to the state, Femmes Démocrates is willing to risk adversarial stances vis-à-vis the state. However, this point deserves some qualification.

Femmes Démocrates is engaged in a daily struggle to maintain its autonomy from and resist co-optation by a hegemonic state that has so far succeeded in stifling dissenting voices. However, to find a balance between irrelevance and appropriation in such an atmosphere, these autonomous activists understand that they must in some way engage the state. Each time ATFD chooses to engage the state, it risks co-optation. Conversely, each time it avoids engagement, it risks complete isolation that threatens the continued relevance of the organization. To avoid the risks of these extremes—appropriation or irrelevance—ATFD attempts to maintain a tenuous balance somewhere in between. This balancing strategy informs how ATFD fares in the arena of state-civil society relations and, as we will see, is also relevant in understanding how Femmes Démocrates negotiates the realm of transnational linkages.

The cautionary point, then, is that although the autonomous activists themselves—not to mention the state—might characterize Femmes Démocrates as adversarial, we should keep in mind the activists' ongoing willingness to engage with state institutions and state-affiliated women's organizations to improve the situation of women in Tunisia. Whereas state-affiliated activists are apt to praise the government for bestowing such an advanced Personal Status Code upon the women of Tunisia, the autonomous activists are likely to push for changes that will make the code even more progressive and egalitarian.[6] In this way, Femmes Démocrates ironically appears to engage the state at a deeper level than the state-affiliated organizations, even as it maintains its autonomy from the state. However, we should also be mindful that opportunities for collaboration are determined by the state—not by the autonomous activists—and when the Personal Status Code is reformed, no accolades are directed to Femmes Démocrates for the role it played in raising public awareness or influencing the government.

Such levels of state control inevitably impact the access to—and ability to freely participate in—transnational women's organizing afforded to women's groups by the Tunisian government. For instance, throughout the 1990s, the more outspoken and active of the autonomous activists—feminist and otherwise—have routinely had their passports confiscated by the state, thus inhibiting their ability to participate in international meetings and conferences or in any sort of transnational or-

6. Most recently, ATFD has launched a campaign to reform the Tunisian inheritance laws that continue to dictate that women inherit only half as much as men.

ganizing. Although in most contexts transnational linkages involve moving beyond the state, in the case of Tunisia, the state refuses to be left behind.

To facilitate this exploration of the relationship between the autonomous feminist movement, transnational linkages, and the state, this paper focuses on three illustrative cases. The first case consists of two regional networks of which ATFD is a member. The Maghreb collective of autonomous feminist activists and organizations was created in 1991 to prepare a unified Maghreb presence at the 1995 Fourth UN Conference on Women in Beijing; the Arab Women's Forum was created in 1993 to build linkages between women throughout the Middle East and North Africa. The second case is the Rihana Network, a temporary and (allegedly) collaborative structure created within Tunisia to facilitate the country's NGO participation at the Beijing Conference. The third case is a center for victims of violence against women, the Centre d'Écoute et d'Orientation des Femmes Victimes de Violence, or Centre d'Écoute, which has served as the central programmatic effort of ATFD since the early 1990s.

Each of these three cases offers insights into questions of autonomy and co-optation and promotes a multilayered analysis of resistance and accommodation in relation to the state. These cases also illustrate various types of linkages that can be grouped under the umbrella of the transnational women's movement. Finally, I hope that these cases shed some light on the need to consider the role of the state in transnational social movements. Before discussing each case in turn, I offer some brief theoretical remarks on the state and transnational linkages.

Theorizing the State and Transnational Linkages

A useful theoretical tool with which to analyze the relationship between autonomous women's activism and the state is Raka Ray's revitalized concept of political fields. Ray applies Pierre Bourdieu's idea of fields to a comparative analysis of women's movements in India, expanding the concept to incorporate two factors that explain variation among fields: the distribution of power and the political culture (1999, 7). As for Tunisia, the political culture is highly homogenous, with a clearly delineated dominant discourse and *pensée unique*. Such a culture fits with Ray's characterization of a political culture that is "rigid, monolithic, and intolerant of difference" (9). ATFD and other state-affiliated women's organizations in Tunisia should be situated within this context that informs not only all levels of formal politics but also the nature of Tunisian "civil society."

Again reflecting the nature of the larger political system, women's organizing in

Tunisia also happens in an atmosphere of concentrated power, with a small group of women's organizations, those groups with close state ties, controlling available resources and political influence. Both the political system and the women's movement in Tunisia are also geographically concentrated and urban based, centered exclusively in the capital city of Tunis.[7] According to Ray, this combination of homogenous culture and concentrated power results in a hegemonic political field (1999, 11). I thus refer to the Tunisian state as "hegemonic" and situate the autonomous feminist movement in a hegemonic political field.

However, we need to avoid adopting too reductionist an argument concerning the hegemonic state power that surrounds Femmes Démocrates. That the activists refer to this repressive environment with the code word *atmosphère* alludes to their belief in the "omniscience" of the Tunisian state, but even those women who have experienced, firsthand, acts of state repression are aware—theoretically and practically—that state power is not an impenetrable wall. Similar to other Middle Eastern states such as Egypt, Algeria, and Syria, Tunisia is best described as a "corporatist bourgeois-bureaucratic state" that has toyed with political liberalization and democratization but remains largely authoritarian (Murphy 1999). Wendy Brown's analysis of the masculine state helps us avoid a homogenous and reductionist view of state power that can be difficult to avoid, particularly when confronted by a hegemonic and authoritarian state. She argues that the state is at once "an incoherent, multifaceted ensemble of power relations and a vehicle of massive domination" (1995, 174). This paradox is of critical importance in the context of authoritarian states where hegemony and incoherence coexist but can be difficult to disentangle on both theoretical and practical levels.

Applied to the experiences of Femmes Démocrates, state power exemplified through the laws of association is different in kind from the authority of the police who ransack activists' homes, which is in turn different from the command of the plainclothes police who surveil the movements of the activists and the events that they host. All of these forms of state power are in turn distinguished from the power exercised through the Tunisian Ministry of Women's and Family Affairs, or any

---

7. As of the late 1990s, UNFT had 27 regional representations and 750 local, rural, and vocational sections across the country. Regional and local activities are very much controlled from above, and a "grassroots" atmosphere is absent from the organization. The local UNFT office is typically located next door to, or in the same building with, Ben Ali's ruling political party. UNFT remains the only women's organization in Tunisia capable of reaching all parts of the country. Femmes Démocrates has attempted without success to establish sections outside of Tunis.

other ministry for that matter, and the power played out within state-affiliated women's groups. Each kind of state power generates a different kind of possible resistance, and thus a more layered conception of resistance and accommodation is necessary to accompany this more nuanced analysis of the hegemonic state.

Turning now to transnational women's organizing, Sonia Alvarez provides a useful frame. Writing about transnational organizing and the impact on local feminist actors in Latin America, Alvarez identifies two "logics" of transnational feminist organizing: an *internationalist identity-solidarity logic* characterized largely by intraregional activism, such as the transnational feminist organizing that has occurred dramatically within the region of Latin America—and within smaller subsets of that region—during recent decades, and a *transnational IGO-advocacy logic* characterized by regionwide and global activism, such as the global organizing related to the UN world conferences and the associated regional preparatory conferences.[8] Alvarez also outlines three distinct reasons that local actors pursue these transnational linkages. First, local actors use these linkages to reaffirm or construct marginalized identities and to establish strategic bonds of solidarity (2000, 31). Second, local actors work across borders to expand formal rights and impact public policy debates. Third, some local actors might organize transnationally because they share a common legal or cultural fate across borders (60n7).

Another useful contribution is by Tunisian legal scholar (and autonomous feminist activist) Hafidha Chekir, who organizes the work of international and regional women's networks into two general categories: exchange and solidarity (1998a). The category of exchange can then be divided into the exchange of information and the exchange of experience. Isis Wicce is a classic example of an international network focusing on the exchange of information between women and women's groups.[9] Networks focusing on the exchange of experience allow for women to examine similarities and differences and compare notes on what strategies have been useful in struggling against women's oppression. The second function of many women's networks, building solidarity, is often seen in the organization of campaigns to denounce certain practices or legal codes that violate women's rights. In-

8. An IGO is an intergovernmental organization.

9. Isis Wicce (Women's International Cross-Cultural Exchange) was founded in October 1974 in Geneva. Its mission is to create solidarity networks and communicate ideas among women in various regions of the world with the goal of overcoming gender inequalities. The network relocated to Kampala, Uganda, in 1993 and operates an exchange program, information and documentation program, and publication program.

ternational or regional campaigns to denounce violence against women would fit into this type of women's networking.

However, missing from both Chekir's dual typology and Alvarez's discussion of the "logics" of transnational feminist organizing is any attention to the role that the state might play in mediating nongovernmental transnational activities. As mentioned above, the specifics of the Tunisian case—a hegemonic state that promotes a paradoxical vision of vibrant yet controlled civic activity—offer us an opportunity to explore the question of state influence and control over access to and participation in transnational social movements, and as such the Tunisian case serves as a unique contribution to the literature on transnational social movements in general and transnational feminist linkages in particular. With the understanding that the role of the state needs to be inserted into Chekir's typology and Alvarez's "logics," we can attempt to apply both conceptual tools to the autonomous feminist movement in Tunisia in each of our three cases of transnational linkages.

The Maghreb Collectif and the Arab Women's Forum

Since the early days of autonomous feminist organizing in Tunisia, Femmes Démocrates has prioritized efforts to form alliances with other like-minded autonomous feminists and feminist organizations in the Maghreb. Prior to the formal creation of Femmes Démocrates, autonomous women's activists in Tunisia hosted three Maghreb meetings in the early 1980s. Femmes Démocrates continued to host meetings once it was officially recognized by the state in 1989. Finally, in 1991, activists in Tunisia, Morocco, and Algeria created the Collectif 95 Maghreb Égalité with the stated goal of preparing a unified Maghreb presence for the Beijing Conference. Specifically, the activists wanted to create a secular Maghreb presence at the conference that would push for ratification of the Convention on the Elimination of All Forms of Discrimination Against Women (CEDAW) and prepare a unified plan of action for promoting gender equality in the Maghreb.

This regional networking is illustrative of Alvarez's internationalist identity-solidarity logic and functions as both a solidarity and exchange network, following Chekir's typology. Autonomous activists across the Maghreb have pursued transnational regional linkages for a number of reasons, making use of all those outlined by Alvarez. Clearly, these activists come together to establish strategic solidarities with those individuals who share "stigmatized values." Autonomous feminist activists in the region are routinely stereotyped as Westernized, secularized divorcées, and those women in Algeria have dealt with life-threatening conditions throughout the 1990s.

I would argue that this first reason is the primary motivation for the continued functioning of the Collectif. But because these activists are committed to CEDAW and advancing their own version of an egalitarian codification of the personal status or family law, Alvarez's second motivation also applies.[10] Expanding formal rights and influencing policy is indeed part of its agenda. Finally, even though family law and women's rights vary within the Maghreb, the region has a common cultural heritage, and, thus, Alvarez's third reason applies as well: women in the Maghreb generally share a similar legal and cultural fate. Indeed, although Tunisian family law may be more progressive than the Moroccan or Algerian codes, political control of civic associations is much more intense in Tunisia than in the other two Maghreb countries (Ziai 1997). The participants in the Collectif understand that no one group of women is fundamentally better off than the other.

This regional identity-solidarity linkage is a crucial site of resistance for Femmes Démocrates. The Collectif has been granted legal status only in Morocco,[11] so simply distributing Collectif documents within Tunisia, where the group is not formally recognized, is an act of resistance.[12] Tunisian activists that I interviewed occasionally alluded to apprehension about the relationship between the Collectif and the state, saying that they were not able to widely circulate the network's documents, fearing reprisals from the state. But Femmes Démocrates has made a strategic choice to avoid the process of applying for official status—because of the quagmire of the Tunisian laws of association and the potential backlash. Understandably, the activists are leery of drawing attention to the activities of the network for fear that the state will then prohibit all related organizing, but they also run the risk of the state finding out about their involvement in an "illegal organization" even without submitting an application to the Ministry of the Interior. For example, on one occa-

10. The Collectif has outlined its version of an egalitarian personal status code in Collectif 95 Égalité Maghreb 1995b.

11. All funding of the Collectif has been funneled through Morocco. The German Friedrich Ebert Foundation has funded the Collectif from the beginning, through its office in Rabat. More recently, the European Union has funded the network, with Friedrich Ebert serving as the partner foundation (the European Union stipulates that southern NGOs must have European partners to qualify for funding).

12. Collectif publications, with titles given in English if a translated version is available, are the following: *Violations flagrantes des droits et violences à l'égard des femmes au Maghreb: Rapport annuel, 1996–97* (1998), *Maghreb Women "with All Reserve"* (1995), and *Women in the Maghreb: Change and Resistance* (1995).

sion the Collectif was determined to hold a meeting at a hotel in Tunis without obtaining a conference visa from the authorities—knowing it was futile to ask for one in the first place. The police arrived at the hotel in short order, told them they did not have the proper permission, and the women ended up regrouping at the Tunis office of the Friedrich Ebert Foundation, the key funder of the network, to finish the meeting.[13]

Fortunately, no severe crackdown on Collectif activities in Tunisia resulted from the hotel incident. So it seems that as long as the state refrains from confiscating everyone's passport, participating in the Collectif allows Femmes Démocrates to organize *regionally* in ways that are barely permissible *nationally.* Furthermore, the Collectif is relatively free from the pressures of state co-optation because it continues to function "off the books" in Tunisia. Of course, another component of this situation is that the work of the Collectif remains essentially unknown within Tunisia.

Another regional linkage that remains officially unrecognized for strategic purposes and unknown by the general population within Tunisia is the Arab Women's Forum, also known as the AISHA Network. Interestingly, both the Collectif and the Arab Women's Forum have received consultative status from the United Nations, thus achieving formal international recognition even while remaining incognito in Tunisia. The Arab Women's Forum was created in 1993 as a response to a perceived lack of solidarity among Arab women. ATFD activists had begun to notice the lack of interaction between democratic-minded women's organizing in the Maghreb ("the West," or North Africa) and the Mashreq ("the East," or the Middle East) and were fully aware of the tendency to look toward Europe for solidarity instead of toward other Arab women in the Middle East. But it was the UN World Conference on Human Rights in Vienna in 1993 that provided this population of Arab women with two key reasons to create an alliance: marginalization by American and European feminist groups and threats against women's rights issued by Islamist forces within the Arab world (Safia Farhat, ATFD activist and AISHA Network coordinator, interview by author, Oct. 16, 1998, Tunis).

Like the Collectif, the Arab Women's Forum functions both as an exchange and a solidarity network and illustrates the internationalist identity-solidarity logic out-

13. This story was recounted to me by Gerd Emil Lieser, resident director of the Friedrich Ebert Foundation office in Tunisia, during an interview on June 4, 1999. Lieser was in Morocco when the Collectif was created and was the one who received the network's first request for funding. He agreed to finance the new group and, even when no longer in Morocco, continued to follow the work of the Collectif. He is very impressed by the work the network has been able to achieve over the years.

lined by Alvarez. With membership open to "all non-governmental Arab women's organizations registered in their respective countries," the AISHA Network links together organizations from Palestine, Lebanon, Egypt, Morocco, Jordan, Sudan, Algeria, and Tunisia.[14] The network holds a general meeting at least once every three years and elects representatives to serve on the Coordinating Committee that meets each year. The Executive Committee is composed of the general coordinator (elected once every three years) and four members (two from eastern Arab countries and two from western Arab countries). Then there are national and local coordinators who work within each member state. Since 1995, seminars have been held annually, and the network has focused on researching the Arab states' ratification of international human rights treaties and specific human rights violations that women in Sudan and Algeria have faced from Islamist movements.

In Tunisia, the AISHA Network's "Solidarity Center" is located a floor below the ATFD headquarters. In December 1996, Tunisian activists organized a conference in Tunis to celebrate the opening of the Solidarity Center, and the event ended up inciting an intense backlash against the autonomous activists that spread through the papers in the form of a negative press campaign. ATFD activists were the subjects of numerous caricatures and were again accused of being prostitutes, lesbians, or simply unmarried women. As the president of ATFD at the time deplored, "Anything you can imagine, we were called it. We were even harassed over the phone" (Bochra Bel Haj Hmida, interview by author, Feb. 25, 1999, Tunis).

Femmes Démocrates has a hard time explaining why a meeting of the AISHA Network incited such a backlash. Most activists believe that it was *not* a result of the network's lack of legal status in Tunisia, since the event was reported correctly by the press as having been sponsored by ATFD. The former president of ATFD tried to explain it by looking at the psychology of the state and the state-controlled media: "There is not true solidarity in the Arab world. Hence, the fact that we, as a small organization, were able to [create this solidarity] resulted in harsh repercussions" (Bel Haj Hmida, interview by author, Feb. 25, 1999, Tunis). ATFD did not press charges against the newspapers, but instead wrote letters and circulated a petition to protest the coverage. Many autonomous feminist activists are convinced that their success in collaborating with other women from throughout the Middle East and North Africa to create the Arab Women's Forum has resulted in a more general backlash against Femmes Démocrates that has persisted since the founding of this network.

For instance, at any particular moment any combination of activists might not

14. Sudan and Algeria have individual activists as members of the network.

have their passports. This confiscation of passports means that women risk missing conferences and meetings that they themselves have helped to plan. Indeed, the weight of the *atmosphère* means that any amount of activism in Tunis, let alone transnational linkages, seems an amazing feat. Yet these two examples of identity-solidarity transnational linkages continue to offer Femmes Démocrates the space to maneuver just beyond the reach of the hegemonic Tunisian state. Certainly, if they plan Collectif or AISHA Network events in Tunis, they by now expect to be harassed by the police. But the autonomous activists are able to collaborate with Collectif members on publications, for instance, that are then published outside Tunisia, thus circumventing the restrictions in Tunisia. Indeed, even hegemonic state power is incoherent, and Femmes Démocrates works strategically to negotiate the fissures and inconsistent terrain.

The Rihana Network

The Ministry of Women's and Family Affairs managed Tunisia's official governmental preparation for the Fourth UN Conference on Women. However, to prepare for the parallel NGO meeting, the state-affiliated Union National des Femmes Tunisiennes initiated the creation of a preparatory NGO network in 1992. This Rihana Network proceeded to meet once every two weeks in the years leading up to the conference.[15] Nine organizations, including ATFD, agreed to participate.[16] However, the Rihana Network was not the first time that members of ATFD and UNFT set aside ideological differences and attempted to cooperate on projects, nor was it the first time that both groups participated conjointly in transnational organizing.

Thanks primarily to strategic thinking on the part of the state, both autonomous feminist activists and state-affiliated women's activists mobilized against the Islamist movement in the early 1990s. Part of Ben Ali's efforts to consolidate power and cripple the Islamist opposition involved rallying women against the threat of retrograde changes in the Personal Status Code that would likely result

15. The word *Rihana* comes from the name of a traditional necklace worn by Tunisian women.

16. In addition to UNFT and ATFD, these organizations participated in the Rihana Network: Association des Femmes Tunisiennes pour la Recherche et le Développement, Association Tunisienne des Mères, Women's Commission of the Ligue Tunisienne des Droits de l'Homme, Women's Commission of the Union Générale des Travailleurs Tunisiens, National Chamber of Women Business Leaders, Women's Commission of the National Federation of Women Farmers, and the Women's Commission of the National Lawyers' Council. In 1995, the Red Crescent Women's Committee joined the network.

from the increased political power of an-Nahda, the now outlawed Tunisian Islamist organization. However, though both organizations—UNFT and ATFD—
spoke out against the Islamist movement and the potential threat to women's rights,
the adversarial and autonomous position of Femmes Démocrates allowed it to
maintain a firm stance against the human rights abuses suffered by an-Nahdha
members and their families at the hands of the state security forces.

This instance of collaboration between ATFD and UNFT did not have an overt
transnational dimension, but it does call attention to an additional cross-border
linkage, outside the domain of the transnational women's movement—but allied
with it—that Femmes Démocrates has consistently been involved with over the
years: international human rights activism, in collaboration primarily with European human rights activists from Amnesty International.

A second example of collaboration between ATFD and UNFT that occurred
prior to the Rihana Network happened in the context of antiwar protests during the
first Gulf War in 1991. ATFD and UNFT, along with nonaffiliated activists, formed a
coalition for unified action against the war and in support of the people of Iraq. This
women's antiwar coalition was a very prominent part of the larger antiwar movement that coalesced in Tunisia during the Gulf War, and included activities such as
publishing communiqués, declarations, and articles; organizing meetings; and participating in public demonstrations against the war (Labidi 1991).

These two examples of collaboration between autonomous and state-affiliated
women's groups suggest that such levels of cooperation occur as long as the target of
the coalition activities is not the Tunisian state. Condemning opposition to Islamist
activities, protesting a foreign war, and showing solidarity with the people of Iraq
are permissible subjects for unified mobilization. UNFT played a key role in antiwar
organizing and coalition building, both within Tunisia and transnationally, during
the first Gulf War, and UNFT was also the group that initiated the Rihana Network.
However, as the case of Rihana will demonstrate, occasionally the state has to re-
assert control even with the hallmark state-affiliated women's group already at the
helm.

In the years leading up to the Beijing Conference, members of the Rihana Network—Femmes Démocrates and the array of state-affiliated women's organizations—participated in the drafting of the *National Report*, the centerpiece of the
official Tunisian delegation to the conference, and they also participated in regional
preparations for the meeting. Another task was to agree upon a common platform
on the issues relevant to the conference and plan events and activities that would
occur once at the meeting. Unlike the regional networks discussed above, Rihana is

an example of Alvarez's second logic of transnational IGO-advocacy because it existed only to prepare for participation in a much larger UN-sponsored interregional event. However, even with the expected conflicts between groups, the network also served to foster a certain level of solidarity among Tunisian representatives to the conference, and thus mildly fits Chekir's description of a solidarity network.

At the conference, ATFD and UNFT found themselves on the same side of the debate on women's rights and Islamist movements, owing to the secular nature of both organizations. In fact, one of the most meaningful demonstrations of solidarity between autonomous and state-affiliated activists occurred during the women's parliament hosted by the Collectif 95 Maghreb Égalité, when Rihana delegates took similar (secular) positions in debates with Islamist women. Femmes Démocrates was also given enough leeway to be able to host its own events at the conference, such as a workshop on violence against women. The autonomous activists also understand that the efforts of the Rihana Network translated into greater visibility for Tunisian women's groups at the conference.

However, autonomous activists remain ambivalent about their decision to participate in the network. Ultimately, Femmes Démocrates felt marginalized within the network and believe that its efforts were largely co-opted by the state, especially given the events immediately prior to the conference and the complete lack of follow-up after the conference. Although the activists maintain respect for the efforts of individual participants in the network, the general assessment is that on the eve of the conference, the state moved in and tightened the control that it already had over the network. Rihana delegates were informed on the way to the Beijing Conference that the woman who had directed their efforts through three years of meetings, then president of UNFT Faiza Kefi, had been replaced as director of the network by a male government official. Autonomous activists who participated in the network and traveled to Beijing recounted stories of nightly meetings, coordinated by this Tunisian government official, that involved ensuring a unified "NGO" plan for the next day's activities.

Post-Beijing, autonomous feminist activists were startled not only by the lack of follow-up but also by their systematic exclusion from any public relations materials or media coverage of the Rihana Network. Initially, Femmes Démocrates chose to participate in this network in an effort to actively engage the state and avoid the isolation—and potential irrelevance—of the autonomous feminist movement. In retrospect, however, most autonomous activists regret participating because their hard work within the network led to new levels of co-optation and marginalization of the autonomous feminist movement. As autonomous activists recounted in numerous interviews, the Rihana Network functioned as a thinly veiled attempt by the state to control all Tunisian NGO activities at the Beijing Conference.

Furthermore, while the autonomous activists felt marginalized and co-opted by the state usurpation of the Rihana Network that was *already* dominated by state-affiliated women's groups, they also felt marginalized by Western feminist hegemonies that still tend to dominate international conferences. As Hafidha Chekir points out, autonomous activists from Tunisia feel marginalized at these international conferences much like they feel marginalized at home (1995). State-affiliated women's groups that function as extensions of their respective governments receive preferential treatment—not only from their governments but frequently from foreign funders as well—that translates into an increased presence at international events. Rather than opening up a space for building solidarity, as was seen with the regional networks, international forums easily overwhelm autonomous activists with the perception of a dual force of marginalization and co-optation.

Thus, Femmes Démocrates remain wary of the potential for positive outcomes from this "transnational IGO-advocacy logic" in the same way that it remains skeptical of the potential for positive collaboration with the state structures that attempt to mediate this transnational logic, such as the Rihana Network. Indeed, the autonomous activists' participation in the network meant that their participation at the actual NGO conference was almost entirely mediated through hegemonic state structures. Thus, the Rihana Network serves as an example of how authoritarian states conspire to hinder transnational NGO linkages or, at a minimum, severely control the images and discourses that women's organizations can employ while participating in international conferences—even when the organizations are *not* part of the official national delegation.

The Center for Victims of Violence Against Women

Since its emergence as a topic for transnational activism in the early 1980s, violence against women has gone on to become a central unifying issue of the transnational women's movement as well as a key concern of the international human rights community (Keck and Sikkink 1998). Women's organizations in Tunisia began addressing violence against women in their programs in the early 1990s. Today, a variety of women's organizations have programs that claim to address the issue of violence against women through general social service programs, but ATFD is the only women's group in Tunisia that has a program designed exclusively to assist women who are victims of gender-based violence. The centerpiece of this program is the

Centre d'Écoute, a multifaceted support center for victims of violence located in ATFD's main office in Tunis. The daily operation of this center has been the most ambitious project of Femmes Démocrates since the center's creation in 1993.

Interestingly, this third case of transnational linkages straddles Alvarez's transnational logics. Because of ideological differences between Femmes Démocrates and state-affiliated women's groups on the question of how best to confront violence against women, the autonomous feminist movement has turned toward its sister organizations in the Maghreb, such as the members of the Collectif, to build solidarity and collaborate on this issue. Thus, the issue of violence against women has reinforced the regional identity-solidarity logic of the autonomous movement's transnational linkages. However, the act alone of taking up the issue of violence against women—so central to the transnational women's movement—illustrates the participation of Femmes Démocrates in the transnational IGO-advocacy logic. Furthermore, this second transnational logic is at play in the funding relationship between Femmes Démocrates and the European foundations that fund the Centre d'Écoute.

The energy that the Femme Démocrates devotes to violence against women is therefore a rich site of transnational linkages, even though the Centre d'Écoute is a local project. Autonomous feminist organizing around the issue of violence against women also offers us insight into questions of autonomy and co-optation and promotes a multilayered analysis of resistance and accommodation in relation to the state. To illustrate this point, some background information on the Centre d'Écoute is necessary.

Just one year after obtaining legal status as a formal women's organization in Tunisia, ATFD's Health Commission began examining violence against women as a physical and emotional health issue. One year later, in 1991, Femmes Démocrates launched Tunisia's first public-awareness campaign on the issue of violence against women. However, their first poster campaign in May 1991, described to me by one member as "too much too fast," was almost immediately taken down by state authorities. By December 1991, ATFD had protested the censuring of the first poster and successfully put up a second one, reaching areas outside Tunis such as Sousse, Sfax, Gabès, and the Cap Bon region. The poster depicted a woman with a black eye and the caption "Breaking the walls of silence." That same month, ATFD organized a press conference announcing their awareness campaign and hosted a debate on the subject of violence against women.

Shortly thereafter, in 1993, the organization established the Centre d'Écoute et d'Orientation des Femmes Victimes de Violence. Today, the Centre d'Écoute is staffed by ATFD activists who function as counselors and crisis advocates and by professional lawyers, social workers, and psychologists. The mission of the Centre d'Écoute is to provide a secure space for women who are victims of any form of gender-based violence. As of 2000, the Centre d'Écoute had assisted a total of 789 women.[17] The great majority of the women who come to the Centre d'Écoute are victims of domestic violence, but others are victims of rape, incest, and sexual harassment. In addition to the direct support of victims of violence at the Centre d'Écoute, ATFD has hosted various seminars and workshops targeting various populations, such as the police, judges, media, and doctors.

For most of its existence, the Centre d'Écoute has functioned within a complete media blackout. Echoes from the initial public-awareness campaign were heard on television and read about in the newspapers until about 1994 or 1995 (Association Tunisienne des Femmes Démocrates 1999). Since then, the Centre d'Écoute has received essentially no media coverage. ATFD's press releases are no longer published in the newspapers. The only recent exception to this media blackout was an article in the Tunisian magazine *Réalités* on a legal assistance case being managed by ATFD's former president for a seventy-year-old woman who had been illegally repudiated by her husband (Oumrane 1999). The implication of this media blackout is that the Centre d'Écoute functions by word of mouth and, presumably, by referrals from state institutions and organizations.[18]

No state-affiliated women's organization or state institution in Tunisia has a program that is devoted exclusively to the issue of violence against women like the Centre d'Écoute. However, in the years since Femmes Démocrates established its center, a number of state-affiliated organizations and state structures have inserted the issue into already existing social service or legal assistance programs. Most of these projects take the form of a general "hotline" that women can call when they need advice. Ironically, although such programs are incredibly weak efforts compared to the Centre d'Écoute, it is these small projects that receive the media coverage.[19] In any case, however hard state-affiliated groups attempt to ignore the

17. On average, the center assists 100 women each year; 1993 was the busiest year, with 135 new clients. Additional data can be found in Association Tunisienne des Femmes Démocrates 2001.

18. Official data are not kept on the extent to which women are referred to the Centre d'Écoute from various government social service agencies or from other state-affiliated women's organizations that have social service programs.

19. In the late 1990s, the president of UNFT's Alliance Juridique had a call-in radio show to provide legal advice to women.

achievements of the autonomous activists, it is difficult to deny that Femmes Démocrates was the first women's group in Tunisia to assist victims of violence and difficult to discount the importance of the role the autonomous feminist movement played in initially spreading awareness of the issue and in inspiring these other organizations to do the same.

The level of collaboration that presently exists in Tunisia on the issue of violence against women is minimal. The lack of formal collaboration around the issue of violence against women has numerous potential causes, one being conflicting ideas on how best to confront the issue. ATFD focuses explicitly on empowerment and the health and safety of the woman. Other institutions, such as UNFT and the Ministry of Women's and Family Affairs, focus on reconciliation and the sanctity of the family. Beyond conflicting ideology is the fear of co-optation foremost on the minds of ATFD activists and the fear of being outperformed that weighs in the calculations of state structures.

However, while the various state-affiliated women's groups compete among themselves—part of the state's divide-and-conquer strategy, most certainly—to see who has the better hotline, the Femme Démocrates is more than willing to cooperate with state agencies offering the services needed by the women they are assisting. ATFD works closely with the ministry in the management of specific cases of violence against women, setting aside ideological differences to ensure that a woman receives the social or psychological assistance that she needs.[20] Indeed, the autonomous feminist activists believe that the Tunisian state should be more involved than it presently is in guaranteeing services to women who are victims of gender-based violence. Arguably, the level of cooperation that exists between ATFD and the ministry and the obvious state ties between the ministry and UNFT result in the semblance of an informal network on the issue of violence against women in Tunis. However, this vague informal network is imbued with a level of competition and defensive posturing that makes true collaboration unlikely.

Fortunately for Femmes Démocrates, it can look to transnational linkages within the Maghreb, just as it does with the Collectif, for moral support and solidarity with other autonomous feminist activists on the issue of violence against women.[21] In the Maghreb, the German Heinrich Boll Foundation funds the "Project

20. Legal assistance for Centre d'Écoute cases is typically handled exclusively through ATFD, thanks to the organized team of lawyers that is affiliated with the center.

21. The Collectif has addressed the issue of violence against women. See Collectif 95 Égalité Maghreb 1998.

Hotline" that appears to hold great potential for formal transnational collaboration within the region. This Maghreb project is a group of three programs, one being ATFD's Centre d'Écoute, that have been created exclusively to help victims of violence against women; the other programs are located in Morocco and Algeria.

Although no formal regional network exists specifically on this issue, Femmes Démocrates feels a greater affinity with the like-minded autonomous activists in Morocco and Algeria who are also organizing around the issue of violence against women than it does with other state-affiliated women's groups in Tunisia who have attempted to implement "hotline" projects. Collaboration outside Tunisian borders also opens up the opportunity for Femmes Démocrates to make the connection between different forms of violence. Its organizational literature draws a clear relationship between the political violence that autonomous activists bear—the tapping of activists' phones, the confiscation of passports, the searching of activists' homes—and the various forms of violence against women. Such crucial connections cannot be discussed in collaboration with state-affiliated women's groups in Tunisia. In this way, then, the hegemonic state serves to inspire transnational linkages rather than hinder them.

The heavy dependence of ATFD—and the Centre d'Écoute in particular—on foreign donors such as the Heinrich Boll Foundation has not escaped the critical analysis of autonomous activists. A key component of the transnational IGO-advocacy logic is the North-South constellation of power asymmetries that encompasses the relationship between northern funders and southern women's organizations. Autonomous women's groups are especially vulnerable to dependence on foreign donors because of the lack of government support, as is the case with Femmes Démocrates. This reliance on foreign foundations for everything from daily operating costs to funds for conferences raises anew the question of autonomy for Femmes Démocrates. Indeed, a number of autonomous activists question the substantial influence that a small number of German foundations have had on the programmatic decisions of the organization, including the decision to accept the funds to create the Centre d'Écoute in the early 1990s. ATFD had to confront the harsh reality of the lack of financial autonomy as their grant from the Heinrich Boll Foundation faced expiration and they searched for new funding for the Centre d'Écoute.[22]

---

22. This situation was as of February 2003.

Conclusions

The three cases discussed in this chapter illustrate some of the ways in which the autonomous feminist movement in Tunisia negotiates transnational linkages and its relationship with what we have been referring to as the "hegemonic" Tunisian state. One hope is that a dual interrogation of transnational linkages and the state offers some insight into questions of autonomy and co-optation and the tension between resistance and accommodation as they apply to the autonomous feminist movement in Tunisia during the 1990s. Another hope is that this dual interrogation sheds some light on the need to consider the role of the state in mediating nongovernmental transnational activities.

The first case of the two regional networks, the Collectif 95 Maghreb Égalité and the Arab Women's Forum, or AISHA Network, reveals some hidden space for resistance. As long as Femmes Démocrates does not draw too much attention to its involvement in both of these identity-solidarity networks, the autonomous activists are able to use these linkages to organize regionally in ways that would be impossible within their own borders. As mentioned above, Femmes Démocrates collaborates on Collectif publications, all of which are published outside Tunisia. Although they cannot risk widely distributing these documents within Tunisia, and are thus unable to reach a broader population, the activists are at least able to take leading roles in the creation of the documents. Indeed, this collaboration with like-minded women within the Maghreb and the rest of the Middle East and North Africa plays a crucial role in maintaining the spirits of the autonomous activists in Tunisia when the levels of state repression defy explanation.

The second case of transnational linkages, the Rihana Network, is representative of the transnational IGO-advocacy logic. More crucial to our purposes here, this network serves as a key example of how hegemonic states conspire to hinder free and open participation in transnational NGO linkages. The Rihana Network ostensibly aimed to facilitate a diverse NGO presence at the Beijing Conference—and arguably succeeded in this attempt to the extent that any NGO delegation from Tunisia can be considered "diverse." However, after a prelude of open discussions that included the full participation of Femmes Démocrates and an effort to prove some sort of distinction between the state itself and state-affiliated women's organizations, the state maneuvered to take control of the NGO network—going so far as to usurp the power of the queen of state-affiliated women's groups, the Union National des Femmes Tunisiennes. Tunisian NGO participation in the Beijing Conference was thus mediated through hegemonic state structures, illustrating the potential hindrance that hegemonic states in particular pose to transnational feminist linkages. Femmes Démocrates remains wary of participating in similar state-affiliated networks in the future, fearing that years of work will once again be co-opted.

The third case of transnational linkages, ATFD's centerpiece program on violence against women, the Centre d'Écoute, demonstrates ATFD's engagement with the transnational IGO-advocacy logic by force of having chosen to take on an issue that is today central to transnational women's organizing. Thanks to the autonomous feminist movement, awareness of violence against women has spread to state-affiliated women's groups in Tunisia, many of which now include the issue in their social service programs. However, owing to a mix of ideological differences; societal, cultural, and political constraints; and state repression of autonomous organizing, no formal NGO collaboration on violence against women exists within Tunisia. Instead, Femmes Démocrates turns again toward regional linkages. In this way, the Centre d'Écoute illustrates the identity-solidarity logic of transnational linkages as well.

The Centre d'Écoute also functions as a nexus for the two power constellations highlighted in this paper. Organizing around the issue of violence against women in Tunisia requires resisting the effects of the state-sponsored media blackout and the attempts of state-affiliated women's groups to discount the achievements of the Centre d'Écoute. Because of the absolute reliance on external funding, resistance is also directed against the "tyranny" of foreign funders. This position represents the North-South constellation of power and the third arena of autonomy that Femmes Démocrates increasingly debates. With the male-dominated political left increasingly irrelevant and the struggle to maintain autonomy from the state a decades-old, highly refined battle, the relationship to foreign funders may well become a crucial site of debate and resistance for the autonomous feminist movement. This third arena of autonomy similarly affects members of the Collectif.

These three cases reveal a hegemonic Tunisian state that indeed has the potential to mediate transnational linkages, but not only with the effect of hindering them, as we observed with the Rihana Network. The autonomous feminist movement's participation in transnational identity-solidarity linkages at the regional level unearths an unintended *promotion* of transnational linkages. Femmes Démocrates turns to regional solidarities precisely because the hegemonic state atmosphere so drastically limits its options for action within state borders. It looks toward international linkages but knows to be wary of how the state might attempt to mediate these linkages if the related events are high profile and its image stands to be tarnished in front of a large global audience.

As such, Femmes Démocrates negotiates both the state and transnational linkages so as to avoid the extremes of co-optation and irrelevance. Femmes Démocrates represents one of the only examples of vibrant autonomous organizing in Tunisia—indeed, one of the only pieces of evidence that even mild dissent is permitted within Tunisian borders. Because the group poses no direct threat to the regime, it would appear that the state has no good reason to hinder any transnational linkages that the autonomous feminist movement wishes to pursue. Indeed, by loosening its hold, the Tunisian state stands to improve its image not least within the human rights community. But as Femmes Démocrates already knows, hegemony does not imply coherence.

7 Women, Communications, and Democratization in Morocco

LOUBNA H. SKALLI

> The New Communications Technologies are development tools. While growth is conceived of now mainly under the banner of newer Information and Communication Technologies, women still lack their most basic rights. . . . Democratization of social life involves the democratization of family life as well. Our recommendations for bringing changes to the Personal Status Code (Moudawana) seek to establish a legal framework guaranteeing a balanced relationship between the spouses. That is why we demand raising the marriage age for a girl from 15 to 18; canceling the tradition of legal tutoring and polygamy; establishing court divorces; unifying the conditions for child custody for the parents; and an equal sharing of property accumulated during marital life.
>
> —Messages advertised by the Spring of Equality, a
> network of women's organizations in Morocco

SINCE THE UN'S FOURTH WORLD CONFERENCE on Women, in Beijing in 1995, two contradictory phenomena have been observed.[1] On the one hand, there is an increasing awareness of the growing "digital divide" not only among and within world nations but also across gender, race, and age lines. On the other hand, more hope is invested in the democratic impulses and development potentials of the new communications that are expected to "facilitate information sharing and knowledge creation, and increase the transparency, accountability, and effectiveness of government, business and non-profit organizations."[2]

1. I wish to thank Val Moghadam for her editing of an earlier draft of this chapter. For the epigraph, see the French-language daily in Morocco, *Le Matin,* June 11, 2002, 12.

2. UNDP Thematic Trust Fund, "Information and Communication Technology for Development," http://www.undp.org/trustfunds/TTF-ICTe.PDF.

In this chapter, I explore the uses of communications by women in the democratic transition of Morocco. In particular, I focus on the gender dimension of such a transition by documenting ways in which women's nongovernmental organizations (NGOs) with strategic feminist interests use communications both as a tool and as a strategy in the conduct of their activities and the pursuit of their objectives.

The process of democratization in Morocco that began in the late twentieth century has attracted much scholarly attention.[3] Existing scholarship has analyzed the sociopolitical and historical context that has contributed to the "rebirth" and effervescence of civil society, the scope of freedom it enjoys, and the challenges it faces. Few studies, however, have focused on the gender dimension of civil society. Those studies that have done so have traced the historical emergence of women's organizations in Morocco and analyzed their profile as well as range of activities.[4]

However, despite the pertinence and quality of existing scholarship, none of the studies has explored the role of communications, old and new, in the development and dynamism of civil society. We know virtually nothing about how and if communication and information technologies have facilitated the work objectives of civil-society organizations in general. We still wonder whether they have contributed to widening the scope of women's intervention or increased their efficiency and visibility at the international level. There is an equal absence of documentation on the communication strategies utilized by women's organizations for reaching their publics and building meaningful networks.

This chapter complements existing scholarship by focusing on the gender dimension of civil society and the uses of communications by women's organizations. Three sets of questions are addressed: How accessible are the technologies of communication and information to the NGOs that promote women's political, socioeconomic, and legal rights? What communication tools and strategies are these advocacy NGOs using to publicize their activities, increase their visibility, and reach their targeted publics? And what are the specific needs of and challenges facing NGOs as far as communications are concerned? The questions were answered through sixteen in-depth interviews with members of nine nongovernmental women's organizations based in Rabat and Casablanca. The selection of the NGOs for this study is based on two criteria: the focus of their activities (that is, women's issues and gender equity) and their willingness to participate in the research. The

3. See, for example, el-Aoufi 1992; Deneoux and Gateau 1995; Ghazali 1989; Layachi 1995.

4. See, for example, Belarbi 1989, 1997; Brand 1998, 29–69; Zirari and Ouakrim 1998.

analysis and conclusions also draw on the extensive literature provided by the NGOs during the visits and interviews conducted between February and June 2002.

Women's Organizations in Morocco: Actors in the Democratic Transition

The contribution of women's organizations in the establishment of a democratic society in Morocco has been a long and even painful process.[5] Such a contribution has taken place within a historically patriarchal environment in which women have been marginalized and the portent of their work minimized if not hampered by the dominant masculinist ideology. Moreover, since the early formation of the Moroccan feminist consciousness in the mid-1940s, there has been a remarkable diversity in the political positions, priorities, and demands of the women activists. True, nearly all of them targeted the education of young Muslim girls and campaigned for raising the consciousness of women and improving their living conditions. Yet their political and ideological alliances often determined their work agenda and approaches that, up until the mid-1980s, kept them under the tutelage if not paternalism of the political parties to which they were affiliated.

The mid-1980s, however, saw the emergence of a new generation of women's organizations operating outside the formal political circles. As women's educational and work opportunities increased and frustrations within their parties mounted, they began to organize outside the conventional political arena that alienated them and marginalized their needs. Feminist consciousness and political commitment for women's emancipation gained serious momentum mostly during this period. Women started pressing gender-based demands with more audacity, autonomy, and a clearer vision as to their priorities. Women's organizations comprised mostly, but not exclusively, middle-class, professional, and left-wing political activists with a feminist agenda targeting all expressions of gender inequality and subordination.[6]

Many researchers have tried to provide a categorization of Moroccan women's organizations by relying on their economic, political, or sociocultural orientations.[7] However, such categorizations could get confusing when the NGOs' orientations are diverse and overlapping, as is often the case. It is probably more useful to apply a dis-

5. For a thorough historical overview of women's movements in Morocco, see Belarbi 1995; Daoud 1993, 237–345.

6. For more on this composition, see Lewis 1993.

7. See Belarbi 1989, 1997; Deneoux and Gateau 1995.

tinction that organizes them around "practical gender interests" and "strategic gender interests."[8] The first can be seen as organizations that respond to women's immediate economic needs and fight for economic survival. The latter are gender strategic organizations with feminist demands that target issues of rights and gender equity. Nearly all the organizations included in this research belong to this category.

In the late 1990s, there were at least thirty-five officially recognized nongovernmental women's organizations in Morocco.[9] Only five of these organizations were established before 1970. Between 1970 and 1984, some twenty-seven new organizations were added, and many more were to emerge during the mid-1990s. Eighty percent of these NGOs are located in the capital city of Rabat, while the rest are situated in Casablanca. Many of these organizations have regional sections and offices in other urban centers.

One of the most significant means of communication used by NGOs before and during the 1980s was the written word, namely, newspapers, magazines, journals, and periodicals.[10] The choice of such a tool may appear to be unwise, given the high rate of illiteracy among the Moroccan population (67 percent for women and 47 percent for men) and the fact that the most effective medium for reaching the larger public is the oral medium. The choice is strategic, however, because the national scene has been characterized by, on the one hand, a long tradition of men's monopoly over information and knowledge as well as the channels of disseminating them and by, on the other, an equally long tradition of women's "silence" and absence from the public scene. Indeed, one of the achievements of the Moroccan women's movement in the 1980s was precisely their growing confidence in using the tool of writing. Greater educational opportunities made women realize that the power of the written word could be effectively used to demystify the hegemonic world of power. In many ways, writing and mass publishing grew to signify an active participation of women in the process of knowledge production and control, the reinterpretation of social reality, and the struggle over power. Although the written word is

8. See Molyneux 1985.

9. This total is the official number communicated by the Ministry of Employment and Social Affairs. These groups are defined as "non-governmental associations whose major concern is the promotion of women and the recognition of their social, economic, cultural, legal and political rights." See Royaum du Maroc 1997, 213.

10. For a complete background on the nature and role of women's magazines in Morocco, see Skalli 2000.

not directly accessible by the majority of Moroccan women, it has nonetheless created transforming and transformative communication spaces for publicly discussing and debating issues of immediate concern.

Some of the important titles from the 1980s include the Arabic-language monthly *Thamania Mars* (8 Mars), published by the Union of Feminine Action; *Nissa' al-Maghrib* (Moroccan Women), a monthly published by the Democratic Association of Moroccan Women; and the French-language monthly *Kalima*, published by an independent group and edited by Hind Taarji, a Moroccan writer and (investigative) journalist. Such publications contributed to opening up new discursive spaces by and for women to critique oppressive power differentials. Equally important, they have turned women into producers, users, and consumers of information over which they have a more or less greater degree of control.

These magazines were among the important instances in which women's organizations and activists used technologies of information and communication to transform women's silence into public knowledge and action. Mirroring the case of other Muslim contexts, communications have contributed to redefining a new "public sphere" for the marginalized and the socially discriminated against. And, as has been often noted, it is not so much the novelty of the technology that has made all the difference but the creativity in using the old and newer communications that has carved out democratic spaces.[11] A close analysis of the uses of communications by the nine case-study women's organizations reveals how these actors of Moroccan civil society struggle to participate in the democratic transition of the country.

The Promises and Limitations of Communications

There is an increasing awareness that civil society in Morocco generally lacks the adequate communication skills for producing, sharing, and disseminating information among a larger segment of the Moroccan population. Most civil-society organizations admit that they not only lack a clear vision about which communication strategies to use to maximize the impact of their intervention or work but also fail to use the newer communication technologies (such as the Internet) to their full potential.[12]

11. See, in particular, Eickelman and Anderson 1999; Sreberny-Mohammadi and Mohammadi 1994.

12. Rachid Jankari, "ONG et Internet: Le Fossé "associatif" Marocain," Sept. 3, 2002, http://webzinecnd.mpep.gov.ma/article.php3?id_article=56. These observations emerge from most of the re-

The women's organizations that I studied do not seem to fare better. If anything, they reveal an ambivalent attitude toward communications. Their spokeswomen all have expressed a strong belief in the democratization of information and knowledge, the need for a larger participation of citizens in their programs and projects, and the establishment of important networks between and among national and international organizations advocating gender equity. In reality, however, they face serious challenges both in devising meaningful communication strategies to meet the above stated objectives and in fully exploiting the benefits of newer technologies. In the discussion that follows, I document both their achievements and their challenges.

Organizations' Use of Communications

"Communication and information are the throbbing heart of all NGOs," comments a woman activist. "We need them, we use them; but I am not sure we have the expertise or vision about how to maximize their benefit." This statement by the former president of a leading women's NGO echoes similar views expressed during the interviews with different members of women's organizations. The concept of a communications department or a communications director or coordinator is fairly new to the women's organizations. Although all of them expressed an urgent need for such a department as well as a keen interest in setting up a structure and personnel that would respond to their communication needs, few of them actually acted upon their decisions. Explanations often provided include limitations in financial and human resources.

All the organizations examined, however, have their own facilities, complete office equipment (including computers, fax machines, telephones, and photocopiers), and a minimum of two permanent hired staff. It is important to make this clarification because limitations in the use and application of communications are often attributed to the absence of facilities, equipment, or human resources. In fact, most of

---

search on civil society in Morocco. Similar comments also come up in the NGOs' self-evaluation during the study days, colloquia, and roundtable discussions organized by the Espace Associatif in Rabat on the nature and limits of associative life in Morocco. See, for example, the following publications by the Espace Associatif: *Action associative au Maroc,* vol. 1, *Elements de diagnostic* (1998), and vol. 2, *Elements de strategies* (1999); and *Relation du mouvement associatif aux acteurs politiques et socio-économiques* (2002), available online at http://www.caasnet.net.ma?applicationsNS/articles/index.asp?p95Article_ID=8039&m_select=technologie.

the organizations studied do not seem to prioritize expenses for communication needs in their overall budgeting. The ones that did had in fact started the tradition only six months prior to my research and were in the process of redefining their communication strategies. This fact suggests that there has been a lack of coordination and efficiency, as the opening epigraph reminds us.

When asked about the communication technologies used for organizational purposes and other informational needs, nearly all the organizations ranked the telephone first, the fax second, slow mail third, and the Internet last. Various reasons have been advanced for such an order of priorities. First, Moroccan culture in general favors immediate, person-to-person communication and an oral mode of transmission. Despite the high cost of phone calls, people prioritize the telephone as a reliable medium for transmitting and receiving information. Second, maintaining the human dimension of communication permits an important degree of familiarity that provides a moral guarantee for the transmission and diffusion of the message. Faxes and mailing come second and third because they are perceived to have a fairly high degree of "trustworthiness," to which is added the possibility of saving copies "for the record."

If the Internet does not constitute a major tool of communication yet, the "written" medium remains relatively weak as well. Although most NGOs are made up of educated middle-class members, many have not yet developed the habit of committing everything to writing, whether we are talking about minutes of meetings, reports of activities and events, or any other form of organizational publication. The groups that do admit that they are not very regular about it. This situation is taken by most of the organizations as one of the main obstacles for collecting, sharing, and disseminating information in Morocco. I return to this point in a later section.

The organization's financial profile, the availability of technical skills, and the perception of cost-effectiveness are usually the factors determining the use of the Internet. More than half of the organizations studied had at least one staff member with adequate computer literacy and the technical skills for using the Internet. Technical training in these cases was either paid for by the staff before joining the organization or provided by the organization itself within the framework of its partnerships with multiple governmental or international organizations.

However, in none of the organizations has e-mail become a routine part of day-to-day communication with members of the organizations or national stakeholders. None of them uses conferencing or a wide range of Internet tools such as search engines and the World Wide Web on a regular basis. In general, access issues—such as infrastructure limitations and costs to connect—rather than lack of interest or motivation are behind the expressed reasons for the slow adoption of the newer technologies. None of the organizations sees the Internet, and electronic mail in particular, as a cheaper alternative to point-to-point communication tools that offers a possibility of reaching a larger number of people.

Here again, the specificities of Moroccan culture are held accountable. There is a special "attitude to technology," an interviewee explained. "People prefer the relational side of communication. Even in places where the technology exists, it is not used that much inside the country." All the interviewees confirm that they use electronic mail to reach "the outside world," meaning to reach individuals, organizations, or stakeholders outside Morocco. Within the country, the tool has little appeal, at least in the associative world: "People do not reply to the ones we send them. So you send an e-mail, and you have to follow up with a phone call."

Even the professionals of the media do not seem to have fully integrated newer technology into their regular correspondence with people. In the words of another interviewee, "People do not answer mails. For example, if I send press releases via the Internet, only 10 percent will get published; when the same document is sent by fax or snail mail, the chances of publication are much higher." This observation is pertinent because all the main newspapers in Morocco have an online version. It seems that "the culture for this technology does not exist yet," as an interviewee suggested.

Most of the organizations have their own Web pages. They provide a brief online history of the organization, its objectives and achievements, as well as basic contact information. However, none of them has any feedback on their home page or a mechanism for assessing the number or profile of their cyber visitors. There also is no regular updating of the information included in the early design of the page.

Building and Sharing Information Resources

Most of organizations I studied are making significant contributions to building information resources on women. However, financial constraints or organizational priorities or both have kept them from utilizing newer information technologies to do so. None of the organizations has developed databases or listservs for online resources. Many "connected" members of the organizations act as bridges to the rest of their fellow activists or researchers. In these cases, they access online information first and then share what they deem pertinent through such traditional communication channels as print, fax, or telephone.

Important initiatives for creating online resources have come, interestingly enough, from sources other than the organizations included in this research. For instance, the Espace Associatif houses the Web pages of leading women's associations in Morocco and offers links to relevant databases.[13] A Moroccan Internet user designed a Web site (http://www.lamarocaine.com) that provides an exhaustive list of women's organizations and links to databases on all activities, publications, and events related to Moroccan women.

Women's organizations rely in general on other traditions for building and sharing information. Half of the offices visited have a small but growing resource center that contains the organization's own publications, if nothing else. Moroccan organizations have a well-established tradition of holding national and international conferences, study days, seminars, and colloquia on a fairly regular basis. The proceedings of these encounters are often published and either offered gratis or sold to readers, researchers, and members of other organizations. This documentation constitutes an important "capital" of information and research to be shared with the reading public. In addition, the centers house the published findings of sociological and legal studies based on fieldwork research undertaken by the same organization or by others. The range of topics covered is as wide and varied as the interests of the organizations. They often include, but are not limited to, such sensitive issues as sexual harassment, domestic violence, the problem of young female housemaids, unresolved divorce cases and contradictions in women's legal status, as well as the feminization of poverty.

Building Communication Strategies and Networks

Persistent resistance to gender equality in Morocco and the increasing marginalization of women from human sustainable development have convinced the women's organizations that they cannot afford to either remain atomized (carrying out isolated efforts) or work in a disorganized or uncoordinated fashion. This realization has resulted in a growing recognition among women's organizations that serious ef-

13. Espace Associatif is a Rabat-based NGO founded in 1997 to coordinate the activities of civil-society organizations. Its Web site is http://www.espaceassociatif.org.ma. See also espasso@iam.net .ma. I wish to thank the communication and public relations director of Espace Associatif for providing useful information and publications for this study.

forts must be directed toward devising a clearer communication strategy to achieve their immediate and long-term objectives. There has also been a sense of urgency about building bridges across ideological or institutional differences. They feel pressured to reorient their interventions and improve on their spirit of solidarity, cooperation, and networking.

A strategy adopted by one of the organizations was a gradual revision of their vision, mission, and work methods. In the words of its former president, the result was that "we are now an organization with strategic interest. We try to have an impact on the *verrous* [sites of resistance] that have multiplying effects, such as changing the political vision, legal texts, and the mentalities with them." Since 1995, this organization has developed and implemented a long-term program called "Education for Equality" that targets strategic publics with appropriate communication and information tools. They include manuals and workshops that gender-sensitize schoolkids, youth clubs, vocational trainers, policy makers, educators, social workers, and media professionals. Relatively similar efforts are reproduced by three other organizations included in my study.

However, if devising new strategies for communicating the culture of gender equality is a project in process, developing the spirit of solidarity and networking remains a serious challenge. This fact is best summed up in the statement of an interviewee: "There are serious problems working with other associations and building a network. We have problems with our partners and other associations. We have the same objectives, but we do not agree on the same strategies. And we know that all is based on power relations. In order to have impact and weight, we need to deal with and face these difficulties."

One of the difficulties often mentioned by organizations is what is called "information retention." Various interviewees reported that all attempts at networking and solidarity building were defeated because organizations have a general tendency to "withhold" information from others and monopolize it for their own benefit. Competition for receiving funding from the same donors usually puts a high price tag on information perceived by organizations to be pertinent for obtaining funding. The information withheld offers a competitive edge for acquiring more project funding from local, national, or international donors. In an effort to overcome the counterproductive effects of competition and divisiveness, recent attempts have been made to achieve common objectives. The uses of communications in these instances have been most interesting and are worth describing in brief in order to assess some of their implications.

On July 19, 1999, a group of leading women's organizations and human rights activists announced the creation of Chabaka, which means "network" in Arabic.[14] Chabaka comprises at least two hundred Moroccan NGOs supporting the demands of women's organizations. The objectives of the initiative were threefold: to inform and sensitize Moroccan public opinion about the contents of the Action Plan for the Integration of Women in Development; gain the support of most citizens, government agencies, and civil-society organizations for the plan; and constitute a follow-up committee to press for the implementation of the plan.[15]

The coordination committee of Chabaka developed a five-stage communication strategy to achieve its objectives. First, it used the mass media in all their forms, mainstream and alternative, to inform the national public about the action plan. It then organized at least thirty-six information-sensitization meetings across the country to build regional support networks for Chabaka. The third stage targeted specifically the government, the parliament, and political party leaders with whom meetings were organized for "oral pleading" in defense of the plan. This step was followed by the stage of "written pleading" to the same decision makers: open letters in the press and recommendations for gender-sensitive revisions in the legal texts were used here. The final stage, during which strong resistance to the plan "froze" the intervention of the government, involved reinforcing as well as expanding solidarity and support networks across the nation.

Chabaka multiplied its efforts and creative strategies to reach the larger public through press conferences, appearances in the mass media, opening up of discussion forums and roundtables in closed spaces (offices and centers) as well as open public sites (streets). This work culminated on March 8, 2001, during which all the supporters of the plan were invited to wear a pin in support of the theme of the cam-

14. The information used in this section is drawn from personal communication with one of the main coordinators of Chabaka, an active member of an NGO included in this study. She is also the writer and editor of Chabaka's magazine, published under the same name.

15. The Action Plan for the Integration of Women in Development is a large-scale development project for ending all forms of discrimination against Moroccan women at the economic, legal, sociocultural, and political levels. The plan was the product of collaboration between the Moroccan government and civil-society organizations that press for gender equity. The same organizations that spearheaded Chabaka participated in developing the action plan. When announced by the prime minister in 1999, the plan was met with strong opposition and virulent criticism from conservative religious centers that considered demands for changes in women's legal status a violation of the spirit of Islam. In the face of this organized opposition, the plan was shelved by the government.

paign, "TOGETHER FOR EQUALITY." Chabaka published a magazine under the same title in an effort to fully document the historical evolution of the plan.

In the second example of a coordinating effort, preparations for the celebration of International Women's Day on March 8, 2002, inspired a committee representing more than thirty-five NGOs, including women's organizations, human rights groups, trade unions, youth groups, and cultural associations, to launch a sensitizing campaign under the theme "Citizenship, Equality and Dignity for Women." The campaign targeted primarily the general public in Rabat and surrounding towns Sale and Temara. The coordination committee used posters, leaflets, and banners to transmit its messages. Representatives from women's organizations organized activities in high schools, universities, neighborhoods, administrations, and production plants.

The Spring of Equality

In 2001, seven leading NGOs for the promotion of women's rights established an "advocacy structure" lobbying the most controversial aspect of the Action Plan: revisions of the Family Law, known as the Moudawana, which came to be known as the Spring of Equality (Printemps de l'Égalité). The communication campaign was organized for this purpose had three phases. The first was launched on April 15, 2002, and involved the publication of a series of press releases, posters, and articles in the national dailies explaining the discriminatory provisions of legal texts in matters of repudiation, divorce, child support, domestic violence, and so on. The second phase used billboards in five of the major urban centers in Morocco with the aim of raising the consciousness and understanding of public opinion. This step was followed by the distribution of flyers and publication of articles in the press featuring real-life cases of victims of legal discrimination. The choice of the victims was very strategic: it was meant to represent women from all walks of life, while each case pushed for revising the specific law that the women's organizations were targeting.[16]

16. Some of the cases taken up are the following: a fifteen-year-old girl forced into marriage by her father, her legal guardian; a twenty-six-year-old divorcée with two children who was forced to return to her parents' home in the absence of alimony; a thirty-two-year-old upper-middle-class architect who was a victim of domestic violence but could not obtain a divorce in the absence of the required number of witnesses to the acts of violence; and a sixty-eight-year-old woman with three children and four grandchildren expelled from her marital home by her husband and without financial support for having refused to cohabit with the new wife of her polygamous husband.

Discussion and Recommendations

Women's organizations in developing countries are still struggling to apply the newer information technology in their internal functioning and external relations. Although they face formidable obstacles, women are making great strides in adopting different communication tools and strategies to participate in the democratic transition of Morocco. This progress is best illustrated by the above-mentioned examples of networking and campaigning.

The Spring of Equality initiative came as a complement to and reinforcement of the objectives and efforts of Chabaka. Some interviewees called the campaign the "first professional and best communication project developed to promote the culture and values of gender equality in Morocco." For other interviewees, however, the entire structure and work of Spring of Equality are not so much a success story as they are a symbol of the "perennial divisions among women's movements and a failure of many NGOs to rise above personal agendas and self-interest." Points of dissent include the foreign funding of this communication campaign and the tendency of this new structure to overshadow if not marginalize the achievements of Chabaka.[17]

For a while it appeared that the ultimate objectives of both initiatives would not be met, because the plan was officially shelved by the government in the face of a massive Islamist resistance. But a royal commission recommended that the Moudawana be reformed, and the king's decree of October 2003 led to parliamentary approval in January 2004. In any event, the results of the activists' combined efforts have created a new dynamic in the democratic transition of Morocco. First, they have transferred discussions around women's rights and status away from the usually closed circles of women's organizations out into the public sphere in a way never seen or experienced before. Now, the voices of women activists are mingled with the voices of progressive and conservative citizens, political and religious decision makers, as well as the different representatives of civil-society organizations. Second, the "sacred" aura surrounding the Moudawana was unveiled and even challenged by real-life cases of discrimination and injustice against women. Major steps were taken toward building a coalition and solidarity among various civil-society organizations. For the first time, most of them united behind one cause, gender eq-

17. See the views expressed by Latifa Jbabdi, president of the Union of Feminine Action, one of the two NGOs that withdrew from the Spring of Equality project, in *al-Ayam,* no. 34 (May 25, 2002).

uity, and adopted large-scale communication campaigns in a systematic and strategic fashion.

However, greater efforts need to be made not only in the utilization of newer technologies but also in the cultivation and promotion of a more democratic vision of information and knowledge sharing. This need applies to two critical areas in which women's organizations in Morocco have to seriously rethink their communication choices: cooperation and grassroots participation. Cooperation and networking are on the agenda of virtually all NGOs. But competition often leaves them vulnerable and amenable to co-optation by other forces and agendas. Competitive conditions for receiving funds from national and international donors have often been cited by interviewees as among the key causes aborting major efforts at cooperation and transparency among NGOs. Hence, there are frequent cases of information retention among civil-society organizations and the tendency of most to engage in what may be called "selective communication." No doubt, these considerations have vexing results, among which are poor coordination of action among organizations, duplication of projects and programs already proven fruitless elsewhere, and an unnecessary waste of experiential knowledge that could be invested in furthering common goals. Sharing reliable information among all stakeholders is an essential basis for good governance at the NGO level. Without aiming at greater transparency in information sharing, women's organizations could fail to constitute a solid lobbying force regardless of the novelty of the communication tools used or the originality of the strategies devised.

What organizations need to realize, therefore, is that *communications* should not be reduced to a narrow understanding of a mere technology and tool for promoting immediate political, economic, or ideological ideas or interests. Communications are part of a much larger human sustainable development project that enables individuals and communities to form a cohesive unity around a social project beneficial to all.

This point leads to the second critical area that women's organizations need to develop: using communications to inform, involve, and mobilize a greater segment of the population, male and female alike. Moroccan women's organizations have often been criticized for being elitist structures for the middle- to upper-class urban few.[18] Information and knowledge produced by organizations usually remain locked within these closed circles and do no reach the grassroots level they are sup-

18. See, for example, Daoud 1993; Deneoux and Gateau 1995; Zirari and Ouakrim 1998.

posed to address, benefit, or represent. Women's organizations, and specifically those groups with strategic interests, do not penetrate the lower social strata to explicate to them their organization's vision and mission in the appropriate medium. Nor do they establish regular connections with them. Poor, working-class, and rural women are not the ones who are invited to or participate in urban-based conferences or roundtable discussions. Nor do they understand the immediate relevance of communication campaigns targeting changes in the legal texts if they have not been informed about how those texts harm them in the first place.

The communication void at this level exacerbates the marginalization of these important stakeholders and alienates them from the projects carried out in their name. Women's organizations often fall into the trap of reproducing mechanisms of exclusion whereby only the educated and the initiated participate in debates and actions for gender equity. More important, women's organizations risk losing the battle with the conservative and patriarchal groups in society over how to better connect with and recruit from the grassroots level the largest number of people for their own ideological projects.

The lessons to be learned from Chabaka and the Spring of Equality initiatives are indeed interesting and should be taken seriously by many civil society organizations. The establishment of broader solidarity bases, beyond and above ideological differences, is a rewarding exercise that promises constructive results. The adoption by the Moroccan government of the revised Family Law on January 25, 2004, is certainly a case in point. Although the revisions in the Moudawana are the product of many decades of relentless struggle, they are also a reflection of women's increasingly mature approach to advocacy and activism.

Further, the adoption of the revised legal text does not and should not signal the end of women's struggle. As Moroccan political analyst Mohamed Tozi observed, "The act of reform itself is revolutionary . . . only if it is combined with the massive education of young girls. One should not expect that it will change society. It will go along with social change" (quoted in Rachidi 2003). One of the main challenges facing women's organizations is still related to information circulation and knowledge sharing: the question now is how to promote legal literacy among the educated as well as the illiterate segments of the female population and the general public. The illiterate female population is particularly vulnerable to misinformation and misguidance given the fact that they lack any form of power that comes with the knowledge of their own rights and privileges.

The conservative forces that sought to bury the action plan relied precisely on such a vulnerability to further their agenda. Campaigns for misinformation by the opponents of the plan were more successful in recruiting and convincing a greater number of women who marched against the plan in the Islamist-organized March in Casablanca in March 1999. Many women did not realize that they had been misled or misinformed until well after they had protested against changes in their own favor: "We were told to march in defense of equality between men and women."[19]

The truth is, nearly 86 percent of Moroccan men and women in both rural and urban centers admit to not being familiar with the contents of the Moudawana. These results were published by a study on legal literacy in Morocco conducted by the Democratic Association of Moroccan Women. The study itself was not conducted until opposition to changes in the Moudawana had become disturbing.

Women's organizations need to understand, therefore, that exchanging information and sharing knowledge in a democratic fashion should become a *strategy in and of itself*, because information shared enhances the sense of belonging to and identifying with a community of shared ideas, values, and beliefs. Technology must be reappropriated by women to serve this aim if a broad-based movement is to be conducted in favor of meaningful changes in women's lives. This strategy is how women's organizations can achieve their democratic ideals of justice and equality not only at the local level but at regional, national, and global levels as well.

19. See *Espace Associatif,* no. 6 (Feb. 2002): 5.

PART TWO

Economic, Social, and Cultural Participation

8 Women's Empowerment in India

Rhetoric and Reality

AHMAD SHAMSHAD

GENDER INEQUALITY has been a feature of all human societies, from antiquity to contemporary times.[1] In recent years, women's empowerment has been recognized as a goal in the development process and has been placed on the agenda of many governments, including India's. The Indian government's stated policy is that all measures should be taken to guarantee women equal access to and full participation in decision-making bodies at every level, including the legislative, executive, judicial, and corporate, and in statutory and advisory bodies. Affirmative action measures such as reservations and quotas and women-friendly personnel policies are to be considered wherever necessary on a time-bound basis. However, although a broad framework for women's empowerment exists at the policy level in India, implementation remains slow, and the social realities do not always match the stated policies. Women are nowhere near to being full and equal participants in public policy formulations that affect their lives. This lack of adequate participation in decision-making bodies deprives women of important rights and responsibilities as citizens, while their points of view and perspectives tend to remain unheard or underrepresented and in some instances ignored.

This chapter provides an analysis of the Indian government's official policy on women's empowerment, the mechanisms for its implementation, and the continuing constraints to gender equality. I begin in a conceptual and definitional vein, followed by a discussion of mechanisms for women's political empowerment. I then turn to women's economic participation in the formal and informal sectors. The chapter ends with some policy recommendations for women's political, economic, and social empowerment in India. These dimensions of empowerment are linked, I

1. Sincere thanks to Dr. Valentine Moghadam for her comments and edits.

139

argue, but more emphasis on women's economic empowerment rather than reserved seats in Parliament may be the best way to advance both national development and women's participation and rights.

What Is Empowerment?

The greatest problem in India stems from the fact that the primary producers at the grassroots level have little control over the means of production or its distribution. This pattern reproduces the country's great social inequalities. Likewise, the vast majority of women lack control over their lives, reflecting and reproducing gender inequality in the household as well as in the society. Intellectuals, activists, and policy makers have long recognized these problems, but today the stated solution is "empowerment."

Empowerment is often employed loosely, but definitions and understandings abound. One is that people achieve true empowerment through their own efforts. According to Robert Chambers, "Empowerment means that people, especially the poor people, are enabled to take more control of productive assets as one key element. Participation, decentralization and empowerment enable local people to exploit the diverse complexities of their own conditions and to adapt to rapid change" (2005, 8). Marilee Karl notes that empowerment is a process rather than something that can be given to people. She further says, "The process of empowerment is both individual and collective, since it is through involvement in groups that people most often begin to develop their awareness and the ability to organise to take action and bring about change" (1995, 15). The World Bank defines empowerment as "the process of increasing the capacity of individuals or groups to make choices and to transform those choices into desired actions and outcomes. Central to this process are actions which both build individual and collective assets and improve the efficiency and fairness of the organisational and institutional context which govern the use of these assets" (1996, 1).

Empowerment is a multidimensional process and refers to the expansion of freedom of choice and action in all spheres (social, economic, and political) to shape one's life. In the current academic and political discourse, it refers to a process or strategy whereby a qualitative and sustained improvement in people's lives is brought about. Three interrelated prerequisites of empowerment need to be borne in mind. First, empowerment needs to be viewed in an integral, holistic framework, including economic and political processes, social and cultural dynamics, the constitutional and legal framework, education, human rights, the role of central and state governments as well as voluntary agencies, and the perception and participation of the group or the community that is the beneficiary of empowerment. Second, a distinction needs to be drawn between the ideal of empowerment and the prevailing reality of disempowerment. Third, empowerment is a normative, value-laden concept. Therefore, all discussions of empowerment must come to grips with the bearing of political, social, and moral values on the goal as well as strategies of empowerment (Prasad 2002). For women, empowerment is a process, not an event, that challenges traditional power equations and relations. Thus, the empowerment of women requires a set of assets and capabilities at the individual level (such as health, education, and employment) and at the collective level (such as the ability to organize and mobilize to take action to solve their problems and in political representation) (Kabeer 2001; Moghadam and Senftova 2005).

Empowerment of Indian women is intrinsically linked to their status in society. Though over the years there has been a slight increase in the total female population (495.7 million in 2001, from 407.1 million in 1991), life expectancy at birth (65.3 years in 1996–2001, from 59.7 years in 1989–93), and sex ratio (933 in 2001, from 927 in 1991), yet demographic imbalances between women and men continue to exist. There is a strong preference for the male child in India, as sons are perceived to be future breadwinners and the old-age security for their parents. It has been well documented that the girl child in India faces discrimination from birth until death, especially but not exclusively in poorer households. Indian women and girls often get less priority in education, are deprived of proper food, and lack access to health care. Women's empowerment in India is further complicated by intervening factors like gender discrimination, low level of work participation, violence against women, and poor health. Another major hurdle in empowering Indian women is widespread poverty. Women constitute nearly 70 percent of the total population living below the poverty line and are very often in situations of abject poverty. The ongoing poverty alleviation programs are expected to address specifically the needs and problems of such women, as poverty affects women more than men.

The social empowerment of women is a long and difficult process, as it requires a change in the mind-set of the people. The mind-set is often reinforced by poverty, illiteracy, and lack of social and gender awareness. Sincere efforts are needed to break the vicious circle and thus help eliminate poverty and enhance the status of women in the family and the society. Both the pace of development and the process of democratic decentralization depend on women's empowerment. To that end, a number of mechanisms have been established in India.

Mechanisms for Women's Political Empowerment

The Seventy-third Amendment to the Indian Constitution, established in 1992, is epoch-making, inasmuch as for the first time in the country's history, it provided for a minimum number of seats and political offices in the Panchayats for women.[2] In the context of meager representation of women in the state and national legislatures vis-à-vis their population, reservation of not less than one-third of the total number of seats and chairmanships of the Panchayats should be considered a significant landmark in the process of political empowerment of women. As explained by K. S. Subrahmanyam, Clause (3) of Act 243-D inserted in the Indian Constitution by the Seventy-third Amendment Act provides that "not less than one-third (including the number of seats reserved for women belonging to the *Scheduled Castes* and *Scheduled Tribes*) of the total number of seats to be filled by direct election in every Panchayat shall be reserved for women and such seats may be allotted by rotation to different constituencies in a Panchayat."[3] Similarly, Clause (2) of the same article provides that "not less than one-third of the total number of seats reserved (for the Scheduled Castes and Scheduled Tribes) shall be reserved for women belonging to the Scheduled Castes or, as the case may be, the Scheduled Tribes." Moreover, the provision under Clause (4) that deals with reservation of offices of the chairpersons in the Panchayats for the Scheduled Castes and Scheduled Tribes and women stipulates that "not less than one-third of the total number of offices of chairpersons in the Panchayats of each level shall be reserved for women" (2002, 28, 29, 30)

The Seventy-third Amendment has contributed to the political empowerment of women and marginalized communities in rural society and has thrown open political opportunities in the Panchayats to these disadvantaged sections. There were,

2. *Panchayat* literally means "a council of five." It refers to a village council or court of elders entrusted with executive and judicial powers for the governance of community affairs. It is based on the Panchayati Raj, a three-tiered system of democratic decentralization introduced in free India in 1959. It aims at taking democracy to the village level, by delegating substantive power to people's organizations. It received legal status in the Seventy-third Amendment to the Indian Constitution in 1991–92.

3. The caste system is India's traditional system of social hierarchy and inequality. The castes were ranked traditionally using a *verna* hierarchy of Brahmans (priests), Kshatriyas (warriors), Vaishyas (traders and artisans), Sudras (agriculturists and service groups), and outcastes (the untouchables or those individuals outside the caste hierarchy). Today, certain castes and tribes are scheduled, or specifically mentioned, in the Constitution of India, hence the terms *Scheduled Castes* and *Scheduled Tribes*. *Backward classes* or *weaker sections* are general terms applied to three different categories of people who have been singled out by the government of India for special treatment.

of course, skeptics, mostly men, who were not favorably disposed to the proposition of women leadership. Guided by their traditional dominance in a patriarchal society, the skeptics cited women's high rate of illiteracy, family responsibilities, poverty, and lack of experience, exposure, awareness, and communication skills as inhibiting factors for their effective participation in the decision-making process at the local level. Similar arguments were made in regard to the reservation of political offices to the Scheduled Castes and the Scheduled Tribes. The upper-class/caste males were indeed apprehensive of the very idea of political empowerment of women and weaker sections, and they frantically searched for methods through which their traditional hold in the rural sector could be retained. And initially, even many women and the marginalized rural communities were not very confident of their abilities to assume leadership in the Panchayats. The leadership that emerged had to cope with many problems, including their own traditional socialization.

At the national level, women have held important political and administrative positions in independent India. For instance, Indira Gandhi guided the destiny of the country as prime minister for more than fifteen years. Women have also served as governors, chief ministers, ministers in union and state governments, presiding officers of legislative bodies, judges of the high courts, and secretaries to the government of India. Yet despite the fact that Indian women have held important positions both on national and international levels, women's participation in the political arena and in the country's decision-making bodies is not in proportion to their population.

Political representation was initially based on the premise that it deals primarily with individuals, regardless of sex, and equal opportunities should be granted for power and influence in society. It was believed that though very few women were actually joining politics, given time the overall change in terms of education and employment opportunities would necessarily percolate into the political sphere too, and their representation would increase. However, as is apparent from table 8.1, the representation of women in the Lok Sabha, the lower house, has not exceeded 10 percent. In the First Lok Sabha there were only 22 women, constituting 4.4 percent of the House. It increased marginally over the years, until a slight decrease in the Fourth Lok Sabha, a severe drop-off in the Fifth Lok Sabha and a further decline in the Sixth Lok Sabha, when the House had only 19 women members. In the Thirteenth Lok Sabha there were 49 women members; however, in the Fourteenth Lok Sabha, again the strength of women has come down, this time to 45. Similarly, in the case of the Rajya Sabha, the upper house, the percentage of women members has never exceeded 12 percent, which is shown in table 8.2. In the 2004 elections, out of

Table 8.1
Number and Percentage of Women Elected
to the Lok Sabha, 1951–2004

General Election	No. of Women Elected	Percentage
First (1951–52)	22	4.4
Second (1956–57)	27	5.4
Third (1962)	34	6.7
Fourth (1967)	31	5.9
Fifth (1971)	22	4.2
Sixth (1977)	19	3.4
Seventh (1980)	28	5.1
Eighth (1984)	44	8.1
Ninth (1989)	28	5.29
Tenth (1991)	39	7.02
Eleventh (1996)	40	7.36
Twelfth (1997)	44	8.07
Thirteenth (1999)	49	9.02
Fourteenth (2004)	45	8.25

Source: Lok Sabha Secretariat, Who's Who Lok Sabha.

245 members, only 28 women (11.4 percent) were elected to the Rajya Sabha (Narayan, Sahu, and Lakshmi 2005).

The data also show that very few women actually participate in the elections. In the first Lok Sabha election, the total number of candidates was 2,439, only 70 of which were women; in the fourteenth elections, the total number of contestants was 5,435, only 355 of which were women. Though the number of women participating in the elections may be increasing gradually, they continue to constitute a very small percentage of the total number of contestants.

It is unfortunate that in India after fifty-five years of independence and a progressive Constitution, we find that women are still fighting for their empowerment, fighting to gain equality of status and to secure a role for themselves in the decision-making bodies. What may be needed is more support from political parties to increase the number of women members, candidates, and legislators. Political parties can provide legislative space to women in public life. Their due share in the representative bodies at the state and the national levels must be accorded top priority by the political parties.

Since 1996, almost all preelection party manifestos contained promises to implement 33 percent reservation for women, and in September 1996 the Eighty-first

Table 8.2
Number and Percentage of Women
in the Rajya Sabha, 1956–2004

Year	Number	Percentage
1956	20	8.62
1958	22	9.52
1960	24	10.25
1962	18	7.62
1964	21	8.97
1966	23	9.82
1968	22	9.64
1970	14	5.85
1972	18	7.40
1974	18	7.53
1976	24	10.16
1978	25	10.24
1980	29	11.98
1982	24	10.16
1984	24	10.24
1986	28	11.98
1988	25	10.59
1990	24	10.34
1992	17	7.29
1994	20	8.36
1996	19	7.81
1998	19	7.75
2000	22	9.01
2002	25	10.20
2004	28	11.43

Source: Rajya Sabha Secretariat, *Who's Who Rajya Sabha.*

Constitution Amendment Bill seeking 33 percent reservation for women was introduced in the House. Heated debates and dissenting opinions were aired, and the bill was referred to the Joint Select Committee, consisting of 31 members from both houses of Parliament.

Chaired by Geeta Mukherjee, the committee presented its report on December 9, 1996. It had in all received 102 memoranda from various associations and organizations, including representatives of the women's organizations. The committee in its report noted that Subclauses (1) and (3) of proposed Article 332-A of the bill provided that seats should be reserved for women in the Legislative Assembly of every state. The committee believed that those clauses did not cover the National Capital Territory of Delhi, though it had a Legislative Assembly. Similarly, the Union Territory of Pondicherry was not covered, though it had a Legislative Assembly. Furthermore, the committee recommended that the bill be amended so as to provide that one of the members nominated from the Anglo-Indian Community be a woman, by rotation. The committee noted that the bill did not contain any provision for reservation of seats for women in the Rajya Sabha or the Legislative Councils of the states. The committee thought that there should also be reservation of seats for women in the Rajya Sabha and the Legislative Councils.

As the Eighty-first Constitution Amendment Bill fell through on December 14, 1998, the Eighty-fourth Constitution Amendment Bill seeking reservation for women was introduced. The bill could not be passed by the Twelfth Lok Sabha, so again on December 23, 1999, the Eighty-fifth Constitution Amendment Bill seeking 33 percent reservation for women in legislative bodies was introduced in the Thirteenth Lok Sabha, which also lapsed with the dissolution of the House.

In order to view the problems of women in the national perspective and to develop a holistic approach to their development and progress, the National Perspective Plan for Women (1988–2000) was drafted. It sought to increase women's participation and presence at decision-making levels and local self-governing bodies, state assemblies, and Parliament. Women's participation in elections is to a great extent dependent on the mobilization of efforts of the political parties, general awareness among the community of the importance of exercising franchise, and the overall political culture. The effectiveness of the plan to prepare women to meet the challenges depended on the presence or absence of a political will. However, despite government rhetoric and the establishment of mechanisms to increase women's political participation and representation, women's political empowerment has been furthered postponed. This delay is partly because values encouraging the political participation of women coexist with the notions of the traditional role of women vis-à-vis the family and society. The focus on women's roles in development and their access to economic resources, therefore, may be a more feasible route to women's empowerment.

Economic Participation and Empowerment

Women received government attention right from the beginning of Indian Planning. However, the shift from "welfare" to "development" of women took place in the Sixth Five-Year Plan (1980–85). The Eighth Plan (1992–97) promised to ensure that the benefits of development from different sectors would not bypass women.

The First Five-Year Plan set up the Central Social Welfare Board in 1953 to undertake welfare activities through the voluntary sector. The Second Five-Year Plan anticipated development from the grassroots level partly through women's organizations (*Mahila Mandals* in Hindi), and the third, fourth, and interim plans arranged for women's literacy and education, along with maternal and child-care services. In the fifth plan there was a shift from the welfare to the developmental approach, and it was only in the sixth plan that women's uplift and their role as agents of development received priority attention. In fact, the sixth plan included a separate Chapter on Women and Development, with a multidisciplinary approach focused on women's health, education, and employment. In the seventh plan, the objective was clearly stated to bring women into the mainstream of national development, and in the eighth plan for the first time the shift was made from development to empowerment. Among other initiatives, the Rashtriya Mahila Kosh (National Women's Fund) was set up in 1993 to meet the credit needs of poor and assetless women.

The ninth plan (1997–2002) stated empowerment of women as a strategic objective and was accompanied by the *National Policy for Empowerment of Women (2001)*. The tenth plan (2002–7) made a major commitment toward empowering women as the agents of socioeconomic change and development. The *Approach Paper of the Tenth Five Year Plan (2002–7)* called for a women's component as a part of the plan of each sector to identify the impact of intended programs on women (Government of India 2002). The plan ensures that at least 30 percent of funds and benefits from all development sectors flow to women. Based on the recommendation of the National Policy for Empowerment of Women, the tenth plan suggests a threefold strategy for empowering women: through economic empowerment, social empowerment, and gender justice.

Economic Empowerment

To ensure provision of training, employment, and income-generation activities with both forward and backward linkages, with the ultimate objective of making all women economically independent and self-reliant, the plan includes some programs for poverty eradication, microcredit, support services for women, and women's roles in agriculture and industry.

Social Empowerment

The plan aims to create an enabling environment through various affirmative developmental policies and programs for women's advancement besides providing them easy and equal access to all basic services—such as education, health, nutrition, clean drinking water, sanitation, and adequate shelter—to enable them to realize their full potential.

Gender Justice

According to the tenth plan, all forms of discrimination against the girl child and violation of her rights are to be eliminated by undertaking strong measures both preventive and punitive within and outside the family. These measures would relate specifically to strict enforcement of laws against prenatal sex selection and the practices of female feticide, female infanticide, child marriage, child abuse, and child prostitution. Removal of discrimination in the treatment of the girl child within the family and outside and projection of a positive image of the girl child will be actively fostered. The plan states that there will be special emphasis on the needs of the girl child and earmarking of substantial investments in the areas relating to food and nutrition, health and education, and vocational education. In implementing programs for eliminating child labor, there will be a special focus on girl children.

THE PLAN SEEKS to eliminate all forms of gender discrimination and thus allow women to enjoy legal rights and fundamental freedoms in all domains—civil, political, economic, social, and cultural. This approach is necessary, the plan explains, because globalization has presented new challenges for the realization of the goals of women's empowerment and gender equality. Microlevel studies that were commissioned by the Department of Women and Child Development indicated a need to reframe policies for access to employment and quality of employment. The benefits of the growing global economy have been unevenly distributed, it reported, leading to wider economic disparities, the feminization of poverty, and increased gender inequality, along with deteriorating working conditions and unsafe working environments, especially in the informal economy and rural areas. According to the National Policy for the Empowerment of Women, strategies would be designed to enhance the capacity of women and empower them to meet the negative social and economic impacts that may flow from the globalization process (Government of India 2001).

There is a need to improve Indian women's socioeconomic participation and rights. Women in the economically active age-group fifteen to fifty-nine constitute 58.4 percent of the total female population, but they are generally viewed as economic burdens, and the contributions they make to their families are overlooked. Though there has been a slight increase in the female economic participation rate from 19.67 percent in 1981 to 25.68 percent in 2001, this level is still much lower than the male work participation rate in both urban and rural areas (see table 8.3). Women make up less than one-fourth of regular workers and a higher proportion of marginal workers and nonworkers than men (see table 8.4). In the organized sector, too, women are a minority.

The employment of women in the organized sector (both public and private sectors) as of March 31, 2001, was about 4,949,300, or about 18 percent of the total organized sector employment in the country (Government of India 2004a, table 2.11). In 2003 women's employment in the organized sector had increased only very slightly. States with higher female literacy rates have higher proportions of women in organized-sector employment.

Women in the informal sector receive special attention in the Tenth Five-Year Plan as they account for more than 90 percent of workers in that sector and are still

Table 8.3
Work Participation Rate in India (by Percentage), 1971–2001

Year (% Total/Rural/Urban)	Percentage Rate	Males	Females
1971 (Total workforce)	34.17	52.75	14.22
(Rural)	35.33	53.78	15.92
(Urban)	29.61	48.88	7.18
1981 (Total workforce)	36.70	52.62	19.67
(Rural)	38.79	53.77	23.06
(Urban)	29.99	49.06	8.31
1991 (Total workforce)	37.68	51.56	22.73
(Rural)	40.24	52.50	27.20
(Urban)	30.44	48.95	9.74
2001 (Total workforce)[a]	39.26	51.93	25.68
(Rural)	41.97	52.36	30.98
(Urban)	32.23	50.85	11.55

Source: Government of India 2003, 13.
Note: Excludes Assam, where the 1981 census could not be held, and Jammu and Kashmir, where the 1991 census was not held.
[a]Figures for 2001 are provisional.

Table 8.4
Rural and Urban Employment in India by Sex and Status, 2001

Employment Status	Sex	Total Number	Rural	Urban
Total workers		402,234,724	309,956,070	92,278,654
	M	275,014,476	198,839,153	76,175,323
	F	127,220,248	111,116,917	16,103,331
Regular workers		313,004,983	229,186,552	83,818,431
	M	275,147,813	169,101,251	71,046,562
	F	72,857,170	60,085,301	12,771,869
Marginal workers		89,229,741	80,769,518	8,460,223
	M	34,886,663	29,737,902	5,128,761
	F	54,363,078	51,031,616	3,331,462
Nonworkers		626,375,604	432,534,569	193,841,035
	M	257,142,296	182,763,521	74,378,775
	F	369,223,308	249,771,048	119,462,260

Source: Government of India 2004a, 11.

continuing to struggle in the most precarious working conditions without any legislative safeguards. It calls for efforts to ensure both minimum and equal wages for women on par with men, toward fulfilling the constitutional commitment of "equal pay for equal work." To this end, the tenth plan is to extend important labor legislation to the informal sector.

While formulating necessary policies and programs for the betterment of women in the informal sector, the findings of the Fourth Economic Census (2001) as well as the unrealized recommendations of the National Commission on Self-Employed Women and Women in the Informal Sector (Shram Shakti) are to be taken into consideration.

India's 2001 national census found that in the informal or unorganized sector, the vast majority are women engaged in agriculture and allied activities. Unskilled workers constitute 90 percent of rural and 70 percent of urban women workers. All poor women, especially those women below the poverty line, have to perform domestic duties as well as supplement the family income. Unskilled and without any principal occupation, they are subjected to economic exploitation by low and discriminatory wages (Government of India 2004a, 20). Women head only 10 percent of the total households; ownership of land and other assets is mainly in the name of the male members of the family. Hence, women have hardly any ownership of resources or autonomy to make decisions.

The participation of women in income-generating activities for the family has been increasing over time, and it is important that this trend continues. Female work participation not only increases their family income but also brings economic independence for women in the household. It helps them to participate more effectively in intrahousehold decision making and have better access to information. Moreover, where women are economically active, female children are perceived as potential wage earners, and they receive a higher share of household resources than where women are economically unproductive. But female work participation alone cannot ensure true economic empowerment, as the ownership of resources may still lie in the hands of the male members. Thus, the female work participation rate is a necessary condition but is not a sufficient condition for the economic empowerment of women. The economic empowerment of women is possible only when women have full autonomy to spend their income and also control resources. Such empowerment is possible through paid employment but also entrepreneurship.

Entrepreneurship and Women's Empowerment

If an entrepreneur is a person who organizes and manages a commercial undertaking, women entrepreneurs may be defined as those women who initiate, organize, or run business enterprises (Naik 2003). The government of India has defined a woman-owned enterprise as an industrial unit where one or more women entrepreneurs have not less than 51 percent financial holding. Since the 1990s, many women in India have shown themselves ready to take risks and face challenges in the hitherto male bastion of business ownership and management (Khanna 2001).

Entrepreneurial development among women can be considered one approach to the economic empowerment of women. A woman as an entrepreneur is economically more powerful than as a worker, because ownership not only confers control over assets (and liabilities) but also gives her the freedom to make decisions. Through entrepreneurial development, a woman will not only generate income for herself but will also generate employment for other women in the locality. It will have a multiplier effect in the generation of income and poverty alleviation. Development of entrepreneurship among women has become an important aspect of overall economic development.

Many organizations at the central and state levels, financial institutions, commercial banks, and nongovernment organizations (NGOs) engage in financing and promoting entrepreneurship among women. For example, the National Bank for Agriculture and Rural Development (NABARD), to promote economic development of rural women through gainful employment, has introduced an exclusive scheme called the Assistance to Rural Women in Non-farm Development. It is a single-window scheme to take care of the credit and promotional needs of groups of rural women in nonfarm development either for their own activity or for group activity. The scheme envisages an umbrella support for NGOs and other promotional agencies. The scheme has a credit component and grant component. The credit component is extended through banking channels, and the grant component is provided by NABARD directly to the sponsoring agency. In order to encourage women entrepreneurs, NABARD is implementing a scheme titled Assistance for Marketing of Non-farm Products of Rural Women, to provide credit and promotional exposure to agencies engaged in providing services for the marketing of goods produced by rural women. The scheme covers promotional grants and revolving fund assistance to women's organizations, NGOs, and development agencies for the provision of marketing arrangements, refining marketing skills, capacity building, quality-control equipment, advertising, sales outlets, and mobile vans. NABARD has also been supporting promotional institutions and NGOs for the conduct of the Rural Entrepreneurship Development Programs, skills training, and the setting up of artisans guilds and common service centers for rural women.

NABARD has been working as a catalyst in promoting and linking more and more self-help groups (SHGs) to the banking system.[4] The Micro Finance Development Fund has been constituted in NABARD. This fund would be utilized for scaling up the SHG-linkage program and supporting other microcredit initiatives. Special emphasis is provided for building the capacities of the poor, with particular emphasis on vulnerable sections including women, Scheduled Castes, and Scheduled Tribes (Kamalakannan 2005).

The National Small Industries Corporation Ltd. has introduced a new scheme for granting composite-term loans for the benefit of tiny industries. The composite-term loan is to be granted for the acquisition of machinery and equipment, land and buildings, and working capital to tiny units, with total assistance up to Rs. 25 lakhs (2.5 million rupees). The minimum amount of assistance under this scheme is 2.00

4. A self-help group is a group of people who meet regularly to discuss issues of interest to them and to look for solutions to commonly experienced problems. It acts as a forum for members and provides space and support. SHGs comprise very poor people who do not have access to formal financial institutions, and they enable members to learn to cooperate and work in a group environment. SHGs may or may not be promoted by governmental or nongovernmental institutions but are considered as one of the most significant tools in the participatory approach to economic empowerment.

lakhs, though for women entrepreneurs the amount is Rs. 0.50 lakhs (Yadav 2005). This scheme will be initially implemented for the benefit of the tiny sector industries being set up in women's industrial parks under development in various locations. The National Small Industries Corporation is playing an important role in promoting women entrepreneurs' small-scale units. It conducts technical training and entrepreneurial development programs in its various technical service centers for the identification, training, and development of women entrepreneurs.

Assistance to women entrepreneurs in rural sectors is one of the objectives of the Small Industries Development Bank of India (SIDBI). The SIDBI has formulated a number of special schemes for the benefit of women entrepreneurs, such as the Refinance Scheme for Women Entrepreneurs, the Mahila Udyam Nidhi (Working Women Fund), Mahila Vikas Nidhi (Women Development Fund), Entrepreneurship Development Programs for Women, and Assistance to Associations of Women Entrepreneurs.

All nationalized banks have a women's unit that deals with women entrepreneurs only. The functions are to monitor the progress made by the bank in financing women entrepreneurs and to collect and disseminate information to branches about the various resources provided by SIDBI, NABARD, the Khadi and Village Industries Commission, and government agencies to women entrepreneurs. They also organize entrepreneurial training programs for women entrepreneurs, explore the possibilities of bringing about specific schemes for women entrepreneurs, and establish liaisons with NGOs, microcredit institutions, and SHGs (Peerzada and Prande 2005).

Besides financial institutions and banks, a number of nonfinancial institutions and voluntary bodies are also engaged in this field. At the state level, the State Technical Consultancy Centres and District Industry Centres are conducting entrepreneurship development programs for women. The National Alliance of Young Entrepreneurship has been conducting entrepreneurship development programs for women entrepreneurs since 1975, and its women's wing assists women entrepreneurs. The Self Employed Women's Association is also promoting entrepreneurship among women. The National Institute for Entrepreneurship and Small Business Development has plans for a number of awareness and motivational programs to be organized for women.

Government-sponsored programs for the promotion of entrepreneurship in general and particularly among women include the prime minister's Rozgar Yojana, Swaranjayanti Gram Swarozgar Yojana, District Rural Industrial Project, Rural Employment Generation Programme, Support to Training and Employment Programme for Women, and Construction of Technology Parks for Women. Others are Indira Mahila Yojana, now recast as the Integrated Women's Empowerment Project, along with the Rural Women's Empowerment and Development. Their purpose is to ensure that no less than 30 percent of funds and benefits flow to women from other development sectors and to organize women into self-help groups and equip them with services of awareness generation and income generation through training, employment, credit, and marketing linkages to small entrepreneurs.

To equip women of rural areas with the necessary skills in the modern upcoming trades that could keep them gainfully engaged beside making them economically independent and self-reliant and to increase access to credit through setting up of a development "Bank for Women Entrepreneurs" in small and tiny sectors, the corpus of Rashtriya Mahila Kosh is being enhanced for this purpose. The Support of the Training and Employment Programme provides a comprehensive package for upgrading skills through training, extension inputs, and market linkages in the traditional sectors like agriculture and handicrafts. Training is also provided for the poor and needy women in the age group of eighteen to forty-five in the upcoming nontraditional trades. The Socio-Economic Programmes provides work and wages to needy women, and the Condensed Courses of Education and Vocational Training provide new vistas of employment through continuing education and vocational training for school dropouts.

It is important to note that the Parliamentary Standing Committee on Human Resource Development is currently focusing attention on the issue of making India's budgetary processes more sensitive to women's issues. In this context, the committee is aiming to stress the need for greater availability of microcredit facilities to the women's self-help groups spread over large parts of the country for their economic well-being and empowerment (Chattopadhyay 2005, 29).

Women entrepreneurs in India face numerous problems in establishing as well as running their businesses. During the start-up phase, women are reported to encounter more problems than their male counterparts, both within their families and as part of the larger society that discriminates against them. For instance, problems cited pertain mostly to obtaining financing, delays in the process, and providing collateral security, often as a consequence of insensitivity to the particular situation of women or owing to gender biases. It makes marketing of products difficult for women entrepreneurs. Nonetheless, it is widely acknowledged that in the present era of economic reforms, women's economic empowerment is necessary for the elimination of poverty and the overall development of the economy. Entrepreneurial development and income-generating business activities are feasible solutions for women's empowerment and for social development.

Government planning also acknowledges a role for women in the environment and conservation. Considering the impact of environmental factors on their livelihoods, women's participation will be ensured in the conservation of the environment and control of environmental degradation. The vast majority of rural women still depend on the locally available noncommercial sources of energy such as animal dung, crop waste, and fuel wood. In order to ensure the efficient use of these energy resources in an environmentally friendly manner, development policies will aim at promoting nonconventional energy resources. Women will be involved in spreading the use of solar energy, biogas, smokeless *chulas* (ovens), and other rural applications so as to have a visible impact of these measures in influencing the ecosystem and in changing the lifestyles of rural women.

Education and Women's Empowerment

Education in general and higher education in particular are insurance against economic need. Access to higher education and technical and professional competencies guarantee economic independence leading to social status and hence empowerment to women. It not only changes the lives of women at the personal level by altering the pressure of dependence, hierarchy, and domination through economic autonomy but at the social level also has the effect of cracking the patriarchal social order.

Literacy campaigns have spread in various parts in India, and the government spends about 30 percent of the gross national product on education. Still, the literacy rate remains low, and India has the largest number of illiterates in the world while also having the highest number of graduates. Only 40 percent of India's population above fifteen is literate. The weaker sections of the society, namely, Scheduled Castes and Scheduled Tribes, are in a more pitiable condition insofar as their literacy is concerned. Girl children are particularly disadvantaged in this area.

According to the government's women's empowerment policy, and in keeping with India's commitment to the Millennium Development Goals, equal access to education for women and girls will be ensured. Special measures will be taken to eliminate discrimination, universalize education, eradicate illiteracy, create a gender-sensitive educational system, increase enrollment and retention rates of girls, improve the quality of education to facilitate lifelong learning, and develop women's occupational, vocational, and technical skills. Reducing the gender gap in secondary and higher education is a focus area. Gender-sensitive curricula are to be developed at all levels of the educational system in order to address sex stereotyping as one of the causes of gender discrimination.

India is home to the largest number of illiterate women in the world. As far as women's education is concerned, it is a combination of parental apathy, sociocultural norms, direct and indirect costs, market failure to capture the true costs and benefits of girl's education, lack of enforcement of the law, inadequate and inappropriate educational infrastructure, as well as low participation of women in the system that have made female education trail behind the education men. In rural India, out of every one hundred girls who enroll in Class I, only one enters Class XII. In urban areas, the position is only slighter better, with fourteen girls entering Class XII. Out of one hundred girls who enroll in Class I, fewer than forty join Class V, an attrition rate of 60 percent. The literacy rate among women, which was 24.3 percent compared to 46.39 percent among males in 1981, increased to 39.29 percent for females and 64.13 percent for males in 1991. The literacy rate for rural areas was only 44.7 percent vis-à-vis 73.1 percent for urban areas in 1991. Female literacy in rural areas, at 30.6 percent, is still very low and is less than half of the literacy rate of females in urban areas (Government of India 2004c).

The access of girls to secondary education is minimal. According to provisional figures of the Department of Education, there were only fifty-five girls per one hundred boys enrolled in the secondary level (Classes IX-X) in 1993–94. Similarly, the dropout rate for girls at the secondary level was 74.54 percent (for boys it was 68.41 percent), calculated as a percentage of intakes in Class I. Although according to the Sixth All-India Educational Survey there was a 50 percent growth in girl's enrollment at the secondary level, vis-à-vis a 21 percent increase for boys, in terms of percentage of enrollment the figures are still quite small—just 36.15 percent in 1993. At the higher secondary level, girl's enrollment registered a 53.97 percent increase from 1986 to 1993. In terms of percentage of total enrollment in Classes XI-XII, girls constituted 34.69 percent in 1993 (Govinda 2004) (see table 8.5).

The ratio of dropouts for girls at different levels of education is more than what it is for the boys. To remedy the situation, the Central Board of Secondary Education has made a provision in its Examination By-Laws that girl candidates who are bona fide residents of the National Capital Territory of Delhi can appear in Class X and Class XII examinations of the board as private candidates. In order to further promote education for girls, an amendment in the Affiliation By-Laws of the board has now been made that all the affiliated schools will grant full waiver of all fees (includ-

Table 8.5
Percentage of Girls' Enrollment to Total Enrollment by Stages, 1950–2001

Year	Primary (1–5)	Middle (6–8)	Sec/Hr. Sec (10+2/Inter.)	Higher Education (Degree and Above)
1950–51	28.1	16.1	13.3	10.0
1955–56	30.5	20.8	15.4	14.6
1960–61	32.6	23.9	20.5	16.0
1965–66	36.2	26.7	22.0	20.4
1970–71	37.4	29.3	25.0	20.0
1975–76	38.1	31.3	26.9	23.2
1980–81	38.1	32.9	29.6	26.7
1985–86	40.3	35.6	30.3	33.0
1990–91	41.5	36.7	32.9	33.3
1991–92	41.9	38.2	33.8	32.3
1992–93	42.6	38.8	33.9	32.3
1993–94	42.9	39.3	34.3	33.5
1994–95	42.8	39.9	34.8	35.2
1995–96	43.1	39.0	35.3	37.1
1996–97	43.4	39.8	36.3	37.2
1997–98	43.6	40.1	37.4	36.4
1998–99	43.5	40.5	37.8	36.8
1999–2000	43.6	40.4	38.9	39.86
2000–2001	43.7	40.9	38.6	36.9

Source: Government of India 2004c.

ing tuition fees and all other fees under any heading except the meals and transportation fee) charged by them from Class VI onward to each girl student who is also the single child of a parent. Similarly, it will be appreciated if the schools also consider extending a 50 percent concession in these fees for every girl student who is one of two daughters who are also the only two children in a family. In addition to the above, the school on its own can also waive such fees as the transportation and meal fees (as applicable).

Conclusions and Recommendations

India is indisputably committed to the cause of empowerment of women. The need to strengthen policies and laws aimed at elimination of all forms of discrimination against women has been emphasized. A broad framework and a perspective for empowerment of women exist at the policy level in India. However, the journey toward progress is long and arduous. In a world of challenge and competition, both the state and the society have to constantly attune themselves to the changing needs. Women's participation in the process of development is of crucial importance from the consideration of both equity and development. There still exists a wide gap between the enunciated goals and the situational reality of the status of women in India.

The 2001 National Policy for the Empowerment of Women admits that there still exists a wide gap between the goals enunciated in the Constitution, legislative policies, plans, programs, and related mechanisms, on the one hand, and the social reality of Indian women, on the other. Noting that the empowerment of women has been recognized as a central issue in determining the status of women, the policy sets the objectives of promoting women's advancement, development, empowerment, and equal access to participation and decision making at all levels. However, the need of the hour is to translate these ideas into actual numbers in legislative bodies and other representative institutions. Women are underrepresented in governance and decision-making positions. Even today, women occupy less than 9 percent of parliamentary seats, less than 6 percent of cabinet positions, less than 4 percent of seats in high courts and the Supreme Court, and less than 3 percent of administrative and managerial positions.

Despite the Indian government's numerous programs and policies for the political, economic, social, and cultural empowerment of women, the data show that much remains to be done. Sustainable development needs women's empowerment. Unless women acquire equal status and dignity in all spheres, the development and advancement of any society or country cannot be considered complete. We end by looking at the recommendations by the Committee on Empowerment of Women, whose mandate is to examine the measures taken by the central government to secure women's equality of status and dignity in all matters. The committee's suggestions for women's empowerment include the following:

• There should be adequate reservation for women in the houses of Parliament, Legislative Assemblies, and Legislative Councils so as to give representation to all sections of society.

• Given the vital role that parliamentarians can play in the process of social change and the critical importance attached to accountability to the legislature in the Platform for Action, it is important to build their capacities, strengthen their networks, and equip them with resources.

• The continued engendering of census and data-gathering systems should be a priority.

• Gender sensitization of enforcement mechanisms, the judiciary, and central and state ministries is to be a priority and needs to be matched with resources.

• The reform of laws to address gender-based violence should be closely monitored.

• The fulfillment of the Ninth Five-Year Plan objective of the empowerment of women and the strategy of sectoral women's component plans need to be closely monitored, and women's voices and perspective should be a part of this monitoring.

9 Girl but Not Woman

Garment Factory Workers in Fez, Morocco

M. LAETITIA CAIROLI

OVER THE PAST THREE DECADES there has been a global surge in female industrial employment, most notably in garment production. Throughout the world,
gender ideologies emphasizing the docility, submissiveness, and dispensability of
girls and women have allowed employers to maximize profits by recruiting young,
often unmarried females at costs far below the wages of their male counterparts.
This feminization of the factory has been well documented, as scholars have used
this phenomenon to question the effects of women's participation in production
and the relationship between women's role in wage labor and in the household and
family.[1] Would the participation of girls and women in these new forms of labor
mark their liberation from local patriarchies, or would it introduce a new kind of
enslavement to the demands of foreign capital?

The region of the Middle East and North Africa has participated in the globalization of capital and expansion of the world market that began to accelerate in the
1970s. In several countries of the region, most notably Morocco and Tunisia, the appearance of labor-intensive factories has drawn females into industrial labor; most
often, these girls and young women represent the first generation of female factory
workers in their societies. Because the region is characterized by patriarchal ideologies (common indeed throughout most of the world), the region provides a sort of
test case for asking questions about the effect of the integration of women into
wage-labor systems on the women themselves and on the culture generally.

In this chapter, I provide an overview of the economic restructuring of the Middle East and North Africa of the past several decades, with an eye to its effect on the
labor of women and girls. Then, I look more specifically at the case of Morocco and

---

1. See, for example, Nash and Fernandez-Kelly 1983; Ong 1991; Safa 1988.

at the economic context in which females there have been drawn into the industrial labor force over the past three decades. Finally, using data from research on industry in Fez, I return to the question of how wage labor affects the position of females. The entrance of females, en masse, into the garment factories of Fez is a practice that contrasts vividly with local ideals of gendered behavior. I contend that the convention of hiring young, unmarried girls rather than mature, married women helps ameliorate the contradictions inherent in allowing females to labor in what is a public, and more legitimately male, role. I assert that mature women are not acceptable employees to factory owners because their elevated status as wives and mothers threatens the authority of men and of the factory itself. Researchers have noted that women's role in the reproductive realm is integrally linked to their role in production. Here I explore the specific cultural meanings that influence and help determine *which* females—daughters or mothers, sisters or wives—will labor outside the home and on the shop floor, and I conclude that it is the power inherent in women's traditional role inside the home that hampers their ability to participate on the shop floor.

I conducted the fieldwork for this study in the city of Fez from August 1994 to August 1995. The fieldwork involved intensive ethnography. I interviewed owners in some twelve of the twenty-five then operational garment factories in Fez. I informally interviewed workers both inside and outside the Fez factories: I met with workers in the streets outside the factory gates as they stood waiting to find work and as they exited after the day's labor. I met with many of these same workers in their homes, visiting with and interviewing their family members. I carried out two random surveys in separate garment factories whose owners permitted me access to their workers, in one of these factories interviewing all 150 workers. I was granted permission by the owner of this same factory, where I interviewed the 150 workers, to labor on the shop floor as a garment worker; thus, I spent three months working, observing, and interviewing workers within this factory. This participation in the factory regime provided me insight into the nature of factory work and the everyday experience of the factory workers. The ethnographic data provided in this chapter and the quotations drawn from factory workers are all derived from this 1994–95 period of intensive ethnographic research in the city of Fez.

The Context of Women's Industrial Labor in the Middle East

The region of the Middle East and North Africa has long been characterized by the low labor force participation of females. Girls and women represent less than 20 percent of those individuals employed in nonagricultural positions in the countries of the region, as compared with 35–45 percent in most developing countries (Moghadam 2003, 1998). Although there is a tendency to "blame Islam" and overemphasize cultural factors in this region of the world, economic factors are at work here: the region of the Middle East and North Africa has a comparatively low level of industrialization, and this fact itself limits women's participation in the labor force.[2] Although the area continues to lag behind others, females have been increasingly integrating into the workforce since the 1960s.

The rate of industrial expansion in the Middle East remained slow until the mid-1950s; between 1955 and 1975 industrialization throughout the region was characterized by import substitution, in which governments of the region were geared toward heavy capital investments. Oil-producing countries particularly followed a pattern of industrialization that was heavy in capital-intensive technologies and low in labor; throughout the oil-boom era of the 1960s and 1970s, high wages were available to men in these countries—a set of conditions that has generally precluded the involvement of women in the workforce, particularly in manufacturing. Valentine Moghadam (1998) observes that in those economies less dependent on oil revenues, women's involvement in the labor force has been greater. Throughout the region generally, it has been noted that "although women were recruited for factory labor in the early part of the century, the large-scale industrialization schemes of the twentieth century have not, by and large, involved the use of female labor: women's participation in industrial production has been minimal" (Tucker 1999, 106).

The speed of developments in several countries in the region since the 1980s has rendered this statement increasingly less accurate, particularly for specific locales. In the context of a widely felt economic recession, a number of countries in the region adopted structural adjustment policies under World Bank and International Monetary Fund auspices: Morocco in 1983, Tunisia in 1986, Jordan in 1989, and Egypt in 1990. Syria and Iran independently restructured their economies (Moghadam 1998). All of these countries moved away from a state-based development strategy toward liberalization of their economies and a focus on export-led growth. Throughout the 1990s, this trend has continued, with governments throughout the region privatizing state-owned industries and encouraging indus-

2. Nadia Hijab (1988) argues that women's participation in wage labor fluctuates with economic conditions. Valentine Moghadam (1998, 2003) shows the importance of the oil economy and argues against the notion that religious and cultural factors somehow weigh heavier in the region than in other regions.

trialization. It is the nonoil economies in particular that have most aggressively pursued the strategy of export-oriented manufacturing and agriculture. And, as has been observed throughout the globe, a focus on export orientation in industry is accompanied by the movement of females onto the factory floor. The countries in the region with the highest levels of manufacturing exports are also the ones with the greatest number of women and girls involved in factory production. These countries include Israel, Turkey, Tunisia, and Morocco. An analysis of the impact of this economic shift on the lives of women in Morocco is the aim of this chapter.

Before beginning to look at the rise of female factory labor in Morocco, however, it is important to add a codicil to this general overview on economic developments in the Middle East and North Africa: although the formal economic participation of females throughout the region has been historically low, women's economic opportunity there has varied significantly in time and place. In terms of their current participation in industry, for example, women in the Arab Gulf states play almost no role in factory production, whereas females in Morocco and Tunisia represent as much as one-quarter and one-fifth, respectively, of their nation's factory workers. Whereas female wage earners in the region tend to be concentrated in the fifteen-to-twenty-nine-year age category, Kuwait and Qatar see high rates of mature women, ages twenty-five to forty-nine, participating in wage labor (most of them professional women), and women throughout all age categories labor for pay in Israel and Turkey (many of them in agricultural tasks) (Moghadam 1998).

As everywhere, class position has shaped women's access to employment possibilities. The majority of Middle Eastern women who work for a wage are concentrated in professional occupations and in public service, because throughout the twentieth century educated women from elite families have been the women most likely to become employed. Factory work has traditionally been seen widely as inappropriate for women throughout the region (Tucker 1999). Moreover, it has been women of the middle and upper classes who could benefit from the expansion of education systems and the public sector that opened up opportunities for women in civil service and public-sector factories in such countries as Egypt, Iran, Syria, and Tunisia. During the era of oil wealth, the migration of men from Jordan, Egypt, Lebanon, and North Yemen made positions available to the women left behind, and well-educated women particularly were able to benefit. Female employees in the public sector often received valued benefits, and labor laws in countries throughout the region protected female employees from dismissal during pregnancy or maternity leave. During the period of rapid growth owing to oil wealth in the region, some governments were particularly generous: some states even provided for workplace nurseries and breast-feeding breaks. These sorts of privileges accorded women in public-sector employment are not widely attained by women working in private-sector industries. Morocco provides a case in point, as will be seen.

Industrial Development in Morocco and Its Economic Context

In 1983, Morocco launched a series of stabilization and structural adjustment programs, the first country in the region of the Middle East and North Africa to do so. This economic strategy ultimately transformed the nature of Moroccan industry and the makeup of its industrial labor force; the emphasis on labor-intensive manufacturing for export resulted in the wide-scale incorporation of females into Moroccan industry. Today, 25 percent of Moroccan girls and women are in the paid labor force, according to official statistics. Among Arab countries, Morocco has the highest level of female participation in industry, and within the region Morocco is noticeable for its large number of women and girls in paid labor (Moghadam 1998).

The Moroccan economic restructuring initiated in 1983 was prompted by its creditors—the International Monetary Fund and the World Bank—and included provisions for slowing growth in public-sector employment, wage freezes, and reduction of food subsidies. Throughout the decade of the 1980s, the textile, leather, and agroindustries sectors grew rapidly, while the government reduced its social spending. The Moroccan government in recent years has made no commitment to increasing its social spending on housing, welfare, or social security. The overwhelming majority of Moroccans have no access to any sort of social security benefits. Government spending on basic health care, schooling, and infrastructure services is low, and many of the basic social indicators—infant nutrition, female literacy, and mortality—compare poorly with other nations in the region. In the late 1990s, official figures put the unemployment rate at a little more than 15 percent, although unofficial observations rate the levels much higher. (Officials with whom I spoke ventured that the proportion of un- and underemployed Moroccans was as high as 40 percent.) Officially, 30 percent of the urban poor and 20 percent to 25 percent of women were unemployed. At the same time, between 17 percent and 22 percent of all households were headed by women, mostly divorced or widowed women (Moghadam 1998). Many of these women would likely be relatively uneducated, as the mean year of schooling for adult women was less than two years.[3]

3. Morocco is taking steps toward rapidly closing the gender gap in education. As of 2000, 46 percent of primary school students and 44 percent of secondary school students were female (World Bank

In the context of these generally low economic indicators, female employment in the industrial sector in Morocco has undergone a dramatic rise, in large part owing to increases in garment manufacturing. The jobs that girls and some women have obtained, however, have tended to be low-wage, low-skill, and flexible or temporary. At a time when the male breadwinner role is not guaranteed, government provides few services, wages are low, and women are left as unofficial heads of households, the Moroccan garment industry seeks females to staff its factory production lines.[4] Will women's participation on the shop floor subvert, intensify, or transform local patriarchy?

Although researchers have looked to the rising educational attainment of women and women's increased awareness of their own rights because of the activities of local feminist movements as factors that precipitate women's movement into the labor force, I contend that these factors had little influence in pushing Moroccan women onto the factory floor. Given the above-mentioned indicators of the relative poverty of many Moroccans, it seems that government policies of export manufacturing, which created a demand for cheap and flexible labor, coupled with economic deterioration, which prompted households to seek income from every means possible, are largely responsible for pushing Moroccan females onto the factory floor.

The Garment Industry in Fez and Conditions of Work

Morocco's industrialization has followed a trajectory similar to the economic development pattern described for the region of the Middle East and North Africa as a whole: slow industrial growth during the 1950s, state-sponsored import substitution industrialization through the 1970s, and economic liberalization with the concomitant growth in export industrialization beginning in the 1980s. During the course of the 1990s, Fez became Morocco's second most important industrial hub (after the Casablanca-Mohamedia industrial complex) and a leading garment-producing center. Until the 1980s, the vast majority of Fez factory workers were males employed in the city's state-run textile firms. Females began participating in Fez's industry in the late 1970s, when garment manufacturing entered the city's in-

Group, Data and Statistics, "GenderStats"). Whereas adult women have relatively low rates of literacy overall, young women are more widely educated.

4. I use the term *unofficial* to refer to the fact that the factory girls I interviewed did not identify their (generally) widowed mothers as heads of household, but instead usually claimed that an older brother, or in some cases an uncle, had taken charge.

dustrial scene. The economic adjustments of 1983 helped transform Fez's garment industry into a booming export-driven industry that hires females (Fejjal 1987). Today, Fez's sewing factories employ more than a third of all factory workers in the city, and nearly all of the garment workers are females. If Fez's female garment factory workers are counted together with the women and girls working in the city's food-processing plants, it becomes evident that approximately half of all of Fez's factory workers are female.[5] Morocco's economic development during the 1980s produced in Fez (as in Morocco generally) an industrialization that is overwhelmingly female. Women and girls flood the labor-intensive, export-oriented manufacturing enterprises such as the garment factories, a dramatic contrast to the situation that existed less than two decades ago, when the town's factory workers were men.

In Fez, there is a small number of foreign-owned and several well-established Moroccan firms that are well-known for following Moroccan labor laws and for providing adequate wages, benefits, and working conditions. The vast majority of the Fez garment factories, however, disregard Moroccan labor legislation, which is modeled on French law and would be progressive if it were enforced. The law most commonly disregarded in Fez factories is requiring all workers to be provided with employee identity cards, which legally establish the worker's status as an employee in an enterprise that is registered with the government. These identity cards assure workers that they will receive the benefits and protections Moroccan labor laws guarantee. Very few of the garment workers in Fez hold identity cards, partly because the majority of the city's garment factories do not register workers officially and thus avoid the necessity of providing workers with the rights, wages, and benefits outlined by law. Nearly all the factories in Fez are thus, in a sense, "unofficial"— and operate outside of the labor laws.

Although Moroccan labor law prescribes a nine-hour workday with a maximum forty-eight-hour workweek and overtime pay at a higher rate, factory hours are typically erratic, and overtime without pay is a standard feature of employment. In factories notorious for requiring workers to work through the night to meet shipping deadlines, workers speak of "sleeping at the factory." Most workers receive no sick leave or paid vacation, benefits stipulated by labor law. Workers have no job protection, and often lose their jobs without warning when the factories shut down, as they frequently do. Workers are commonly fired after several years' service by factory owners who fear the workers might demand the seniority benefits that Moroccan labor law guarantees. Though Moroccan labor law defined the minimum wage

---

5. See Royaum du Maroc 1995a, 1995b, 1997.

at an hourly rate that would equal twelve hundred dirhams per month (in 1995), workers throughout Fez reported earning anywhere from three hundred to, at most, eight hundred dirhams a month. Thus, they received, on the whole, somewhere between one-quarter to two-thirds the minimum wage prescribed by law.[6]

Morocco has signed the UN Convention on the Elimination of All Forms of Discrimination Against Women, and Moroccan labor law entitles women to twelve weeks' maternity leave at full salary. As will be discussed presently, the typical hiring policies of factory owners preclude recruitment of older girls and married women; thus, those women most likely to become legitimately pregnant (married women) are generally excluded from factory employment. The issue of maternity benefits is never considered. However, given the flagrant disregard of labor laws that factory owners demonstrate, it is difficult to imagine that married women were considered burdensome workers owing to the benefits they might demand, a point that will be taken up later.

Conditions inside the factory are difficult. The workday is long, and workers are rigorously controlled throughout the day. The more rigid factory administrators might prohibit them from leaving their assigned places, or even speaking, during work hours. Workers are frequently kept at the job long after quitting time and told they will not be permitted to leave until the day's quotas are met. They know that to leave the factory without their superiors' permission is to forfeit the job. Workers recognize the difficulties of habituation to the seemingly unending routine inside the factory. When asked how they like the work, they consistently respond that "it is difficult to get used to." In my own first days as a worker inside the Fez factory where I carried out my in-depth participant observation, workers urged me to "be patient," saying that in time my legs would no longer hurt from standing all day and that eventually I "would not feel the cold so much." I would, they assured me, "slowly become accustomed to the system."

Many longtime garment workers in Fez factories believed that labor conditions

---

6. Although Morocco has several well-established labor unions that have fought for garment workers' rights in other cities and at different time periods, during the period of research garment factory workers in Fez did not participate in union activism. Workers did report participating in wildcat strikes and walkouts, although these events were apparently not orchestrated by organized labor. Longtime garment workers reported significant participation in organized labor unions during the late 1980s. This activism declined, Fez residents believed, after the Fez workers' strike that occurred on December 14, 1990. Workers themselves attributed the decline in labor activism to the widespread fear that factory owners would carry out their threats to shut down factories and depart Fez, leaving even more of them jobless.

within the factories had undergone a serious decline because of the workers' strike of December 14, 1990. This strike erupted into rioting, looting, and civil unrest that lasted several days. It is widely believed that large-scale factory closings resulted from the strike; Fez locals assert that, since the strike, one-third of all Fez's factories have been shut down.

It is difficult to assess the extent of factory closings resulting from the strike and the effect the strike actually had on the quality of work conditions in the garment factories of Fez. Nonetheless, women who had been longtime employees in the garment workforce consistently described working conditions before the strike, and during the 1980s, as far superior to the circumstances of the present. Workers themselves believed the decline in conditions to be owing to the reduction in the availability of garment factory jobs. With fewer positions available to an ever growing number of poor and unemployed young females, owners are better able to deny workers their legal rights to equitable wages and fair working conditions. Workers consistently reported significant participation in organized labor unions and labor activism before the strike, which was no longer apparent among garment factory workers in Fez in 1995.

Work in the garment factories is tedious and physically exhausting, yet workers complained most bitterly of the fact that garment factory work is shameful. They spoke of being treated with a lack of respect by high-level factory staff and of being treated like "cows," "prostitutes," or "maids" inside the factory. They protested that in the public eye they are not respected for their labor, as are educated female bureaucrats who work in schools and offices. As one worker noted, "People see you in the street and say that you are just a factory girl, that you have no value."

Garment factory workers indeed are generally demeaned by Fez inhabitants for their participation in factory labor. Factory labor is in itself poorly regarded because it is manual labor, neither autonomous nor artisanal, and participation in factory work connotes a low-class status. But for females, it suggests as well a lack of family honor and the real or potential loss of personal virtue. Girls who engage in factory labor are assumed to be related to males who are unable to appropriately support and protect them. The glaring presence of factory girls on the streets of Fez is often cited as proof of the inadequacy of families to adequately control and monitor their daughters. Nonetheless, as I argue below, this lack of control over girls who are daughters is far less threatening to the community than the potential lack of control over women who are wives. Moreover, in their status as unmarried females, young girls do not have the moral authority to confront the authority of men. Married

women, and particularly mothers, do. And thus we find the widespread employment of young, unmarried females in the factories of Fez.[7]

The Category of Factory Girl

In Morocco and in Fez specifically, not all females are considered eligible for garment factory work. Moroccan garment workers are almost invariably unmarried
young girls who live at home with their parents and unmarried siblings; it is relatively rare for married women to carry out garment factory work, particularly if
they have children. Moroccans widely recognize this fact and refer to garment factory workers as girls (binet), making the linguistic and social distinction between a
female who has not yet married and one who has (and who is thus forever referred
to as a woman).

The research I conducted revealed that the garment workers are generally
daughters in lower-class households that, in comparison with others of their class,
are relatively poor and suffer high rates of male unemployment. According to my
surveys, 76 percent of workers surveyed were never-married females, 16 percent
were married, and 8 percent were divorced. Nearly all of the workers surveyed (92
percent) were between the ages of thirteen and twenty-five. (I encountered only two
girls as young as thirteen during the research period, in marginal jobs such as picking threads from finished garments. Again, this practice contravenes Moroccan
labor law, as do many of the labor practices, as mentioned above.) Never-married
and divorced workers (84 percent of the total) almost invariably lived as daughters
in their natal households (divorced young women return to their natal homes when
possible). One-quarter of these households were female-headed households, in
which the father was absent, largely owing to his death. The 16 percent of workers
who were married were either newly married and as yet childless or were destitute
women with young children whose husbands were unable to work.

As noted above, workers generally earned anywhere from three hundred to
eight hundred dirhams per month, and 89 percent of workers reported contributing some or all of their salary to the family. At the time of the study, twelve hundred
dirhams represented the legal minimum wage for a month of labor, and thus the average factory salary fell severely short of meeting the needs of any single family.

7. The predominance of "factory daughters" in the feminization of the factory has been well documented for Asia. See, for example, Nash and Fernandez-Kelly 1983; Ong 1987; Salaff 1995; Wolf 1992.

Nonetheless, these salaries were considered significant in lower-class households where men found difficulty securing steady work. The strategy in factory households is to send all eligible family members to work and to combine the meager incomes earned to allow for household survival.

Daughter but Not Wife

In Morocco, the phenomenon of females working in industry is just two decades old. Women's work on the shop floor contradicts revered ideologies, widely held to be Islamic, that set the model for gendered behavior. In some social contexts these ideologies are changing; nonetheless, they retain significance for many, particularly for those individuals in the traditional lower class, the class from which garment workers are drawn. According to Moroccan gender ideals, a woman's proper role is as a wife and mother, a position that is essentially noneconomic and correctly played out in the privacy of the domestic sphere. Men appropriately take the position of breadwinner and operate in the economic realm outside the home. A family's honor is embedded in its ability to keep women inside and protected, thus maintaining the divide between male and female that is at once a separation between private and public, kin and nonkin, home and business.

These notions of gendered behavior reinforce, and are reinforced by, the structure of the patriarchal family. In factory households the ideology and practices associated with the classic patriarchal family retain a fierce hold. Traditional patterns of respect of younger for elder and of female for male prevail. Wives defer to their husbands and children to their parents. Older siblings advise and direct younger ones, and sisters heed the authority of their brothers. Girls serve and wait on fathers, mothers, and elder brothers, and they do not openly resist their parents. As junior and female members of the household, unmarried daughters are granted the least authority and expected to demonstrate an attitude of deference and servitude.

Male authority in the family is legitimated by the notion that women are economically dependent, subservient, and in need of control. The intrusion of females into Fez factories, then, could potentially threaten male authority by placing females in wage-earning positions traditionally held by men. This outcome has not been the result of women's incorporation into the garment industry in Fez, at least partly because the females hired are single girls, still living in their fathers' households in the role of daughters, rather than older women laboring in the role of wives. Sending daughters (rather than wives) to work might actually help impoverished families preserve the ideal family structure.

Factory workers and their families point proudly to the definition of marriage as an economic union characterized by male financial support and female dependence, a notion of marriage that they perceive as specifically Islamic. They are familiar with the Moroccan legal statutes (based in Muslim codes) that assert that men owe their wives material support and cannot command them to contribute to the family economy. A woman who does work for a wage is not obligated to give her salary to her husband and has the right to keep her earnings for herself if she so chooses. One of the grounds for which women can legitimately petition for divorce is nonsupport by the husband. Female garment workers and those individuals in their communities perceive these aspects of Moroccan family law as assurances that women, as wives, will be provided economic protection in marriage.

Because the law gives women rights over their own wages, a husband has no dominion over his wife's earnings. In sending wives out to work, then, men risk losing authority over their wives, an authority based at least partly in the male's position as economic provider. Men in Fez today overwhelmingly disapprove of the idea of wives who work and make efforts to ensure that the women they marry will not work for a wage after marriage. Particularly for those individuals in the lower class, sending a wife out to work is shameful, as it suggests not only that the man is unable to play his proper role as economic provider but also that he has lost some dominion over others in his household.

Although they proudly defend the notion that women as wives have legal rights to their own salaries, however, factory families unanimously believe that daughters have no right to argue for control of the wages they earn. It is assumed that young, unmarried daughters, as junior and female members of the household, will provide support and services to their parents; daughters can work for a wage as part and parcel of the other kinds of services they are accustomed to providing the household. Sending daughters to work, then, allows families to take advantage of the income-earning opportunities they need. At the same time, working daughters do not pose the same kind of threat that working wives present husbands, for they do not upset the balance of authority and dependence around which marriage and family are structured. The wage labor of daughters is more easily assimilated into family power hierarchies than the wage work of wives.

Thus, families send their daughters to the factories, allowing husbands and fathers to maintain some sense of honor by continuing to protect their wives. Daughters willingly go out to work knowing that, at least, they are sparing their mothers the indignity of labor outside the household. As one informant explained, "It would be disrespectful for a mother—an older woman who has worked her whole life for her children—to go out and work when her children stay at home. . . . So long as the children are not in school, it is for them to go out and work, out of respect for their mother, because she is old and weak."

As noted above, the overwhelming majority of factory workers reported handing over their salaries to their parents, specifically to their mothers. The salary was most often used to pay for household necessities, including food. Most workers reported that whether they were permitted to keep a portion of their salaries, and how significant this portion might be, depended on the urgency of the household's needs in any given month.

Workers reported that their sense of duty to the family compelled them to comply with their parents' requests and that they willingly handed over their earnings; many presumed that they had no right to withhold their earnings from their parents. Although it was rumored in Fez that working girls attempted to pocket their earnings without telling their parents (many workers are paid in cash, sums of money that vary monthly), workers widely asserted that attempts to keep a significant portion of the salary would be fruitless. As one observed, "A girl can try to hide her money, but then what can she do with it? If she buys anything, like a dress, for example, her mother will surely see it and ask her, 'Where did you get this dress?' Her mother will know she has taken the money." Given the general lack of space and privacy in lower-class households, it is indeed difficult for the workers to secretively keep a meaningful sum of money. Moreover, given the overwhelming needs of most factory families, it is troublesome for many young workers to argue against their parents' demands. Indeed, the money is most often used to support the households where they live, and upon which they themselves depend.

Thus, the factory worker labors to support her family, much as she performs the housework assigned to her as a daughter when she is at home. Her contributions to the family economy do not significantly alter her role or her status in the household. In word and in deed the factory worker retains her position as a dependent, junior person in the household who holds no authority over others. Workers report that despite their contributions, a girl never "governs herself." They unanimously insisted that a father and brothers have the right to control a girl's behavior, even in the case where she is financially supporting them. As one worker explained, "If a girl wants to go to a café, her brother will say no, even if she is earning money. And he has the right to do this. She will not defy her brother or her father." The cash the worker earns does not override age-old patterns of respect for those individuals whose age or gender places them in authority. The following sequence of events, drawn directly from field notes I recorded after a visit to a factory worker's home, aptly characterizes female workers' roles in their households.

> I sat waiting for my friend to return from work as her mother readied the evening tea. The girl's brothers, one younger and the other older, sat with us, watching television. The mother kept urging the younger boy to go out and purchase the milk needed for coffee, but the boy kept putting her off. She did not ask her older son, who was in his late twenties and unemployed, for assistance. It was after six when my friend entered the room, tired from a day spent standing at the factory, very eager to sit down. Her mother whispered to her as she kneeled at the table, and she quickly jumped up and disappeared. She returned some minutes later with milk.

Factory girls remain faithful to their roles as daughters within the household. This point is not to suggest, however, that their work inside the factory has no wider impact on their lives. Indeed, a worker gains latitude, simply because work outside the home takes her away from the protective watch of her family. En route to the factory, and in stolen moments and sometimes afternoons spent away from the factory, under the pretext of work obligations, working girls can gain some freedom of movement. But these liberties are pilfered, not earned. Wage labor does not legitimately afford the daughter the right to control the money she earns; neither does it provide her the autonomy to make decisions for herself, or for others.

Fez residents acknowledge that there are several features of factory work that combine to ensure that a girl's wage labor in garment factories does not earn her the status and influence associated with the role of breadwinner. The income the factory girl brings in is not steady—the family cannot rely on her factory work from month to month; often, because of factory shutdowns, the working daughter finds herself unemployed and marginal to the family finances. The amount she earns, moreover, is low, and although the money is often needed, rarely does the girl singlehandedly support the household. And because factory labor is so poorly regarded, her occupation gains her no prestige, as it might if she were an educated, respected bureaucrat.

Thus, despite their toil and efforts in support of their families, garment factory workers are widely rumored to be "only girls" who "work for makeup," or face cream, or fashionable clothing. This myth does more than dismiss the reality of exploitation within the garment factories. Reiterated time and again by Fez residents, the idea helps to reinforce the position of the young garment workers as daughters

.thin their households and thus to preserve the primacy of the structure of the patriarchal family. As girls who labor only for frivolity, these workers do not risk disturbing traditional authority patterns within their households.

Protecting Women and Honoring Men

If married women were hired within the factories, there would be a greater potential for alteration in the structure of the patriarchal family, and consequently in patterns of gendered authority in the community generally. Only 14 percent of garment factory workers I surveyed in Fez were married; some 60 percent of these married workers labored because their husbands were ill, unable to support them, and had no alternative solution to family poverty.

Normally, when young women become wives, their participation in factory labor comes to a halt. Indeed, the critical importance of a wife's work within the home partly explains this phenomenon. Most of the factory families surveyed lived in nuclear family households; only 20 percent of factory households were made up of extended families; thus, women who were working would not necessarily be able to depend on help from other older females at home. Garment factories do not provide for child-care arrangements or other maternal benefits. Moreover, men in Fez generally uphold the notion that a married woman ought not work.

In Fez, many factory owners discriminate against hiring older, married women. Hiring practices help ensure that it is unmarried females, daughters and not wives, who staff the garment factories of Fez. In my interviews with Fez factory owners, they frequently asserted that they did not wish to hire older women, that is, married women. Indeed, it is rare to find a woman over the age of thirty working in the garment factories of Fez. (Despite trends toward the rising age of females at first marriage, most Moroccan women are married by this age.) Older and married women report that they are often sent away from the factory door when inquiring about work, a dismissal they attribute to their age. Workers themselves claim that it is not uncommon for girls to be fired for "growing old"—working too many years at a single establishment.

Why are owners of Fez factories so reluctant to hire mature, married women to labor in their factories? It might be assumed that factory owners in Fez wish to avoid paying maternity benefits, although noncompliance with labor law seems to be an assumption on the part of both owners and workers alike. When questioned about their reluctance to hire mature women as workers, owners assert that older women are less nimble and learn the production system less rapidly than young girls. Obviously, females do not, in reality, begin to lose their capacity to labor in the factory at an age as young as thirty. I believe that the owners' assertions belie the real reasons women are not hired. They have to do with ideas about gendered authority, marriage, and the status of females—girls and women—in the community. As noted above, the Fez community generally perceives the labor of females in garment factories as immoral. The employment of women who are mothers and wives is perceived as even more dishonorable than the employment of girls who are daughters. This condition is true for several reasons.

It is true that young and as yet unmarried girls are more amenable to factory control owing to their social and chronological age—because they are children and not adults. This fact holds universally and explains the frequent employment of young girls on global factory-assembly lines. But in Morocco, the role of wife holds a particular kind of meaning. The woman as wife ideally remains submissive to her husband. It is in her ability to properly play out her subservience to him that she demonstrates not only her own honorability but also the integrity of her husband, his family, and her own natal kin. Whereas for the daughter work in the factory implies servitude to the father, for the wife factory work hints at female autonomy, rather than proper dependence. (Again, this condition is owing to the fact that married women have legal rights over their own salaries.)

Yet Moroccan society sustains an unspoken yet palpable contradiction: the incongruity between the ideal of male dominance and the centrality of women's position as mothers. Although married women are believed to display their high status by striking a pose of submissiveness to the husband's authority, it is as mature, married women—most likely mothers of sons and daughters alike—that women attain a personal power strong enough to counter, or at least speak to, the authority of men. Women as mature wives and mothers could traditionally gain control of the household finances, of their children's marriages, and of their own movements.[8] They are often implicitly understood to be in control of their own homes. As one worker described the difference between her own and her mother's life: "My mother has lived a life where she gets up in the morning, she prays, she makes breakfast for her children. . . . In the afternoon she goes to visit her friends. . . . She has no one ruling over her, she works as she pleases, when she pleases. I do not have this kind of

---

8. A wealth of literature describes Middle Eastern women's lives and the changes in their position in the household as they age and mature. For example, Susan Schaeffer Davis (1983) describes a mature, married wife handling the family finances in a Moroccan town, arguing that the older woman's control of the purse strings is a source of power in the rural Moroccan context.

life. . . . I have someone ruling over me at work. My mother never had anyone controlling her, she managed her own work, at home, in peace."

The implicit contradiction between factory authority—male dominance—and the universally recognized value of women as mothers threatens factory regimes. Women in their reproductive role, women who assert their need to tend to their duties as wife and mother, can undermine the work of the factory. Thus, it is safer, and far easier, for owners to choose to hire females who have no such source of personal power—females in their roles as daughters.

The woman as wife, in word and deed submissive, has an elevated role to play. It is in this role as wife, and eventually as mother, that women gain a kind of religious status. As wives and mothers, Moroccan females play a central role in religious practice, making possible the quotidian and the annual ritual expressions of Moroccan Muslim identity. Married women are experts in preparing and managing the necessary ritual processes. It is the respectful and traditional wives who prepare couscous every Friday at noon to mark the Muslim holy day, sometimes producing extra portions to give to the poor. Through the month of Ramadan it is women as wives and mothers who skillfully cook the evening meals that make the duty of fasting possible for their husbands and families. They prepare the breakfast meal for the "Aid el-Fatur" that marks the end of the holy month. Wives have the knowledge needed to properly prepare and cook the ram men slaughter for the sacrifice marking the "Aid el-Kebir." Altogether, in their roles as wives and mothers, women make it possible for the Muslim community to carry out the central rituals and practices of Islam. This role has a quasi-religious dimension, and through it females attain a social worth above the status of unmarried females.[9]

An incident I witnessed in one Fez factory speaks to the position of married women in the factory community, and in the community at large. This episode illustrates how the elevated status of married women, a status higher than of an unmarried girl, demands the respect of factory owners.

9. I do not imply that it is true of women only in the Moroccan or Muslim context. In all the world's patriarchal religions, including Christianity and Judaism, women have traditionally been excluded from positions of textual authority and power but have been incorporated in religious ritual as supporters, responsible for managing tasks necessary for the completion of ceremonies and celebrations marking important spiritual moments and lifecycle transformations. In successfully playing their role, often overlooked as routine aspects of child rearing or housekeeping, women everywhere have found spiritual expression, satisfaction, and enhancement of their own moral status. See, for example, Hoch-Smith and Spring 1978; King 1993.

This incident occurred on a Friday, several days after Ramadan had begun, in the factory where I was laboring as a worker, carrying out intensive participant observation. Most Moroccan institutions alter their working hours to accommodate the fast, and this factory had adopted an 8:00 A.M.–3:00 P.M. schedule during the month of fasting. The mass of factory workers appreciated the shortened workday but begrudged the early morning hours more than usual. For them, much of the joy of the month is in the evening hours spent feasting, watching television specials, and perhaps venturing out for walks in the night. Below is a description of the Ramadan incident drawn directly from field notes I recorded after a day of intensive participant observation inside the factory:

> This morning the factory administrator announced that the administration was considering changing the Ramadan work schedule on behalf of the married women, who had requested more time off in the afternoon in order to prepare the *harira* for their family's breakfast meal. The newly proposed workday would go from 7:30 A.M. to 2:30 P.M. rather than the previously instituted 8:00 A.M. to 3:00 P.M. The administration asked for the workers' opinion on this change.
>
> The crowd of workers went into an uproar. It seemed that every girl was shouting, "No, we don't want this. . . . We are all girls. . . . We don't need to cook *harira*! . . . We need to sleep in the morning!" The workers argued loudly against the proposed change that would force them to wake one half-hour earlier. The workers sat at their tables and counted the number of married women working amongst them—"There are no more than three here in this section!" voices near me shouted. Despite the majority's vocal objections to the proposed changes, the administration instituted a revised Ramadan schedule to allow married women enough time in the afternoon to return home and prepare the soup with which Moroccans break the fast. Although the married workers represented a seemingly insignificant minority of employees, their needs were swiftly accommodated by the factory administration. The wishes of the unmarried workers, the vast majority, were totally disregarded.

In the Ramadan incident, factory administrators had little choice but to accommodate women in carrying out their most revered role, their role as Muslim wives. And it is for this reason that mature women in Morocco, the majority of whom are wives, are less desired as workers by factory owners. The factories cannot as easily exploit married women, for their husbands would be shamed and outraged. If a married woman is kept at the factory into the wee hours of the night, if she is prevented from returning home to cook the evening meal, as young working girls often are, not just the woman herself but also the status of the husband and of the family is diminished. The woman's importance as wife and mother legitimately counters the work of the factory.

In one incident in the factory where I worked, a worker was slapped in the face by a male supervisor, and she slapped him back. The most shameful aspect of the incident, one worker bitterly commented, was that the worker involved was a married woman, working not because she was destitute but because she chose to work for the material benefits her personal income allowed her. Through her actions, this woman had shamed not only herself but also her unwitting husband and family, I was told. Women's role in reproduction also implies their role as status bearers for their families.

Fewer married women are employed in the garment factories of Fez partly because fewer married women seek work in these factories, not only because of the resistance of their husbands but because of the burden of their work at home as well. Researchers have long noted that women's role in the reproductive realm hampers their participation in production, and it is certainly a factor in Morocco, where fertility rates remain high and married women are almost invariably mothers who bear sole responsibility for the care of children. On the other hand, married women are not welcomed into the garment factories, because factory owners do not wish to engage in the social politics of hiring them. The employment of wives is considered less appropriate, and perhaps more immoral, than the employment of daughters. Factory owners are able to use, and to exploit, the labor of unmarried young females with minimal outcry from the community. Subjecting married women to the toils of the factory would be an insult to their husbands, families, and the moral community as a whole. Moreover, factory owners know, as they demonstrated in the Ramadan incident, that married women themselves can use their status in the household, the power they feel and the respect due to them in their role as wives and, more important, as mothers, to counter the demands of men—factory owners—and the factory regime.

Conclusion

Over the past decades, the Middle East and North Africa have participated in global trends that have resulted in the integration of females into industrial labor. Morocco, because it was the first nation in the region to undertake the sort of economic restructuring that promotes export industrialization and the concomitant employment of women in factories, provides a good place to ask questions about the effect of industrial labor on a patriarchal system. Factory owners in Fez rebuff the efforts of mature women to work in the city's garment factories. It is everywhere acknowledged in Fez that older women who wait at factory doors seeking work will most certainly be turned away. Although I recognize the real restraints that the duties of motherhood place on women's participation in production, I argue that the strength of their status in the reproductive realm, the centrality of their position as mature wives and mostly as mothers, poses a threat to factory owners. The position of women in the household affects their position in the realm of production, albeit in an unexpected way: women's value and power as older wives, and as mothers, counter the value and power of the factory.

It is said in Fez that the females who staff the garment factories are willing to work under such difficult conditions, and for so little pay, because they are "only girls." The local claim that workers are amenable to the poor work conditions because of their position in the reproductive realm coincides with Marxist-feminist explanations of why females are so often participants in poorly paid factory labor. The role and status of women inside the household is inextricably linked to their roles outside the household. Specific cultural assumptions about what it means to be a daughter and a sister, and what it means to be a wife and mother, help determine female participation in work in the garment factories of Fez—and elsewhere.[10]

---

10. I do not claim that cultural and ideological factors in Morocco are inflexible or that they override economic factors. As noted at the start of this chapter, mature women have long held highly regarded professional positions throughout the Middle East, positions they maintain as wives and often as mothers. In addition, young girls in Morocco have manipulated the ideologies associated with honor and female seclusion in order to work in the factory while maintaining their own personal virtue. Similarly, Naila Kabeer (1994) describes how Bangladeshi women "take their purdah with them" to the factory. Likewise, the ideals and practices of motherhood might be manipulated for economic gain, if factory work were financially more worthwhile. Given the lack of benefits, insecurity of the work, and low pay, I would argue that the married women of Fez are not motivated to struggle for the right to work in the garment industry.

10 The Status of Rural Women in Turkey

What Is the Role of Regional Differences?

AYŞE GÜNDÜZ-HOŞGÖR

and JEROEN SMITS

THERE HAS BEEN INCREASING AWARENESS that the agricultural policies in the Turkish Republic had different impacts on women and men in the countryside. The available studies indicate that women in rural areas have been affected mainly in three ways by the governmental policies: through modernization in farming technology and commercial marketing, through migration, and through the compulsory and free primary-education reforms.

Most previous research has focused on the first and the second issues. Those studies, for example, indicate that the modernization of farming technology in agriculture and commercial marketing tended to reproduce and intensify the sexual division of labor to the disadvantage of rural women. The change from traditional to modern farming tended to enhanced men's prestige and power at the expense of women's by widening the gap in the level of knowledge and training. The influence of men thus increased both within their households and within the local centers of power (Tunaligil 1980; Azmaz 1984; Ertürk 1987; Ilcan 1994). The effect of migration, on the contrary, may have been a strengthening of the position of women. Both the early national migration and the later international labor migration to western Europe, which began in the 1960s, were movements of male labor. For example, 91 percent of the workers placed in a position abroad by the Labor Placement Office between 1967 and 1992 were male. As many of these men were married (SIS 1994), a large number of married women stayed behind in rural Turkey and had to take care of themselves and their children, though they also gained some autonomy.

The small-scale case studies on which the above conclusions were based provide little insight into the way in which the impact varied among regions. Turkey exhibits large differences across regions in level of economic development, natural resources, history, and culture. Comparing the effects of the modernization process among these regions, therefore, might provide new insights into the way in which economic and cultural factors influence the process of modernization in rural areas.

In this chapter, we study the regional differences in the impact of modernization on the position of rural women in Turkey, using national representative data for the year 1998. We focus on the differences among five regions of Turkey: the West, South, Central, North, and East (including Southeast) (see map 10.1).[1] We compare women in two basic stages of the modernization process: women living in the countryside (called from now on "country women") and women living in towns (called "town women"). We focus on differences in degree of freedom or autonomy between women, as measured by a number of socioeconomic, demographic, and cultural indicators. More specifically, we want to discern differences among rural women from the different regions in Turkey and within the regions between country women and town women in their access to and use of education facilities, their labor-market positions and occupations, the degree to which they reproduce patriarchal ideologies, the degree to which they experience traditional norms, and their attitudes toward family planning.

We begin with a description of the differences among the five regions of Turkey, the relevant historical developments pertaining to Turkish women, and the differences between rural women living in the countryside and rural women living in towns. To frame the chapter conceptually, we also provide an overview of the most influential perspectives within the women/gender and development literature. The empirical part of the chapter starts with a discussion of the data and variables, after which the results are presented. Finally, the results are summarized and discussed.

Regional Differences in Turkey

The West is the most advanced region of Turkey. It is also the most densely populated and urbanized region, as it includes Istanbul (the country's largest city and one of the largest metropolitan areas of the world with around thirteen million inhabitants) and Izmir (the third-largest city). This region is the center of the industry,

1. This map illustrates six regions: the West, South, Central, North, Southeast, and East. However, because the data for the East and the Southeast could not be separated in our data set, in our analyses these regions are combined and referred to as the East.

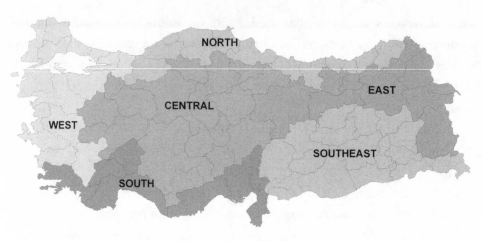

10.1. Regions of Turkey

commerce, and finance of Turkey. It has a dynamic economy, in which industrial activities, especially manufacturing industry, play a key role. The highly diversified and rapidly growing manufacturing industry attracts many people from the less developed parts of Turkey to the cities of the region. The driving force behind the local economy is capital investment, whether national or local private capital. In this region, the infrastructure necessary for regional development (such as roads and schooling) was built up earlier than in the other parts of Turkey. The Aegean area has a very important agrarian sector. Mechanization of agriculture and its connection to the market economy already took place here in the 1950s. Because of the favorable climate, this region produces and exports many valuable agricultural products, such as cotton, sunflowers, and citrus fruits. In the coastal areas, tourism is a booming business. Overall, the western region contributes most to the gross domestic product of the country.

Like the West, the South of Turkey includes highly fertile agricultural areas as well as industrial centers, like Adana, and a growing tourist industry along the coastline, like around Antalya. Although there is some internal variation, the South is a densely populated and urbanized region, characterized by relatively high levels of per capita income. It includes a highly diversified, dynamic, and rapidly growing manufacturing industry and, because of this fact, has experienced in-migration from the less developed parts of Turkey to its cities. In its market-oriented agriculture, a wide variety of products are cultivated, of which the cotton and citrus-fruit production provide high export earnings for the region. Other distinctive features of agriculture in this region are its high level of mechanization (probably among the highest of Turkey), of tenancy (land leased out for cultivation), and of seasonal migration. The agricultural holdings in the region are relatively large. There are signs of a mild polarization of landownership between, on the one hand, a few big landowners and, on the other hand, a majority of small landholders.

In the Central region of Turkey, we find Ankara, the capital and the second-largest city in Turkey. The local economy includes government activities and related expenditures. Another contribution of Ankara is in the area of cultural capital, as the city includes many educational institutions and universities. With the exception of some minor industries located around Ankara, the industrial production of this region is low. The agricultural production is less diversified than in the West or the South, because the climate and geography of Central Turkey are more restrictive. The Central region includes arid grazing areas where mostly cereal (wheat and barley) is produced by mechanized agricultural techniques. Given the dry climate, husbandry is a common economic activity in the countryside of the region. Although close to the capital, the countryside of Central Turkey has no well-developed infrastructure. Within the region, there is much migration from the countryside to the larger city centers.

The North of Turkey has a fertile coastal area and receives much rain, although its width in some parts is only a few kilometers. The coastal area is isolated from the rest of the country by high mountains and forests. Therefore, the North was connected relatively late to the market economy and lacked infrastructural development. Within the region, substantial differences can be observed. For example, the western provinces have extensive coal reserves and were a center for mining and steel industry (like the city of Zonguldak). In the northern parts, on the other hand, the mechanization of agriculture was hindered by the geographic circumstances, and there was much out-migration of males. The women who were left behind in the region had to carry out intensive agricultural work (such as hazelnuts and tea production). The village structure in the northern region differs much from the countryside villages in other parts of Turkey; the houses are apart from each other (especially in the northern part of the region, there is no close community structure), and, because of this condition, the main social community is not the village itself, but rather the extended family and other relatives.

The East of Turkey is the least-developed region of the country. It can be divided broadly into an eastern and a southeastern part. In the eastern part, the terrain is highly mountainous, and, therefore, the most important economic activity is husbandry. The winters are long and snowy, and the summers are short and mild. Generally, crops are produced only for household consumption, not for marketing. Wheat and maize, the most important items of a subsistence economy, are the dominant agricultural products. The average size of the agricultural holdings is small compared to other regions, and the lands are mainly cultivated by the landowners. Another important feature of its agriculture is the low level of mechanization, as is evidenced by the low rate of tractor usage. In the East, the number of people living in urban areas is very low. Also, the rate of population growth is low. In some parts it is even below zero because of out-migration. Per capita income is the lowest of all regions of Turkey. The few industrial activities are mostly geared to local needs and do not play a role of significance in the local economy.

The southeastern part shows similarities with the eastern part in terms of lack of industrialization and infrastructure. In the Southeast, the villagers live either in the high mountains or on the plains. The climate is rather unfavorable (very hot summers and very cold winters). In the mountains, the majority of the villagers own the land on which they work, whereas on the plains the tribal leaders, or *aghas,* own the land. Until recently, an important characteristic of the villages in this region was their tribal structure, and most people lived under the authority of their religious leaders (sheiks). Because of economic insufficiency, the region experienced high levels of internal migration to the larger cities. In some regions (especially in Diyarbakir), this migration process was strengthened in the past decades as a result of the conflict between the Kurdish Worker Party and the state's security forces. The Southeastern Anatolian Development Project has begun to improve the economy of the region, and there are plans to stimulate the agricultural development further through irrigation and hydroelectric power. In this way, it is also hoped to reverse (or at least to bring to a halt) the migration flow from this region to the rest of the country. However, at the moment the region is still very poor in terms of agricultural production.

The Position of Women in Turkey

Since the establishment of the Turkish Republic in 1923, the state has been concerned with the economic and social development of the country. To that end, the Kemalist regime implemented a number of legal and social reforms in the first two decades of the republic. In 1924, the caliphate was abolished, and by 1926, the sharia, the religious law, was replaced by the secular Civil Code, which was adopted from the Swiss Civil Code. The laws in the new Civil Code established women's rights in the areas of marriage, divorce, inheritance, and property ownership. Family law made polygamy and marriage without the agreement of the partners illegal, and civil marriage was made the only legally valid form of marriage, while religious marriage remained an additional option to those individuals who are married by civil authorities; the minimum marriage age was raised to the legal age of majority, eighteen, for both sexes; "consent of both parties" was made a requirement for a valid marriage; divorce by repudiation was prohibited; equal inheritance rights to men and women; as well as women's right to freely own and dispose of property were granted as fundamental consequences of the secular civil legislation that was adopted. In addition, the principle of "equal pay for equal work regardless of sex" was recognized, and women were actively encouraged to have higher education and careers. Women received the right to vote in municipal elections in 1930 and to vote and stand for election in municipal and national elections in 1934 (Browning 1985).

The introduction of the new legal framework was intended to transform the nation into a secular, "modern," and industrial state. Women were considered central to the success of the new secular and modernizing ideology. For this purpose, they had to be freed from the traditional Islamic values, because Islam and women's rights were considered to be incompatible. "State feminism," therefore, supported women's rights and encouraged education and employment of women (Moghadam 2003).

To increase the schooling opportunities for women, several measures were taken. Early on, coeducation was established at the primary and university levels (Tan 1981). Families were obliged to send their daughters to primary schools, and compliance was monitored by the Ministry of National Education. Although these Kemalist measures opened up new doors for women, the system provided limited opportunities for rural women, and especially for the women who were living in the East and Southeast, where the modernization attempts were blocked by the religious and ethnic tribal leaders. Those women also had (and many still have) another disadvantage: they were speaking their local languages at home, which meant that the ones who did not attend school missed the opportunity to learn the principal language of the country, Turkish. To this day, about a quarter of the Kurdish and Arabic women of Turkey are not able to speak Turkish and are dependent on their male household members (who almost all speak Turkish) for information about Turkish society and their legal rights (Smits and Gündüz-Hoşgör 2003).

Theories on Women and Development

Research has shown that the impact of development—or lack of development—differs between men and women. In their attempts to answer the question of whether development improves the relative status of women in "third world" countries, social scientists have focused on economic, social, and cultural transformations. Two major theoretical perspectives have emerged: the modernization approach, called "women in development" (WID), and the Marxist-inspired perspectives known as "woman and development" (WAD) and "gender and development" (GAD) (Rathgeber 1990).

The WID approach is closely related to Western liberal feminism and modernization theory and does not necessarily address the existing gender structures. It assumes that development leads to female liberation by involving women more in social and economic life. According to Janet Z. Giele, the factors that the WID approach considers as most crucial for gender equality are a technologically advanced or industrial economy, a kinship system based on a nuclear rather than the extended family, a democratic state and an egalitarian class structure, and a secularized religious tradition or worldview (1992, 5). The classic WID approach views women's relative "backwardness" as a function of traditional attitudes and simple technology. As industrialization (along with urbanization) leads to more educational facilities, job opportunities, and social services, it is considered to be a major factor leading to the improvement of the status of women. In other words, economic development brings female liberation by integrating them more into economic life through education.

The more recent evidence indicates that *values* are part of what needs to change in order for the society to become modern. Instead of arguing that cultural values derived from developed nations bring modern ideas conducive to development, the recent "culturalist" modernization perspective argues that modernization involves both modern and traditional values. This acknowledgment of the importance of cultural factors is an important strength of the WID approach (Kandiyoti 1977, 1984, 1988; Berik 1987; Afshar 1985; Moghadam 1992).

These studies indicate that the expansion of paid employment has bypassed rural women in, for example, Turkey, Iran, and Afghanistan and denied them the opportunity to take control over their lives (as the earlier WID approach would predict). Both "classic patriarchal" and "Islamic-patriarchal" controls persist.

A major weakness of the WID approach is its lack of focus on structural variables and relations of production. The importance of these "material" factors is much more acknowledged by the Marxist-oriented approaches to the position of women in the developing world, which point that development may affect men and women of the same class in different ways (Boserup 1970, 1977; Saffioti 1978; Safa 1983; Ward 1984; Joekes 1987; Finlay 1989; Taplin 1989; Moghadam 1992). Within this group, the WAD approach focuses on the economic roles of women. However, this approach focuses mostly on class divisions and tends to ignore the domestic roles of the women at home. These roles are better addressed by the GAD approach, which involves a detailed review of the intersection of household and public structures to discover "why women have systematically been assigned to inferior and/or secondary roles" (Rathgeber 1990, 494). According to this socialist-feminist approach, the oppression of women will stop only if women participate in nonhome economic production—under conditions of equality between the sexes—and men are more involved in household activities (Rathgeber 1990).

According to both Marxist approaches, gender inequalities emerge from and reinforce the relations of production. During the transitional (early) stages of development, the economic and social marginality of women increases, partly because they reproduce the labor force and consequently are less involved in earning wages themselves. In later stages, women contribute to the economic development as cheap laborers. Both WAD and GAD see the disadvantaged position of women as being to a large extent caused by their lack of access to critical resources. Both approaches also acknowledge the importance of patriarchal ideologies and structures for placing the women in a subservient position at home and in the workplace. To enhance the status of women in development, therefore, they consider it necessary that those women get better access to critical resources and that patriarchal ideas be undermined.

Both the WID approach and the Marxian approaches start with economic factors and the work that women do. They examine the work of women, both at home and in the labor force, and also the needs of families and employers. Both perspectives come to the conclusion that the domestic mode of production in which women exchange their unpaid domestic services for their upkeep is the origin of patriarchy, which within feminist literature is generally defined as a dual system in which men oppress women and men oppress each other (Mackie 1991). However, they differ in their view on the basis of patriarchy: according to WID it is culturally based, whereas according to WAD and GAD it is materially based (Gündüz-Hosgör 2001).

None of the approaches provides a complete analysis of the relationships between women-gender and development. Following A. Portes (1980), who suggests that in the development literature there are convergences between the modernization and Marxist theories, we combine "structuralist" concepts from WAD and GAD with "cultural" concepts from the WID approach to derive hypotheses about the evolving status of women in different regions of Turkey.

Differences Between Town and Countryside

There are marked differences in the lives of rural women and the degree of mobility and autonomy they experience. Women living in the small villages of the country-side generally have more freedom of movement and greater access to public space, as long as they stay within the borders of their own villages. As the WAD and GAD approaches suggest, this condition is related to their mode of production. Women in villages work in the fields or in the barns or both from spring to the end of au-tumn. In some regions, they do outside domestic activities together, like washing clothes, baking bread, or preparing food for winter. They also may get together in front of their houses as leisure-time activity.

In the towns, the freedom of women is more restricted. Town women are gener-ally marginalized from economic activity—as many of them are housewives—and their access to the public space is much more limited. For example, the daily shop-ping activities are carried out mostly by men. Patriarchal control is stronger over town women than over village women, which may be related to the strength of the social norms within the issue of migration from countryside to the towns. Because women represent the honor of their families, their interaction with outsiders tends to be limited when they migrate to an unfamiliar environment. This argument also applies to young women. However, in contrast with the older women, living in a town may have a major advantage to the younger ones: the educational facilities and hence the opportunities to become economically independent generally are much better in the towns.

Data and Methods

We use data from the 1998 Turkish Demographic and Health Survey (TDHS). This survey is part of the Demographic and Health Surveys (DHS+), which provide data and analyses on the population, health, and nutrition of women and children in de-veloping countries (DHS+ 2003). The DHS+ surveys use nationally representative samples of households and consist of at least a household survey and a women's sur-vey. In the current chapter, we use the data from the TDHS women's survey. The fe-males in the data set are a representative sample of all females ages fifteen to forty-nine in Turkey. The males for which information is available are the husbands of married females. The total number of married women in the data set is 6,152.

Variables

In this chapter, rural women are defined as women living in settlements of 10,000 or fewer inhabitants. On the basis of the TDHS definition, they are divided into "town women" and "countryside women." The five regions we distinguish include the following provinces: *West:* Edirne, Istanbul, Kirklareli, Tekirdag, Balikesir, Kocaeli, Sakarya, Canakkale, Bursa Yalova Izmir, Denizli, Manisa, and Aydin; *South:* Mugla, Burdur, Isparta, Antalya, Hatay, Adana, Icel, Gaziantep, Kilis, and Osmaniye; *Central:* Cankiri, Corum, Yozgat, Tokat, Amasya, Bilecik, Eskisehir, Usak, Kutahya, Afyon, Ankara, Kirsehir, Nevsehir, Bolu, Konya, Kayseri, Nigde, Aksaray, Karaman, and Kirikkale; *North:* Trabzon, Rize, Giresun, Ordu, Artvin, Samsun, Kastamonu, Zonguldak, Sinop, Bartin, and Karabuk; and *East:* Mardin, Diyarbakir, Siirt, Hakkari, Bitlis, Van, Batman, Sirnak, Kars, Bingol, Agri, Mus, Erzurum, Ardahan, Igdir, Sanliurfa, Malatya, Adiyaman, K. Maras, Sivas, Tunceli, Elazig, Erzincan, Gumushane, Bayburt (TDHS 1999).

Besides "urbanization" and "region," a number of other variables are used. *Socioeconomic characteristics* are educational level and literacy of the woman, whether she is employed, her occupation, her husband's education and occupation, and the household income. *Sociocultural factors* are whether the woman speaks Turkish, reads a newspaper at least once a week, or has always lived in the same place. *Gender-role attitudes* of the women are measured with dummy variables indicating whether (1) or not (0) she agrees with the following pronouncements: "Important decisions should be made by men," "Men are wiser than women," "Women should not argue with men," and "It is better for a male than for a female child to have education." As *traditionality of marriage variables,* dummies are used that indicate whether (1) or not (0) the woman married before age sixteen; there is a blood relationship with the husband; the marriage was arranged by the family; there was a bride price paid for the marriage; and there was only a religious marriage ceremony. *Family-planning issues* are measured with dummy variables indicating whether (1) or not (0) the women approve of family planning, consider family planning to be against religion, use no family planning, have five or more children, would be unhappy if they became pregnant, want more children than their husbands, find family-planning information in high schools acceptable, have husbands who approve of family planning, and have husbands who want more children than they want themselves.

Part of the marriage and gender-role variables is used to indicate whether the women grew up in traditional and patriarchal families. We expect women who were under age sixteen when they married or when they had their first child, women with five or more children, women who have a blood relationship with their husband, women whose marriage was not arranged by themselves, women for whom a bride price was paid at their marriage, women who had only a religious marriage ceremony, and women who agreed with the traditional gender-role pronouncements to have a higher probability of being raised in a traditional and patriarchal family than other women.

Results

Table 10.1 shows that, overall in Turkey, almost 35 percent of the women in the countryside have not completed primary education. This figure drops to 25 percent for the towns, which indicates that women in towns have more chance to go to school than women in the countryside. The proportion of countryside women who did not complete primary education is highest in the East (64 percent) and lowest in the West (15 percent). Thus, the women in the East seem to be the most disadvantaged group in terms of access to formal education.

There are also substantial differences among the regions in terms of reading easily. Again, the women in the eastern countryside are the most disadvantaged group, followed by the women from the eastern towns. In fact, there are considerable differences between this region and the rest of the country. With regard to education, the most surprising figures are of the countryside women in the North. Even though the settlements of the houses in some parts of this region are not only apart from each other but also away from the schools, the female literacy rate is even higher than in the South and the Central region of Turkey. Identifying the factors behind this fact requires further analysis, which is not the focus of this study.

Regarding participating in the labor force, table 10.1 makes clear that women in the towns are economically more marginalized than women in the countryside. In the countryside, 47 percent of all women are housewives, against 70 percent in the towns. Only in the East, the percentage of countryside women who are housewives is not much lower than in the towns.

Of the country women with a job, only 16 percent are engaged in nonfarm activities. In the towns, this percentage is 53 percent. If we take into account that in the towns only 30 percent of the women are employed, we find that no more than 15 percent of the town women have a nonfarm job. This result makes clear that in the rural areas of Turkey there are very little nonagricultural employment opportunities for women. Only in the more industrialized western and southern regions of

Table 10.1

Socioeconomic Characteristics of Married Country Women and Town Women in Turkey, 1998

Characteristic	Location Type	South	East	Center	North	West	All	Number of Women
Education less than primary	Country	36.9	63.5	24.4	39.0	15.4	34.6	2,016
	Town	29.8	51.1	22.9	24.0	13.6	25.4	885
Reads easily	Country	59.3	31.6	66.1	60.1	78.7	59.7	2,013
	Town	69.2	48.2	69.5	72.8	85.0	71.5	882
Employed	Country	50.8	26.8	56.5	69.7	65.2	53.0	2,012
	Town	19.2	23.4	33.8	39.0	30.5	29.6	882
Employed in nonfarm occupations	Country	8.8	3.7	8.0	5.5	15.7	8.5	2,012
	Town	13.1	13.1	11.4	17.1	21.4	15.8	882
Education of husbands less than primary	Country	10.9	27.5	5.2	11.8	11.0	13.0	2,005
	Town	8.4	16.9	8.9	5.8	3.5	7.9	882
Husband employed in farming	Country	43.8	44.4	46.6	24.7	42.3	41.8	2,009
	Town	12.6	9.0	17.8	2.9	5.7	10.0	871
Household income < 50 million TL	Country	46.3	51.4	41.9	25.8	30.6	39.9	1,991
	Town	29.2	33.6	31.4	16.3	6.9	21.9	873
Speaks no Turkish	Country	4.1	33.0	0.0	0.4	0.4	7.8	2,014
	Town	3.8	16.8	0.0	0.0	0.0	3.2	882
Reads a newspaper at least once a week	Country	8.1	4.6	11.0	14.7	22.0	12.1	2,011
	Town	27.5	11.7	14.6	29.8	42.5	26.8	883
Always lived in this place	Country	49.8	48.2	50.5	51.7	43.7	48.6	1,837
	Town	32.2	33.3	23.9	19.4	21.4	25.2	825

Note: Figures are percentages of women with the respective characteristic. Percentages are based on data for 2,016 countryside women and 885 town-dwelling women.

Turkey does the situation seem to be better, with about 70 percent of the employed town women engaged in nonfarm employment.

In all regions, the educational level of married men is considerably higher than the level of their wives. The difference is lowest in the West, where 15 percent of the countryside women have less than primary education against 11 percent for the countryside males. In the East, however, the respective figures are 64 percent for the women and 28 percent for the males. This educational difference between husbands and wives may result in more dependency of women on their husbands.

A similar difference pattern between men and the women also exists in terms of occupations. Especially in the towns, husbands are occupied much more in non-farm economic activities, whereas a large part of the employed women continues to be engaged in agriculture, where their work often is considered as unpaid family work. In the towns the proportion of men employed in nonfarm occupations is 90 percent for Turkey as a whole, whereas the proportion of women is 53 percent (of the 30 percent of women that are gainfully employed). Comparable differences are found in all regions.

These figures indicate that in the early stages of social development, men enter nonfarming economic activities much easier than women, who are either marginalized (become housewives) or continue to exchange their labor as use value in the sector of agriculture. The reason might be partly related to the low educational level of women or even to the nonability of speaking Turkish for ethnic women. But, generally speaking, these figures are in line with the WAD and GAD argument that women are marginalized during the early stages of social development.

The figures on household income make clear that in all regions the proportion of households with an income below 50 million Turkish liras is substantially higher in the countryside than in the towns. Surprisingly, the proportion of countryside households with a low income is in the North lower than in the countryside of any other region of Turkey, and the towns of the North rank second in this respect after the towns in the western region.

In the East of Turkey, still a substantial number of women are not able to speak the dominant Turkish language. In the countryside this proportion is 33 percent. Very few women in this region read newspapers, but it seems not in the first place a language problem, because in the rural areas of the other parts of Turkey there are also very few women who read a newspaper once a week.

With regard to geographic mobility, almost half of the respondents in the countryside of all regions declared that they had always lived in their villages. Women in the towns are much more mobile than women in the countryside. The highest geographic mobility is observed among the town women of the North.

Gender Role Attitudes of Women

The results for the questions on the gender-role attitudes of the women are striking. In all of the regions about half of the countryside women agree with the statements that "Important decisions should be made by men" and "Men are wiser than women" (table 10.2). In terms of the argument "women should not argue with men," the percentage is even higher (63 percent). Only with regard to the statement that "It is better for a male child to have education" is the proportion of women who agree much lower (37 percent).

Among town women, the proportions of women who agree with the statements are clearly lower than in the countryside. Still, on average 34 to 48 percent of the women in the towns agree with the first three statements. These figures make clear that the women themselves play a central role in the reproduction of the patriarchal ideology to the next generations. The fact that substantially fewer women agree with the statement about the education of female children might be interpreted as a relative success of the Kemalist educational reforms.

Traditionally in Marriage

In table 10.3, we observe that getting married below age sixteen is mostly experienced by countryside women in the eastern region. Similarly, among those women there is much more often a family relationship with the husband, a bride-money payment, or only a religious marriage than in the other regions. The last point, "only having a religious marriage ceremony" almost lost its importance in the countryside of the West and North (2 percent and 4 percent, respectively) and was reduced to about 10 percent in the countryside of the Center and South. This result can be interpreted as a considerable improvement, because women who have no civil marriage have no legal inheritance rights. Unfortunately, the figures make clear that in the countryside of the East, this unfavorable situation is still a daily truth for one-third of all married women. For all indicators and regions, traditional relations within marriage are stronger in the countryside than in the towns.

Table 10.2
Gender Role Attitudes of Married Country Women and Town Women in Turkey, 1998

Statement of Attitude	Location Type	South	East	Center	North	West	All	Number of Women
Important decisions should be made by men	Country	53.6	57.9	58.0	49.8	46.9	53.8	1,965
	Town	41.1	45.8	50.9	36.6	28.9	39.8	869
Men are wiser than women	Country	46.8	59.2	48.3	46.7	43.1	49.1	1,914
	Town	29.5	37.1	51.6	26.0	22.6	33.7	852
Women should not argue with men	Country	65.5	61.1	68.1	69.4	51.8	62.7	1,953
	Town	51.6	50.4	59.9	49.0	37.1	48.5	854
It is better for a male child to have an education	Country	32.8	41.1	34.3	40.5	34.8	36.5	1,983
	Town	17.8	26.1	25.6	19.6	14.6	20.3	868

Note: Figures are percentages of women who agree with the statement.

Table 10.3

Traditionality in Marriage of Married Country Women and Town Women in Turkey, 1998

Characteristic	Location Type	South	East	Center	North	West	All	Number of Women
Married below age 16	Country	20.2	32.9	19.8	17.3	16.3	21.6	2,013
	Town	14.6	26.3	17.2	12.5	9.1	15.1	883
Family relationship with husband	Country	33.7	40.2	31.4	27.9	13.2	29.1	2,015
	Town	22.1	36.5	27.0	18.3	11.2	21.6	884
Couple arranged marriage themselves	Country	23.2	29.6	26.8	27.6	34.9	28.8	2,015
	Town	38.5	33.6	25.2	35.6	42.5	35.3	882
Bride's money paid	Country	19.0	67.1	32.7	33.3	16.9	34.6	1,998
	Town	18.5	45.9	26.6	15.5	9.6	21.6	872
Only religious marriage ceremony	Country	11.1	34.6	9.9	4.1	2.0	12.8	2,016
	Town	4.6	21.9	2.6	1.9	2.8	5.9	884

Note: Figures are percentages of women with the respective characteristics.

Family Planning

In terms of some of the family-planning indicators, we observe similar differences as we found for the other indicators between the regions East and West (table 10.4). A striking difference is related with the number of children. In the countryside of the West, only 12 percent of the women have five or more children, whereas in the countryside of the East, it is the case with 41 percent of the women. In the towns of these regions these percentages are 5 and 29, respectively. We also observe that in the West more families are using a family-planning method. In spite of these contrasts, the large majority of the respondents in both regions approves of family planning and finds teaching family planning at the high schools acceptable.

A final interesting finding is that in the countryside of the North only 17 percent of the women consider the use of family planning as being against religion, which is even a little less than in the West.

Multivariate Analysis

The results presented so far show that there are important differences among regions and between countryside and towns for almost all of the variables studied. However, because many of these variables may be related to each other, the presented percentages do not show us which of the factors are more important and which are less important in explaining the regional differences in, for example, the adherence to traditional values among women. The fact that in the East more women agree with the traditional gender-role statements may, for example, be related to their lower educational level, their more traditional family background, poverty, or the fact that they are more controlled by their family. It is, therefore, possible that when controlling for these characteristics, the differences in traditionality of gender-role attitudes among regions and between towns and countryside disappear.

To gain more insight into this possibility, we conducted a multivariate logistic regression analysis in which the simultaneous effects of all relevant factors were studied for two indicators of traditional gender-role attitudes: whether the women agree with the statements "Important decisions should be made by men" and "It is better for a male than for a female child to have education."

The results of these analyses are presented in table 10.5. For both dependent variables, two models were estimated, Model I with only the region and urbanization variables and Model II with all the relevant variables. To keep things simple, we

Table 10.4
Attitudes Toward Family Planning of Married Country Women and Town Women in Turkey, 1998

Characteristic or Statement of Attitude	Location Type	South	East	Center	North	West	All	Number of Women
Respondent approves of family planning	Country	92.3	79.1	95.0	91.6	96.0	91.2	1,876
	Town	94.1	83.2	97.2	95.9	96.8	94.5	832
Husband approves of family planning	Country	84.9	70.5	89.0	82.5	90.3	84.1	1,726
	Town	86.6	73.9	90.5	89.8	92.7	88.1	773
Use of family planning is against religion	Country	23.6	46.9	20.3	17.4	17.9	25.7	1,773
	Town	13.9	38.3	20.3	12.9	5.9	16.8	788
No family planning method used	Country	47.1	69.9	37.4	39.3	28.0	44.0	2,015
	Town	41.2	57.7	36.3	32.0	30.4	37.9	883
Has five or more children	Country	25.6	41.1	18.2	29.2	12.1	24.3	2,014
	Town	16.8	29.0	13.2	13.5	5.3	13.7	885
Unhappy if would become pregnant	Country	69.1	79.0	74.7	79.7	73.9	75.2	1,598
	Town	72.7	73.8	85.6	76.3	68.1	75.1	695
Husband wants more children than wife	Country	17.6	29.6	18.5	17.9	13.7	19.6	1,837
	Town	21.7	36.3	14.3	18.2	15.1	19.5	806
Wife wants more children than husband	Country	16.4	13.7	12.9	13.1	13.0	13.6	1837
	Town	17.4	12.9	13.8	14.1	17.4	15.4	806
Finds family planning info in high schools acceptable	Country	89.4	70.7	89.5	88.1	90.0	85.7	1,781
	Town	91.5	78.0	92.4	90.7	93.5	90.4	819

Note: Figures are percentages of women with the respective characteristic or who agree with the statement.

Table 10.5
Logistic Regression Coefficients of Selected Independent Variables on Agreement of Turkish Women with Two Gender Role Statements

Country	Important Decisions Should Be Made by Men		Better for Male than for Female Child to Have Education	
VARIABLE	MODEL I	MODEL II	MODEL I	MODEL II
Intercept	-0.22**	0.71**	-0.73**	0.19
Age	—	0.00	—	0.00
Education				
None	—	Reference	—	Reference
Incomplete primary	—	-0.41*	—	-0.04
Completed primary	—	-0.66**	—	-0.72**
More than primary	—	-1.95**	—	-1.97**
Household income				
< 50 million TL	—	Reference	—	Reference
50–100 million TL	—	-0.18	—	-0.38**
> 50 million TL	—	-0.47**	—	-0.57**
Woman employed in nonfarm occupation	—	-0.11	—	-0.19
Others present during interview	—	0.17	—	-0.07
Husband away from home	—	-0.31*	—	0.16
Wife related to husband	—	0.15	—	0.08
Couple arranged marriage themselves	—	-0.23**	—	-0.30**
Bride's money paid at marriage	—	0.20*	—	0.37**
Married below age 16	—	0.13	—	0.11
Only religious marriage	—	0.40**	—	0.33*
Living in town instead of countryside	-0.51**	-0.26**	-0.78**	-0.51**
Region				
West	Reference	Reference	Reference	Reference
South	0.36**	0.15	-0.01	-0.35*
East	0.54**	-0.10	0.39**	-0.44**
Central	0.61**	0.45**	0.16	-0.19
North	0.20	0.02	0.30*	0.04
N—Total	3,000	2,804	3,028	2,804
N—Agrees with statement	1,404	1,319	901	833
Model Chi-Square (DF)	87.2 (5)	354.0 (19)	90.7 (5)	325.6 (19)

* $p<0.05$
** $p<0.01$

interpret the logistic regression coefficients in table 10.5 only in terms of their sign, their size, and whether they are significant or not. For both statements, Model I shows that women living in towns agree significantly less than women living in the countryside. For the statement on "important decisions," women in the West agree significantly more than women in South, East, and Central Turkey. For the statement on "female education" women in the West agree more than women in the East and North. Thus, as expected, women in the countryside and women in the East tend to accept the traditional gender-role attitudes more often than women in the towns and women in the West.

When the other characteristics are included (Models II), the effect of urbanization becomes smaller but remains significantly negative. However, for the "region" the change is much more substantial. For "important decisions" only the difference between Central Turkey and the West remains significant. For "female education" the change is even stronger, with women in South and East Turkey agreeing significantly less with this statement than women in the West. These results indicate that the regional differences in traditionality of the women found in Models I were to a large extent caused by the differences in the distribution of other relevant characteristics of the women among the regions. Women with less education or household income and women who did not arrange their marriage themselves, at whose marriage bride money was paid, and who had only a religious marriage agree significantly more with the gender-role statements than other women.

These results make clear that the reproduction of traditional gender roles goes together with women's lower education, a traditional family background, and poverty. The fact that, after controlling for all other factors, women in the East are least traditional with regard to girls' education suggests that in regions where women are disadvantaged in many respects, there might be more awareness of the importance of education for the improvement of the situation of women than in other regions.

Interestingly, for the statement about "important decisions," women where husbands were away from home agreed less than other women. This finding is in line with the idea that women whose husbands are often away (as in the North) have more say in their nuclear family than women whose husbands live in the same household.

A final important conclusion we can draw from table 10.5 is that the answers of the women were probably little influenced by the presence of others during the interview. At least, the answers of women where other adults were present during the interview are not significantly different from the answers of others with similar characteristics.

Discussion and Conclusions

Using national representative data for the year 1998, our study has examined differences across five regions in Turkey in terms of the impact of modernization on the position of rural women. We found important differences between women living in the countryside and women living in towns. In terms of completing primary education, for example, our results make clear that women in towns have more opportunity to go to school than women in the countryside. The countryside women in the East of Turkey are the most disadvantaged group. Almost 64 percent of them have not completed primary education, whereas it is the case with only 15 percent of the countryside women in the West. There are also very striking differences between these two regions in terms of household income and number of children. In the West, families earn more and have fewer children than in the East.

Women living in towns are better off with regard to educational opportunities and household income, but at the same time they seem to be more dependent on their husbands than are countryside women, because fewer of them are gainfully employed. Of the countryside women more than half declare themselves to be gainfully employed, whereas it is the case for only 30 percent of the town women. Of course, it should not be forgotten that women in the countryside are mostly engaged in (unpaid) farming activities. Nevertheless, regarding participating in the labor force, a clear finding of this study is that women in the towns are marginalized compared to women living in the countryside; that is, the majority of them have dropped out of the labor force and became "housewives." Generally speaking, these results confirm the WAD and GAD argument that women are marginalized during the early stages of the social development. In terms of the socioeconomic differences, the gap between men and the women may temporarily widen to the disadvantage of women.

The situation of the women in the East of the country is much worse than in other regions with regard to almost all indicators of women's status used. The situation of women in this region may be particularly unfavorable because a substantial part of them are not able to speak the official and dominant Turkish language and one-third of them has not had a civil marriage, which makes them dependent on their family members and puts them in a disadvantaged position in terms of legal inheritance rights.

The North of Turkey shows similarities with other regions, but it is also different. Although this region is on the priority list for development by the Turkish State

Planning Organization, the proportion of the households with a low income in the countryside is lower than in any other part of Turkey, and the towns of this region rank second in this respect. These figures may have to do with the fact that in the North much more than elsewhere the husbands are working in nonfarm occupations. Many of the husbands in the North also work away from home. This fact may explain the high level of labor-force participation of women in the countryside of this region and the fact that almost all of these women are working in agriculture: while the husbands are away, the women are running the farm and the market activities. Another explanation may be related to the crop diversification and the natural settings of those villages. Women in the North are usually out of the house for most of the year and carry out their forestry-related economic activities mostly alone. Also, cultural and religious differences may play a role. For example, our study indicates that in the North "only having a religious marriage ceremony" almost lost its importance and that few women consider "the use of family planning as being against religion." Referring to a study in the northwest of Turkey, Chris Hann suggests that maybe in the past "Islam did not play a major part in the daily lives of most of the inhabitants in this region" (cited in Beller-Hann 1991, 260). Also, besides Turks, other ethnic groups are living in this region (for example, Lazis, Hemsins, Georgians, Circassians), and each of these groups has its own local language. However, according to the results of our research, unlike eastern Turkey (where besides Turks, mostly Kurds and Arabic ethnic groups live), not speaking Turkish is not a major concern of the women in the North.

Our findings also indicate that women themselves play a central role in the reproduction of the patriarchal ideology to the next generations. About half of the countryside women and some 40 percent of the town women agree with the statements that "Important decisions should be made by men," "Men are wiser than women," and "Women should not argue with men." The fact that at the same time the majority of those women disagree with the statement "It is better for a male child to have education" might be interpreted as a "success" of the Kemalist educational reforms.

Regarding women's rights, another success of these reforms is related to the prevalence of civil marriage. With the exception of the East, "only having a religious marriage ceremony" to a large extent lost its importance. This fact can be interpreted as a considerable improvement, because without civil marriage women have no legal inheritance rights. On the other hand, our figures make it clear that in the countryside of the East of Turkey, about one-third of the married women remain in a disadvantaged position.

Taken together, our results make clear that there are substantial differences among the regions of Turkey in many aspects of rural women's "status" and that the country still has a long way to go in the area of rural women's emancipation and empowerment.

11 Education, Tradition, and Modernization

Bedouin Girls in Israel

SARAB ABU-RABIA QUEDER

EDUCATION IS WIDELY RECOGNIZED as a key ingredient in national development, community advancement, and women's empowerment. Around the world, educational attainment rates have increased, but problems remain. More women than men remain illiterate, and dropout rates tend to be higher for girls than for boys. Illiteracy and undereducation have wide-ranging ramifications for citizens in general, but women and girls in particular can find themselves in states of dependence and poverty.

This chapter discusses the problem of female Bedouin dropouts from the Bedouin school system in the Negev region of Israel and links the problem to discourses of tradition and modernity. The data were collected from two population groups: Bedouin girls who dropped out of school and their parents and Bedouin girls who did not drop out and their parents. The purpose was to discover why members of the first group terminated their studies and the girls in the second group did not.

The testimonies of the groups investigated reveal a mismatch between modern features that the Bedouin educational system has been forced to accept, especially coeducation, and Bedouin traditions that remain the cultural ethos of the girls' fathers. This mismatch creates conflicts between modernity and tradition among fathers and is one of the most important factors in girls' dropping out of school.

Introduction

Israel has a very high dropout rate (Horowitz 1992; Weizman and Freidman 1994). However, dropping out by female Bedouin from the educational system in the

Negev region is a new phenomenon that has not yet been studied. Although several studies about the Bedouin educational system have been carried out (Abu-Saad 1991, 1995, 1997; Meir and Barnea 1988; Melitz 1995), none deals in depth with the dropout phenomenon in general and female dropouts in particular. The few studies about the dropout problem have been written largely by foreign or male researchers (Ben-David 2000; Hos and Kenan 1997; Meir 1986). This chapter is the first study that explores the female dropout issue from the point of view of a Bedouin female researcher who had an opportunity to investigate the girls directly—an especially important advantage in this sex-segregated society.

Various studies (Ben-David 1982; Katz 1998) indicate that Bedouin females have some of Israel's highest dropout rates. The report by Katz points to dropout rates of 10 percent in the Jewish sector, 40 percent in the Arab sector, and more than 67 percent in the Bedouin sector. According to Abu-Saad (1996), who based his findings on data from the Israel Ministry of Education, more than 80 percent of Bedouin girls do not complete high school. This figure is correct in both recognized and unrecognized settlements. Several neighborhoods in Rahat, the first Bedouin city in Israel, had dropout rates of 100 percent, whereas in Rahat itself dropout rates reaches 40 percent (el-Hosael 1997, table 9). The Katz report suggests that the number of female students rises every year but that the size of the increase declines every year with the rise in class level (see also Central Bureau of Statistics 1999, 78, table f/9).

This chapter explores the reasons for girls dropping out of school by directly investigating the dropouts and their parents. I show that historical factors affecting the situation of the Bedouin minority in Israel and its educational system have a direct effect on dropping out in general and on dropping out of females in particular. It is the clash between these traditional values and modern values, as evinced in schools, that prompts female students to drop out. My study also sheds light on the clash between tradition and modernity and asks what the modern state has done to respect and understand the traditional needs of Bedouin society. I offer a new perception on the traditional nature of society and a way to reach an appropriate solution for the Bedouin, especially for women.

Ethnicity and Education in Israel

Studies on dropouts in various countries (Blackorby and Kortering 1992; Fitzpatrick and Yoel 1992; Klinov 1996; Rumberger 1983, 1987) trace the dropout phenomenon to two main sets of factors: push effects originating in school-related

factors and pull effects stemming from the community and the family. These studies also indicate that political factors affect dropout rates among minority groups
around the world (Colabrese and Poe 1990; Uday 1991). When looking at the
Bedouin society, the main factors for female dropout relate more to pull effects,
originating in the family and the political system, which will be discussed further.

The historical periodization of the Bedouin is directly related to the educational
system that serves this population group. Abu-Saad (1995) divides the history of the
Bedouin and their educational system into three periods: before the State of Israel
was established (up to 1948), from the establishment of Israel until the abolition of
military administration in Bedouin communities (1948–66), and from the abolition of military administration to the present day, including the construction of
seven settlements for the Bedouin.

Before Israel was established, the Bedouin did not receive formal education.
There were no educational programs, and the Bedouin were not interested in learning about issues that were not relevant to their nomadic lifestyle. Instead, they participated in daily processes in a type of informal education called Kutab, in which
boys ages five to twelve acquired basic literacy and the fundamentals of Islam in
classes of twenty.

When the State of Israel was established, the political, social, and economic
order of the Bedouin was disrupted. Most of the tribes were driven off their lands
and moved to Egypt or Jordan. The tribes that remained in Israel lost their freedom
to move about, and the Israeli government recognized only nineteen tribes. Under
the military administration, the Bedouin were distanced from other Arab population groups in the country and were denied access to education and employment
opportunities except where special approval was obtained. During this period, most
schools in the Negev region closed down and relocated to the North. Thus, a whole
generation of Bedouin tribes had no access to formal education.

In 1966, the abolition of military rule led to a welcome turnabout in Bedouin
life. For the first time, the Bedouin were able to interrelate with relatives in Gaza and
the West Bank, and these relations had a positive effect on their attitudes toward education. Before and after that watershed year—from the early 1960s to the late
1970s—the government built seven settlements to modernize the Bedouin. The
modernization drive included the introduction of school systems that practiced coeducation. Despite the change for the better, however, the Bedouin still faced discrimination. Klinov (1996) suggests that the Israeli policy prioritized the needs of
the *mizrahi* ("Oriental") Jewish minority over the Arab citizens and that this preference was expressed at the Resources Division of the Ministry of Education.

Abu-Saad (1998, 1995) explains this situation by offering several examples. First, whereas the Jewish educational system was divided into two subsystems (state and state-religious), the Bedouin educational system had only one. In 1991, 79.9 percent of students in Israel were Jewish, and 20.1 percent were Arab. Second, the recently introduced long school-day program was not implemented in all schools countrywide. Of the schools chosen for the new policy, 135 were Jewish and only 11 (2 percent) were Arab. No Bedouin school in the Negev region was chosen. Furthermore, 95 percent of vocational-inspector hours were allocated to Jewish schools; only 5 percent went to the Arabs. Some 99 percent of counselors' hours went to Jewish schools as against only 1 percent to the Arab sector. Third, Bedouin schools that were built in unrecognized villages were temporary; they had no electricity, running water, scholastic aids, laboratories, or sports equipment (Abu-Saad 1991). Fourth, although the Bedouin localities are connected by roads, the distance between school and home limits access to schools, especially for girls. Many students walk to school every day under difficult topographical and climatic conditions. As a result of all these factors, Bedouin students do not share in learning processes that other students in Israel take for granted (Meir 1997).

Furthermore, the number of professionals responsible for the treatment of dropout students among the Jewish sector covers 53 percent of the needs, compared to only 15.3 percent of the Bedouin's educational system needs. For example, in the Bedouin village of Kseifa, there is only one-half of a standard salaried position, compared to the fourteen positions required by the law. In another Bedouin town, Rahat, there is only one standard salaried position compared to the legal requirement. Out of a budget of 61 million NIS (New Israeli Shekels) required for youth services in the entire country, only 337,000 NIS is allocated to the Negev region. These services operate in ninety-nine local authorities in Israel, thirty of which serve the Arab-speaking sectors, sixteen in northern villages, ten in Druze villages, five in Arab-Jewish villages, and three in recognized Bedouin villages. The local authorities claim that it is not enough. In the Kseifa village schools with a total population of 4,600, some 2,300 hundred of its students come from outside of the village, that is, from unrecognized villages. Fifty percent of these students drop out of school every year and do not receive any remedial services.

Another problem is called the "data problem." This problem indicates that the reported dropout rates by the Ministry of Education do not match the reported data from the local authorities. For instance, in Rahat they report a dropout rate of 40 percent, meaning 337 students out of 526 studied in the twelfth grade in the year 2001 (Beily 2002). However, the Ministry of Education reports a dropout rate of

26.9 percent for students between the ninth and the twelfth grades. This variance raises questions about the quality of the data and the magnitude of the problem. Clearly, there are discrepancies in the calculation of the dropout problem. Whereas the Ministry of Education reports the dropout rates for four grades (from ninth through twelfth), the local authorities report these rates for each grade every year. The Ministry of Education reduces the true dropout rates by reporting only the average for four years.

In any event, comparative data show that the Bedouin have the country's highest dropout rates and lowest rates of high school graduation. Between 1990 and 1995, only 3 to 4 percent of the Bedouin students graduated, as against 16 to 22 percent of Arabs and 37 to 40 percent of Jews (Katz 1998).

Women's Status in Traditional Bedouin Society

In Bedouin society, community policy and members' mobility and prestige are determined by perceptions of honor and shame. A family that has an interest in improving its mobility fulfills its aspirations by confining women to the home so that they may marry, bear children, and increase the family size (Kressel 1993).

Abu-Lughod (1986) suggests that woman's inferiority is a result of her sexuality. Sexuality is associated with reproduction, and reproduction is considered natural. Thus, women are associated with natural things, thus limiting their opportunity to be equal to men. Women lose control over their bodies through sexuality and reproduction. The best way to conceal sexuality is the veil, but the honor perception of the Bedouin also restrains women's behavior by means of *tahashum,* a term denoting bashfulness and modesty (Abu-Lughod 1998). The honor code places limits on Bedouin women in adulthood. Upon puberty, women's appearance in public is limited, and the socialization process continues through the mother only (Emrys 1990; Abu-Ajaj and Ben-David 1988; Kressel 1992). Additionally, Bedouin women are strongly protected under Bedouin law. Any offensive conduct toward them may result in revenge. Women's purity is likened to a glass: once broken, it is difficult if not impossible to restore (Bar-Tzvi 1991).

Girls continue to attend school as long as they are young, although their attendance rates are low because they are required to participate in the family's domestic work (Meir and Barnea 1986). However, gender segregation, covering sexual shame and limiting women's appearances in public, increases females' propensity to drop out of school. Many parents refuse to enroll their daughters in school after they reach puberty because they are afraid that contact between the sexes in school will harm the family's code of honor (Hos and Kenan 1997). Fathers are reluctant to send daughters to school because of the long distances that the girls must cover, either on foot or in mixed-sex buses (Ben-David 2000; Abu-Rabia 1993, 2001).

Thus, the Bedouin regard the educational system as an attempt to instill modernization in a traditional community. Although traditional values remain dominant at home, the educational system enforces different and contrasting values, especially in regard to girls (Abu-Saad 2001). It is this clash between traditional and modern values, coupled with discrimination against this ethnic minority, that eventually results in female dropout.

In this chapter I suggest an alternative for the problem that has been discussed in the mentioned studies.

Research Methodology and Findings

I conducted ethnographic interviews with two generations of women from two groups: educated and dropout girls and their mothers and fathers. To ensure that Bedouin women had an opportunity to express themselves, I used a qualitative research method that bases itself on the actions and meanings of the individual person, who can be understood best through his or her language and attitudes (Berg 1995). This method helped me get to know the interviewees' proximate world, which had not been explored in research thus far. Another advantage of this method was its ability to allow me to ask questions not asked before. Two considerations were kept in mind during the interviews: that all participants should speak the same language (the interviews were conducted in Arabic) and that the questions should be phrased in a way that carried the same meaning for all.

The process of locating the girls, especially the ones in the less educated group, met with obstacles because fathers were sensitive to the issue being studied and were afraid of females' exposure. To locate the dropout girls, I first asked for the names of seventeen-year-old dropouts from the local high school. Finding that inaccuracies in registration undermined the locating process, I carried on by locating dropouts' relatives on the basis of surnames in a "networking" process (Feldman 1981). To induce people to respond to me, I used my role as a teacher in the community and, through my colleagues, was able to visit dropouts at home. Sometimes I had to ask men's permission to interview their daughters and wives. To reach the girls' fathers, I had to ask other males in the community to help me make the initial contact. Most fathers refused to open up or even to meet me because I was a Bedouin woman. It took me a year to locate twelve dropout girls whose parents agreed to participate.

The girls were interviewed in their homes, sometimes in the presence of their mothers and sometimes alone. All interviews with fathers took place at their homes with at least one additional family member present.

I accessed the schoolgirls—all of whom were seventeen years old and had dropped out of school between grades seven and nine—through the local high school. These interviews took place at the school in a classroom that the principal made available to me. To reach their parents, I asked the girls to obtain their parents' permission. At this stage, too, I had to replace one girl with another whose parents would agree to have her interviewed. On the one hand, my status as a Bedouin woman helped me in my access to the community; on the other hand, I could not interview the men without the presence of another family member, owing to the honor code and the segregation norm.

My sample consisted of two groups of interviewees:

• The *educated group* had mothers with nine years of schooling; a few of the mothers had had no education at all. Their average age was forty to forty-five, and they had between seven and nine children. All their husbands were employed; most had finished high school.

• The *less educated group* had mothers with no education at all. Their average age was forty to forty-five, they had more than ten children, and 40 percent of their husbands were unemployed and had an average of seven to nine years of schooling.

What my interviews showed was that the two groups have different attitudes toward and perceptions of females' education and dropping out.

As table 11.1 shows, most of the educated girls (70 percent) decided to attend school because it was their personal wish, which they expressed in different ways: "I want to prove a point not just to my family but for my self-gratification. I get pleasure from it." "I want to be a teacher or something; I feel a desire to continue my studies." "It's my parents' wish and mine, too." "It's my goal to get a professional job that will benefit me." "I really want to succeed in school so that I'll have work, so that I'll be something." and "I love to study. Without a diploma you're worth nothing. An educated person does not experience prejudice. An uneducated person won't solve the problems of violence in life." Thus, most of the girls attend school because of their own inner drive and for their personal and professional satisfaction.

When their mothers were asked, "Why does your daughter go to school?" they spoke about the utility of education, which they expressed in several ways: "Education is the spine of life; when I go to the store I don't understand a thing." "What else? Should I let my daughters be ignorant, like me? That's why I want them to get an education." "It's useful; if her husband dies and she's left with her children, she can

Table 11.1
Educated Girls' and Parents' Attitudes Toward Girls' Education (by Percentage)

Reason for Education	Girls	Mothers	Fathers
Intrinsically important	0	20	40
In daughter's interest	0	20	0
Own wishes	70	0	40
Economic utility	30	60	20

help herself. With an education she can make a living and do well for herself." "Because it's her weapon." "Knowledge is a weapon. If you're educated can read the note by yourself." "Modern times require an education." "It'll help her to help herself and her home in the future." These expressions indicate that since the mothers are undereducated or illiterate, they want their daughters to get an education as a path to a life better than their own.

Fathers were of two minds. Some 40 percent of them supported their daughters' decision to attend school because the girls wished it, as they explained: "She wanted it; if she's interested we don't have any objection." And "As long as she loves studying, her mother and I will support her." Another 40 percent supported the daughters because they value education: "She studies in order to be educated for her own future." "Education is one of life's necessities; as long as she wants it, I approve." Mothers also valued education, but only 20 percent expressed this belief: "She had to be educated. A girl without education isn't worth a thing. It was her decision and ours, too." And "She's good at school. Education is light. We're proud of educated people." It does seem that girls will not attend school unless they wish to do so and unless their fathers support their decision.

Table 11.2 shows that 50 percent of girls blame their school for their decision to drop out: "I knew I wouldn't succeed." "I felt like a stranger." "I didn't like school." "There are boys there who do not respect girls." Thirty percent of the girls trace their dropping out to family factors, that is, a male authority figure who prevents them from attending school: "There were rumors about girls who do things with boys and go out with them behind their parents' back. In my family they don't let any girls go to school. My father told me to stay home, and I didn't disobey him. I did what he said and stayed home." And "It's because of my husband's parents; they didn't want me to go to school." And "My uncle didn't want me to stay there." Twenty percent of the girls left school to help with domestic duties owing to a mother's illness. These

Table 11.2
Attitudes of Dropout Girls and Their Parents Toward Reasons
for Dropping out (by Percentage)

Dropout Reason	Dropout Girls	Mothers	Fathers
Family factors	30	40	60
Domestic duties	20	20	0
School factors	50	10	40
Economic situation	0	10	0
Personal wishes	0	20	0

girls take care of younger brothers, do domestic chores, and act as little mothers in lieu of their own.

In contrast to what the daughters say, 40 percent of mothers believe that their daughters dropped out because of family-related factors: "It's because of Bedouin norms, not because of me. I can't disapprove of my husband's word. This is the how the Bedouin make decisions. It's their custom and it's nothing unusual." And "Her relatives deceived us. Her husband didn't agree that she should stay in school after she got married." "Her uncle and father prevented her from studying, a girl who goes to school gets hurt by gossip and bad rumors because of other girls who ran away with their lovers." "Her father stopped them all. That's the Arab nature; they don't let their girls finish school. Her uncles and relatives also prevent her and her sisters from doing so." The family decision makers, it seems, are not mothers but the male figures: husbands, fathers, and uncles.

Twenty percent of mothers claim that it is their daughters who refuse to go to school: "She didn't want to go." "No one forced her to drop out; it was totally up to her."

Sixty percent of fathers claim that it is a male figure who prevents the girls from attending school: "After ninth grade, we stopped sending her to school because there were young boys there who distracted her." "It's a usual thing among us that she gets married when she reaches ninth or tenth grade." "We made a mistake with her life; many men asked for her hand, but we preferred that she get married instead of having men visit her every day. I don't want there to be gossip or bad rumors about her." Most fathers admit that they wish to stop their daughters from attending school because of early marriage customs.

In sum, fathers and mothers blame family factors for female dropout, but half of the girls view reality differently, blaming their schools, while 30 percent blame the family. How can girls who live with their parents have a dissenting view of reality? My assumption is that it is their way of rejecting the domination of a male figure. It is an act of sublimation; they find it easier to blame schools for their situation than to confront male domination.

In another finding, 20 percent of dropouts—who were married at age fifteen and had children—completed their studies at a women's basic-education institute in town. They did so with their young husbands' approval, and their goal was to earn a diploma and find a job.

What do these findings tell us about females' education in a traditional, sex-segregated society?

Discussion and Recommendations

Bedouin girls drop out of school because of a clash between traditional values (sex segregation) and modern values (coeducation), in a distinct example of marginalization of women as passive victims in the process of modernization in a traditional society—a process linked to globalization. The case at hand shows that when a modern state offers the Bedouin an education as part of the modernization process, it fails to consider the needs of women in this community and the community's traditional values. Bedouin girls have a high dropout rate because of Israel's coeducational policy. By pursuing such a policy, Israel helps to discriminate against women by setting new conditions for them, conditions that men do not face in their efforts to access educational institutions. The modern concept of coeducation is not beneficial to a society that forbids women to appear in public. The state has, in fact, extended a limitation of the private sphere to the public sphere. I argue that the concept of modernization in traditional societies should be subverted.

El-Saadawi (1997) explains that women in third world and postcolonial countries are the persons most severely harmed by the globalization processes that are being imposed by Western capitalist countries. These women are torn between two representative models: On the one hand, they surrender to the influence of globalization by imitating modern values, even though they do not change in essence. On the other hand, the traditional community calls for the preservation of traditional values. This tension may be resolved only through the creation of local feminine thought that exists as a part of the local culture and in consonance with its own values.

In the case of Bedouin women, too, the solution should be devised within the culture and the community and should use traditional tools, even if these tools seem to be anything but modern. To lower the female dropout rate, the solution that would bring some girls back is the establishment of sex-segregated schools. It would create choice and opportunity for fathers who are afraid to enroll their daughters in mixed-sex schools. In this fashion, the Bedouin community would at least avoid the loss of an entire generation of educated women. The reenrollment of 20 percent of married dropouts in a sex-segregated institute would be an appropriate solution for a sex-segregated society. It would encourage women who cannot fulfill their wishes in the modern school to obtain an education without subverting social norms.

Another strategy, used by schoolgirls' fathers, is the preservation of modest attire in the public domain. This practice extends the concealment practices from the private sphere to the public sphere. An additional example, this one used by mothers, is to view economic utility as an answer to the needs of women as women; this strategy makes it easier for them to accept the intermingling of boys and girls, and of members of different tribes, in schools.

This kind of thinking does not exist among families of dropouts. Because of their lack of education and their state of unemployment, they are unfamiliar with the daily difficulties of life and the importance of education as a tool for social mobility. It may also be stated that girls cannot attend school without the approval of the dominant male figure at home. Even married dropouts depended on their husbands' support.

The approach that this study wishes to promote is called "entryism" (a term coined in Helie-Lucas 1993)—a feminist strategy for women's action that flows from the community and its traditional values. Entryism is suitable for women who wish to introduce changes in their communities but cannot use revolutionary approaches that contravene local traditional values.

Studies by women on the Middle East (Afshar 1997; Ahmed 1982; Nelson and Altorki 1998; Tucker 1993) are highly critical of modernization in the case of traditional societies. They dispute the claim that modernization spares women from discrimination. Many traditional Muslim women struggle with and disapprove of the modern Western solution, which charges them a high price that they are not willing to pay. They prefer to seek another path that would be more acceptable. Only by returning to traditional roots will such women be able to progress in their lives. Unable to cross patriarchal limits, they must create new alternatives. The solution that comes out of the local values that does not match modern-global values, is indicative of the otherness discourse that occurs between the other and the self from an ethnocentric perception of the self. In this study it is represented by the Israeli view toward the other—the Arab-Bedouin minority. This perception sees the Bedouin as the other as it is perceived in the colonial discourse. This discourse sees the other's values, needs, and culture from a Western perspective and thought.

Bhabha (1994) claims that this discourse is racist because it is made of boundaries, differences, and discrimination. Bhabha perceives the aim of this discourse as
producing cultural, historical, and political differences and ignoring them at the
same time. It also produces disadvantaged and subordinated subjects who should
be saved, relieved, and improved by the civilized Western colonial mission. But in
the name of this mission, the subordinated subject is pushed to the margins.

Furthermore, Sharabi (1990) claims that the social knowledge of the non-
Westerns was developed, by intention, in political-analysis categories in order to understand the other. When the hidden aim of these categories is revealed, it shows
how cultural binaries between the other and the self are made, that is, the binaries of
primitive-civilized and traditional-modern. These differences serve the West's attitude toward the "Other." Here, two hidden assumptions are made. One is that the
non-Western other will always be behind and will catch up the modern Western; the
other is that this Other has a different destiny and will always be "the other." Sharabi
asserts that the first assumption is built on the Western experience toward "change";
Westerners see it as a process of progress toward modernism, science, and technological development. The second assumption is built on the perception that non-
Western cultures belong to another existence and develop through different
impulses.

Applying this framework helps us to understand how and why notions of modernization have not "liberated" Bedouin women. When "modern education" is imposed on the Bedouin community by the colonizer, women pay the price. Bedouin
females drop out of school as a result of a clash between the other and the self, that
is, between the Bedouin's perception of themselves and the Israelis' perception of
the Bedouin.

In the Bedouin case, the solution should come from the state. It is the state's obligation, because the Bedouin in Israel are an ethnic minority that faces discrimination and lacks the means to create alternatives. If the state fails to provide the right
solution, Bedouin women will remain torn between two states and two forms of
"Otherness": as women in traditional society and as an ethnic minority in modern
thought. Although the release of this otherness requires a new discourse, a postcolonial discourse that challenges the colonial mission and thought, there is still much
that the Israeli state can do to encourage equity and empowerment in the Arab-
Bedouin community, and especially for the women. It must draw on the cultural resources of the Bedouin and increase financial resources to the community.

12 Museum Feminization?

Women and Museum Employment in Jordan

CAROL MALT

MUSEUMS ARE AN IMPORTANT FORCE in the cultural past, present, and future of the Middle East. They also contribute to the independence and economic support of women. Although women are participants in the founding, development, and management of museums today, in the past several factors have traditionally worked against their representation and participation in museums throughout the world. Women were not often perceived as a legitimate constituency by museum administrators, or by women themselves. And even today, they are often considered legitimate only if they are involved with the usual women's interests of jewelry, costume, and the decorative arts or as they relate to a famous spouse or relative. Further, women in museum leadership have tended not to view history, their history, as empowerment.

The literature provides ample evidence of the value of museums as storehouses, entertainment centers, and educators as well as the changing role of museums and how they are agents of democracy. For example, George Hein and Mary Alexander reveal the contributions of museums to the educational system in *Museums: Places of Learning* (1998), while John H. Falk and Lynn D. Dierking investigate how museums serve communities in *Learning from Museums: Visitor Experiences and the Making of Meaning* (2000). Flora E. S. Kaplan, in *Museums and the Making of "Ourselves": The Role of Objects in National Identity* (1994), points out that museums seem to thrive best in democracies, and Jorge E. Hardoy, in *The Popular Sum of Knowledge and the Museum* (1986, 17), continues the premise that a museum, a place for collective thought, analyses, and discussion, presents the most direct path to development for a country and the most direct support that can be given to a democracy. There are few references in the literature, however, to the role of women in the museum profession.

Internationally, the late 1990s were challenging times for museums and for the

women who served in them. Museums were beginning to play an active role economically and educationally in the Middle East and were also being credited as
agents of democratization. Women, as they assumed leadership in the museum domain, were contributing to these changes in museums. Along the way, women were
benefiting economically, participating in the workforce, and helping to bring
women's history to the forefront.

At the Freer Gallery in Washington, D.C., during a meeting of the North American Historians of Islamic Art several years ago, Islamic art scholar Dr. Esin Atil surprised me with the question: "Did you know that there are more women curators
and administrators working in museums in the Middle East than there are in the
United States and Europe combined?" The creation of museums has been an important goal of Middle Eastern countries. The fact that women have been involved
in the development and administration of museums in the Middle East may seem
inconsistent with Western perceptions of that part of the world, however.

Why is it that women have been such an important force in the founding and
management of museums in the Middle East? Who were these women, why did they
choose the museum profession, what obstacles did they face, and how have they affected society through museum programs on issues such as women's history and
national identity? These questions led me to pursue research on women and museums in Jordan and Palestine in 1998–99. This chapter, which focuses on Jordan, addresses these questions.[1] In Jordan, twenty-four of the thirty-six museums have
been curated or administered (or both) by women, and seven of the museums were
founded by women. Those numbers grew with the opening of three new museums
in 2002: the Numismatic Museum of the Jordan National Bank, the City Hall Museum, and the Royal Car Museum.

Women and Work in the Middle East: An Overview

In the Middle East, the role of women as workers outside the home has changed
greatly over the centuries, expanding or diminishing as the economics and customs
of the area changed. The degree of their participation also changed according to
their social status and ethnic or tribal group. Historically, women have been excluded from the power structure as their society became economically divided into
public and private sectors. Eventually, traditions and customs gained legitimacy, be-

1. The research was made possible by a Fulbright-Hays grant. This paper is based on my book
Women's Voices in Middle East Museums: Case Studies in Jordan (2005).

came entrenched, and solidified the separateness of these domains. Globalization and urbanism have had a dramatic effect on the treatment of and the opportunities for women.

Although women had achieved recognition for their work in specialized professions since pre-Islamic times, it was not until the nineteenth century that intellectuals and the emerging middle class began to advocate the public education and participation of women. However, is the education that women now have only a veneer under which women's traditional role remains unchanged? Will her identifiers always be her family, her virginity, her marriage, her ability to bear sons, and her relationship with her mother-in-law? Director of the Sakakini Cultural Center in Ramallah, Adila Laidi, conceded, "The reality is that one isn't a self-contained unit. You are part of a family, your husband, and his reputation. If a woman isn't married, it could be a problem. You aren't considered by yourself here. Your competence isn't on the strength of your résumé. You are a package" (interview, Feb. 25, 1999, Ramallah).

Many educated women who work in Jordan's museums are aware of the dichotomy they represent. They are spokespersons and perhaps role models for the goals of the kingdom, the development of the economy, and the modernization of traditional society. They interact internationally with their peers in the West or Far East, yet at the same time they are charged with the responsibility of bearing the moral and cultural values of their society as child bearers and symbols of traditional conservatism. This dual responsibility to themselves and other women, particularly in the younger generation, can be confusing. Museologist Hanan al-Kurdi in Amman acknowledges, "Overall, women are confused now that they are 'outside the house' " (interview, Apr. 13, 1999).

In England in 1998, speaking at a Lord Caradon Lecture on women and Islam, Jordan's Princess Sarvath proclaimed that Jordan's laws were conducive to women attaining a status in keeping with the essence of the religion and the aspirations of the leadership of the country. She confirmed that Islam "gave women the right to paid work, to own, inherit and bequeath property, and to learning . . . and that women are involved in many aspects of leadership in the country, they stand for election, serve in Parliament, hold responsible government positions and are actively involved in every sphere of life" ("Princess Sarvath" 1998). Jordan's Princess Basma has spent years developing women's awareness and participation in society and now chairs two women's organizations. These two women show the very public support of the government and the royal family for women's political, educational, and economic advancement.

During the past few decades, as educational opportunities increased for women, an overall shortage of professionals encouraged the employment of all the middle class, both men and women. But the kinds of work offered to women of the lower classes were limited, and often these women were relegated to job situations that kept them in the kitchens or in the traditional women's arenas of craft making, teaching other females, or nurturing. Development usually favors men, and women are often relegated to noncompetitive work. Women may freely participate, but only in the limited arenas designated as "women's professions." The middle classes in Jordan found better opportunities, less opposition to participation in the growing economy, and higher levels of acceptance by both their families and the public than did the lower classes (Quinn 1977, 185). But women in 1999 still constituted less than 16 percent of the labor force, and their average work period was approximately 3.7 years in comparison to 44.8 years for men (Hamdan 2000, 3).

In her foreword to Nawal el-Saadawi book *The Hidden Face of Eve: Women in the Arab World,* Irene Gendzier discredits the notion that modernization and development automatically improve the status of women (1982, x). She argues that just as economic development is not identical with growth, neither is the increasing participation of women in the labor force in itself an automatic guarantee of improvements in women's status. Abla Amawi points out that women in the Jordanian workforce are "comparatively skilled and well educated. Of the Jordanian women who work outside the home, 46.4% are in professional or technical jobs. . . . [O]ther data suggest that the smaller female workforce is much better educated and skilled than its male counterpart and . . . that legally . . . women enjoy equal protection with men under Jordanian labor law and civil service regulations" (1996b, 85).

Changes in women's rising economic status often involve allowing them to enter new work arenas and undertake new roles. In addition to their employment as staff in civil service jobs, two other areas of women's participation that have grown dramatically are in nonprofit women's organizations such as the Queen Alia Foundation and the Noor al-Hussein Foundation and in museum work.

What seems to make museum work an acceptable, even desirable, profession for women? Could it be the exclusivity or the perceived idea that curating, collecting, displaying, and inventorying constitute women's work, a women's profession? Are there few other creative opportunities for women professionals? Is it the controlled environment—is it an allowed profession? Or is museum work the only nonphysical option for women with a degree in archaeology? Is it acceptable because it is a motherly profession in a patriarchal society and noncompetitive with men? Could this choice of profession stem from a passion for order or a statement of pride in one's heritage? In fact, all of the above are true.

Judith Tucker points to the major influence that women have had on the development of cultural life in the Middle East, especially in the realm of high culture. Further, she cites the upper-class tradition of educating women that produced several "women of letters" in the nineteenth century (1999, 88). That tradition laid the foundation for women to play a central role in the development of new art forms in the twentieth century, including the visual arts and the establishment of museums. Women in Jordan have become leaders in museum work; in addition, Adila Laidi, director of the Sakakini Art Center in Ramallah, confirms that women are active in the arts in the Palestine Territories (interview, Feb. 25, 1999).

The Feminization of Museum Work?

Why are women represented in such a high percentage in Jordan's museums? Museum work is among the career options available for university archaeology graduates, but is availability the reason it is chosen? Love of history and a desire to be near the artifacts of history were given as reasons, as were love for one's heritage and a passion for research. "You have to love your work—why else would you put up with the smell of this naphthalene?" said the curator of the Museum of Popular Traditions in Amman (interview, Huda Kilani, Mar. 24, 1999). "Museum work? It's a polite job," explained the administrator of the museum at the University of Jordan (interview, Manal Awamleh, Mar. 14, 1999, Amman).

Studies have shown that there appears to be a very low preference by females in Muslim countries for becoming sales workers. It is an occupation in which the possibility of indiscriminate contact with outsiders is highest. This fact might reinforce the thought that women who work in museums are in some way protected from public contact or that there is an aura of isolation or exclusivity about the work. Perceptions such as "Only nice people come to museums, so it's a career women are safe in" reflect the idea that there is an association of respectability about museums, which is why women are attracted to them and men deem them acceptable (interview, Jafar Tukan, Dec. 21, 1998, Amman). Further, few men work in museums.

Who are the women in Jordan who founded, support, or work in museums? The founders are Hidea Abaza, the Folklore Museum; Princess Wijdan Ali, Ph.D., the Jordan National Gallery; Naeimeh Asfour, the Stamp Museum; Nazmieh Rida Tawfiq Darwish, the King Abdullah Museum; Aida Naghawieh, the Islamic Museum; Suha Shoman, the Darat al-Funun, and Sa'adieh al-Tel, the Museum of Popular Traditions. More recently, Queen Rania has championed the Children's Museum that is under construction at Al-Hussein Park in Amman.

Twenty-four women have been involved with Jordanian museum work as curators and administrators. Those women I interviewed included Ruba Abu Dalu, Irbid Archaeology Museum; Manal Awamleh, University of Jordan Museums; Temara Bermamet, Jordan Archeological Museum; Sawsan al-Fakhri, Aqaba district administrator; Hanan Gammoh, Haya Cultural Center; Muasar Hadidi, Salt Folklore Museum; Lubna Hashem, Museum with No Frontiers; Hyat al-Kadi, Jordan Archaeological Museum; Alia Khasowne, Irbid Archeology Museum; Huda Kilani, Museum of Popular Traditions; Wafa'a Mansour, the Museums at Madaba; Arwa Masaadeh, Kerak Museum; Jan Mufti, Darat al-Funun; Eman Oweis, Jerash Archeological Museum; Eman al-Qudah, Folklore Museum; Zahida Safer, Central Bank Numismatic Museum; Nihad al-Shabar, Yarmouk University Museum; and Suhair Shadid, Geological Museum. In addition, I also met women arts activists, collectors, art educators, and nonadministrative workers affiliated with museums in the context of this research, interviewing an additional thirteen women.

All of the women I interviewed held university degrees. Many held a bachelor degree in archaeology from the University of Jordan, and several held higher degrees in that field. Others had degrees in law, art history, fine arts, education, geology, or political science. Four held a Ph.D. Their ages varied. Some began their involvement with museums in the 1970s; however, the majority of women were in their thirties.

Both ethnicity and religion were identified in this study. Of the thirty-six women I interviewed working in or affiliated with Jordan's museums, twenty-six were Muslim; among that group, three wore the *hijab*, and ten were from the Circassian ethnicity. Circassians (both men and women) make up a large percentage of professionals in the broad cultural workforce in proportion to the entire population. Nine of the thirty-six women were Christian. Two of them, who did not wish to be quoted, believed that Islam restricted them. They believed that they had to conform to the Muslim way of life publicly and that their career opportunities may have been hindered because they were a minority. However, they added that their professional relationships with Muslim women in the museum workforce were religion-blind.

Several women in my study were discouraged from a career in archaeology or museology. Nazmieh Rida Tawfiq Darwish confided that her professor at the university questioned her desire to go into archaeology, telling her: "That's a goat's life."

She rebutted, "I want to be a goat" (interview, Apr. 1, 1999, Amman). She subsequently became the director of the new Directorate of Museums.

Many achieved their education in spite of the great economic hardship on their families. Others seemed destined to work in museums: artist and art historian Wijdan Ali, when she saw the need for a place to showcase Jordan's fine arts; likewise, artist Suha Shoman, when she saw the need for a place where artists, writers, and musicians could freely interact and explore creativity, and knew with the support of the Arab Bank, she could develop such a place. Arwa Masaadeh seemed destined for her work in a museum (interview, Apr. 6, 1999, Kerak). She followed in the footsteps of her parents. Although they had no professional training for their work in Kerak's museums, they were an early support system for her and helped define her goals. Others had told her that archaeology was not for girls, and coming from a small town, she faced many obstacles in pursuit of her career. While conducting fieldwork for her degree, she would go to work at five in the morning and return home covered with dust. Initially, townspeople criticized her and told her that her work was for a man. But the next year they stopped her in the street and asked her what she was doing. They grew used to her, but always asked her if she had found the gold yet.

For Huda Kilani, museum work was also an early goal. She recalled visiting the Museum of Popular Traditions in Amman while still a student at the University of Jordan. She met founder Mrs. Tel and was told they needed help. That was all it took. She soon became committed to museum work: "I've reached my goal. To be a curator was my dream. And you don't get your goals easily" (interview, Mar. 2, 1999, Amman).

Interest in Jordan's history and in the material culture of the past was the reason Eman al-Qudah of the Folklore Museum in Amman chose museum work: "I'm interested in the traditional life in Jordan" (questionnaire, Jan. 15, 1999, Amman). Working in a museum allowed her to be near the objects. Eman Oweis has worked many years in the museum at Jerash. "Initially I wanted to study philosophy, later history. I wanted to know more about the past" (questionnaire, Apr. 2, 1999, Jerash). Museum work has allowed her to combine her many interests.

Other women were inspired by the abundant antiquities around them, including Lubna Hashem, who credited her family for instilling a love of museums in her and recalled how she accompanied them when they traveled abroad and visited museums. Siham Balqar, former curator of the Jordan Archeological Museum, drew upon her experience of living in a land rich in antiquities in choosing her career. For her, working in a museum seemed to have many assets: dealing with the objects, the visitors, and the research.

All of the women interviewed believed that women had special or unique apti-tudes that they could bring to museum work. As women, most thought they were better suited for the job of curator than a man. In Aqaba, Sawsan al-Fakhri noted that women have a "touch." They save things in the home, and they know how to decorate—something they learned from their mothers. And as a mother herself, she could talk to children. Huda Kilani also recognized women's unique aptitudes: "Mu-seums need a woman's touch, and women are more suitable for this work." She also added, "Men are better at administration" (interview, Mar. 24, 1999, Amman). Eman Oweis concurred: "Women have a way . . . to show the objects, to show them well. I make the displays; we women sew. And for the tourists, women can speak well . . . and be friendly" (interview, Apr. 2, 1999, Jerash). Arwa Masaadeh mentioned that she added a feminine touch to her museum environment. She brought plants into the office, helped to redecorate when she came, and cleaned often because the men did not notice those things (interview, Apr. 6, 1999, Kerak).

Could these comments imply that curatorial work in museums *is not* a man's job and that museum administration *is* a man's job? Director and curator of the new Numismatic Museum of the Jordan National Bank, Dr. Nayef Ghassous, observed that there were "Many women in numismatics. They have more patience. Addition-ally, working women are men and ladies at the same time, because of their obliga-tions in the home and the workplace" (interview, Apr. 6, 1999, Amman).

Working Conditions

What are the conditions that these women work under? Do the same labor laws and government policies apply equally to men and women in Jordan's museums? Of the twenty-nine positions in government-sponsored and university museums, thirteen were held by women. In both discussions and on questionnaires, the women in my research group denied government policies of preference for men, citing the equal pay scale for men and women and mentioning the fact that any preference "is not necessary now . . . or, maybe it was before, with older men" (questionnaire, Muasar Hadidi, Mar. 20, 1999, Salt). Concerning preferences for male workers, Eman Oweis thought it was the contrary: "Women hold higher positions in most museums in Jordan" (questionnaire, Apr. 2, 1999, Jerash), and Ruba Abu Dalu thought "the op-posite was right. That they prefer women in museum jobs more than men" (ques-tionnaire, Dec. 12, 1998).

Two women, however, acknowledged that men might have been given the ad-vantage for jobs right after the draft ended, when the peace treaty with Israel was signed. Siham Balqar concluded: "In general, men in Jordan have the advantage of employment—but not in museums." She believed, however, "it would never happen that a lady becomes director general of the department" (interview, Apr. 12, 1999, Amman). Only one former curator, Hanan al-Kurdi, who had just returned from Canada with a master's in museology, believed that preferences might exist at the upper management levels (interview, Apr. 13, 1999, Amman). Twelve in my research group desired further training in museology, which they acknowledged would put them in a position of consideration for advancement, but could not balance their work and their family life and continue their education.

Given these attitudes, did the women in this study believe they had the same goals or opportunities as their male coworkers? Among the older women (age group forty to fifty) in government museums in Salt, Jerash, and Amman, several agreed. But others differed. Two curators thought that although the incentives to work were the same, such as equal pay, they were not interested in adding more administrative responsibilities to their jobs: "I don't want to be the director. There's too much responsibility. I have enough at home" (interview, Temara Bermamet, Dec. 30, 1998, Amman), and "It is not part of my personality to be on the top" (interview, Huda Kilani, Mar. 24, 1999, Amman). But quite the opposite view came from two women from private museums who asserted: "I am competitive. My goal is to be assistant director or director" (interview, Hanan al-Kurdi, Apr. 13, 1999, Amman), and another declared her "ambition was to go solo" (questionnaire, Jan Mufti, Apr. 4, 1999, Amman). Many women curators in government museums, including Temara Bermamet, expressed their personal goals through reference to the goals of their institution: "to help visitors, especially children, understand the history of Jordan" (questionnaire, Apr. 12, 1999), and Eman Oweis, who wanted to help plan a "garden inside the ruins of Jerash . . . and a hotel and a whole new museum for mosaics, marble statues, and inscriptions" (interview, Apr. 2, 1999, Jerash).

What kinds of support did women curators and administrators receive in pursuing their education and in their museum work? Although many women gave credit to their mothers as being an inspiration, only two curators, Hanan al-Kurdi and Arwa Masaadeh, admitted to having nonfamily mentors, both of whom were men. Eman Oweis in Jerash and Sawsan al-Fakhri in Aqaba mentioned that their fathers supported their decision for higher education and choice of profession. Al-Fakhri's mother thought it would be too hot under the sun for her daughter to have a career in archaeology, but her father prevailed. Oweis credited her husband for his support of her career.

Arwa Masaadeh, one of the youngest curators, gave credit to her director, Dr.

Bisheh, for his support. "I felt strange. I was a girl, unmarried. I had to prove myself. My director said I would be good at the job—to phone him if I needed help—and a couple of times when the men here didn't like what I planned I called him and he backed me up" (interview, Apr. 6, 1999, Kerak). Since 1983 her mother, Fowzia Zayyaden, had worked in various jobs at the Kerak museum. She had no formal schooling after secondary school and bore eight children. When they grew up, she went to work. Her husband insisted that all the children get an education, even the girls. "My husband worked at the museum in the morning, me in the afternoon. He died six years ago. All my children are getting an education. I must work to get this education for my kids. I've asked myself why I suffered with a big family—two or three are enough in these hard times. Nowadays, girls must have an education for the future—if she doesn't marry, she has to take care of herself" (interview, Apr. 6, 1999, Kerak).

What advice did these curators and administrators give to women just entering the museum profession? Some gave practical advice; others shared personal thoughts. "Read a lot. Work from the heart," advised Eman Oweis (interview, Apr. 2, 1999, Jerash). "Have a lot of patience and a good command of foreign languages," and, Temara Bermamet added, "If they work in a government-sponsored museum, they should know that not all the things they wish will come true" (interview, Apr. 12, 1999, Amman). "They should believe in what they are doing," said Huda Kilani (interview, Mar. 24, 1999, Amman). Muasar Hadidi advocated specific study to include museology, being more social than any other women, having good experience, participating in educational events and lectures at institutions, and following the local mayor and his activities (questionnaire, Mar. 20, 1999).

Ruba Abu Dalu challenged newcomers to the profession: "Loving this work as a thing private and special; trying to know and learn as much as possible about museum work, then everything will come" (interview, Dec. 12, 1998, Irbid). Suha Shoman's advice was to pass things on to the next generation and credited Princess Fahrelnissa Zeid for giving her the vision to do so (interview, Jan. 26, 1999, Amman).

Women, Work, and Family

There is a pattern to the age of women who successfully participate in the museum workforce today. Older women are more successful and dynamic in achieving their goals. That judgment seems a logical conclusion about the professional working woman, but in addition, there seems to be a connection between the amount of power a woman has in general in Middle Eastern society and her age. Obviously, women in the workforce, married or not, are often given increased responsibility as they grow older, but this fact does not reflect just the passage of time. Some of this personal accomplishment relates to their husbands' success and to their sons, but not all. Also, older women holding administrative positions in the government or the private sector may not be perceived as a threat to the social or cultural disintegration of the country as long as they are wives and mothers or make symbolic concessions of behavior toward gender segregation and dress in the workplace.

In addition, for educated, unmarried, or married women of the middle class, there is less of a conflict between their personal choice of lifestyle and career and the restraints of religion or tradition after menopause. Norma Yessayan, former assistant at the Jordan National Gallery who once ran as a candidate for Parliament, pointed out that as an older woman she had no problems working with other male staff. "We never talked about the fact that I was a woman. I am older, so it's easier" (interview, Nov. 1998, Amman). Likewise, in midcareer, Hanan al-Kurdi equated the advantage of age to when people begin to take you seriously.

Regardless of their education or position, all the women interviewed agreed that women in the Middle East live and work first and foremost as members of their own families. Within this family unit, most women are totally responsible for the care of children. These working women handle their child care and family responsibilities differently. Within the Department of Antiquities there were no provisions for such care at any museum site. However, many women mentioned their maternity-leave benefit of forty to sixty days and that child-care service might be under consideration at the department in Amman (for example, interview, Aida Naghawieh, Jan. 27, 1999, Amman).

At the Numismatic Museum of the Central Bank, two women employees, both married with children, had different solutions to the problem of child care. Both worked from 7:45 A.M. to 4 P.M., with Fridays and Saturdays off. Ghada Gordlow, a Christian and a young mother of two, had a maid to help with the children while she was at work. Her coworker Rabiha Qorani, a Muslim, had four children, the youngest seven years old. She had no hired child-care help. She balanced her work and domestic responsibilities by rising early each morning, helping her family off to school and work, then preparing their dinner before leaving home. Ruba Abu Dalu in Irbid had two young children who were in a nearby school. If there were any problems, she counted on her mother for help. Curator Temara Bermamet in Amman often relied on her mother-in-law and said it was difficult for women, especially during the holidays, when they worked. "Where to put my children? The nursery school is closed, so I have to give my son to my mother-in-law" (interview, Temara Bermamet, Apr. 12, 1999, Amman). Many working women without domestic help found that astute planning, coupled with work hours that often ended at 2 P.M., allowed them to continue traditional family schedules.

Although the women in my study in Jordan have won the right to work, they have not been relieved of social stereotypes or domestic responsibilities. The fact that women were participating economically in their family's future had little effect on the traditional expectations or demands of their families. They were still expected to maintain domestic duties. Many women mentioned they were considered role models and believed they had to be exemplary, even better than men were, on the job.

True, as women, they received equal pay, but what about the other aspects of their jobs, like opportunities for advancement or personal-goal achievement? In calling for a balance between the traditional and the new, Ruba Abu Dalu provided an interesting perspective. She believed that women must fully participate in society, and a way to do so was through women's organizations. "All women need more political and legal background . . . advice on how to transcend their traditional roles while maintaining the support of their families and community" (interview, Dec. 12, 1998, Irbid).

In the early 1980s, Nawal el-Saadawi discussed indicators of job equality in the broad Middle Eastern arena: "Women who are employed in government administration or elsewhere in the public sector are paid equal wages as compared to men. However, they are not afforded the same opportunities for promotion, or for appointment to responsible jobs or for training directed towards the preparation of employees for the higher positions" (1982, 187). Twenty-five years later, the situation seems not to have changed significantly. Though women who work in museum-related government jobs in the Department of Antiquities in Jordan confirmed that they receive equal pay, upon further discussion they revealed that men in their department whose wives did not work received fifteen Jordanian dinars more. In addition, after a female employee's death, her children cannot receive her retirement pension. However, when a male retiree dies, a wife can receive his pension until her death, and their children can do so until they are eighteen (interview, Aida Naghawieh, Jan. 27, 1999, Amman).

Discussing equality in the workforce, Temara Bermamet acknowledged equal pay and added that women received other kinds of benefits, including maternity leave. She added, "Women can leave work one hour early to breast-feed their children—for up to one year." Asked what her male coworkers thought about this benefit, she answered, "They are happy they don't have to do that!" (interview, Apr. 12, 1999, Amman).

To many of the women interviewed in government museums, the issue of individuality—the focus on personal satisfaction—was an unaccustomed goal and an uncomfortable one. "Individuality" was also sometimes thought of as an indulgent Western goal or a form of narcissism, whereas "identity" for them is contained in the collective selfhood found in their society through kinship ties and the extended family. Further, "individuality" was often equated with "more responsibility." Curators revealed their feelings in many ways. For instance, questions about career goals were often answered by collective ways to better their departments or were directed toward the needs of their peers. In Amman, for example, Lubna Hashem was comfortable only as a team member and was dedicated to the concept of her virtual museum and focused on making it a success. Although many women actually held no power over long-range policies or decisions in Jordanian museums, they assumed responsibility for the day-to-day success of museum operations. They also recognized that advancement meant involvement in the male world of politics and bureaucracy, areas that they were not trained for.

Dealing as it was with educated women of the middle and upper classes, this research involved women who acknowledged they had already achieved many of their professional goals. They had the benefit of hindsight because there were no such career opportunities in the past. Progress is comparative and situational; so is perspective. In my study, only Hanan al-Kurdi actively challenged the system. At that time, she was looking for a position in museum work. Three offered suggestions for change in their reports but received no responses—suggestions such as monthly meetings for staff, operational computers, training seminars, and budget reform. For almost all of these women, professional inequality and gender bias seemed to be outside their area of concern. One curator thought that "being a woman was a plus. I never felt discriminated against. We were protected . . . even when we archaeologists went out in the desert. But with other women, we were competitive" (interview, Aida Naghawieh, Jan. 27, 1999, Amman).

Did the fact that these women had achieved so much blind them to equality for other women? The usual avenues for developing sisterhood awareness such as clubs, literature, affinity groups, and conferences were not promoted or available. Moreover, there was a paucity of networking and mentoring activities. Rula Qsoos at the Department of Antiquities argued, "We have no time to change the world" (interview, Jan. 15, 2000, Amman). Mentoring activities were at best subtle between women and almost negligible between women and men. Two female administrators admitted they preferred hiring men: Zahida Safer at the Central Bank and Suha Shoman at the Darat al Funun. Both explained that women leave jobs because of personal or family reasons more often than men do, and employers see it as a loss of invested time and training.

Did the women I interviewed know about feminist or women's organizations in Jordan? Yes, all were aware. Did they support these organizations? Two-thirds of the respondents to my questionnaire said yes, they did. Many of the women I interviewed in the museums of Salt, Kerak, and Amman were sympathetic to feminist issues and believed they should be active, but were not. Only two said they belonged to Jordanian women's organizations; however, some were members of the United Nations Women's Guild and the International Council of Museums through the Department of Antiquities. The most common response to membership or involvement in women's empowerment organizations was that they had no time for such activities. Women's organizations in Jordan exist on several levels for different purposes, mostly as support groups in the nonprofit sector whose concerns are politics and social welfare. Other international service organizations, such as Rotary, serve women in the business community. There is no Jordanian professional union or organization for museum workers. The professional women in my study have not developed or utilized such organizations fully as resources for mentoring, socializing, or networking.

Summary and Conclusions

The research interviews and questionnaires showed that women are represented at the administrative level in twenty-four of Jordan's thirty-six museums—approximately 67 percent—confirming my premise that this profession holds much promise for women in Jordan, and perhaps elsewhere. The majority of the women I interviewed were between the ages of thirty and forty; the second most active age group was forty to fifty. They were predominantly Muslim (72 percent), and three of these women wore the *hijab*. Seventy percent were Jordanian natives, and 13 percent of this group were Circassian. Seventeen percent were Palestinian. All of the women held university degrees, most often in archaeology; 25 percent held a master's degree. Seventy-one percent of the administrators and curators in my study were married. Two-thirds were sympathetic to women's organizations in Jordan, although only two were active in them, while three believed the organizations were unnecessary or a waste of time.

The women in my study all believed that they held special or unique aptitudes for museum work. Many believed they were better suited for the job than men. Others expressed the opinion that the administrative or bureaucratic operation of museums was better served by men, abdicating a leadership role and subjugating themselves to the system. Nevertheless, the women were goal oriented. For example, two founder-administrators of private museums who had set their own goals, spoke of the future: Wijdan Ali's objective was "the promotion of world peace through the advancement of the arts and the eradication of cultural apartheid" (curriculum vitae, 1999), and Suha Shoman referenced President John F. Kennedy's concept of service: "We should be doing something for the country. We are, as artists, witnesses of our time; we are the true historians. We should be doing something for the country" (interview, Jan. 26, 1999, Amman).

It is evident from this research that women are attracted to museum work, that men allow this career choice, and that the profession is perceived as safe and honorable. Although women in Jordanian society still identify with the traditional careers of educator or nurse, today there are more options for them to consider, and working in museums is certainly one of the employment possibilities.

13 Feminism and Censorship in an Islamic Republic

Women Filmmakers in Iran

IBRAHIM AL-MARASHI

IRANIAN FILM has always flourished despite the fact that the Pahlavi regimes of Reza Shah and his son Mohammad Reza Shah banned or restricted any film that was deemed threatening to the security of the state. After the 1979 Iranian Revolution, the newly emergent clerical ruling establishment did not regard the medium of film as sacrilegious, despite Islamic prohibitions against artistic representations of the human form. Rather, it attempted to use film to support the ideological agenda of the Islamic republic, and encouraged directors to depict the social injustices of the shah's regime. In fact, in some respects, directors had more freedoms than under the previous government. For example, directors were now authorized to use regional dialects and minority languages in film, which had been forbidden prior to the revolution.

The clerical establishment regulated and imposed restrictions on all prerevolutionary movies and prohibited expressions of political dissent in any future productions. In the 1980s, film directors were free to produce movies dealing with social issues as long as they did not violate Islamic virtues. The censors did not permit scenes that threatened "public decency," such as women with their hair exposed and physical contact between people of the opposite sex. At the same time, film has been one of the only media that allowed one to explore contemporary Iranian private life, as well as the complexities of women's lives. However, the intimate issues of many feminist movies have been checked by a rigid censorship regime that edited any element of a film it deemed un-Islamic. As a result, Iranian women directors have been circumscribed by a uniquely Iranian set of rules and regulations, which has limited the freedom of expression in films yet has also resulted in the emergence of an indigenous and innovative contemporary Iranian film industry.

The censorship regime has posed formidable obstacles to film directors, whether male or female. First, a director must submit a short film outline to the Council of Screenplay Inspection. Afterward, the Council for Issuing Production Permits examines a working version of the screenplay and scrutinizes the list of cast and crew. Then, the Council of Film Reviewing views the final film and then decides on what changes and deletions should be made. Their decisions can be challenged by the director, which can be appealed to the High Council of Deputies, which issues an irrevocable judgment. Finally, the ministry gives the film a final grade based on ideological factors, with A being the highest and D being the lowest. Grade-A films are given the widest distribution and promotion in major cities, whereas grade-D films are shown on smaller screens and receive no official promotion.

The rigid censorship restrictions changed when Ali Akbar Hashemi-Rafsanjani assumed power in 1989, after Khomeini's death, allowing a moderate liberalization of film standards. Mohammad Khatami, elected in May 1997, launched a reformist platform that included greater political and social freedoms in Iran's rigid theocracy. In fact, Khatami was the former head of the Ministry of Culture and in this role had encouraged Iranian directors to test the limits of state censorship (Frodon 2001). During his presidency, he appointed officials who were more tolerant of film themes. For example, the cleric responsible for overseeing movies in Iran remarked in a foreign television documentary on the Iranian film industry that "cinematography is excellent for the development of the mind" (219). After Khatami's election, filmmakers began producing works focusing on serious social problems that may have been considered taboo by censors working under the former administration. Previously banned films were now shown, such as *Two Women* by Tahmineh Milani, which became one of the most profitable and talked-about films in Iran.

Nevertheless, certain film policies have not changed. For example, women actors must wear the *hijab* (head scarf), concealing the hair and any body curves, throughout the entire film. Even in the home, the private sphere, where most Muslim women remove their *hijab,* films must show actresses wearing their headdress. Women cannot sing or dance in films. The film *Az Karkheh ta Rayn* (From the Karkheh to the Rhein) about an Iranian woman living in Germany who has to care for her brother injured during the Iran-Iraq War, showed women wear wigs in the foreign version, whereas the actresses donned the *hijab* for domestic consumption. The foreign release of Rakhshan Bani Etemad's film *Nargess* featured a woman's song solo, whereas the Iranian version relied on a chorus for the soundtrack.

Thus, female Iranian directors must deal with unique challenges that make their films some of the most innovative in the world. First, they work in a society where men have dominated film directing. Second, the majority of the censors are men, suspicious of films with a feminist message. Third, restrictions on the freedom of action of Iranian women in film have forced directors to use creative techniques with actresses or to use child actresses to circumvent religious regulations. Finally, women, as well as men, directors have made an art form of using encrypted codes or symbols to express an idea or political dissent that the censors may fail to capture but that local Iranian audiences may comprehend.

This paper examines these challenges in the careers of three Iranian film directors: Tahmineh Milani, Samira Makhmalbaf, and Marziyeh Meshkini. What unites all these directors is not the fact that they are women, but that they are prominent directors in a male-dominated industry who have tried to convey feminist themes in their films, while at the same time satisfying the rigid conditions of the censor boards. They have been the pioneers in this revolution of contemporary Iranian film by dealing with gender issues from a culture where gender is the most sensitive and controversial of social issues.

I have chosen these three directors because they have had the greatest impact inside of Iran as well on the foreign market. However, there are other Iranian woman directors whose works have not yet reached international acclaim yet still deserve attention in this paper. Mariam Shahriar's *Daughter of the Sun* offers insight into the inequality between men and women in rural Iran. In the film, a young woman defies religious and social law by cutting off her hair and dressing as a male to work as an apprentice weaver to support her impoverished family. The woman spends hours at her loom, only to be imprisoned in her home during night. The main character must remain silent as she looks on, as the women she works with are terrorized by the master weaver.

Ziba Mir-Hosseini and Kim Longinotto's *Divorce Iranian Style* is a humorous documentary on the Iranian divorce courts. It provides a unique insight into the intimate circumstances of Iranian women's lives, as the producers follow Jamileh, who is seeking a divorce from her abusive husband; Ziba, a sixteen-year-old trying to divorce her thirty-eight-year-old husband; and Maryam, who is desperately fighting to gain custody of her daughter. This film documents the strength and perseverance with which these women confront biased laws and an imposing judicial system, dispelling images of Iranian women as passive victims of an overbearing system.

Tahmineh Milani

Two Women covers the fate of Fereshteh and Roya. The film opens at Tehran University, when the girls were students during the turmoil of the revolution and formation of the Islamic republic. Fereshteh comes from a lower-middle-class rural background outside the central city of Isfahan, while Roya is from the middle class of Tehran.

The time frame is not mentioned directly in the film, and the director avoids any political reference, although encoded signals indicate when this film takes place. In a conversation in the beginning of the film, Fereshteh offers Roya driving lessons, and afterward they casually refer to rumors that the universities will be closing. This comment is an indirect reference to the cultural revolution that is about to begin, the two-year period shortly after the Iranian Revolution when the universities were closed to investigate students and faculty to determine if they had the necessary Islamic credentials for readmission to the reconstituted university system. During this time, too, the university curriculum was revamped. The universities were closed to both women and men, but for young women without a degree it was especially problematic. They often had families who had been willing enough to let them study on their own but with the education and political instability wanted their girls to return to their homes. This conversation between Roya and Fereshteh foreshadows the fate of the latter.

In the film, Roya helps Fereshteh fight off an aggressive stalker, who then turns violent. Fereshteh finds little sympathy from her family and is forced to drop out of school. Her father assumed that the stalker was her lover, and her father forbids her from studying again, saying, "You are coming home with me! Our family has lost enough honor." Once she returns to the village, Fereshteh continues to study independently, but the hopes of returning to her university are dashed, as all colleges are closed in this postrevolutionary purge of "un-Islamic" elements. Thus, Milani employs the indirect method of criticizing the government's cultural revolution by showing Fereshteh's tragic fate as a result of these policies. One can infer that she is criticizing the state's former policies, but by making no direct mention of the cultural revolution, she escape the censors' cut.

As Fereshteh has no prospects of pursuing her education, she is married to an older merchant. At this time, the popular ideology of the Iranian Revolution emphasized a traditional domestic role for women. Even young women who had been raised in a Westernized and modernized middle-class social environment (coeducational schools, mixed parties, the liberationist texts and music of the seventies) found themselves newly pressured by families having second thoughts about the cultural trends they had encouraged in their children, especially now that the whole nation seemed to be in backlash against them. As a last resort, many young women got married, like Fereshteh (Moruzzi 2001). Her jealous husband prohibits her from using a phone or reading books, literally imprisoning her in the house. He forbids her from returning to the university when classes resume in 1984. The once ambitious overachiever is now reduced to a subject of her jealous husband.

The passivity of Fereshteh was not only in response to her husband and her father but her society as a whole. She is trapped, not simply by her marital situation but also by her national context. As an individual she is helpless in changing the nation. Thus, the film is a damning indictment not only of Fereshteh's father and husband but also of the restrictive social norms toward women that were emerging at the period of the cultural revolution. Again, the director's indirect condemnation of postrevolutionary society is symbolically conveyed through the actions of Fereshteh's husband and father.

Fereshteh tries to plead with her husband, but when all efforts fail she seeks a divorce. In the court, she is questioned as to her reasons for her desire to separate from her husband: "Does he hit you? Does he avoid paying the bills? Is he unable to perform his manly duties?" the court asks. Her answer is no to all these questions. The court finally asks why she is seeking a divorce. Her answer is, "Because he doesn't let me grow." The court refuses her request, since Iranian law allows only the husband the right to divorce a woman. The court can grant a divorce to a woman only if there is evidence that the man abuses his wife physically.

Roya, on the other hand, has become a prominent architect in Tehran. A scene shows her giving orders with confidence to construction workers. In contrast to Fereshteh's mate, Roya's husband is gentle and sympathetic. After fifteen years have passed, Fereshteh and Roya meet once again. The reunion demonstrates the gap between the lives of both women, where Roya, with her cellular phone and loose-flowing head scarf, is a stark contrast to the pale, lifeless Fereshteh.

The fate of Fereshteh is suddenly transformed. The psychopathic stalker, newly released from prison, tracks her down in an empty alley. She falls to her knees, screaming, "Kill me, kill me!" but the stalker instead declares his love for her and kills the husband, who shows up at that moment. She is now freed from her husband's control by the actions of her stalker. She shows no grief over his death, but her only concern now is how she will survive on her own. "What will I do?" she asks in desperation. "How will I live? What about my children?" She then becomes determined to reconstruct her life, saying, "I will go back to university" and take computer classes. At the end of the film she declares that she will catch up with her friends. As her society is changing, she decides that she also needs to change herself. At the end of the film she says, "I have no time, I have to hurry."

Fereshteh tells Roya that she is ready to put her life back together, even ready to learn to drive. Early in the film Roya was offering to give her friend driving lessons and a key middle scene involved her driving a car. These women are no longer trapped. They have changed, as has the society. The film functions as a powerful cathartic experience through the portrayal of a national political experience in personal terms.

Milani's message is that women have little control over their own lives, and their destinies are determined by a patriarchal society. Her lesson is that if Iranian women want the freedom they deserve, they must grab it themselves.

Milani always adhered to Islamic ideals and safe topics for her films. Yet Milani's style always met resistance at the Ministry of Islamic Guidance and Culture. Many of her films had been banned, and on numerous occasions she was barred from making movies again.

Milani had produced a film, *Kakado,* a story of a young girl's growing pains. She produced a film about children and the environment, hoping that the topics would be suitable to the censors. "I thought I had satisfied everyone, because I made a film about the environment," Milani said. "I thought it was impeccable and it was praised by the public." However, the censor Hamid Khakbazan forbade its release until all provocative images in the film had been edited. His objection was that the main character in the film, an eight-year-old girl, did not wear the *hijab* throughout the film, despite the fact that girls in Iran are not expected to wear the head scarf until turning nine. Khakbazan wanted to cut so many parts of the film that Milani would have had to edit most of the film to meet his requirements. "He believed women should not bend in films, they should not run and they should not be shot in close-ups," Milani has said of the censor. "He was so sick, he thought everything was erotic—and he caused movies to be cut to pieces." The ordeal devastated her personally and cut short her career. "I want you to see what happens to a woman who wants to be outspoken and active in society. They want you to believe that women can be filmmakers in society—but look at me. . . . There are so many people who will be brought to their knees if they can't make their films" (quoted in Cohn 1997). At times, Milani received threatening phone calls from local government employees, who warned she could be flogged for her films.

Another objection to *Kakado* was that a corrupt character had the name Hassan, which the censors considered an insult to Imam Hassan, the grandson of the prophet Muhammad. The complaint about using the name Hassan was dropped. Milani also argued that the girl was not old enough to have to wear a scarf under Islamic law. Milani intentionally used a girl who would not be obliged to wear the scarf. "I disagree that little girls have to wear the scarf. Children should be free to run around, jump up and down. . . . We have to show them how they really are in real life," Milani said.

Referring to the absurdities of censorship, Milani pointed to a rule that characters of the opposite sex may not touch. "You see a scene where a woman faints and collapses and her husband calls the [female] neighbour to pick her up," the filmmaker said. "This is very damaging to the film." She said there are ways that filmmakers can follow the rules and still be allowed to have realistic movies. For instance, women can wear wigs instead of scarves, and married couples can play husbands and wives on film. "We use unbelievable symbolic images. A love scene can be portrayed by wrapping a scarf around a hat," she said (Faramarzi 1997, D11).

When Milani approached the film censorship board in 1995 with the film *Two Women,* the predominantly male committee banned it outright. "I think many of the men on the board saw themselves in the movie and it was too sensitive for them," Milani said (Molavi 2000, 217). When Khatami assumed the presidency, film restrictions were soon relaxed, and her film *Two Women* was released in Iranian theaters to wide acclaim.

Samira Makhmalbaf

Samira walked out of school at the age of fifteen because she thought her teachers were not teaching her anything new. She asked her father to tell her about filmmaking, and three years later she made *The Apple,* becoming the youngest director to compete in the official section of the 1998 Cannes Film Festival.

The Apple is a true story of an impoverished sixty-five-year-old Tehran man named Ghorbanali Naderi, married to a blind woman, who virtually imprisoned his eleven-year-old twin daughters, never allowing them out of the house. Makhmalbaf was able to persuade the man and his family to play themselves in a work in which the line between fiction and documentary is blurred, as the characters all "play" themselves. Makhmalbaf got Naderi's cooperation because when the imprisonment of his daughters became first a local and then a media scandal, he felt dishonored when it was falsely reported that he had kept the girls chained hand and foot, and he wanted to set the record straight. Yet he is unable to comprehend the widespread outrage directed at him.

Makhmalbaf was able to start shooting only four days after the story broke in the press and shot her entire film in eleven days. Her ability to get this particular family to behave naturally and without self-consciousness is quite an accomplishment.

The Apple tells us about life for women and girls in Iran today, yet the father is not vilified for what he has done, as the film struggles instead to understand and explain his actions. He says he is simply doing his best, however misguided, to protect his daughters according to the teachings of the Qur'an. As it is, the family subsists on charity, and the father, Ghorbanali Naderi, is afraid to let them out of the house. The deeply religious Naderi is so conservative that he believes that should he allow his daughters to play in the tiny, walled yard in front of their small house, they might be dishonored if one of the neighborhood boys were to so much as touch them. Because the boys play in the narrow street in front of the house, they sometimes climb over the wall to retrieve a ball. "My girls are like flowers. They may wither in the sun," Naderi asserts. "A man's touch is like the sun." But the film also shows that their home confinement has stalled the girls' development.

The film records the girls' first steps into the world beyond the bars of their home and their awakening to the wonders of ordinary life. They are grinning and hopping about the streets of Tehran, reenacting their own experiences for the camera. In depicting the girls' discovery of the outside world, Makhmalbaf sets up a series of situations and shows how the girls react. For example, a boy approaches them selling ice cream bars, but the girls want an apple instead. The girls have never seen ice cream before and have no concept of paying for an ice cream bar.

At the heart of the matter, of course, is that the twins represent the extreme oppression of women in Iran, yet Makhmalbaf is careful to suggest that the angry reaction to their plight reveals that the status of women is improving within a patriarchal Islamic society. *The Apple* leaves to us to ponder why it took neighbors so many years to petition Tehran's welfare organization to investigate the twins' dire situation. At the moment, they receive a monthly allowance from the profits of the film and are now studying at school.

Although some may think that Samira's father, Moshen Makhmalbaf, was really the director of his teenage daughter's film, the release of her next film, *Blackboards,* consolidated Samira's position as the youngest woman director in the world, winning her the Grand Prix du Jury at Cannes in 2000.

Blackboards opens with a group of teachers walking the mountains between Iraq and Iran, their blackboards on their backs, in search of students. The film follows a batch of teachers sent into the mountains of the border like missionaries of ancient times. Instead of using the huge blackboards strapped to their backs for teaching, they are used for protection against bullets and the elements. Forced to hide from the helicopters that patrol the border, the teachers separate. Whether they are Iranian or Iraqi helicopters is uncertain. One teacher, Said, meets a group of nomads who are trying to head for their homeland. They have no use for a teacher, but they use Said's blackboard as a stretcher on which to carry an old man who cannot urinate. Said is encouraged to marry the old man's daughter, Halaleh, whom Said tries to teach how to write "I love you." In a bizarre wedding ceremony Said marries Halaleh, with his blackboard, which is his sole source of income, as a dowry. On one occasion, it is used as a screen to ensure privacy for the main teacher, whose progress we witness, when he makes love to his mute, shell-shocked new "wife." When the nomads reach the border, Said splits from the woman and gives his blackboard to her. The nomads wander to the border with the words "I love you" still written on the blackboard strapped to her back.

Any doubts that Samira directs her films herself were dispelled by a documentary screened at Venice last year titled *How Samira Made "Blackboards."* Makhmalbaf spent four months shooting the film in the Kurdish mountains near Halabcheh, a city on the Iraqi border where the Iraqis gassed the Kurds during the Iran-Iraq War. She dodged land mines daily and used a cast of two hundred local villagers, with just two professional actors taking leading roles. The film depicted her rehearsing with the actors, frustrated by some who were unwilling to adapt themselves to their characters, and her willingness to wade waist-deep into obviously freezing water to encourage her collaborators. "It was one of the best experiences I had, living with those people," she says. "Because I loved them. They were humans, good humans, suffering from different things. It was a deeper kind of life compared to most of the other places I've lived" ("Young, Gifted" 2001).

Blackboards, shot in the mountains without the permission of the Iranian authorities, and the subject Samira chose were extremely controversial—the plight of the dispossessed. The assumption is that these people are Kurds who are denied places within Iranian society, and the very fact that a film can be made that focuses on such a disadvantaged minority group is something of an eye-opener. There is an implicit criticism of a system that causes young and old alike to wander the dry, unforgiving mountains and of the shortcomings of education. Of necessity, Makhmalbaf withholds pieces of information that would have made the motives of her characters clearer.

Marziyeh Meshkini

Meshkini's *The Day I Became a Woman* consists of three concise vignettes. The first story revolves around a girl, Hava, who awakens on her ninth birthday and discovers that she is now a woman and cannot play with boys and must also wear a traditional chador. Hava's grandmother drives a playmate away with the line, "She's not a child anymore. She's nine today." Hava argues that if she was born at noon, she should have until that hour to be a child. Her grandmother, who warns God will not forgive her if she crosses that boundary, shows her how to tell time with a stick wedged into the sand. When the shadow disappears, it will be time to go home. When the shadow disappears, her life will change. Hava measures out her hour of childhood with the makeshift sundial. She feeds a friend some licks of lollipop through a window, then helps two boys build a boat from petrol cans, contributing her brand-new chador as a sail. Time is the ultimate symbol in this piece, as yesterday, she was a girl and had her freedom. Today, she is a woman and does not have her freedom.

The second story is about a woman named Ahoo who is competing in a bike race, much to the anger of her husband. One of a flock of female bicyclists in black chadors, she pedals madly along the Persian Gulf coast, pursued on horseback by her brothers, her father, fellow tribesmen, and her husband—who divorces her at thirty-five miles per hour. This vignette takes place entirely in the course of a bicycle race. First, the husband appears on horseback next to the bicycle trail to order her off the bike and back to their marriage. When she defiantly refuses to stop, her husband vows to divorce her—then and there. To the others, who resemble old-fashioned nuns with their black fabric billowing in the breeze, the husband chauvinistically asks, "Why are all you riding? Don't you have a man?" He then brings an angry mullah who says, "What you are riding is not a bicycle; it's the devil's mount." Finally, her father arrives on the scene and forces her off the bike and back to a household, where she will return as a divorced woman.

In the third story, an elderly woman arrives at Kish International Airport and hires a local boy to chauffeur her around a very modern mall and shopping district as she engages in a spending spree. Snippets of fabric are tied around her fingers to remind her of all the things she always wanted and now can afford. She gathers an entourage of children as porters for a whole showroom's worth of wares. "All my life, I wanted cold water," she says, which is why a refrigerator is her first purchase. Leading a picturesque parade of boys and men bearing large cardboard boxes, she stops at the beach to survey her goods and figure out what she has forgotten. The sight of a stocked refrigerator and ironing board on the sand is as shocking as it is surprising and memorable.

The three characters could represent a single woman at different stages of the life course. The second woman could be the first girl, now that she is grown up and wants to experience everything for herself. The old lady could be the same woman who lost her innocence in childhood and her means of advancement in her twenties and now craves gadgets and appliances that she can afford—but not understand or truly use.

The Day I Became a Woman, shot on the Persian Gulf island of Kish, uses mainly nonprofessionals. The children in the first and third stories are especially charming in their unpracticed manners; the young girl toys with her hair and occasionally stumbles over her words, and the boys on the beach delight in playing with the old lady's vacuum cleaner or jumping on her bed. Meshkini made her film as three shorts rather than as a feature, because "short films do not require government script approval. On the other hand, you can't buy film at reduced rates or rent government-owned equipment." The film has played only one theater in Iran, Meshkini said; the poster—of Ahoo on her bicycle—has been banned. As her step-daughter Samira Makhmalbaf said, "Censorship isn't just a committee, it's a system" (Anderson 2001, D2).

Conclusions

Not only are Iranian women film directors under the observation of a strict censorship regime, but they also have been able to thrive in this atmosphere and produce films that have swept international film festivals.[1]

Despite censorship restrictions, these women directors have produced innovative films that share many similarities. *The Apple* and *The Day I Became a Woman* use children as one way of getting through the strict censorship that limits the way filmmakers can deal with adult subjects. The powerlessness of children is a profound way of engaging with the nature of life in such a society, a world where everyone feels as helpless as a child. The strictures on female performers in Iranian productions have created a cinematic opening for young girls, who are freed from the religious obligation to wear the *hijab.* Girls can avoid the potential—or perceived—sexual tension in adult relationships, making these prepubescent protagonists the most popular performers in recent years.

Two Women and *The Apple* portray women being controlled and abused by possessive husbands or fathers. In *Two Women* and *Divorce Iranian Style,* the heroine has to argue for a divorce to release her from her oppressive marriage before a mullah who represents an unsympathetic legal system. In both cases, the man symbolizes the nation that intervenes and prevents them from reaching their full potential.

1. For further reading on Iranian cinema, see Dabashi 2001; Mir-Hosseini 2001; Naficy 1994, 2001; Tapper 2002.

PART THREE

Violence, Peace, and Women's Human Rights

14 Depression in Nepalese Women

Tradition, Changing Roles, and Public Health Policy

DANA CROWLEY JACK

and MARK VAN OMMEREN

THE WORLD HEALTH ORGANIZATION estimates that by the year 2020, depression will become the second-leading cause of the global disease burden. Women in both high-income and low-income countries experience depression at a rate almost double the rate of men;[1] currently, depression constitutes women's leading cause of disability in the world. In Nepal and most low-income countries, almost no attention has been focused on women's depression, even though the World Health Organization ranks depression as the most important women's health problem in the world overall (Cabral and Astbury 2000; http://www.who.int/mental_health.org). This chapter reports on research conducted on gender and depression in Nepal in 2001.[2]

1. Women experience higher lifetime prevalence rates of major depression than men at a ratio of approximately two to one in twelve general population studies carried out in a range of countries, including Hong Kong, Taiwan, Korea, Germany, France, Puerto Rico, the United States, and Canada. See Piccinelli and Homen 1997.

2. This research was carried out by Dana Jack and was supported by a Fulbright Scholar grant to Nepal in January–July 2001. The research could not have been undertaken without the help of the following: Dr. Bhogendra Sharma of CVICT, Kathmandu, introduced me to the two participating psychiatrists, Dr. Nirakar Man Shrestha and Dr. Vidaya D. Sharma, and was supportive in every step of the process. Dr. Sharma and Dr. Shrestha both arranged the demanding schedules at their respective outpatient clinics—Tribhuvan University Teaching Hospital and Patan Mental Hospital—to accommodate the interviews for depressed patients. Our conversations about depression were essential to understanding its specific manifestation in Nepal. The Nepalese interviewers, Pooja Sharma, Shiva Dhakal, Archana Rai, Rushmi Joshi, Birbahadur Lama, and Jyoti Shrestha, interviewed with respect and empathy. My deep gratitude also goes to the women and men who willingly told the stories of their

243

Women's Depression in Nepal: The Social Context

Nepal is an attractive country with a rich culture, warm people, and strong, coherent communities with a wealth of social resources. However, the status and treatment of many Nepalese women are causes of serious concern. Women's depression must first be put into the context of social issues affecting all women in Nepal. Women's overall health picture is very poor as reflected in their lower life expectancy than men's (53.7 versus 55.2 years, respectively), partly owing to experiencing one of the highest maternal mortality rates in the world (515 per 100,000 live births) (Nepal National Planning Commission, His Majesty's Government of Nepal, and UNICEF 1996, 3) and a high incidence of suicide.[3] Women's poor health is influenced by social factors such as extreme poverty (an estimated US$210 annually), low levels of girls' education, literacy (female 23 percent compared to males 57 percent), heavy work burdens, and early marriages (in 1993, about 60 percent of marriages occurred before age 18).[4] Women are primarily involved in agriculture, comprising 65.7 percent of the agricultural labor force and contributing 60 percent of the agricultural production. Yet women control only 6.4 percent of total landholdings. Trafficking of girls and women, estimated for the year 1999 to affect approximately 5,000 to 7,000 females between the ages of 10 and 20, carries disastrous consequences for victims' physical and mental health (Forum for Women, Law, and Development 1999, 6–7, 17–20).[5]

Nepal has a patriarchal system that is reflected through legal discrimination

---

depression and offered their perspectives on their distress. We hope their interviews provide the basis for deeper understanding of the difficult problem of depression and can help others.

3. There are no official rates of suicide in Nepal, primarily because of social taboos, fear of legal complications, lack of medical care, and complicated reporting requirements. Dr. Nirakar Man Shrestha, director of Patan Mental Hospital, says that "suicide is always underreported and underreporting has been reported to occur to the extent of a third or to a fourth of the real occurrences" (personal communication, June 2001). Rates by gender are not reported, but violence against women is widespread and known to result, in most cases, in mental anguish and stress, and in some cases suicide. See SAATHI 1997. SAATHI (which means "friend" in Nepali) is a nongovernmental organization (NGO) working to prevent violence against women and girls, formed in 1992 in Nepal.

4. The level of absolute poverty is very high, at 45 percent of the population. Unofficial estimates describe the situation more gravely and calculate the ratio at 60–70 percent (*Nepal Human Development Report* 1998, 5). See esp. 3 (poverty), 113 (education), and 123–24 (literacy rates).

5. Rescued victims face violence, intimidation, STDs, AIDS, and abandonment from families and society.

against women in many areas: property inheritance rights, citizenship rights, employment, business, and contractual rights as well as laws affecting marriage, divorce, adoption, abortion, and rape. Domestic violence is a widespread problem in Nepal, and the linkage between violence against women and depression is well established by studies in many cultures.[6]

In the midst of these obstacles, Nepal's women are experiencing new possibilities resulting from an increased focus on gender equity and a heightening social awareness of women's rights. Opportunities for women exist in higher education and in government leadership for literacy training within their villages.[7] Yet the unsettled political situation resulting from the murder of King Birendra and the royal family in 2001 and the government response to the Maoist insurgency have diverted attention from Nepal's beginning efforts toward women's empowerment.

Mental health in Nepal is a largely neglected area and faces numerous barriers to improvement, including social stigma, inadequate resources such as personnel and health facilities, and a virtual absence of formal mental health services in isolated rural areas where the vast majority of the population lives. Most of Nepal's people depend on traditional ways of understanding and treating mental problems, primarily turning to traditional healers. Long-standing cultural practices and even some laws discriminate against those individuals with mental problems. For example, the husbands of women who are considered "mad" (the local slang for mentally troubled, which includes severe depression) can take a new wife (Sangroula 200).[8]

Very little is known about women's mental health in Nepal, particularly regarding their subjective experiences and perspectives on what is causing their distress. So

---

6. See, for example, Cabral and Astbury 2000. Regarding Nepal, a 1997 SAATHI study found that violence "cut[s] across women and girls of all class, caste, age and ethnicity with 95 percent of respondents attesting first hand knowledge of violence against women and girls incidents. In 77 percent of the cases the perpetrators were reported to be members of the family. . . . In the case of domestic violence, nearly 58% reported it as being a daily occurrence" (ii).

7. Nepal's government requires that at least 5 percent of the total number of candidates contesting any election in the country be women and has reserved three seats for women in the National Assembly, out of a total of sixty seats. The amendment of the Local Self-Government Act with 20 percent reservation for women is another special measure adopted by the government to increase women's participation in local government, which has resulted in some forty thousand women participating in local governments. SAATHI (1997): 5.

8. See also Forum for Women, Law, and Development 1999, which states that the law allows a man to marry a second wife if a woman becomes "physically disabled, does not produce children or if the children do not survive after 10 years of marriage, of if she becomes blind or otherwise disabled" (39).

far, all published studies of women's depression have been conducted with nonvalidated questionnaires, offering data that do not present a clear picture of social factors related to depression in women. We sought to complement these quantitative studies by listening to women's own perspectives on their depression with the goal of helping foster interventions focused on women's realities.

Women's Depression in Global Context

Gender affects the material and symbolic positions people occupy in societies as well as the daily experiences that condition their lives. Women's inequality affects their exposure to risks, for example, to sexual and physical violence and also affects their power to manage their own lives, to cope with such risks, and, thus, to influence their own health.

The common consensus is that depression results from interacting biological, psychological, and social factors. However, the influence of social factors tends to be ignored in research, clinical practice, and public mental health policy. Overwhelming evidence points to the significance of social factors in the onset of women's depression; such factors include their greater exposure to poverty, domestic violence, negative life events, chronic difficulties, lower education, and heavier workloads than men.[9] These social factors are translated into depression through emotional experiences of humiliation, hopelessness, entrapment, lack of control, feelings of inferiority, and loss of self. Factors that can protect women from depression are having the ability to experience some control when confronted with severe events, which requires having access to some resources, and having support from a close relationship. Poverty is a recognized risk factor in the pathway into depression for women, especially when combined with negative life events, ongoing difficulties, and the lack of a confiding relationship and support.[10]

9. In a study in four countries undergoing economic restructuring, strong associations among female sex, low education, and poverty with common mental disorders was found in Goa, India; Harare, Zimbabwe; Santiago, Chile; and Pelotas and Olinda, Brazil, revealing how gender inequality is linked to economic inequality and rising income disparity. See Patel et al. 1999. See also Cabral and Astbury.

10. Social theories of women's depression emphasize the interaction of life events; vulnerability factors, including parental loss before the age of seventeen, particularly the loss of one's mother before age eleven; the presence at home of three or more children younger than fourteen; a poor, nonconfiding marriage; and the lack of full- or part-time employment. See Brown and Harris 1978.

Silencing the Self, Relationships, and Women's Depression

Research around the world finds that in most instances, the severe events provoking women's depression involve a core relationship. Women, as a group, place a higher degree of importance on the quality of their personal relationships, and the quality of such relationships centrally affects women's sense of self, self-esteem, and self-regard. The importance that women place on their relationships with husbands and partners, combined with women's inequality, leads them to avoid conflict and suppress anger in order to preserve those relationships. Inequality leads to a form of self-censorship that Dana Jack has metaphorically called "silencing the self" (1991). A woman's economic dependence on a man who may leave her for many reasons—she fails to produce a son, she becomes "mad"—increases her fear of abandonment and her self-silencing. Silencing the self, in turn, is hypothesized to contribute to a fall in self-esteem and feelings of a loss of self, inner division, and depression. Trying to keep relationships by pleasing others, or at least by complying with their wishes, a woman experiences a hidden self that is resentful, angry, and, likely, increasingly hopeless. Yet her anger cannot be expressed for fear of retribution or abandonment.

Silencing the self fits with how women internalize subordination; muting one's voice and anger works to reinforce subordination. Being female coincides with having a lower rank in society; as the UNDP's 1995 *Human Development Report* observed, "No society treats its women as well as its men." In Nepal, as in many cultures, girls are likely to internalize this social fact from birth on, and it influences their self-perception. Social inequality becomes part of one's felt worth and sense of standing in the world. For example, the restrictions on women's physical movement, self-expression, and sexuality are internalized and work as a form of self-inhibition and self-surveillance. They restrict women's imagination about their already limited choices; many women berate themselves or feel anxiety if they think they have "stepped over the line" of acceptable behavior. Submissive, dependent, and nonassertive behaviors are still considered desirable feminine traits by many societies, including Nepal. Trained in girls and expected of women, such behaviors are also found to be associated with depression (Allan and Gilbert 1997).

The Silencing the Self Scale (STSS) was designed to measure self-silencing and internalized subordination as it manifests in interpersonal behaviors, specifically self-sacrifice, self-silencing, pleasing, and seeing oneself through others' eyes. It also assesses a person's endorsement of presenting an outwardly compliant self in relationships while feeling inwardly angry and asks respondents to describe the stan-

dards they use to judge themselves and feel they fail to live up to.[11] The STSS correlates with women's depression across studies in numerous countries, including
India, Hong Kong, Greece, Puerto Rico, Canada, England, and in various ethnic
groups within the United States.

The Depression Study: Goals and Description

This exploratory study of gender and depression in Nepal was designed to examine
what women seeking help at outpatient clinics identify as the sources of their depression, their symptoms, help-seeking patterns, and how social factors affect their
depression. The study included comparison samples of men in order to examine
gender differences with respect to these critical issues of depression.

Participants

Data for the study were collected from women and men attending outpatient clinics
at two government-supported hospitals in Kathmandu. When diagnosed with
unipolar major depression by Nepali psychiatrists, patients were informed of the
study after their first appointment. Those individuals consenting to be interviewed
were seen immediately. The consecutive sample, interviewed between April and
June 2001, consisted of thirty-four women and sixty-two men. The larger number
of men than women seeking help may reflect Nepalese society, where families are
more willing to spend money and time on male members and where males are more
free to seek help themselves.

Women ranged in age from 18 to 68, with a mean age of 37; men's ages ranged
from 15 to 73, with mean of 30. Fifty-seven percent of women were illiterate,
whereas 11 percent of men were illiterate; 15 percent of women and 14 percent of
men were literate through nonformal education; 3 percent of women and 16 percent of men had attended college. These educational patterns reflect Nepal's wider
practice of schooling boys more often and longer than girls.

Seventy-six percent of women and 66 percent of men were married; 15 percent
of women and 34 percent of men were unmarried. Women's age at marriage ranged
from 10 to 25, with the mean age of 16.3 similar to what is reported for Nepalese
women in general. Men's age of marriage ranged from 13 to 32, with a mean age of

11. The STSS is published in *Silencing the Self: Women and Depression* (Jack 1991). The psychometrics and scale construction study are reported in Jack and Dill 1992.

21.2. Only unmarried women had no children; all married men had children. Fifty-three percent of women and 57 percent of men lived in joint families; women lived with a mean of 6.2 of family members, men with a mean of 7.7 of family members. Only 12 percent of women earned money through employment, whereas 56 percent of men were wage earners. Seventy-six percent of women and 66 percent of men described their income as low relative to other Nepalese.

Measures

A *semistructured interview* inquired into each person's perspective on the causes of their psychological distress and into known factors that affect women's depression. Questions about physical and emotional symptoms and help-seeking patterns were also asked. The interview was translated into Nepali, reviewed by the participating psychiatrists, pilot tested, and revised before use in the study. Trained Nepalese interviewers conducted the interviews with each patient; the interview lasted approximately one hour.

A measure of depression, *Section E of the Composite International Diagnostic Interview—2.1* (hereafter referred to as the CIDI). The CIDI has been developed for international use and served to develop a picture of depressive symptoms in Nepal as compared to other countries. The CIDI has been translated into Nepali and utilized in a study of Nepalese-speaking Bhutanese refugees (van Ommeren et al. 2001).

Questions from this measure were asked verbally by trained Nepalese interviewers. The CIDI was scored for point prevalence of DSM IV *(The Diagnostic and Statistical Manual, Version 4,* American Psychiatric Association) major depression, that is, how many people were experiencing the symptoms of major depression within the past two weeks.

The Silencing the Self Scale (Jack and Dill 1992). The STSS is a thirty-one-item self-report measure that assesses cognitive schemas about how one "should" interact in order to develop and maintain interpersonal relationships. Respondents rate their agreement or disagreement with items on a five-point Likert scale. STSS items reflect the four subscales that make up the construct of self-silencing. Higher STSS scores indicate a greater degree of self-silencing.

The STSS was translated and adapted to Nepalese culture with the use of the Translation Monitoring Form (van Ommeren et al. 2001). After translation and blinded back-translation, the STSS was then tested with four focus groups with women, both literate and illiterate, to make sure the instrument was clearly worded and relevant to women's lives. It was then tested-retested with the group of master's students to establish reliability and basic scale psychometrics for Nepal. STSS test-retest reliability for women was .92 (p < .001); for men it was .54 (p < .005). Scale alpha for the women was .79; for men it was .69. Convergent validity was established by predicted correlation with DSM IV major depression as measured by the CIDI: women (N = 39) .56, p < .001; men (N = 56), .28, p. < .05.

The semistructured interview, the CIDI, Section E, and selected items representing the four subscales of the STSS (nos. 2–9, 15, 16, 19, 25, 29, and 31) were administered to the hospital outpatients who participated in this study.

Results

The correlation of total depression symptoms on the CIDI, Section E, with STSS scores were as follows: females (N = 34), .23 (p > .05); males (N = 62), .48, (p > .001). The correlation of the STSS and the CIDI in the male participants requires a follow-up examination of the meanings Nepalese men attach to scale items; that study is now under way. The four focus groups with women established the usefulness of the scale to capture their experience in relationships; similar focus groups are currently being conducted with men.

Qualitative Analysis of Interviews

Responding to the question, "What brought you to the clinic?" patients overwhelmingly listed physical symptoms, including persistent headaches, weakness, and bodily pain. Their expression of symptoms through physical distress corresponds to symptom expression found in many societies in which physical complaints serve as the idiom for depression.[12]

When identifying what they think is causing their symptoms, both women (70 percent) and men (50 percent) most frequently describe problems in their relationships.[13] Women are much more likely to point to problematic relationships with their spouse (40.1 percent of women, 18 percent of men) and with in-laws (women 35.3 percent, men 0 percent). In these relationships, women describe financial de-

12. See Kleinman and Good 1986.

13. Written interviews were typed and imported into Ethnograph software, which allows systematic analysis of themes. Five students were trained to code interviews; the following analysis results from the codings.

pendence, social roles that require them to serve men and in-laws, and, for many, early marriages or widowhood that bring severe difficulties. Men describe tension around the roles they are expected to play within the family, particularly in providing economic support, or feeling disapproval from family members, or being distressed by family members' nonconforming behavior.

As each sex describes their relational problems, women's narratives powerfully reflect the impact of their inequality on their lives and on their depression. For example, among the thirty-four women coming to the clinics, the following situations were reported as precipitating their psychological distress: rape at age twelve, being regularly beaten by husbands or in-laws, living as a daughter-in-law in an oppressive joint family with a heavy work burden and no freedoms, being widowed with low status and no emotional support, living separately from husbands who send money sporadically, living with husbands who take second wives or threaten to do so, and health problems. Each of these situations is affected by women's unequal legal status, lack of economic independence, early marriages, lack of education, male child preference and its corollary of girl children as liabilities to parents, and lack of social resources to support women who wish to leave abusive relationships.

The violent structure of married relationships that affects many of these women's mental health appears in the following representative examples from women's narratives:

#1812–55 (age thirty-five, three children, illiterate, married at fifteen): "My husband is the main cause of my illness. . . . When I got out [of the hospital] my husband beat me as I was unable to do house chores, and my husband never loved me. I have three children, and he still beats me when he is drunk."

#1812–558 (age thirty-seven, three children, nonformal literacy, married at seventeen): "My older son is very troublesome. . . . [H]e beats me and has no respect for me. I have been suffering from this disease for years. When I had the sickness I was beaten by my sister and father; my husband also beats me."

#2728–057 (age twenty-seven, two children, illiterate, married at sixteen): "There is no peace at home, only fighting with my husband. He drinks all the time. Whenever he is drunk he beats me. He even kicks me out of the house at midnight. He had sexual relationships with other women, and he had [an] STD. Because of him I also got [an] STD. I don't trust my husband. If I ask him not to drink he beats me."

#5238 (age twenty-three, one child, high school education, married at twenty-one): "I have family problems with my in-laws and my husband. My husband works outside Kathmandu and comes home only on holidays. Whenever he comes home, my in-laws poison his ears by saying all sorts of things about me. He believes them and starts fighting with me and even beats me. He is talking about [a] second marriage; I am always thinking about killing myself, but I think of my little daughter."

Sixty percent of the women who identified problems in relationship with their husbands reported repeated physical beatings; others described emotional abuse and abandonment. Three additional women described physical beatings by in-laws.

Some of the men's narratives provide another view into violence against women within marriages. When the 18 percent of men talked about problems in relationship with their spouse, only two identified such problems as the cause of their psychological distress. The representative excerpts below reveal men's attitudes about male dominance and women's roles in marriage:

#2171 (age nineteen, no children, in college, married at eighteen): "My parents found me a girl [wife] who was older than me. She is big and mature, and I am smaller and immature. . . . I feel trapped. I always regret this marriage."

#3188 (age fifty-three, two children, nonformal literacy, employed, married at seventeen): "I don't share my feelings with my wife because I am male, and how can I lower myself in front of a woman? Men are to rule women. Women should be kept under our feet."

#3539 (age thirty-one, university education, unemployed, married at twenty-eight): "I am unemployed but my wife is a lecturer, so I feel dominated. Because of my unemployment we usually have fights and arguments. . . . My wife is employed, and she tries to dominate me."

#526–058 (age forty-five, two children, employed, married at twenty): "I do not like to see my wife. When I do, I automatically want to kill her. [When I am angry] I run to cut her with a knife."

#5781 (age twenty-eight, one son, middle school education, employed, age of marriage missing): "I can't stand my wife. I become irritated whenever I see my wife. I want to fight with my wife. My friends tease me because my wife works and earns more than I do. . . . I feel like my wife tries to dominate me, so I beat her."

#748–058 (age thirty-two, two children, illiterate, employed, married at sixteen): "I beat and abuse my wife."

Only four men identify violence or its threat as a problem that brought them to seek help. Three of these men had been threatened or beaten by male nonrelatives; one man's step-uncle regularly beat him. When men described violence against their wives, they did not regard it as a problem. Rather, the subject most often came up in response to the question, "What do you do when you get angry?"

Numerous researchers in developed and developing countries have identified the powerful effect of violence on women's depression. The 1997 SAATHI report on violence against girls and women in Nepal found that 95 percent of respondents had firsthand knowledge of such violence, with nearly 58 percent reporting domestic violence to be a daily occurrence. In studies from North America, battered woman are four to five times more likely to require psychiatric treatment and five times more likely to attempt suicide that nonbattered women.[14]

Economics. Inadequate income was the second factor most frequently identified by both sexes as the perceived cause of their symptoms. Fifty-six percent of women and 50 percent of men described problems around inadequate income as central to their distress. Only one of the thirty-four women seeking help lived on her own, worked as a salesperson, and had control of the money she earned. Since women's complete financial dependence on others restricts their ability to leave abusive relationships or take care of children, the overlap of relationship and economic problems occurs commonly: 79 percent of the time in women's narratives. For example, #2728–057 (age twenty-nine, two children, illiterate, married at seventeen) said: "Two years ago he [my husband] started drinking. At first he used to come home at midnight; sometimes he didn't come home the whole night. I was very worried about him. I couldn't sleep the whole night. He started beating me. We have a small furniture shop. He doesn't work much, so now we don't have enough income. Because of the tension I became ill." Economic dependency blocks her escape, reduces her choices and sense of control, and contributes to hopelessness.

Health. Health problems, other than the symptoms that brought them to the hospital clinics, were described by 35 percent of women; in this group of women, 58 percent described health problems as overlapping with economic and family problems. For example, #166–058 (age twenty-nine, three children, literate, nonformal education, married at seventeen) says, "I have had a pain in my heart for a long time. Because of my heart problem I cannot work and have become so weak. I have very young children. If I die from this sickness, what will happen to my children? Because of this problem, I am feeling worse and worse. Since I am not able to contribute to the family work, I feel humiliated. Every member of the family says, 'What type of problem are you facing that does not have any solution?' I used to work in a rice mill, but now I can't, due to this illness."

Self-Silencing and Anger Expression. When asked "What do you do when you get angry?" women overwhelmingly said they keep quiet, cry, give others the silent treatment, stop eating, or beat their children. Several women said that nothing

14. See Stark and Flitcraft 1991.

makes them angry. Suppressing anger or expressing it aggressively has been associated with depression.[15]

The following examples from the hospital study illustrate the relation of social factors to women's depression. All names are fictitious.

Childhood Rape, Loss, and Humiliation. Sirjana, age thirty-six, came to seek help because of physical symptoms. She was terse and uncommunicative in the interview until asked, "Was violence used against you as a child?" She then told the story of being raped at age twelve by a friend of her father but being too frightened to tell her parents. She did not want to marry because of the rape. At nineteen, when both her parents died, she began working in sales. She encounters sexually abusive behavior from men daily: "People come to buy things try and touch me, here and there, and behave with me in a very bad way." Sirjana has a daughter and lives alone with her. She says, "Whenever I remember that day [of the rape] I feel very angry, very angry for not being able to protect myself. I am happy because you are the first person I have told about my rape. I have never told anyone." The events in Sirjana's life illustrate how violence, humiliation, entrapment, and self-silencing converge to create her depression.

Domestic Violence, Marriage, and Local Values Regarding Daughters-in-Law: Internalized Subordination. Laxmi is twenty-two, married with four children, the first born when she was fifteen. She lives in the Terai region and was referred to the Kathmandu clinic by physicians near her village. Laxmi is the oldest daughter-in-law in a joint family of ten people; their income is low. She has never attended school and is illiterate. She lists physical symptoms that have brought her to the clinic: "Terrible headache, dizziness, and a heart ache—I feel like my heart is moving."[16] With further inquiry, Laxmi talked about her family situation. Married at fourteen to a man twelve years older than she, Laxmi has lived with her in-laws and apart from her husband from the beginning, meeting him briefly only every two to three months. He has beaten her from the time they first met and during their reunions. He works in a hotel in Kathmandu and sporadically sends money home to support the family. Laxmi's goals for her life are "to have my own house. I wish I could stay with my husband." At this point, Laxmi's dream seems impossible since her husband's income is very low, and they cannot afford to all live in Kathmandu.

Laxmi's case illustrates themes common to the sample of depressed women:

---

15. See Jack 1999; Sperberg and Stabb 1998.

16. The interviewer wrote the account in the third person, because Laxmi's husband was speaking for her. I have changed the account back to the first person to make it readable.

marital violence, subordination, marriage as an instrument to create kinship with the husband's family, the lowly status of daughter-in-law, and woman's economic and emotional dependence on a husband. Laxmi does not speak as if her husband should not beat her; she yearns to live with him apart from her in-laws.

Early Marriages, Suicide, Trauma, and Sense of Self-Worth. Raju, age thirty-seven, unmarried, illiterate, is the youngest daughter in a joint family of six people. She lists physical symptoms with her mouth and jaw as the reason for seeking help. She thinks that God is punishing her for some sin; she blames herself for the death of her best friend. Raju went on to tell the interviewer the story that she had never before shared with anyone. Raju's friend wanted to marry a man she loved, but her parents were against it. Her friend asked Raju to buy kerosene; in front of Raju, she doused herself, lit a match, and killed herself. Since then, Raju has blamed herself and repeats that she does not want to live. She never married because her parents have no son, and she wanted to stay to help them. Now she cannot work and feels useless.

Raju's depression was precipitated by the trauma of her friend's death and reveals one possible consequence of rapid social change. Traditional cultural norms dictate that Nepali parents (mainly among the Hindu, who comprise roughly 85 percent of the population) arrange the marriages of their children. Yet increasingly, young Nepalese who have access to television and radio are exposed to media that present the new cultural alternative of love marriage. Further, the numbers of young women entering into secondary school and higher education, as well as into jobs outside the home, are increasing. Such changes, combined with arranged marriages occurring more often at sixteen and above rather than younger, mean that young women encounter opportunities to form love relationships and thus to experience a clash between traditional values and their personal preferences.

The suicide of Raju's friend reflects a despair that can result from conflicting loyalties that appear to have no resolution without significant loss: either a young woman forgoes obedient loyalty to parents and loses their affection and trust, or she marries the man of their choice and loses her own love relationship and dreams. Feeling that all exits from the situation were blocked, her friend took the only way out she saw and left Raju feeling traumatized and responsible. Adding to Raju's sense of loss and sin is her inability to fulfill her role of working to help her family.

Conclusions and Recommendations

This chapter has described how social inequality, violence, and specific adverse social factors are overwhelmingly present in the lives of Nepalese women who seek help for depression. Most of these women are trapped in difficult life circumstances, including violent marriages, because of economic dependence and little to no education. They have limited possibility of escape, either through employment, return to natal family, or help from social organizations. The anger that results from violence and devaluation is most often silenced out of fear of consequences, and thus humiliation is suffered. Ongoing life difficulties associated with poverty and poor health bring repeated crises. Cultural expectations that daughters-in-law are subservient to the husband's mother and his family reduce possibilities for young married women to have a close and confiding relationship within their new families unless it exists with their husbands. All these factors add to women's vulnerability to depression.

The fact that self-silencing correlates significantly with depression in Nepalese women and men carries implications for interventions. First, relationships are critically important to both women and men: both sexes most frequently pointed to problems in their relationships when asked what they think is causing their symptoms. But further scrutiny demonstrates that women's self-silencing is owing primarily to their inequality and fear of consequences. Mental health professionals need to inquire about a woman's situation, particularly in regard to the violence and humiliation she may be suffering. Doing so will give her a safe opportunity to talk, and also may be the first chance she has to problem-solve regarding her family situation. Nepali culture does not encourage sharing one's troubles outside the family, but from our study, it was clear that outpatients found relief in discussing their life situations. Many of the women said it was the first time that they had been respectfully listened to or had shared traumatic events or both. As found in other studies, self-silencing and attempting to bury one's distress correlate with the risk of depression. Thus, one inexpensive alternative for treatment of depression in Nepal is to create groups where depressed women can share their feelings, find commonality, and support each other as they consider ways to improve their situations and envision new options together.

These interviews underscore how important it is not simply to use a biomedical framework to address women's depression and ignore the underlying social factors. Psychological counseling is extremely rare in Nepal. Nonformal mental health care is mostly provided by traditional healers. Their methods for treatment of depression are varied, and their effectiveness is unknown. Further, many traditional healers share the values of their culture that women are subservient and inferior to men. Most formal mental health care has a biomedical orientation, psychiatrists at government outpatient clinics can only spend from seven to twenty minutes with a patient, and patient loads are enormous. As a result, most clinical depression is treated with medication only. But treating depression with medication without addressing social situations may be simply a temporary bandage, and may possibly help abused women only adjust to existing circumstances.

Nepal is caught in a bind. The government is preoccupied with fighting a Maoist insurgency. Many nongovernmental organization programs for women's empowerment and development, particularly in the Terai and the far west, have been suspended or interrupted because of the ongoing conflict. In the meantime, public policies must be formulated to help women either avoid depression or overcome it. Government agencies and NGOs can play a critical role by including a relevant psychosocial component for depression in their programs for women. Women's empowerment programs, for example, could address depression and improve women's psychological coping as they help women gain economic independence and offer literacy training. Through gender equity programs, women need to learn their rights and gain self-respect; men need to learn that physical abuse is illegal and culturally unacceptable.

One hopes that the government's National Mental Health Policy, adopted in 1999, will be fully funded and implemented. In the long run, however, in order to offset women's depression in Nepal, their social inequality must be redressed. As the 1998 *World Health Report* states, "Women's health is inextricably linked to their status in society. It benefits from equality, and suffers from discrimination. Today, the status and well-being of countless millions of women worldwide remain tragically low. As a result, human well-being suffers, and the prospects for future generations are dimmer" (World Health Organization 1998, 6).

15 The Menace of Dowry

Laws, Interpretation, and Implementation

POONAM SAXENA

MARRIAGES IN INDIA are usually arranged by the parents or the guardians of the parties. Though a girl of eighteen and a boy of twenty-one years can legally marry without the consent of their parents, in reality such marriages meet with strong social disapproval, and it is primarily the decision of the parents that rules the marriage. It is therefore arranged and negotiated by the parents of the respective parties, and the disparity in the status of a girl and a boy is perhaps most evident at the time of such negotiations and until the solemnization of marriage and continues afterward.

Marriage, the primary aim of every Indian girl's life as she is often told, comes with a heavy price, that is, dowry. Instances are plenty where the houses have been mortgaged to raise funds for the marriage expenses of the daughters. Dowry includes presents given by the bride's parents to not only the bridegroom and his parents but to many of his other relatives as well. It could take the form of money, clothes, jewelry, land, costly household appliances, furniture, a scooter or car, and sometimes even a flat or a house. It may be given willingly or can be demanded by the bridegroom or his family members.

The concept of dowry, which originally might have had its sanction in the religious texts, is so central to our lives and society that a majority of Hindus find it difficult to reject it, even though it is now governed by market forces. Unmarried girls commit suicide for the inability of their parents to arrange sufficient money for their dowry. Newly married girls may be burned to death for their failure to meet the expectations of the dowry demands of the husband and his family members. Yet the practice continues. Eyebrows are raised when the media highlight such murders, yet no one is against accepting money or gifts from the bride's family under the garb of gifts made out of love and affection. The father or even the brothers of a girl would sell their property to marry her off and would wait for their turn to get a comparable return from their wives or their fathers. This vicious circle continues, and the economic exploitation of the bride and her family is strengthened further, along with the bride's ill treatment, humiliation, and abuse. Despite legislation and its subsequent amendments, the plight of the girls in India continues.

This chapter analyzes the legal provisions relating to dowry, the response of parliamentarians and society in general toward the practice of dowry, and the attitude of the courts when they deal with cases of dowry deaths and dowry-related harassment of young wives, under the newly inserted provisions. Questions that this chapter addresses are: Have these provisions been adequate to curb the menace of dowry? Is the attitude of the judges who adjudicate dowry cases compatible with the spirit of the enactment? Does the punishment match the crime? To what extent are the parents of the girl responsible for her death, when knowing full well that the girl is in trouble if they refuse to have her back and still insist that she remains with the husband, eventually meeting a tragic end? How is it that the parents are prepared to spend a substantial amount of money on the wedding of their daughters but would not teach her to be economically independent or self-reliant? What steps can be taken to prevent a bride from being burned? What can ensure her a meaningful life with dignity and independence?

Dowry: Background and Overview

The ancient texts condemn in the strongest possible terms the passing of any money, however small its quantum may be from the bridegroom's side to the bride's parents, while the converse is not only approved but is actually recommended. An agreement to pay a sum of money to the father of the girl in consideration of giving his daughter in marriage is opposed to public policy and therefore invalid, but a promise to make a gift in consideration of the bridegroom agreeing to marry the daughter was considered valid and enforceable (Mayne, Hindu Law, 108, 116).

The Dharamshastras (the ancient Hindu texts that are the primary source of Hindu laws and are considered divine in origin) provided for the attire of the bride at the time of the marriage and also that she be honored with presents and jewels. These presents and jewels were later confused or conflated with *var dakshina* (presents meant for the bridegroom), which is the genesis of dowry. Jurists and historians believe that it might have been intended as a security for the newly wedded couple. It seems unlikely, however, given that in the days of large joint families the security afforded by dowry could hardly have benefited the couple alone. Though no longer obligatory, these dictates that are a result of a selective reading of the ancient texts are still referred to by the dowry seekers to justify the continuance of the practice.

Marriage, too, has its distinctive features in India. Even among the educated and upper class, the parties in marriage are not treated as equal. Those individuals associated with the bridegroom enjoy respect regardless of their conduct, whereas the relatives of the bride are humble, accommodating, and respectful, anxious to please the bridegroom and his entire entourage with gifts and polite behavior and to win them over with good food. The reason is a traditional belief that the girl and her parents are lower in status than the boy and his family, and the bridegroom does a favor to the family by accepting the hand of their daughter.

Dowries can be very large and an onerous burden on families. In cases of lower-income families, where loans are taken out to pay the dowry, brothers have been known to put themselves in bonded servitude until the loans are repaid. Special schemes are launched by the banks and insurance companies for investments and loan facilities for the marriage of the daughters. Even the Hindu Dharamshastras permit the sale of joint family property by the *karta* (manager) without the consent of its other co-owners, if the sale proceeds are to be utilized for the marriage expenses of the daughter.[1]

In upper-income families, marriage and the dowry constitute an occasion for people to spend lavishly and indulge in a display of their wealth or prestige. But this display of wealth has a disastrous effect on the middle-class community. These lavish expenditures, often incurred by influential politicians and rich businessmen, inspire a common man to accord legitimacy to his more modest demands. For him, it becomes the most convenient way of getting rich overnight at the cost of the young bride and her vulnerable father's purse. In addition to these demands, it is the wasteful expenditure incurred through huge marriage feasts (compulsorily hosted by the parents of the bride), which is substantial. It is no wonder, therefore, that the biggest worry of the parents in the patriarchal society is the arrangement of money for the marriage of their daughters.

Legislation on Dowry

The media, women's organizations, and parliamentarians have been attuned to the ugly nature of dowry for some time. The Dowry Prohibition Bill was introduced in

1. Under classical Hindu law, the *karta* is empowered to sell the joint Hindu family property without the consent of its co-owners in three specific situations: legal necessity, benefit of estate, and performance of indispensable duties. Joint family property can be sold and the proceeds used for the marriage of an unmarried daughter, as it is covered under legal necessity.

the parliament in 1959 and took the shape of an act in 1961. It has since been amended twice with parallel amendments in the criminal law to make the act more effective and the punishment more stringent.

It should be noted that the first antidowry legislation was introduced in a small village in Vijayanagar around four centuries ago. Shyamala M. Iyer (1985) writes of an incident that infuriated the king of Vijayanagar, and he passed an order prohibiting the taking of dowry and subsequent killing of an innocent bride for dissatisfaction with the amount of money brought by her. In 1939 in the province of Sind, the Sind Leti Act was passed. It prohibited the payments of money as part of the contract of betrothal or marriage and so on. Dowry was defined as the payment made in connection with or consequence of the betrothal or marriage and includes the giving of gifts and presents of any kind, or in connection with any festival or auspicious day on account of birth of a child or any ceremony in the families of the bride or the bridegroom. The state government of Bihar enacted the Bihar Dowry Restraint Act in 1950. Some years later, in 1958, the Andhra Pradesh state government enacted the Andhra Pradesh Dowry Prohibition Act. These acts were passed with the sole objectives of eradicating the practice of the system of dowry in the respective states. The central enactment came in the shape of the Dowry Prohibition Bill of 1959, which was the parent bill of the subsequent Dowry Prohibition Act (DPA) of 1961.

The definition has since been amended twice, and the present provisions governing dowry and the related crimes are as follows:

> Dowry means any property or valuable security given or agreed to be given either directly or indirectly by the parents of either party to a marriage or by any person to either party to the marriage or to any person at or before or any time after the marriage in connection with the marriage of the parties but does not include dower or mehr in the case of persons to whom the Muslim Personal Law (Shariat) applies.[2]

The proviso is that any presents given at the time of marriage in the form of cash, ornaments, clothes, or other articles is not dowry. That is, presents made by the relatives or friends out of love and affection should not attract penal sanction.

The law prohibits "cruelty" to a bride in connection with dowry:

---

2. See the Dowry Prohibition Act 1961 s 4.

Whoever being the husband or the relative of the husband of the woman subjects such woman to cruelty shall be punished with imprisonment for a term which may extend to three years and shall also be liable for fine.

Cruelty means any willful conduct which is of such a nature as is likely to drive the woman to commit suicide or to cause grave injury or danger to life, limb or health (whether mental or physical) of the woman, or harassment of the woman where such harassment is caused with a view to coercing her or any person related to her to meet any demand for any property or any valuable security or any person related to her to meet such demand.[3]

Indian law also defines "dowry death" and stipulates the punishment in the event of a bride's death within the first seven years of marriage:

(1) Where the death of a woman is caused by any burns or bodily injury or occurs otherwise than under normal circumstances within seven years of her marriage; And it is shown that soon before her death she was subjected to cruelty or harassment by her husband and her relatives of the husband for or in connection with any demand for dowry such a death shall be called "Dowry Death" and such husband or relative shall be deemed to have caused her death.

(2) Whoever commits dowry death shall be punishable with imprisonment for life.[4]

The law also provides for presumption in cases of dowry deaths. Section 113 of the Evidence Act stipulates: "When the question is whether a person has committed the dowry death of a woman and it is shown that soon before her death such woman had been subjected by such person to cruelty or harassment for or in connection with any demand for dowry the court shall presume that such person has caused the dowry death."[5] The meaning of dowry is given under Section 498-A, as a willful conduct of a nature to drive a woman to commit suicide or cause grave injury or danger to her life and so on. It may also mean harassment or coercion to her or any person related to her to meet the demand for dowry or on failure to meet the demand for dowry.

Punishment for dowry offenses is made comparatively severe; the offenses are made nonbailable; dowry death was made punishable by consequent amendment

---

3. See Section 498A, Indian Penal Code, 1860.

4. Section 304B, Indian Penal Code, 1860.

5. See Indian Evidence Act s 113.

to the Indian Penal Code, Code of Criminal Procedure Code, and the Indian Evidence Act; a provision for the appointment of a dowry-prohibition officer by the state is made for the effective implementation of the act; and the burden of proof that there was no demand for dowry is shifted to the person who is alleged to have taken or abetted the taking of dowry. As per the rules framed under the act, the law requires a list of presents given at the time of marriage, giving in brief the description of each present, its approximate value, the name of the person giving the present, and his or her relationship with the bride or the groom. Failure to maintain such a list or enter in the list any present can result in the giver and the receiver becoming liable for punishment for giving or taking of dowry. It is also obligatory for any person receiving dowry either before of after marriage or at the time of marriage to transfer it in favor of the woman within three months of the marriage. If they fail to do so, they are supposed to hold it in trust for the wife (Jain 1996, 566, 567).

While the intention of the legislature to consider the offenses as grave and befitting a stringent punishment is evident, the technicalities prevailing and adopted by the courts in judging these offenses are a major hindrance to punishing the guilty, as is apparent from the number of cases that went to the courts and the decisions given in them. In the section below I discuss some of these cases to show how the practice still continues unabated, with the judiciary often adopting a very casual or dismissive attitude toward this harmful practice.

Interpretation of "Dowry Demand": A Review of Some Legal Cases

A situation where after marriage the husband and his relations threaten to break up the marriage if the demands are not met would undoubtedly be a dowry demand. Or a situation where the wife is abused and given to understand that if she brings money she will be treated nicely is clearly a case of a dowry demand. Likewise, where the wife is sent back to the parents' house and told that she will be allowed reentry in the matrimonial home only when the demands for money are met would be a case of dowry demand. Yet the approach of the courts is bewildering, as is apparent from some cases.

In *Shanker Prosad Shaw v. State of U.P.*, the marriage took place on May 14, 1981. The couple lived together for about nine months (CrLJ 2217 [UP]). Thereafter, the father and the brother of the husband began to make illegal demands to bring costly electronic appliances and cash. On failure of the wife to get these articles from her father, the wife was abused in the husband's house, but the demand was not held as an offense under the act. The explanation given by the court was that the bride's father did not agree to give it but rather knocked at the doors of the court. If he had agreed to give the additional dowry, it might have been an offense. This judgment leaves open the question as to whether any payment or presentation of articles by the father of the wife or any of her relations to placate the in-laws is one in connection with the marriage and thus is embraced within the scope of dowry.

The interpretation of the word *dowry* and "the demand in consideration or in connection with marriage" was again considered in *State of Punjab v. Daljit Singh* (1999, CrLJ 2723 [P&H]). The bride of four years died of poisoning. The facts proved before the court were that she was harassed for not bringing fifty thousand rupees demanded by the husband and the in-laws in order to send the younger brother of the husband abroad. She was sent back to her parents' house and was brought back by the husband only two days prior to her death after an assurance was given by her parents about the payment of money. The prosecution proved that she was harassed, which compelled her to end her life. The court observed:

> It is thus proved that on account of demand of Rs. 50000 made by the appellant which was not fulfilled, Lakhbir Kaur was harassed thus compelling her to end her life. . . . [I]n laws of deceased did not want her to die and also did not allow her to live in peace. The court explored the meaning of the term Dowry under the Dowry Prohibition Act, and concluded that it was not dowry related harassment and therefore the accused cannot be held liable under the DPA. The demand for money was proved but for what purpose the demand was made was also an important factor to be considered. Here the demand was for sending the younger brother of the husband of the deceased abroad and according to the court was not related or connected with the marriage of the deceased with the accused. Thus though the demand for money existed it was not in consideration or in connection with their marriage. This was a demand for money, which is different from dowry. Holding that the accused are not guilty under the DPA.

The court also said:

> To illustrate after four or five years of marriage the husband being in some financial difficulties in his business requests or demands some money from his father in law directly or through his wife only with a view that he is able to advance in his life, can such a demand be termed as Dowry? In our view the answer has to be in the negative. Looked from any angle we are of the firm view that the demand of Rs. 50000

made by the appellants so as to send Khushwant Singh abroad cannot be connected with Dowry by any stretch of imagination.

The honorable court failed to note that it was basically to protect the wife from such demands that the Dowry Prohibition Act was passed. No person should be allowed or given a right to advance in his life at the cost of his father-in-law's purse, least of all in situations when the latter is either unwilling or unable to do so. For what purpose the demand was made should not be a material factor. A demand is a demand, and a demand from a person who is unable to pay or unwilling to pay and tormenting his daughter for achieving that demand should be taken very seriously. It is primarily to discourage any such demand where the right to demand stems from a newly created or shortly established marital relationship that the DPA was enacted. It is the reason that demands made even after the solemnization of marriage are included in the DPA.

This case illustrates why statutes passed with a view to eradicate or minimize social evils should be interpreted so as to correct the imbalance in the society. These judgments should serve as an example and act as a deterrent against criminal enrichments by a husband or his relations at the cost of the bride's life and her father's purse. Here, with a narrow and constrained interpretation, the judiciary actually helped the guilty to escape punishment for such a heinous crime.

Elango v. State of Madras was a case about a young woman of twenty-one who within eleven months of her marriage died an unnatural death (AIR 1997 SC 359). There was a demand for a gold watch by the husband. According to the judge, the husband demanded that the wife obtain cash and jewels, including a gold watch, from her parents. The learned court noted that the sum of thirty-seven thousand rupees was made by the father of the bride to the bridegroom, which the latter accepted. Though the draft was in the name of the wife, it was put in the joint bank account of the husband and the wife opened immediately after marriage. The husband claimed that the wife committed suicide because she was frustrated owing to the nonconsummation of their marriage, which was his fault. The facts presented a strange scenario. A frustrated wife and an impotent husband demanding a gold watch, jewels, and money, and accepting thirty-seven thousand rupees from the father-in-law. If he could admit that he was responsible for nonconsummation of marriage because of which the wife's frustration reached a point that she was compelled to put an end to her life, could anyone justify the demand made by him to his father-in-law?

It is shocking that the learned court noted with approval that as far as Hindus are concerned, whether they are rich or poor, "it is known practice prevailing in this State that for one full year commencing from the date of the marriage whenever an important Hindu festival occurs during that time the parents of the bride will always give the traditional and conventional presentations out of love and affection to the bride as well as to the groom." The accused was therefore let off.

In *G. A. Mohamed Moideen v. State,* the wife died owing to hanging, and the husband took the plea that she had committed suicide (1992 CrLJ 111). The accused husband was found guilty of murder by the trial court and sentenced to seven years' imprisonment. His sentence was confirmed by the high court. The revision petition was filed by the accused to the Madras High Court. The husband had stated that the wife wanted him to set up a separate family. The father of the deceased had stated— which was also proved—that the husband had demanded fifty thousand rupees from the father-in-law to set up a shop in the municipal area. The nonpayment of this amount had led to the abuse of the wife and her death. The court in the revision explored the cross-examination and came to the conclusion that as the father of the wife also wanted the daughter to set up a separate family, the demand of money for leasing a shop was not so grave that would be included as dowry demand, and the husband was acquitted of all charges.

For the courts to connect these two things was not correct. It was wrong to come to the conclusion that if the husband and wife want to set up a separate family, the father of the wife would necessarily be responsible for financing the setting up of the shop for his son-in-law. Why should it be the responsibility of the father-in-law? Businessmen have various options available to raise money for the purpose of setting up shops or opening new ventures, and a demand by the son-in-law would not cease to be a demand if the purpose is to set up a shop. It is no different from any other demand. The act does not specify categories or purposes of demands made by the in-laws of the bride from her father. Even a demand to deck out their daughter-in-law in costly ornaments and fine clothes would be a demand within the meaning of the DPA if the bride's father was unwilling to do so. This case is yet another illustration of how attempted enrichments by a husband at the cost of his father-in-law's purse are treated by the courts as acceptable.

In *Jagdish Chander v. State of Haryana,* the wife of four years suffered 100 percent burns and died (1988 CrLJ 1048). The couple had a three-year-old daughter, and the wife was six to seven months pregnant. Her parents alleged that she was constantly being harassed for dowry and that the husband had burned her. The husband was now trying to feign it was an accident. The trial court noticed that there was a delay of two days in filing the complaint by the relatives of the deceased, and the wife when brought to the hospital was semiconscious but unable to make any statement. This delay in filing the complaint and the fact that there was no direct evidence led the court to conclude that the wife might have committed suicide. The husband accordingly was held guilty of abetment to commit suicide. On appeal the high court overruled the judgment of the trial court and said that harassment or use of heated words against the deceased whereafter she commits suicide does not amount to abetment, and therefore no offense was committed by the husband. Hunting for the possible reasons for her death, they said that she might have died because of the bursting of the stove or because of suicide, but it was not owing to any instigation or incitement by the husband. Regarding the victim, they said, "She was probably a sentimental woman and did not like the drinking habits of the appellant who cannot be held responsible for her suicide." The husband was thereby absolved from all the charges and let off. Strange are the views of our highest judiciary. They add insult to the injury. Addiction to drinking despite protests from the spouse should be taken very seriously and is not just the normal wear-and-tear of married life.

In *Sham Lal v. State of Haryana,* the wife suffered 100 percent burns and died. She was married for less than seven years (AIR 1997 SC 1873). It was in evidence that the accused husband and his family members were harassing her for not bringing sufficient dowry. She was sent back to her parents by the husband, and after a year and a half the local Panchayat (the village level court) met both the parties and effected a compromise pursuant to which the husband was persuaded to take the wife back. She was brought back to the house of the husband and within fifteen days died of her burns. Her father rushed to the hospital but could see only the charred remains of his daughter. He testified in court that in the hospital he had asked the husband whether he had burned his daughter and that the latter had nodded yes and had even asked for forgiveness by acknowledging his mistake with folded hands. The trial court deemed that the husband, his father, and grandmother were guilty of committing the murder of the deceased wife and sentenced them all to life imprisonment. On appeal, the first appellate court acquitted the grandmother but confirmed the sentence of the husband and his father. The high court acquitted the father but confirmed the conviction of the husband.

The supreme court absolved the husband of all the charges under Section 302 on the grounds that there was no evidence that immediately before her death, in that short period of fifteen days, she was harassed for dowry. The court opined that to invoke the legal presumption of dowry death it was imperative to prove that soon before her death she was subjected to such cruelty or harassment. Although the court acknowledged the facts of the prosecution's argument, it decided that there was nothing on record to show how she was treated after she came back to her husband's house. The husband took the plea that the wife had committed suicide, as she was unable to adjust to village life and was frustrated at her inability to bear child. Believing these motivations in fact to be the reasons for which she committed suicide, the supreme court held that it was a case of suicide. In overturning the judgment of the lower courts, the supreme court said, "But it is a certainty that Neelam Rani died under abnormal circumstances. It is not a case of homicide. It could be a case of suicide because her death by accident could reasonably be ruled out from all the broad circumstances in this case."

In *Prem Singh v. State of Punjab,* a bride of seven and a half months died under mysterious circumstances (AIR 1997 SC 221). When her husband and his brother brought her body to the hospital, the attending doctor said that her death might be owing to poisoning. The accused pleaded before the court that his wife had committed suicide. Yet at the same time he could not come up with any explanation as to why and what compelled a newly married woman to end her life. The prosecution, on the other hand, was able to prove that both the husband and his brother had beaten the deceased a day before her death. The medical evidence also proved that the death was owing to violence and poisoning. The trial court convicted the husband and his brother of murder under Section 302 IPC r/w Section 34 and sentenced both of them to life imprisonment. The high court confirmed the sentence and dismissed the appeals. The supreme court, however, disagreed with the concurrent findings of both the lower courts and held, "Except this demand of Bullet Motorcycle there is no other evidence adduced by the prosecution that alleged maltreatment meted out to Surinder Kaur (deceased)."

According to the court, there was no dispute that the parents of the deceased had given the husband a motorcycle. But

> having regard to the facts and circumstances of the case we are of the considered view that the prosecution has failed to prove beyond reasonable doubt that Surinder Kaur met with a homicidal death. The defence plea of suicide cannot be ruled out. It is unfortunate that the marriage of Surinder Kaur, which took place seven and a half months before the date of the occurrence, ended in such a tragic death. From the evidence on record we are unable to pinpoint the guilty person although her death is shrouded with suspicious circumstances. It is in these circumstances, we are constrained to give the benefit of doubt to both the appellants.

Again the supreme court paid lip service to the DPA rather than do it justice. They chose to base their judgment on unconvincing loopholes. Indeed, the court went out of its way to hunt for any possible benefit of the doubt for the accused but chose not to question what would compel a newly married woman to end her life.

Attitude of Parliamentarians toward Dowry

All political parties without exception publicly proclaim their commitment to eradicate practices derogatory to woman, yet their personal views and private actions are often completely in contrast to these proclamations. Given below are the views of Indian lawmakers toward dowry and legislation to curb this menace. I begin with statements by those parliamentarians in favor of dowry.

> Somehow or other we seem to be feminine ridden. Somehow or other we have given so much lift to the ladies that when ever any demand comes from them we surrender to them immediately; reason or no reason. That seems to be the law. Whatever be their demand, that is considered to be a reformist demand because the demand is made by the ladies. . . . I suggest that we should not indulge in these smaller matters. Let us leave this matter to the society and take up some other serious affair for the development and progress of the society.

> Dowry will benefit the *"uneducated and not so beautiful girls,"* who could get a good place after taking money with them by way of Dowry. (Tyagi, Lok Sabha Debates, 1959, 799)

> Dowry should be given according to the status of the parent of the girl.

> If nothing is allowed to be given, their financial position would become weak at the starting point of her life. In the Punjab, as far as the peasantry is concerned, we do not want that the girls should succeed to their parents' property. We are very anxious that the rights of the girls in Punjab and all over the country in the whole of India, should be fully safeguarded by allowing the system of Dowry to remain as it is. . . . I can understand a husband choosing a wife thinking that she is a real heiress and that he would get the benefit if he marries her. This thing can not be ignored in our society. Every father wants that his daughter be married in a rich family, similarly every man wants that he may be married in a rich family. Why should you make any obligations as far as these persons are concerned?

Why should the girls feel dissatisfied that the age old custom in their favor should be disturbed in this way? (Thakur Das Bhargava, Lok Sabha Debates, 1959, 3413–54)

I must say that in the ultimate analysis there are to sections of people in the society, parents with more sons and parents with more daughters. Parents with more sons will certainly go against this bill while parents with more daughters will say dowry is not good. . . . So it all depends on the individual integrity, individual spirit and individual opinion. (Kumari M. Veda Kumari, Lok Sabha Debates, 1959, 953)

The committee feels that the evils of dowry system leading to murders, suicides, burning—popularly known as Dowry deaths—harassment and torture of newly married young girls throughout the country are creating a fear psychosis in India, like the Mafia in European countries. (Sh. Jagannath Kaushal, Rajya Sabha Debates, 1984, 319)

The practice of dowry is justified as not only serving a purpose but actually bene-fiting the girls. If there is a poor man, his daughter is not beautiful and has not been educated. She can get a good place by giving money. (Sh. Tyagi, Lok Sabha Debates, 1959, 794)

Parliamentarians like Tyagi fail to note that it is primarily to protect poor people like the one he quoted in his speech that antidowry legislation was enacted. How, according to his "logic," can a father who is a poor man be in a position to pay money by way of dowry to anyone? Would he have to beg, borrow, or steal to give a dowry? Nor does Tyagi question why a girl should be uneducated, and who is re-sponsible? Further, he assumes that a place bought with money would still be "good." According to Tyagi, those individuals who demand dowry are still good. This is the shameful attitude of our parliamentarians toward giving and taking of dowry. Rather than condemning it, they justify it.

Reactions of Parliamentarians Opposed to Dowry

Sir, we found only in Delhi City since last 1st September to 3rd 1984, near about 228 women were dead. Some of them were murdered, some of the women were burnt alive and some of them committed suicides. Because of not giving dowry. At least every day two women are victims of dowry in Delhi city alone. (Sh. Dinkar Rao Govindrao Patil, Rajya Sabha Debates, 1984)

Twenty five years have lapsed since the introduction of the first parent bill in the Lok Sabha, in 1959. Yet the Dowry deaths are on the increase. Almost daily in the newspaper, we see reports of deaths due to so-called "accidental stove bursts," which are anything but accidental. Almost always the persons involved in these tragic incidents are young married women who are done to death in cold blooded, calculated, premediated manner—all for the sake of dowry or because of lack of it. Therefore it is evident that more stringent measures and draconian laws are called for to stamp out this murderous dowry system which has already claimed so many innocent lives and reduced to ashes innumerable young girls in the flower of womanhood and has mercilessly crushed countless young blossoms which should have been nurtured and cherished instead. (Jayalalitha, Rajya Sabha Debates, 1984, 334)

The dowry Prohibition Bill deals with one of the menacing irritants in the leading of harmonious family life. . . . The evil of dowry system has been a matter of serious concern to everyone in view of its ever increasing and disturbing proportions. How this menace is to be checked, curbed and eradicated is something which has to be viewed on a totally non-partisan and non-political basis. (Jagannath Kaushal, Rajya Sabha Debates, 1984, 321–22)

The Judicial Approach

The application of the laws is done by the judiciary. The provisions relating to dowry if interpreted strictly and applied forcefully would send a strong message to dowry seekers. The application should never encourage those individuals who blatantly violate the provisions of the Dowry Prohibition Act into thinking that here is a crime that largely goes unpunished, and even after openly demanding dowry they can fall back upon the redundant provisions of the ancient texts that they have picked up or manipulate the societal sympathy to their advantage. The interpretation to the provisions passed with an eye on social reform must match stringent law. Unfortunately, although as a general rule the judiciary favors a punishment that matches the crime, in dowry cases there is a visible sympathy not with the victim or her family but with the accused. Given below are some observations of judges while dealing with dowry cases. We begin with judgments made by courts that do not pertain to dowry deaths but emphasize the need to interpret the law strictly rather than leniently. We then contrast these strong statements on the law, its interpretation, and its implementation with judicial decisions that acquitted the husband in the case of a dowry crime or passed an inappropriately reduced sentence.

Considerations of undue sympathy in such cases will lead to miscarriage of justice and undermine confidence of the public in the efficacy of the criminal justice system. *(State of Karnataka v. Kishna alias Raju* [1987] 1 SCC 5638)

It will be a mockery of justice to permit an accused to escape the extreme penalty of law when faced with such evidence and such cruel acts. To give a lesser punishment for the accused would be to render the justice system of the country suspect. The common man will lose faith in courts. In such cases he understands and appreciates the language of deterrence more than reformative jargon. (Supreme Court while refusing to interfere with a death sentence, in *Mahesh v. State of M.P.,* AIR 1990 SC 1346)

Inadequate sentences can do harm to the system. Law must meet the challenge so that the criminalization offers. Maudlin sentiments bordering on toteing [*sic*] weakness cannot masquerade or reformative sentiments cannot do service for a rational sentence system. Misconceived liberalism cannot be countenanced. *(Raman v. Francis* 1988 CrLJ 1359 at 132)

Has emphasized that it is the duty of the court toward proper sentences in each and every case with respect to the nature of the offence and the manner in which it was committed. (Supreme Court in *State of Punjab v. Mann Singh,* AIR 1983 SC 172)

If it appeared to the court that the sentence awarded to the accused is grossly inadequate having regard to the gravity of the offence it should not hesitate to impose adequate sentence an the accused even though the effect of the order might be to send the accused back to the jail once again. *(State v. Pritamdas,* AIR 1956 Bom. 559)

In contrast to the tough approach taken to nondowry crimes, we see the soft approach pedaled in cases of dowry-related crimes. In one case, for example, the following statements were made:

Though one would not justify demands for money, it has to be viewed in this perspective. The respondent is a young upcoming doctor. There is nothing strange in his asking his wife to give him money when he is in need of it. There is no satisfactory evidence that the demands were such as to border on harassment.

She is prone to exaggerate things . . . because of her over sensitiveness or because of her habit of exaggeration she has made a mountain out of a molehill.

The wife appeared to be hypersensitive and she imagined too much and too unnatural things.

Though one would not justify demands for money it has to be viewed in the circumstances from a proper angle. The respondent is a doctor. If he asks his rich wife to spare some money, there is nothing wrong or unusual.

Persistent demand for money did not constitute a demand for Dowry which is defined Sec. 2 had to be founded on some agreement. Dowry means any property or valuable security given or agreed to be given. As the girl's father at no time agreed to meet the demand, it was not a "demand for Dowry," but simply a demand for money. *(Shobha Rani v. Madhukar Reddy* 1998 CrLJ 1048)

Other cases, too, evince the soft approach to dowry-related crimes:

The definition of the word consideration leads us to conclusion that the property or valuable security should be demanded or given whether in the past, present or future for bringing out solemnization of marriage. After the marriage giving a property or valuable security by the parents of the bride cannot constitute a consideration for the marriage unless it was agreed at the time of or before the marriage that such property or valuable security would be given in future.

Anything given after marriage (even if given) on account of demand from the boy or his parents or relatives is only a consideration for the continuation of marriage or for happy matrimonial relationship.[6]

Property that may pass hands subsequently, to the marriage even months or years after it merely to save the marriage from being broken or otherwise keep the family of the in-laws better disposed towards her, to smooth the course of matrimonial life or to save the wife from harassment, humiliation or taunts on the grounds that she did not bring enough at the time for marriage is not Dowry. *(Delhi High Court in Madden All v. Amaranth* 1985 CrLJ [Del])

6. See J. Luthra, in *Inder Sain v. State* 1981 CrLJ 1116 at 1118, on the issue of what constitutes consideration within the meaning of the act.

Labeling the death of a young married woman as tragic, the courts very conveniently forget that she was also a young woman full of hopes and desires and ambitions and above all was a human being, with a human right to live with dignity. Be it a case of forcing her to commit suicide or causing her death, the accused should not be allowed to go free or with a comparatively lesser sentence than what is prescribed by law; otherwise, the whole process looks like an exercise in futility. Stringent legislation is hardly helpful if the practical implementation is not brought up to the desired level.

It appears to be a miserable situation. The scene of the crime is the home of the accused. The crime comes to light much after it has already been committed and the evidences destroyed. The accused husband is sure to have established relations with all possible witnesses. However, for the deceased it was a new place, and for her parents it is a totally strange place and with unknown people. The horrifying impact of the sudden shock of the death or murder of the bride is lessened by the passage of time, and by the time the matter reaches the court it is already a thing of the past and ceases to be of interest to the neighbors and other people.

On top of it is the attitude of the society. The worth of the boy is still measured in terms of the amount of dowry that he is able to fetch in the marriage market. His earning capacity and dowry-fetching abilities make him an eligible bachelor, whatever his family's financial background. The desire of all his family members to satisfy their unfulfilled ambitions with the help of this eligible bachelor is the genesis of dowry demands for which the bride has to pay with her life. Wanting to become rich overnight, family members in active connivance of the bridegroom openly put him up for a sale in the marriage market. The boy and his family are never condemned for their demand or for what they get.

A report indicated that the most rampant practice of dowry is among the Indian Administrative Service (IAS) probationers ("IAS Officers" 1987). These young officers who at the very start of their careers violate the government's laws are subsequently entrusted with the job of implementing anticorruption laws and enforcing policies for advancement of the status of women. It is indeed a matter of shame that a prominent politician promised one *crore* (ten million rupees) as dowry to a young probationer from the Uttar Pradesh cadre. In recent years, at least five probationers from Andhra Pradesh and Delhi cadre have been offered dowry up to Rs 5 lakhs (the equivalent of US$10,000). From the Bihar cadre, nearly half a dozen probationers have been given dowry between Rs 25 to 30 lakhs. The report adds, "It is not unusual for a dowry of Rs. 10 to 15 lakhs to be offered. One young probationer was even promised Rs. 10,000 as the *muhn dikhai* [to show his face]. A Maruti car as an engagement present is also a common practice. Nearly ninety percent of the male probationers take huge dowry though the figure varies considerably depending upon the community."

This blatant violation of the antidowry legislation was discussed on July 8, 1987, by the then minister of state for personal and public grievance, who was also urged to institute an inquiry into this matter. The basis of this inquiry was a letter written by eleven lecturers who had visited the academy, who drew the attention of the minister to the widespread and open practice of taking dowry among the IAS probationers. The majority of these fledgling officials after joining the service took dowry negotiated by them or with the knowledge of their parents. Mr. Chidambaram did agree to look into the matter and hoped that something could be done while the probationers were still at the academy, but noted that once they leave it would be impossible to do any checks and added, "Did they really want the government should encroach further into the private lives of the people?"

Ministers, industrialists, bureaucrats, politicians, business persons, and top officials—all of them openly take and give dowry and feel proud to flaunt their wealth. Matters come to light only when the matrimonial relations are broken. The daughter of a prominent politician, Arun Nehru, lodged a complaint with the city's antidowry cell. Her parents had given a fat dowry, which according to her had been retained by her husband when she left his house. What is shocking is that almost no one is against taking and giving of cash and presents at the time of the solemnization of marriage.

Conclusions: Who Is Responsible?

It would be correct to say that the whole society in one way or another contributes to the perpetuation of this practice, yet at the same time the one who suffers most is the girl and then her parents. She loses her life and the parents lose their daughter, yet it would be incorrect to absolve the girl's parents, as they are at least equal contributors to the dowry menace. When a daughter is born, parents are unable to hide their disappointment, owing to the perception of the daughter as an economic burden. She grows up in the father's home learning how to be economically dependent on men. A girl is India is never taught to be self-sufficient or to have self-respect. She is always taught how to respect others, to serve others, and to be dependent on others for her survival. Her own work, though very important for the entire family, remains unremunerated and of a low status. This situation also strengthens her dependency on men who are coached right from their childhood to be providers, career oriented, dominating, and with an unquestionable right to command the services of their sisters and other female members in their household.

Instances are aplenty where girls after finishing primary or even secondary education sit at home helping their mothers in domestic chores, waiting to get married for years together, but would not be encouraged or allowed to go for training or a career. Daughters in India, though perfectly capable and even willing to look after themselves, are forced to become a responsibility and a liability to their parents and then their brothers because of faulty upbringing and society's values and norms. They have to be looked after by their male relations and married by them. The decision-making power is left with the men and is often exercised without consulting the women.

For a roof over her head she is again dependent on the husband during marriage, in other cases on her natal male relations. When it becomes apparent that the bridegroom or his family members want money from the bride's parents before the actual solemnization of the marriage, the latter do not want to break the engagement for fear of social stigma or family prestige. After marriage, when the relations between the husband and the wife become strained because of dowry demands and she either approaches her parents or the parents come to know about it independently, they still insist on a patch-up of the marriage or ask her to adjust. Their hesitation to bring her back is primarily responsible for the tragic end to her life. Parents hope in vain for things to improve, knowing full well that there is little hope for it. Action is filed only after her death.

In the majority of dowry death cases, the wife is economically inactive and a homemaker. It remains a fact that an economically independent woman would not find the problems of survival without a husband as difficult as an economically dependent woman would, nor would she be so easily subjugated as a woman who has no means to support herself. This argument is primarily the reason not much attention is paid to the education of the girl. A woman who can be easily subjugated, is meek and submissive, is not conscious of her rights but is aware of only her duties, brings money by way of dowry and allows her husband to take control of her property, and serves everyone yet is called a liability, such a woman is the product of a patriarchal society and is socialized to serve the patriarchal family institution.

To end the menace of dowry and empower Indian women and girls, and to give real meaning to antidowry legislation, it is imperative that parents and the community do the following:

• change their attitude and treat the girl as an individual rather than someone they nurture for her husband and his family;

- put more stress on her education;
- inculcate in her the ideals of self-respect and self-sufficiency;
- encourage her to opt for a career and be economically active, rather than be resigned to be a homemaker and be dependent on her husband or other male relations financially;
- encourage her to choose her own life partner rather than imposing a parental choice;
- not hesitate to give her shelter in the event of any matrimonial discord;
- and respect her choice of remaining unmarried if she wishes to do so or getting married on her own terms, rather than feel ashamed about it.

16 Islamic Law, Feminism, and Family

The Reformulation of Hudud in Egypt and Tunisia

LILIA LABIDI

HOW ARE VALUES connected with family life and sexuality undergoing transformation in Muslim societies? How is *hudud* (literally, moral boundaries, limits) being redefined? And how do the debates and reformulations reflect societal tensions as well as the influences of the state, religious institutions, the women's movement, and international conventions? In this chapter I examine three practices: the *mahr* (the sum given to the bride by the groom that becomes her personal property), the *diya* (compensation for murder as a substitute for the law of private vengeance), and *al-ijbar* (the father's capacity to oblige his daughter to marry and thus to attain adult status). I also discuss controversies surrounding rape and its consequences, with a focus on public debates and policy reform in Egypt and Tunisia.

Mahr in Contrast to Diya

Why did the Tunisian Personal Status Code (PSC)—which brought numerous positive changes into the lives of women, providing them with a psychological stability that they did not have when they lived in a system that permitted polygamy and repudiation—retain the notion of *mahr* as the foundation of relations between the sexes in the context of marriage? We know that a marriage is deemed invalid if the *mahr* has not been paid. Sexual relations too, even within marriage, are prohibited if the *mahr* has not been paid, with the period of payment indicated in the marriage contract. It is acceptable for the *mahr* to be paid in two portions, one called *mu'ajjil*, the other called *mu'akhkhir*. In the case of divorce after consummation, the woman keeps the full *mahr*, but if it takes place before consummation she keeps only half. Why? To answer this question, let me first turn to a Persian painting, and then discuss an Islamic court's decision in the United Arab Emirates concerning the rape of

278

a Philippine servant by her employer and her murder of him. These two examples are important because they help us understand what lies behind the payment of the *mahr* and the *diya* in a case of rape and, consequently, why it was not possible for Tunisian legislation to suppress it at the time of the promulgation of the PSC in 1956.

In a Persian painting of the fourteenth century by Janayd titled *After the Consummation of the Marriage* (Grabar 1995), which treats the emotions of men and women in relation to virginity, the bride is alone, crying, while the other women examine the stained sheet. Meanwhile, the husband in the midst of other men receives their congratulations; some give him money, others kiss his feet. The bride, melancholic, is shown here undergoing an injury even when the marriage is sanctioned by the community. One wonders what would happen to a girl who, for example, had been raped?

Let us now examine the case of Sarah. In July 1994 in the United Arab Emirates, an elderly employer, armed with a dagger, raped his adolescent employee, Sarah, who, in the struggle, seized the dagger and killed him. Sarah's rape was acknowledged by the court. The judicial process recognized the destruction of the hymen and stated that the perpetrator would have risked a death sentence if Sarah had not carried out the penalty herself. She was awarded *diya,* damages for the rape, to the value of approximately US$27,000. Tried for the murder, however, she was sentenced to seven years in prison. The recognition of Sarah's rape by the judicial authorities did not protect her from the penalty she faced for having committed murder. Shortly thereafter, the head of state called upon the Islamic court of al-Ain, in the United Emirates, to reach a new decision. Here, Sarah was sentenced to death for premeditated murder, a verdict delivered on September 15, 1995, the very day when the Fourth World Conference on Women ended in Beijing and where the Emirates adopted the UN convention calling for the elimination of violence against women.

The death sentence was appealed. As a new trial was set for October 30, 1995, the judges of the court at al-Ain asked the son of the murdered employer to accept the payment of *diya*. (This "blood money" must be demanded within a year after the offense was committed.) The murdered man's son not only refused the *diya* but also asked that the death penalty to Sarah be applied in accordance with Islamic law. Sarah's uncle, also a Muslim, implored the son for clemency, but the son maintained that only her death could compensate the murder. Meanwhile, the authorities were exhibiting, in the corridors of the court, photographs showing the victim lying in his blood and making it clear to viewers that he had been murdered. With this fact having been made public, the son let it be known that perhaps he would now be willing to pardon Sarah, yet avowed that it was a very difficult decision for him to make. Finally, he agreed to accept the *diya*, which would be used, he said, to construct a mosque or as alms for the poor. However, on October 14, before the new trial was heard, the family of the slain man announced that, following the intervention of the head of the state, it would accept the *diya*. Two weeks later, Sarah's sentence was reduced to one year in prison and a payment to the victim's family of US$40,000, a sum that was collected in the Philippines, and she was sentenced to receive one hundred lashes as well.

Why was *diya*, known to be the price of spilled blood and used specifically in cases of murder, requested by the judge here to compensate Sarah for her rape?[1] Was it because the judge saw a kind of murder in the rape? Was the "injury to a beautiful organ" (an Islamic legal phrase)[2]—here the loss of the hymen or subsequent injury—equivalent to a murder in the view of Muslim law?

There is a hadith attributed to Imam Sadeq in which he responds to a question by saying that "a woman's hair and her virginity are part of her beauty. Thus, in the case of the loss of one or the other, the guilty party must pay an amount equivalent to the *mahr* of a woman similar to the victim" (Kazami 1990, 96). Ali Kazami Rached cites Ayat Allah Allamyé Helli who develops an argument that, by extension, we can present in the following way: where a woman has not consented to sexual relations, the act will be qualified a rape, and the perpetrator of it will not only be condemned to pay *diya* for the negative results of his act but also owe *mahr* to the victim as compensation for the act of penetration. Thus, this author proposes a penalty that joins together three elements in the compensation: "the injury done to the genital organ, . . .injury done to the modesty of the woman, a moral prejudice consequent to the rape" (104).

Although there is compensation for both deflowering and rape, Islamic law has taken care to name them differently and, consequently, has distinguished the signif-

---

1. See Gibb and Kramers 1953, 78. The authors treat the two forms of *diya: diyat al-amd* (intentional injury) and *diyat al-khata* (unintentional injury). In the case of rape, the first form is applied. Only murder comes under *lex talionis* (law of retribution); for all other categories of homicide, Islamic law sees *diya* as applicable.

2. *Beautiful organ* is the term used by jurists to designate the body or one part of it. Applying it to the hymen indicates the importance Islamic culture gives to psychological reality in the encounter between bodies. *Diya* is the compensation here to repair the moral injury undergone by the victim when this encounter is against her wishes.

icant content of the *mahr* from that of the *diya*. For example, a hadith reports that the Prophet said to a man in dispute with his wife who had come to consult him about the *mahr* that he had given to his wife, "You have no right to this sum. If what you have said is true, this sum is the price you have paid to enjoy your wife's charms; if what you say is false, you have even less right to this money" (el-Bokhari n.d., 642).

Where sexual relations are mandated by the community, this sum is called *mahr*, inscribing violence as internal to relations between the sexes. Without *mahr*, the marriage is void, and the union is illicit. Before the marriage, the future groom has to pay both the *naqd* (a sum paid to the bride's father to help cover the expenses of the wedding) and the *mahr* (which is the property of the bride). Some men try to postpone the payment of the *mahr* by lowering the amount given at the earlier stage *(mu'ajjil)*, and raising the payment at the later stage *(mu'akhkhir)*, but, in this case, payment must be made within an agreed period. Without this payment, the woman can bring the husband before the judicial authorities, and sexual relations become illicit.

In Tunisia, reformists have been debating this question since the 1930s. Here too an effort has been made to deconstruct the "cultural." Often, discourse on the *mahr* treated with severity families who demanded a high, sometimes prohibitively high, *mahr*. The Personal Status Code that outlawed polygamy and repudiation and required a judicial divorce, and that gave to women the vote and equality to men in the workplace, did not address the question of the *mahr* but accepted the interpretation given by the Prophet Muhammad when he gave a woman in marriage to a man who had no wealth for the *mahr* but knew parts of the Qur'an. Article 12 of the PSC says that the *mahr* may be composed of any licit good that can be given a monetary value. The amount of this *mahr* "must be serious. . . . The Mahr constitutes for the wife something she has full right to use as she sees fit." [3]

During the 1960s and 1970s campaigns were mounted in the press, particularly on the radio—television was not yet widespread at that time—against families demanding a high *mahr*, leading to a change in consciousness among uneducated as

---

3. The various versions of the Personal Status Code differ from one period to another. Whereas the version published in 1966 comes with commentary, allowing us to see the tensions and the tools used by intellectuals to surmount them, the 1999 version appears as a series of promulgated laws (see République Tunisienne 1999 [1966]). In 1966, M. T. Essnoussi transmitted the discussion relating to the *mahr*, where the emphasis is put on the fact that failure to pay the *mahr* cannot constitute a reason for divorce.

well as educated families. Through these campaigns, the *mahr* became synonymous with a sum spent to buy a wife. This idea became very offensive for families who thought that the higher the *mahr* was, the more honor was being paid to their daughters. The marriage of Habib Bourguiba, president of the first Tunisian republic and the prime force behind the promulgation of the PSC, to Wassila Bourguiba in April 12, 1962, both of whom had been divorced, contributed in a major way to the promotion of the "symbolic Mahr," equivalent to one dinar (approximately US$1). Although this gesture was in line with elements of Islamic tradition (Sunna), it also contributed to a sociocultural reformulation of *hudud*. During this period, when the *mahr* was practiced, it often led to the purchase of an apartment, a symbol of urban life (Fakhfakh 1973). The debates around the practice contributed to the development of a new cultural attitude that encouraged marriage between members of different social classes, which had been difficult to imagine formerly. The new masculine elites, reared in the modern educational system but of modest social origins, were in this context able to enter into marriage alliances with the bourgeoisie, permitting at the same time a rise in status for many women who themselves had not been schooled.

The law relating to the *mahr* was amended in 1993 and now stated: "The Mahr can be composed of any licit goods that can be given a money value. It belongs to the wife." The new version of this law speaks neither of a minimum nor of a maximum. Formerly, it was a question of the wife using the *mahr* as she saw fit, but, in 1993, the law left no doubt: the *mahr* belongs to the wife.[4] This reformulation of the *mahr* came in a context where many women, at the moment of divorce, were unable to prove which items had been bought with their contribution. From then on, marrying couples would have to choose between two forms—where goods are held individually or in common. In couples choosing the first option, would the women once again demand the *mahr*?[5]

From the texts of the Sunna we learn that Abu Houraira reported that the Prophet said:

4. The *mahr* in the PSC of 1999 is made up of any licit good that has a financial value, and it belongs only to the wife.

5. Article 1 of law N 98–91 of November 9, 1998, relating to communal goods between husband and wife, is optional: "The couple can opt for this regime at the time when the marriage contract is agreed or at a later date." One also reads that the *mahr* is "the wife's possession," and "it is not included in common goods" (République Tunisienne 1999, 107). There have been as yet no studies examining the question of how couples choose each regime.

—A woman who has already been married cannot be given in marriage except through her own command; a virgin cannot be given in marriage except after giving her consent.

—How will she give her consent?

—By keeping silent, answered the Prophet.

According to Abou Amr, Aicha said: O Messenger of God, the virgin is ashamed.

—Her consent is indicated by her silence, the Prophet Muhammad answered her.

The distinction between the virgin and the woman who has already been married is clear. Whereas the latter is permitted, after her first marriage, to manage her own sexuality, the father must give his virgin daughter in marriage. Her consent, indicated by her silence, conveys that she accepts committing herself to this new relationship. "Her silence," understood here as her modesty facing her fantasies, is the sign of her acceptance of the exchange (el-Bokhari n.d., 569).

Al-ijbar marks the moment when the father separates from his daughter and when the daughter takes for her husband the man who will free her from her infantile fantasies, from her desire for her father and vice versa. How does *al-ijbar* operate so as to fulfill its symbolic dimension? Formerly or today, has *al-ijbar* had the same meaning? Do different groups interpret it differently? Is *al-ijbar* read the same way in two countries of the same region, and if not, why? To respond to these questions, let us examine debates and developments in Tunisia and in Egypt.

Debating *al-Ijbar*

In the 1920s the notion of *al-ijbar* was debated by Tunisian reformists. Tahar Haddad questioned several public figures, judges, and jurists from Zitouna University and from the Islamic Shar Tribunal of Tunis to find out whether a woman had the right to choose her future husband. In what circumstances did this right belong to the guardian? Who would have the final decision? We will present the opinions of three of these figures (Haddad 1978, 105–47).

Habib Bouchnak, professor of theological sciences of the Hanifite rite at the Zitouna University, said:

A free woman having attained legal majority can freely choose her future husband and can conclude the marriage herself. Her father or guardian cannot, in any cir-

cumstances, oppose this marriage nor constrain her to marry another. The principle is the following: One who satisfies the conditions required to dispose freely of
one's wealth has at the same time the right to conclude one's own marriage. Consequently, a woman of legal majority and sound of mind can dispose of her own
wealth. Nonetheless, it would be preferable if she would confide the management
to an agent, as is fitting and proper. Also, Islamic law gives to the father or to the
agent the right to oppose a marriage if he believes it to be a marriage below station.
In such a case, he makes a request to the judge who may declare the marriage dissolved if the conditions of such an incorrect marriage are shown true. The request
is not receivable if the woman is pregnant. (Haddad 1978, 107–12)

Abdelaziz Jait, mufti of Malekite rite at the religious tribunal, said, "When the
woman's father is deceased, she has the full right to choose her future husband. The
role of guardian is limited to confirming this choice, except where this is a marriage
below station. But if the father is living, the choice of the future husband is his responsibility, if she is a virgin and has not entered puberty" (Haddad 1978, 119–22).

Belhassan Najar, mufti of Malekite rite at the religious tribunal, said that the
woman is free to choose the husband she wants (129–37). The two great jurists
made exceptions of cases where the father is living, for there his view carries as long
as she has not reached puberty or majority. However, it is advisable that the father
ask his daughter's opinion. But where her consent is not given, the father's decision
carries.

In fact, Bouchnak proposes that the woman confide the management of her
wealth, and thus her choice of husband, to a suitable agent; Jait limits the father to
having power over virgin daughters who have not reached puberty; finally, for
Najar, the father's decision carries as long as the daughter has not reached majority.
The PSC states: "Marriage is only formed with the consent of the two spouses"
(République Tunisienne 1999, 11). In the discussion that took place among the
ulama (Islamic clergy), the following principle was agreed: every adult is able to
commit to and contract marriage, except in special cases that may be natural or accidental. The natural exception concerns desire to contract marriage with a person
who is underage, that is, a minor.

But it should be noted that consent is not always fully free and that there are tactics to lead the girl to agree. A local proverb says, "She who offers her hand for henna
should also offer it to be cut off," meaning that she no longer has the right to refuse.
This traditional practice put the girl in a position where she was constrained in two
ways. Her expression of agreement was signaled by the application of henna to her

right palm. If she refuses, she is told it augurs ill for her family. Could she possibly refuse in these conditions? Tunisian legislation, in the face of differences between the various schools—the pubescent Shafiʻi girl must submit to a marriage whereas the Hanifi girl must be consulted by her father—and basing itself on Maliki rite, specifies that consultation with the girl is recommended. Article 6 no longer speaks of constraint but of the consent of the father in cases where the girl or boy is a minor. It should also be noted that the legislation does not make a distinction between the sexes. The article reads: "Marriage of a man or woman who has not reached the age of legal majority depends on the consent of their guardian. In cases where this is refused, and where the couple persists in its intention to marry, the case will go to court" (République Tunisienne 1999, 14).

Modification of this article, under the pressure of women's groups, led to a new formulation: "The marriage of a minor depends on the consent of the guardian and of the mother." It is no longer a question of *al-ijbar*. In cases where the guardian or mother refuses, and where the minor persists, the case will go to court. "A decision authorizing the marriage is not subject to appeal" (République Tunisienne 1999, 6). The first reform, revolutionary for its period, gave the right of choice to the girl and the right of consent to the father and made no distinction between the sexes. The second reform weighs the opinion of the mother equally with the opinion of the guardian and speaks only of the age of the subject and not the gender.

Debating Rape

We now turn to debates on *hudud* in Egypt. During the 1990s, Egypt was the scene of two public discussions on matters usually considered private in nature, where the participants included feminists, women's organizations, *ulama,* jurists, judges, doctors, psychologists, and others. These discussions involved female circumcision and sexual violence. It was, of course, not the first time in the region that private matters had been brought into public space. The case involving a Moroccan police commissioner who videotaped himself and his accomplices raping some five hundred girls and women mobilized feminists, the women's movement, and human rights organizations. They acted as a civil party to the trial, which took place in 1993 and resulted in a death sentence for the police commissioner. But I am paying attention to these discussions in Egypt because they allow us to see the change in notions concerning *al-ijbar*—the moment when the father informs his daughter that he is giving her in marriage—a moment that is central to the elaboration of values.

In Egypt, public debate revolved around the case of a young girl who had been raped by a group of men. Her subsequent marriage to one of the rapists canceled the punishment for the entire group, leading to a major discussion of law 291 of 1937, which allowed a rapist to marry his victim, thus absolving him of any crime or liability to *diya*. The social context in which the public debate took place is important. Researchers report that, starting in the 1980s, there was an average of approximately two hundred rapes per year in Egypt.[6] Rapes of young girls and cases of offenses to decency account for 27.4 percent of crimes. Kidnapping with rape accounts for 10 percent of cases, committed in 85 percent of cases by single men. Some 78 percent of rapists are illiterate, whereas this fact is true for only 17 percent of the girls and women rape victims. About 38 percent of rapes are committed by groups (Essadani 1999b).

When Dr. Nasr Ferid Wassel, mufti of the republic, issued his fatwa on the case in 1998, he had recognized from the start that families' expectations were no longer what they used to be.[7] Whereas for many families virginity remained important and violating it would still lead to the spilling of blood if a man refused to marry the girl he had deflowered, for other families this marriage was no longer sufficient compensation. Dr. Wassel explained why it was urgent to reexamine the law of 1937. The social order, he said, is no longer ensured, for which he advanced three main reasons. The first is that the police are no longer able to ensure citizens' protection and do not have the means to combat such crimes. The second reason is demographic: Cairo today has a population of sixteen million, "and in the streets we see only traffic police, many police officers are busy with traffic." The third reason is that the home is no longer a space that protects. Wassel noted that homes are often spaces "without a father, where the mother has to struggle with the responsibility for the family, for her work." He continued: "Rape is a social, economic, cultural and legal problem. Youth of a marrying age are unable to do so [to marry] because they do not have the resources, because they have no work, to finance a marriage, equip a home. . . . We have a crisis, but we have contributed to this phenomenon" (Essadani 1999b).

Sheikh Wassel's fatwa permitting abortion, hymen reparation, and discretion recognized that the young victim of rape had been a virgin before the rape and her life could have become a nightmare because Egyptian society fails to protect her

---

6. See Majdi 1998. The author counts 164 cases in 1986, 200 in 1987, 189 in 1998, 199 in 1989, 180 in 1990, 164 in 1991, 175 in 1992, 162 in 1993, 203 in 1994, 179 in 1995, 188 in 1996, and 193 in 1997.

7. Hanaa al-Makkawi and Khouloud al-Gamal discuss in "La virginité à tout prix" (1998) how the mufti of the republic issued a fatwa authorizing rape victims to abort and recover their virginity.

(Arishie 1998). Wassel noted that a girl who has lost her virginity outside of marriage is for all intents and purposes condemned to death. But then he authorizes the victim to hide her rape from her future husband except, he says, if the husband asks her specific questions about her past. Otherwise, there is no reason for her to admit, spontaneously, this scandal. In addition, should the husband learn about it, the mufti advises him not to be disappointed—his wife has been a rape victim, and she herself has done nothing dishonorable (al-Makkawi and al-Gamal 1998). He explains that repairing the hymen in these conditions is not a deception, because such a repair satisfies very special conditions. Why should a young woman, whose father is blind, be raped on her way to work? "Why should we accept that the victim submit to this humiliation and that she be faced with a choice between two difficult results?" (Younes 1998). What alternatives does she have? To marry her rapist and live with him in humiliation, or refuse to do so and spend the rest of her life with her head bowed, with no one to help her in what is usually a situation of poverty?

Sheikh Tantawi, since 1996 imam of al-Azhar and known for his moderate positions, decreed that the marriage of the victim to the rapist is licit, provided that she has not been forced into this marriage (Essbai 1998). But only a few months later, he declared that rape is a crime situated at the top of the hierarchy of crimes and that he considered that society with all its components, its intellectuals and various specialists, had to fight this crime with all means available. He addressed those individuals who "fight with the pen," those in the medical sector, and those who work in the social sector, asking them to devote their knowledge to the struggle against rape. He argued that rape should be punished with the death penalty and that such a law should not be subject to revision or challenge, since the honor of families and women must be protected. He noted, from a religious point of view, that "in the crime of rape, religion pushes us to invoke *qisas* [retribution] against the rapist, which means that we must retain the death penalty in these cases," and he added that "the punishment must be carried out; what is important in this crime is that the punishment must be executed. After that, it matters little to us whether he marries her or not" (Essadani 1999a).

Supporters as well as critics of this new measure came forward. Issam Ahmed of the Ministry of Justice said that the law has three functions: protection of the family and its honor, social regulation, and inscribing the marriage that follows rape as a special case, because it can be dissolved only after two years. Faouzia Abdessatar, a lawyer, argued that, if the rape victim is a minor, the punishment should be suspended if the marriage takes place legally and if *al-ijbar* is applied (al-Makkawi and al-Gamal 1998). Others, though recognizing that rape constitutes one out of four crimes, prefer to attack the causes for the crime, which has its origin in social and economic sources, rather than attacking the spirit of the law of 1937 (Youssouf 1999). Ahmed Abousina, professor of theology, distinguished between *al-zina* (adultery), which takes place between two consenting individuals, and rape, which is an act of violence. In the case of rape, Islamic law is clear: the rapist should be condemned to death, and an example should be made for the community (Fadhl and Ibrahim 1999).

The rape case galvanized public opinion, and some parliamentarians entered the debate, asking Parliament to suppress law 291 of 1937 because of its internal contradictions. Why limit punishment to cases in which a man rapes a married woman? Why not also punish the rapist of an unmarried, virgin girl? (Hamdi 1998). Rifaat Othman, head of the Department of Comparative Religion, recommended the abrogation of the law because it constituted an anomaly (Kobtani 1999). For Abdelraouf Hassen Kobtani, law 291 encouraged, in the current context, the unemployed to use the rape of a young, honest, educated girl—perhaps a doctor or a teacher—as a means to have her support him. In such cases, marriage is not a punishment but an income source. And if free, who is going to stop him from doing the same thing all over again with another girl? Muhammad Majdi Morjan, president of the court, said that the law was old and outdated in allowing the criminal to escape punishment by marrying his victim. He added that 99 percent of postrape marriages do not last (Fadhl and Ibrahim 1999).

Civil society joined the debate, helping to elevate it to an important dimension of the public sphere. Many women agreed that marriage to the rapist should be refused and agreed also that the rapist should be punished. However, they were divided on the question of hymen restoration. One group of women affirmed from the outset that they were not in accord with the fatwa of the mufti; they rejected the idea of repairing the hymen and demanded punishment of the crime. Others held the view that "it is the act of rape itself, with penetration or without, which is an injury for the women. Sewing up the hymen will not heal the psychological trauma."[8]

8. Ibid. One should also note the great resistance on the part of the medical faculty of Tunis to treat this subject. Only two theses have examined this issue. In 1983, the thesis author looked into medico-legal issues; in 1993 the medico-psychological aspects attracted the author's attention. Psychological trauma following such acts continue to be neglected. Not taking into account the dedicatory note the author addressed to her parents, "To those who know," the professor of psychiatry—a member of the thesis committee of Dhahbi Souad—expressed his reservations at seeing feminist discourse penetrate the confines of the medical school.

This second group, whose views are represented by Amina Aljoundi, president of the Egyptian Council for Mother and Child, was favorable toward repairing the hymen, called for punishment to be made more severe, and rejected the idea of marriage to the rapist (Malakh and Ayoub 1998).

Egypt's parliament listened to the voices of women, and especially those women with the strongest views on rape. "Honor" no longer came to be related to a biological organ. The contract of marriage between victim and rapist was deemed unacceptable. Since that incident and the public debate on the subject, the religious establishment associates such marriages with concubinage (Nafadi 1999).

Tunisia has seen similar problems, though the discussion did not rise in the 1990s as it did in Egypt, because the issue had been discussed as early as the 1920s. Nevertheless, between 1970 and 1990, figures indicate that Tunisia saw a continual increase in crimes of rape: 329 cases were reported in 1970–71, and ten years later there were 9,116 reported cases. In 1983–84 the number reached 12,475, and in 1989–90 there were 9,155 reported cases of rape (Belloumi 1994, 293). We should also point out that many rape cases are not reported to the police and that, often, even when the victim or her family or both do seek legal redress, the police put the complaint in the category of "violence" rather than "rape," perhaps because of the law's severity in rape cases.[9]

Tunisian law signals out violence, and starting in 1958 it began to act against sexual violence. Rape with real violence or armed threat is punishable, according to Article 227 modified by Article 9 of March 7, 1985, by the death penalty. If the victim is under age ten, even if the act is committed without violence or armed threat, the rapist faces the same punishment. If the victim is under age thirteen, the modified law of 1989 provides a sentence of life imprisonment. If the victim is under fifteen, the penalty is twenty years' imprisonment, and if she is over fifteen, the penalty is ten years' imprisonment. Tunisian legislation provides that in cases where the rape is without violence and where the victim is under fifteen, punishment is six years' imprisonment; in cases where the victim is between fifteen and twenty, pun-

9. This remark is often offered by specialists in the Ministry of Interior to explain the difference beween the number of rapes and the number of complaints of rape. The same observation can be made with regard to domestic violence, but in this case family pressure is very important. A woman is culturally discouraged from lodging a complaint against "the father of her children," and when the complaint reaches the judge, it is often withdrawn in order that "the father of her children" not spend time in prison.

ishment is five years' imprisonment. In these last two sets of figures, marriage cancels the punishment, as it does in law 291 of 1937 in Egypt.[10]

In a context marked by the illiteracy of the population, a strong rural imaginary, and an honor/shame culture, legislation could not perform a radical overturning of existing values but was able to continually stigmatize violence. It was not the victim alone who had to pay the price. In these two countries, the laws adopted oblige the rapist to face prosecution and sentencing.

The notion of *al-ijbar* was interpreted in different ways in different periods, and in both societies attitudes have changed significantly. In Egypt, the *ulama* and jurists seem increasingly to take into account the lived experience and the need of the population. They have publicly stated that there has been a change in family behavior with regard to the marriage of a rape victim with the rapist. Already in 1994, during the debate over the circumcision *(khitan)* of girls, Sheikh Tantawi, then mufti of the

---

10. We can say that Tunisian jurists' discussion of rape has gone through two stages, before and after 1958. The first begins following promulgation of the Tunisian law of 1913 (J.O.R.T. N 79, January 1, 1913) where attacks on the modesty of a child not yet in puberty, without violence, and of either sex were punishable by five years' imprisonment. Without the consent of the victim of either sex, the penalty was five years of hard labor, ten years' imprisonment if the victim was not pubescent, and twenty years of hard labor if the victim was not pubescent and the attacker was a near relative. If sodomy falls under none of the preceding conditions, the penalty was three years in prison. The second stage, following 1958, includes four statutory changes between 1958 and 1989 regarding rape: (1) Law of March 4, 1958. Here, Article 227 stipulates ten years of hard labor, twenty if the victim was under fifteen; Article 227 bis, if the sexual act imposed on a female under fifteen is without violence, the penalty is five years of hard labor, if aged between fifteen and twenty the penalty is five years' imprisonment; Article 228, if the act is imposed on either a male or female the penalty is five years' hard labor, ten if the victim is under fifteen; Article 228 bis, if the victim is male or female, under fifteen years of age, and there has been no violence, the penalty is five years in prison. (2) Law of March 29, 1969. Here, Article 227 bis stipulates that the sexual act imposed on a female under fifteen, without violence, carries a penalty of five years' hard labor and five years in prison if the victim is between fifteen and twenty. (3) Law of March 7, 1985. Here, if the victim is under ten and there has been rape with violence or threat or the brandishing of weapons, the penalty is capital punishment. Consent is not taken into consideration for children under thirteen years of age. (4) Law of February 27, 1989. Here, Article 227 stipulates capital punishment for rape committed with violence, threat, or the brandishing of weapons if the victim is under ten; consent is not taken into consideration for children under thirteen years of age; six years' imprisonment if the act is without violence and the victim is female and under fifteen; five years in prison if the victim is between fifteen and twenty; Article 228, without consent and if the victim is either male or female, the penalty is six years in prison, twelve if the victim is under fifteen; the act committed without violence on a person under fifteen carries a penalty of five years in prison and double that figure if the perpetrator is a close relative, with three years stipulated for sodomy.

Egyptian republic, clearly sided with those individuals who were opposed to the girls' *khitan* and favored letting specialists, particularly doctors, make the final decision. Similarly in Tunisia, families no longer support marriage between victim and rapist. A study involving 850 subjects in greater Tunis in 1998 showed that 50 percent of those people questioned knew of cases where the victim or her family preferred to initiate judicial proceedings and see the rapist punished rather than proceed to a marriage to wipe out the shame.[11] This custom has become a practical possibility, as the proportion of crimes of honor have decreased: in Tunisia, they represented 8.8 percent of all crimes committed between 1964 and 1974 but amounted to only 2.6 percent for the period between 1986 and 1996 (Dal 2000, 117). In 1993, law 72 was promulgated criminalizing crimes of honor.

Conclusions

The picture we have traced allows us to guess at the tensions faced by the families in Egypt and Tunisia (and elsewhere in the Arab region). The examination of *mahr, diya,* and *al-ijbar* has helped us understand the reformulation of *hudud.* As we have seen, topics such as *mahr* and *al-ijbar* are no longer the exclusive domain of the male theologians and jurists but increasingly are debated in public space and in formal politics by different social groups, including women and among them lawyers, judges, feminists, and journalists.

What might at first glance seem a contradiction between the views of one group and another, should instead be seen as a sign of the complexity of the history of ideas throughout the region. On the one hand, the largely masculine pre- and immediate postindependence elite, perpetuating its own social class, reared in European universities and moving within the framework of the state apparatus, and, on the other, the elite of the 1970s, mixed in gender and having graduated from the nation's own educational institutions, failed to propose societal models in which law and religion, reflexivity and autonomy, and individual human desire and society would not be in conflict. Therefore, it is not surprising to see the discussion over questions such as the situation of women, the notion of the self, the nature of public opinion, becoming a way to address extremely sensitive issues. The sometimes conflicting, sometimes agreeing, sometimes out-of-phase interpretations of values we have seen from country to country during the twentieth century and into the new

11. Lilia Labidi, "Violences sexuelles." The latter is a survey carried by psychology classes in March 1999 at the University of Tunis, covering the metropolitan area of Tunis.

millennium are certainly a function of each country's sociopolitical context and of the social actors, both men and women, who are promoting the varied reformulations of meaning. They are also a function of the effects of colonialism, the actions of the nation-state, the Islamist phenomenon, the feminist movements, as well as the influences coming from the international level, such as the various international conventions, whether they have been ratified or not.

17 Gender and Violence in Lebanese War Novels

EVELYNE ACCAD

THIS CHAPTER EXPLORES the relationship between war and sexuality through an analysis of gender and violence in Lebanese war novels. I begin with an overview of conflicts in the Middle East and the nonviolent and feminist responses that they have engendered. Arguing that literature is an appropriate tool of social and political analysis, I then examine six Lebanese war novels written by women and men in Arabic and French. Issues considered are the positive and negative actions and resolutions taken by the novels' male and female characters, the differences and similarities between male and female protagonists, and those between male and female authors. I also assess the necessary changes Lebanon had to undergo to resolve its tragedy and to resume the role of melting pot of tolerance and freedom that it had in the region, and is so much needed in the Middle East.

Present and Past War Conflicts in the Middle East

"Children here find refuge in their hopes to die. The fact that death is equated to life is horrifying me. How are we going to deal with this generation in the future, how could we talk about life?" The passage above is from an e-mail message I received in March 2002 from Nadera Shalhoub-Kevorkian, a scholar-activist who works with and for women in Israel and Palestine, and who at the time was working in the Palestinian Balata campus during the Israeli raids. It very much sums up the place we have reached in our present world: children hope to die, the world offers them only despair, injustices are the order of the day . . . How can it go on like this? How can we go on living in such a world?

The situation in the Middle East, which has been left to fester since the creation of the State of Israel in 1948, has degenerated and has manifested itself at many levels now, among them the September 11, 2001, attacks. Israeli prime minister Ariel Sharon, who as minister of defense in the early 1980s spearheaded the invasion of Lebanon in 1982 and was later cited as responsible for the massacres of Sabra and Shatila in the Palestinian camps that left upward of two thousand Lebanese and Palestinian civilians dead, took advantage of Bush's war cry, the so-called war on terrorism, to once again turn on the Palestinian people. In the spring of 2002, watching the televised images of the tanks and heavy artillery against the major cities of Palestine, and against the camps and the civilians, I was reminded of 1991, of the first air raids of the U.S. forces against Iraq, and I was also reminded of Beirut in the summer of 1982. That summer, which I remember so vividly, my sister was in West Beirut, spending most of her nights in the shelter. Israel was bombarding by air, land, and sea, hitting civilian targets, an urban center, and innocent victims. Most nights were filled with the sounds of shells crushing, detonating, burning, with the Beirut sky going up in fires, flames, explosions, and lights. The massacres in the Sabra and Shatila Palestinian camps were to follow in the same manner. The bodies of women, children, old people, young people, their throats slit, their stomachs open, blood flowing in the earth, a holocaust repeated by the victims of holocaust. But in 2002 it appeared worse, and the problems had reached proportions beyond words. And the next year we witnessed the invasion and destruction of Iraq. Today, I feel a sense of urgency and doom I had not felt even in 1982 Beirut.

Connection Between Sexism and the War System

Many important studies by women and men in recent years see a link between sexuality and national and international conflicts. Jean-William Lapierre sees a real "deep connection between masculine predominance and the importance of war" (1981, 21). He argues that most civilizations are based on conquest and war. "The importance of hunting, then of war in social existence, in economic resources, in cultural models (which valorize the warrior exploits), are at the roots of masculine domination and of women's oppression." He explains how in many "modern" societies, politics, industry, and business are a type of war where one (mostly men, and sometimes women imitating men's behavior) must be aggressive to be powerful. It is not only capitalist societies that "carry war like clouds carry the storm, but productivism in all its forms, including the so-called 'socialistic' one. In all societies in which economy and politics require a spirit of competition (while its ethic exalts it) women are oppressed" (22). Similarly, Bob Connell sees a relationship among masculinity, violence, and war. He notes that it is not by chance that the great majority of soldiers are men—of the twenty-two million people under arms in the world in 1976, twenty million of them were men. "Most of the police, most of the prison warders, and almost all the generals, admirals, bureaucrats and politicians who control the apparatus of coercion and collective violence are men. Most murderers are men. Almost all bandits, armed robbers, and muggers are men; all rapists, most domestic bashers; and most people involved in street brawls, riots and the like" (1985, 4). But such connection should not be attributed to biology—which would absolve masculine responsibility and associate men's violence to some human "destiny"— but rather to social and cultural factors.

Georges Corm, analyzing the Lebanese war, showed how violence nourished itself on the Lebanese confessional system. Aggressiveness and violence were founded on the prism of the communities. "Once started, this violence became cumulative, especially in a society where the dead had to be revenged, and in light of a failing State. In the kidnappings and counter-kidnappings, the reprisals and counter-reprisals, sometimes spontaneous, sometimes organized, a ruthless amplification of violence followed, where those who had started the death machine disappeared in the anonymity of the militias; in fact, the militias not only committed acts of barbarism on the territories they controlled, but often instigated them" (1986, 97).

Arab society in general, and Lebanese in particular, has always had pride in the *za'im* (leader, chief, hero). The *za'im* is the macho man par excellence. Not only does he embody all the usual masculine values of conquest, domination, competition, fighting, and boasting, but also that of *shatara* (cleverness). The Lebanese war transformed the *za'im* into the *askari* (man-with-the-gun, militia-man). The *askari* used weapons of war to destroy and seize control of one region or of another group. He participated in looting to benefit his clientele of family and to extend the range of his influence. Given the extension of his influence, he built a system of wealth distribution and gained even more power.

The more men desired omnipotence and the control of others, the more weapons were used. The means of conquest were given a value in proportion to their success. The gun, the machine gun, the cannon—all masculine sexual symbols that are extensions of the phallus—were put forward and used to conquer and destroy. For Adam Farrar, there is a kind of *jouissance*—pleasure in a sexual sense, no equivalent word in English—in war:

One of the main features of the phenomenology of war is the unique intensity of experience. War experience is exactly the converse of alienation. In war, the elimination of all the norms of intersubjectivity produces, not alienation, but the most intense *jouissance*. The machining of events on the plane of intensity (to use the Deleuzian image), the form of desire, is utterly transformed. Power no longer consists in the capacity to redeem the warrants of communicative intersubjectivity. It consists in the ability of the spear, the sword, the gun, napalm, the bomb etc. to manifest "in a blast of sound and energy and light" (or in another time, in the blood of a severed limb or a disembowelled body), the merest "wish flashing across your mind like a shadow." (1985, 66)

Farrar continues, quoting an article by William Broyles in *Esquire* titled "Why Men Love War," that it is at some terrible level, for men, the closest thing to what childbirth is for women: the initiation into the power of life and death (61).

In the despair I felt throughout the Lebanese war and feel again today as a result of the turmoil in the Middle East, I am also inspired and soothed by the writings of feminist scholars such as Cynthia Enloe and Betty Reardon, who have researched the connection between sexism and the war system. Cynthia Enloe writes: "Personal relations are so basic to the dynamics which sustain the military's grip on social policy that militarism cannot be pushed back so long as dominance, control and violence are considered 'natural' ordering principles in relations between men and women—i.e., so long as patriarchy is deemed 'normal' " (1988, 210). And Betty Reardon explains it well when she says: "At a very deep level feminism is recognized as a powerful peace force—not only in the sense of the term as an intervention in a course of violence, but more significantly as a vital energy for peace. Feminism is a force for the transcendence of organized violence, violence rooted in sexism, strengthened by sexist values, and perpetuated by male-chauvinist behavior" (1985, 40). Similarly, writing about Iraq in 1991, Ann Crittenden correctly observed: "It wasn't Iraqi women who ordered an invasion to grab the toys the selfish Kuwaitis wouldn't share. And it wasn't Barbara Bush who turned a laudable resistance to aggression into a deadly game of chicken, played with the lives of more than 400,000 young Americans" (1991, 119). Crittenden quoted polls by Louis Harris and others that revealed a significant gender gap on the issue of military action in the Gulf. For example, on attacking Iraqi forces in Kuwait, women opposed it by 73 percent to 22 percent, and on bombing, American women were against it 63 percent to 29 percent, whereas men had been roughly divided on these two issues, 57 to 40 percent favoring air strikes against Iraq. Crittenden noticed that "these differences were all the more striking in view of the fact that concerning resistance strategies that do not involve loss of human life, women were just as men and opposed giving up some Kuwaiti territory in return for an Iraqi withdrawal" (119).

Nonviolent Active Struggle

During the war and afterward, Lebanese women and some men were very active in organizing peace marches, hunger strikes, sit-ins, petitions, appeals to international and national peace organizations, conferences, and talks between the various communities. Lebanese women often stood between the guns and tried to stop the kidnappings. Wafa Stephan documented how "they tried to appease the fighters by paying visits to refugee camps and military headquarters and putting flowers in the nozzles of guns" (1984, 3). Women one day tried to eliminate the militia checkpoints where people were being kidnapped. Going from East Beirut to West Beirut, from Phalangist checkpoint to Progressive checkpoint, they were speaking in the name of spouses, mothers, and sisters. They wanted the butchery to stop. They had built homes, but contrary to what an Arab proverb says about a boy's positive contribution to home and country, the sons had started destroying the homeland (Polity-Charara 1983, 15). They blocked the passageways dividing the two sides of the capital, organized all night sit-ins, and stormed into local TV stations to interrupt the news in order to have their demands broadcast (3).

Countless Lebanese delegations were sent to various conferences throughout the world and to the United Nations. Numerous vigils, sit-ins, conferences, and peace marches were organized inside and outside the country. I personally witnessed and participated in one of the actions for peace on May 6, 1984, when I taught at the Institute for Women's Studies in the Arab World of the Beirut University College, located in West Beirut. The action was initiated by Iman Khalifeh, a young woman from the institute who also worked in the kindergarten of the school. She woke up one day, telling herself: "Enough! Enough of this useless butchery!" She worked with the population of both sides of the city. The march was to carry as its sole slogan: "No to war, no to the 10th year of war! Yes to life!" It was to unite both sides of the city at the only cross point, known as the Museum passage or demarcation line. Thousands of people were to participate. Unfortunately, the march was stopped by a "blind" shelling (the word *blind* in Lebanon designates any shelling that does not appear to have precise aims or targets but that according to many studies knows exactly what and why it is hitting and what areas it wants to control), which resulted in many victims—dead and wounded—on both sides. Iman had declared: "I was not introducing an original thought—it was not a new idea. But it was the cry of the 'silent majority' voiced aloud by a people that suffered and endured nine years of ugly war and by a people who carried no arms to defend themselves but struggled to avoid death, violence and ruin in order to live, to build and to continue to be" (L. Abdo 1985, 15–16).

Another significant march was by the handicapped, organized and carried out by Laure Moghaïzel, the late woman lawyer and activist in the nonviolence movement and human rights in Lebanon, during the summer of 1987. Asked what she meant by *nonviolence* in an interview, Moghaïzel replied:

> I am not a pacifist, I am revolted, revolted against injustices and violence. This is why I use the term non-violent. There is a nuance. Pacifism is a form of passivity, which non-violence is not. It is a movement which wants peace and which is making itself known through an opposition of unconditional disarmament. . . . Nonviolence is a struggle and who says struggle also says activity, dynamism. . . . It is a political action sustained and energetic which refuses to exercise violence. But it should not be confused with love for the other. We are not in the era of Love. When there is conflict, there is struggle. Non-violence is a theory very little known in Lebanon. (Makarem 1988, 4)

She went about explaining the origins of the movement with Gandhi and Martin Luther King, Jr.—to cite only the well-known names—and the differences and similarities in Lebanon. They were ready to suffer, but martyrdom was not the aim of nonviolence. Their objective consisted in eliminating violence through nonviolence. With dialogue, persuasion, they hoped to modify the actions of human beings.

Do these analyses still make sense when we have reached the crisis we are in today owing to globalization, pollution, the exhaustion of the world's resources, global warming, new diseases, and new forms of identities expressed in new forms of what is called "terrorism" (a word heavily loaded and needs to be reanalyzed and redefined)? I believe that we can learn from the past and that there may still be some hope to our decaying world. This belief is why I now address the subject of gender and violence in the Lebanese war novels.

Is Literature a Good Tool for Analysis?

To illustrate the connection between sexuality and war, I use examples from novels on the war in Lebanon. The questions often asked when illustrating my topic are: Is literature an adequate field to understand political and social realities? Can novels be used as social, anthropological, and political documents? What about the imagination or fantasy of the author? What about his or her "distortions"? My immediate reaction is to say that creative works are more appropriate than other works to be analyzed and give us the "total" picture because not only do they include all the various fields—social, political, anthropological, religious, and cultural—but in addition they allow us to enter into the unconscious and imaginary world of the author, with all the implications in hidden meanings and underlying significance. An author reflects his or her own individual vision, which is linked to the collective imaginary. What he or she says is an image of his or her society. The tension between individual and collective imagination adds complexities and subtleties not found in more direct scientific documents. Literature thus covers the most complete domain. It can make us grasp the whole picture because it is multidisciplinary and reflects the complexities of a situation. In addition, it is artistic and entertaining. It can educate and amuse us at the same time.

A novel has its own internal logic, which can escape both the novelist and "reality." As such, the logic of a novel is one of fantasy. It goes from a reality with one or more characters, or from a certain dimension, and follows their logic to the end. As such, any novel is dated, as the German critic Lucas has shown, analyzing it as evolving from a problem of society. At the same time, it carries the logical dimension of this society to the limit, therefore leaving "reality." A novel is recognized as "belonging" to a society at a given time, but it is not a sociological or anthropological work as such. What is expressed in a novel is the imagination of the novelist, but this imaginary is of someone who belongs to the society under consideration, she or he is its witness, even if she or he is not representative sociologically speaking. On the other hand, the imaginary of a novelist, expressing itself in a work, marks a generation or a society, in a specific way worth discovering. In this sense, the novelist is an actor of her or his society, a privileged actor. The novel is not so much a reflection of a society as it is a witness, an actor, and an agent of transformation.

The Arab war novel has added its distinctive dimension to a body already quite impressive and fascinating in quantity and quality. War creates such conditions of despair that writing becomes a necessity, an outlet, and a catharsis. It helps heal the wounds. It offers another alternative to fighting and destruction. It can become one of the active nonviolent struggles. The war has seen an appreciable increase in productivity, the measure of which becomes quite apparent when one starts putting a bibliography together—without talking about all the unpublished works, which Miriam Cooke has documented.[1]

The themes and forms have evolved and matured. The problems are so intense, urgent, and horrible that new forms are created to meet the needs. For example, writing in a shelter, or while waiting to cross the demarcation line, or kept in a basement as a hostage, has to be done fast and without basic comfort. Short poems, often surrealistic (since they are more difficult to decode), are a form often used. We still find, as in the main corpus, a blend of poetry and prose, realism and symbolism, but the war novels delight in surrealism, the absurd, and extreme irony, as in the works of Vénus Khoury, Ghada al-Samman, and Rachid al-Daeef. Such modes of expression become a refuge from the war's cruelty and inhumanity, the author reversing its effects through distortions, irony reaching the baroque, emphasis on certain aspects bringing out the absurd. In this respect, there is a marked similarity between women and men authors and between those authors writing in Arabic and in French. A notable difference between how women and men authors treat war stems not from the style and techniques, but from the way they view war and the solutions or lack of them they foresee.

Examples from the Lebanese War Novels

The following passages from two Lebanese war novels illustrate my point about differences in male and female writing on war:

> And this city, what is it? A whore. Who could imagine a whore sleeping with a thousand men and continuing to live? The city receives a thousand bombs and continues its existence nonetheless. The city can be summarized by these bombs. . . . When we had destroyed Beirut, we thought we had destroyed it. . . . We had destroyed this city at last. But when the war was declared finished and the pictures of the incredible desolation of Beirut were broadcasted, we discovered we had not destroyed it. We had only opened a few breaches in its walls, without destroying it. For that, other wars would be necessary.

---

1. For an excellent overview and an in-depth analysis of the novels about the war, see Cooke 1988.

This city is like a great suffering being, too mad, too overcharged, broken now, gutted, and raped like those girls raped by thirty or forty militia men, and are now mad and in asylums because their families, Mediterranean to the end, would rather hide than cure . . . but how does one cure the memory? The city, like those girls, was raped. . . . In the City, this center of all prostitutions, there is a lot of money and a lot of construction that will never be finished. Cement has mixed with the earth, and little by little has smothered most of the trees. If not all.

In these two images of Beirut, two opposing feelings are being expressed, and two contrasting visions emerge. The first wants to get rid of the sinner, the whore, who is the source of all evils, decadence, and the problems of modern existence. The total and violent destruction of the woman is seen as the only way out of an inextricable situation. The second feels sorry for the woman, the city, victim of rape, victim of man's violence. Mediterranean customs are accused. Hypocrisy and the oppression of women are presented as the origin of madness and the destruction of the city.

The first quote is by a man, Elias Khoury, author of *The Small Mountain* (1977, 1987, 1990), the second by a woman, Etel Adnan, author of *Sitt Marie Rose* (1977, 1982). This difference between a man's and a woman's visions of Beirut and their ways of expressing them was even more clearly defined one year during the war, as I watched women friends, determined to cross Beirut two or three times a week, pass through the demarcation line—the most desolate, depressing, and often dangerous spot in the city. They went most of the time on foot, as only a few cars with special permission were allowed through. They were convinced that by this gesture, real as well as symbolic, Lebanon's reunification would take place. They did it against all logic, under the ironic and sometimes admiring look of male companions.[2] Defying weapons, militias, political games, women friends told me how that site had become a meeting place where each morning they looked forward to seeing this friend or that one, walking steadfastly in the apocalyptic space of the Museum passage (another name for the no-man's-land dividing the city, because the museum is located there). They smiled at each other as they walked assuredly, conscious that their march was not an ordinary one, that their crossing was a daring act, important and vital to Lebanon's survival.

2. There are also men who, believing in the reunification of Lebanon, make the gesture, crossing the demarcation line, but it seemed to me they were fewer than women—perhaps because men risk more, are more often victims of kidnappings, assaults, murders. Men do it more in a spirit of duty or for professional interests.

I have chosen six novels about the war to illustrate the connections among sexuality, war, nationalism, feminism, violence, love, and power as they relate to the body, the partner, the family, Marxism, religion, and pacifism. These novels do not necessarily represent the entire range of creative works about the war (Cooke 1988). They were chosen for their significance in terms of the issues under discussion and for their availability in languages understandable to the Western reader. The works, originally written in Arabic or French, are by Lebanese women and men authors who have lived or are still living in Lebanon. All of the novels chosen are set in Beirut, in the context of the war. Halim Barakat's *Days of Dust* (1969, 1977, 1983) and Tawfiq Awwad's *Death in Beirut* (1972, 1976)—both works written before the war started in 1975—foreshadow the events. Even though the subject is treated differently, all of the writers show how war and violence have roots in sexuality and in the treatment of women in that part of the world. Most of the characters meet a tragic fate owing to the war, but women are the principal victims of both political and social violence. For example, the heroine of *Death in Beirut* is seduced, raped, beaten, her face slashed, her ambitions smashed, as she tries to gain autonomy and education in the midst of her country's social and political unrest. In Hanan el-Cheikh's novel *The Story of Zahra*, the heroine tries to find a way out of herself and of the civil war that has just erupted by having a sexual relationship with a sniper (1980, 1986). Instead, she becomes the target not only of his sexual weapon but of his Kalashnikov as well, as he eventually kills her. In Etel Adnan's novel, Marie Rose is struggling for social justice and Arab women's liberation and directs a school for the handicapped. She is put to death by Phalangist executioners who first torture her to get rid of their bad conscience. In Andrée Chedid's *House Without Roots* (1985), Sybil dies from a sniper's bullet at the point of possible reconciliation, the place where Kalya advanced trying to save Ammal and Myriam, one of them having been hit by the sniper's death machine as they were starting a peace march. In *Days of Dust*, Pamela, trying to find herself by helping the refugees and protesting against American imperialism, loses herself in a no-exit relationship with the male protagonist. And in Elias Khoury's novel *The Small Mountain*, the female characters are destroyed, disappear, or are trapped in disgustingly hateful marriage routines.

Although both female and male novels make the connection between sexuality and war, their ways of expressing it, and most of all the solutions implied, are quite different. Women writers paint the war and the relationships between women, men, and their families in the darkest terms: sexuality is tied to women's oppression and the restrictions put on their lives; the war brings destruction, despair, and death. The female protagonists look for alternatives in nonviolent active struggles such as peace marches, engagement in causes to help the oppressed and the dispossessed. At the same time, they seek changes in their lifestyles and in their relationships with the men and families around them. Men writers also paint the war and men-women relationships in the bleakest terms, emphasizing the connection between the two. But their depression does not lead them to search for alternatives different from the historically accepted ones: heroism, revenge, and violence as catharsis to men and women's deplorable communication.

In both women's and men's writing, the war is used to break down the patriarchal system and the traditional order. The female protagonists do it through masochism, whereas the male ones use cruelty and sadism. But such action-reaction leads nowhere because the use of war to free oneself from domination and oppression only reinforces the authoritarian order by reproducing the power structure with different colors.

Both women and men writers question God and the use of religion in war. Institutionalized religion is blamed explicitly, while faith and personal belief are praised implicitly and constitute—more specifically in the women writers—strength and a way of overcoming war. So whereas male protagonists justify their fighting through religion or to show how it was used for imperialist purposes, the female ones draw their strength from helping the oppressed, sacrificing themselves for others' welfare and in active nonviolent struggles.

Both women and men writers seem to concur in showing female protagonists whose political outlook and actions are accompanied by similar ways in their personal lives, whereas male protagonists live double standards and exhibit hypocritical attitudes. In male authors, the female protagonists who are concerned and active politically also reject the traditional passive roles and refuse the taboos surrounding virginity and sexuality. They find themselves in situations where they are unable to live this conscious desire to be free because the men around them cannot cope with it. The irony is that these men voice beautiful statements concerning the need to achieve revolution in both domains—the private and the political—but when it comes to actualizing these theories in interpersonal relationships, it is as if they were paralyzed. It leads one to really doubt the effectiveness of what they advocate. Both male and female authors agree in portraying this difference between their male and female protagonists. To this characterization, women authors add an element not found in the men: their female protagonists often affirm themselves and live different lifestyles even if it means being marginalized, having to live in exile, or being put to death.

Another major preoccupation of female and male writers is their outlook on multiculturalism and the question of roots, exile and pluralism mixed with violence and war, and how it is reflected in interpersonal relationships. Female authors tend to see mixity as something positive. Exile often means freedom. The search for roots can be an expression of nostalgia for one's childhood or a need for security and love. Male authors tend to depict mixity as confrontation. Their search is for purity, mixity meaning dishonor. Multiculturalism increases their schizophrenia and makes them uneasy and depressed. Roots are a search for identity, and exile is a terrible fate.

For example, the character Kalya in *House Without Roots*, raises questions about the significance of roots and expresses the importance of grafting within her all the various roots and sensitivities of the cultures she is made of. She insists on the positive aspects of such hybridization and cosmopolitanism and the enrichment, tolerance, and openness it brings. These values are what Lebanon used to represent and what Kalya had come to seek. In contrast, the character Ramzy in *Days of Dust*, despairs at multiplicity, which he associates with loss of identity, and sees it as one of the causes for the war. Ramzy is constantly split between East and West. It leads to schizophrenia and the inability to harmoniously integrate the various sides of his personality.

Intercultural and interconfessional marriages reflect the same outlook. Women authors depict female protagonists who live them harmoniously and with a great sense of achievement, commitment, and possible solution to the war (even when they get killed because of it, as with Marie Rose). Men authors show male protagonists split between a desire to achieve mixity on the political level and an impossibility to live it in their personal lives, even when they have voiced the importance of breaking down tradition on that level. Men authors also depict female protagonists better able to harmonize the personal with the political. Their failure to achieve true liberation stems not from their lack of action but from the males' inability to realize it with them.

Another notion implied by both female and male novels is androgyny. In this domain, there is less contrast between the two genders. Both women and men authors depict the negative and positive aspects of androgyny. Adnan refers to an androgynous mythical past to confront the male protagonists with their corrupted values. Chedid shows women characters who assume traits traditionally viewed as masculine. And Awwad also portrays women who, in order to free themselves, take on a masculine discourse and decide to engage in guerrilla warfare. With these authors, however, the outcome is not positive. It does not engender life, nor is it a solution to war. And Barakat's male protagonist who assumes both the female and the male sides of his personality is not portrayed as having harmoniously integrated the two. He is constantly ill at ease and torn between aggressiveness and masochism, the male side being associated with victory and the female with defeat. The most positive portrayal of an androgynous character is in Khoury. One of the main protagonists is described as androgynous-looking and appears free from society's restrictions. She is obviously a projection of who the central male character would like to be, how he imagines freedom and a way to reject war. This androgynous-looking character laughs, argues, moves freely, captivates the hero, runs toward the sea, and is unattainable because the man is too busy fighting "the revolution." Why did the author choose to construct an androgynous-looking woman to represent freedom? Is he saying that woman and man are doomed to destroy each other and that only the androgynous can escape such fate? The novel as a whole does not seem to imply such a solution. Freedom is never chosen as the answer to men and women's miseries. Instead, destruction appears as the ultimate response to human condition.

The question of poverty and class-consciousness related to war and women's condition emphasizes women writers' awareness, leading them to search for positive alternatives, whereas men writers use it to justify violence. Both male and female authors show the link between the fate of the dispossessed, their struggle to overcome it, women's oppression, and the war. Awwad paints a direct connection between the classes his female protagonists belong to and the degrees of abuse and violence they are subjected to. Chedid shows women characters whose private and political consciousness and commitment give them real awareness and sensitivity to the condition of the poor and vice versa: watching the poor's lives leads them to become socially committed and active for change in their personal as well as political lives. Similarly, Adnan portrays a female protagonist who is socially, politically, and personally committed to women's issues and to the fate of the poor, the dispossessed, and the oppressed in general. As for Khoury, he often talks about "the war of the poor" to describe the link between oppression and war and to justify a revenge of the dispossessed. The crowd, which invades the plush hotel district of Beirut, is coming from camps, ghettos, and the poor areas of Lebanon. Khoury ironically recalls the name they walk on, "France" (there is such a street in Beirut), to show it is also a revenge of the colonized against the colonizers.

Both male and female authors paint the disastrous consequences of virginity rites connected with the notions of honor, ownership of women, and sexual relationships. It is these customs that lead al-Shaykh's female protagonist to despair, madness, and final death. She rejects them from the beginning and revolts against male's views of her body and sexuality. She would like to be freed from them and in control of her body and of her life. She uses the war to break down the taboos and to assert herself sexually. She finds out that the war is much stronger and more destructive than anything she has known before and that the customs she hoped to get rid of through it are only temporarily shifted. They come back with greater strength and more destructive violence. And Adnan uses the narrator's voice to comment on the frighteningly dangerous outcome of the codes of honor related to virginity and how they reinforce tribal confessional sectarianism. As for Awwad, he shows the direct link between the customs of virginity, the exclusive propriety of women leading to violence, and crimes at the foundation of a society built on divisions and an exclusive sense of propriety. In such a system, women are dominated, raped, led to suicide, or killed by men themselves manipulated by political power. It is a vicious circle of power struggles in which women are the ultimate victims. And Barakat, through the interwoven stories of the Hyena and the Flying Dutchman, demonstrates the importance of the concept of virginity and the codes of honor related to women's roles in society, with the strong implications of woman as earth and Palestine as the ultimate woman.

In most of the novels under study, the codes of honor—related to virginity and to crimes meant to wash the family's or tribe's honor-pride in blood—are connected to rape, itself associated with death. Rape is linked to the notion of death. It is the absolute forbidden (especially on women of one's tribe), therefore the absolute temptation of death (when inflicted on women of the other tribe). Men prove their masculinity through sexual acts of violence against women of the other clans. It, therefore, reinforces the system of the clan by making women vulnerable and in need of the men's protection. In al-Shaykh, the major female protagonist is subjected to rapes throughout her sexual life, which ends with death as the ultimate rape. In Awwad, the sexual act, in most of the men's imagination and in their practice, is associated with rape. They seem unable to conceive of it differently; it is part of the system of power where they prove their masculinity and domination. Their way of conceiving sexuality often results in the death, suicide, or annihilation of the female protagonist. And in Khoury, the wish of the central male protagonist is for the city/woman to be raped because she is like a prostitute and incarnates all the decadent moral values of industrial and modern life. But rape is not enough; it has to reach its limits into total destruction, and the devastation has to spread to other cities/women in the world, leading to annihilation and oblivion. Adnan, who also compares the city to a woman, sees her rape and destruction as men's ultimate cruelty, sadism, and violence. She feels sorry for this woman/city and seeks solutions in peaceful nonviolent alternatives, even in the notion of self-sacrifice if it could help alleviate the hate and destruction. As for Barakat, the images used for the Arabs' defeat by Israel are of invasion, destruction, and rape, taking place on the male protagonist's body that is utterly frustrated and depressed because rendered powerless.

Sexual relations conceived in a system of power struggles and a structure of submission and domination will obviously result in rapes and in the abuse of women. Rapes are associated with unwanted pregnancies and abortions. In none of the war novels do we find conception, pregnancy, and giving birth as something positive and happy. Both female and male authors seem to view life conception and creation as impossible and repulsive in the context of the war. The female protagonists are the ones who pay the price, because the male protagonists view women as having to assume the whole responsibility of contraception and pregnancy. The sexual act being, in most instances, one of rape and domination, women appear as mere objects of possession, vessels into which the men pour their anger and frustration, prolongation of the feelings and acts of war. Abortion is the direct result of rape, like destruction is the direct result of war. Life cannot be engendered in such a context.

The novels by both male and female authors end with the brutal death of some of the female protagonists. Their deaths are the direct result of the male protagonists' violence, worse perpetrators of the war. Zahra and the child in her womb die from the sniper's bullet, fired by the father of the child. A gang of young Christian militiamen executes Marie Rose. Young Sybil also dies from a sniper's bullet. Zennoub is cruelly gang-raped, and, as a result, she commits suicide. Miss Mary, who shows real solidarity for her female friends, and who tries to protect Tamima, dies, shielding Tamima from her brother's cruel hand. In only one of the male authors' novels does a male protagonist die; there, it is from fighting, and one does not feel as sorry for him as with the female protagonists' deaths. His death is the result of his own violence and not cruelty inflicted from the outside, as with the women. Even if violence coming from the oppressed holds a certain justification, the death of its victims does not stir our sympathy, as does the death of innocent victims.

In all of the novels examined here, female and male authors concur in portraying their female protagonists as the ultimate victims. Where they disagree is in showing their responsibility or innocence or both. Khoury is the one who holds women responsible for their own victimization. His rage against the victims is so great that he calls for their total destruction. It is as if he were blaming the oppressed for being oppressed and calling for more oppression to get rid of oppression. Fanon's view of violence as catharsis can be compared to Khoury's call for total annihilation. They both call on negative, destructive means for the transformation of society. There is a similar element in al-Shaykh's novel when Zahra, who goes to the sniper, seeks a homeopathic cure against the war. The difference between Khoury and al-Shaykh is that Zahra does it through masochism, thereby emphasizing her own victimization, whereas Khoury inflicts it through sadism, thereby increasing the cruelty and expressing a total lack of compassion for the victims.

Finally, an obvious conclusion to this study is that the fear men have of women leads them to domination and war, while the fear women have of men's violence leads them to masochistic submission to or rejection of the men (or both) and commitment to political, human, and feminist causes. Both the female and male authors agree on this point. For example, the sniper's first reaction to Zahra is rape, as a way of proving his masculinity through control and domination. Fear is one of his primary motivations: fear of life, fear of women's capacity to reproduce and give birth, fascination with death and destruction. He does not want to assume the responsibility of the life he has engendered in Zahra's womb, when he daily kills innocent victims and destroys life. In order to reestablish the chaos, daily drug, and only meaning of his existence, he must kill her. And for Talal in *The Small Mountain*, fighting is like making love to a woman: it is frightening and never fulfilling. The author describes a group of fighters who have lost the meaning of life, a fraternity of men always afraid, attracted and repulsed by women and by war, who know only destruction in which they lose themselves. The hate and fear they feel for women become their ultimate motivations for war. Such fear is epitomized by the relationship the central character has with his wife. The author describes boredom and weariness in their relationship, thereby trying to justify the need for war to bring about necessary changes. The main character has an obvious fascination with death and destruction, which is closely related to his sense of pleasure. He is chained to his wife through habits he can destroy only through war. And he runs away from the other two women in his life, because they represent life and freedom, which he is unable to accept, busy as he is with destruction. It leads to an obsession with destruction, as if destroying the city and the woman it symbolizes brings ultimate *jouissance.* And Zahra, afraid of the violence ripping her country apart, submits herself masochistically to one of its worse perpetrators, thereby hoping to overcome her fears. In contrast, the central women characters in *House Without Roots* live their lives independent from men and with a commitment to bring about the transformation of society through peaceful means. And Marie Rose stands in front of the fascist young men of her country, confronting them with their perverted values, in an act that defies their violence and rejects them altogether. This *chabab* gang is afraid of Marie Rose who epitomizes feminine and feminist values and who dares confront them with words, showing them their corruption while asserting her femi-

humanism and her commitment to the oppressed and the downtrodden. They will have to get rid of her, just like the sniper had to get rid of Zahra.

Thus, whereas women writers are finding a way out, a circle of hell is being perpetuated, each sex fearing the other, the male one starting the chain through violence and domination. Only a different vision, new actions, and altered relationships based on trust, recognition, and acceptance of the other can help heal the wounds and bring about the cure necessary to project a new future for the world. Such a change has already started taking place with personal and political actions aimed at solving the problems rooted in oppression, domination, and the victimization of women. Writing this chapter has been one of these actions.

The connection between sexuality and war is so present in the novels that it is probably one of the most evident unifying themes. It demonstrates how strongly at work it is in the collective imagination or culture of the people and how central it is to an understanding of the situation and the causes of the war. The similarities and differences between the ways women and men express and deal with violence and sexuality can lead us to a greater comprehension of the complexities in the relationship between the two and bring us closer to a solution: the need for a new rapport between men and women, women and women, and men and men, relationships based on trust, recognition of the other, tenderness, equal sharing, and love void of jealousy and possession. My contention being that the personal is political—a vision also dear to feminist movements—and thus changes in relationships traditionally based on domination, oppression, and power games will inevitably bounce back on other spheres of life.

Reflections and Conclusions

What Miriam Cooke writes about the Lebanese women writers' vision of Lebanon as a sick child in need of care became for me a reality. It was the Lebanese war that made me want to go back and try to help. I would not have felt the same concern for Lebanon had it not been for the war and for what I perceived as real suffering in my friends and many of the people I came in contact with. I shared their pain and desire to remedy. It led me to apply for grants to go and teach there. My experiences in living the war—talking with students, teaching, conducting research, traveling in Lebanon, crossing the demarcation line dividing the city, participating in nonviolent peace initiatives, spending time in the shelter when shelling became too violent, sharing the anguish and suffering of friends and relatives—gave me insights I might not have had otherwise. It led to a conviction that only peaceful means could bring about a solution to Lebanon and reunite the country. It also showed me the importance of activism for the transformation of society: peace marches, hunger strikes, consciousness-raising groups, solidarity among women, singing, writing, crossing the divided city, and, most of all, changing the system of rapport between men and women, the values connected with these relations and the confessional structures tied to the concepts of honor, virginity, exclusive property, and oppression.

It also became very clear to me that women's solidarity and an international feminism, uniting women all over the world, are vital in bringing about such changes. I would like to stress the importance of achieving unity in the midst of cultural differences, if we want to provide some hope in ending the war culture that exists all over the world. I became very aware, when in Lebanon, of the strength that the peace initiative started by two women from enemy communities had, first on women and then on the population as a whole, in uniting people toward peace. It is one of the rare times in my life that I witnessed the tremendous impact that values of love and tolerance can have on people.

The kinds of activities that I described above during my time in Lebanon—which also included discussions with students and with people directly affected by the war, writing a novel about it, composing songs on the war, and performing them in public—were undertaken as a result of my concern and suffering over the destruction of my country, but they were also directly involved with the transformation of society. Changing the system and the values behind it requires more time and a long process of in-depth political, economic, psychological, religious, sexual, familial, and social transformations established on an understanding of the different factors, causes, and links among these various fields. My belief that long-term plans to bring about social transformations are necessary to end the war system and bring about hopeful and lasting changes to a world falling apart led me to this analysis of the relationship among sexuality, war, and literature.

18 Iron Breaks, Too

Israeli and Palestinian Women Talk about War, Bereavement, and Peace

ZIVA FLAMHAFT

AT THE TIME OF THIS WRITING, following a particularly violent week in Jerusalem and Gaza, high-level American officials were traveling to the Middle East in an attempt to salvage the road map and begin to implement some of the commitments Israel and the Palestinian Authority made to each other when the peace initiative was inaugurated by President George W. Bush during the June 2003 summit in Aqaba, Jordan. Based on the president's speech a year earlier, and embraced by the European Union, Russia, and the United Nations, the road map envisioned a two-state solution at the end of a comprehensive settlement of the Israeli-Palestinian conflict by 2005.

As a result of the increased diplomatic activity, by July 2003 Israel had relinquished to the Palestinians direct control of the main north-south road that parts Gaza and began its withdrawal from the West Bank town of Bethlehem. At the same time, three main radical Palestinian factions agreed to suspend attacks against Israelis after thirty-three months of violence that killed more than eight hundred Israelis and more than two thousand Palestinians and maimed thousands. These steps were followed by a meeting in Jerusalem between Ariel Sharon, the Israeli prime minister, and Mahmud Abbas, his Palestinian counterpart, who pledges to continue the path toward peace through diplomacy.

Even as ordinary Israelis and Palestinians express skepticism over the likelihood that these conciliatory measures represented the reigniting of a genuine peace process, evidence showed that both groups prefer the end of violence over the futile bloodshed: although they still expected their government to take harsh military measures in the fight against terrorism, 61 percent of Israelis supported the so-called road map, and nearly 60 percent said they would agree to establish a Pales-

311

tinian state in the framework of peace and evacuate all but the largest blocs of Jewish settlements in the West Bank and Gaza. Correspondingly, 55 percent of Palestinians supported the peace plan, while 71 percent supported a mutual cessation of violence providing that Israel would recognize a Palestinian state next to its borders (on the other hand, almost 90 percent or more continued to support attacks on Israeli soldiers and settlers and more than 55 percent continued to support attacks on civilians inside Israel in the absence of reconciliation).[1]

Although observers remained guardedly optimistic about the future of the new peace plan, public opinion reflecting the yearning for reconciliation and change was hardly voiced by civil society on both sides. If such silence was the result of, among other things, a reciprocal dehumanizing process—in itself the outcome of nearly three years of violence and a diminished mutual trust that was so carefully if cautiously built during the preceding decade of the Oslo years—rehumanizing the other for the purpose of reconciliation nevertheless was possible. The group best equipped to be entrusted with that undertaking was—and remains—a unique body of women who have suffered the consequences of the Arab-Israeli conflict for decades.

This proposition rests on three assumptions: First, because of their unique status in their societies, these women are able to influence public opinion on peace and security matters. Second, the majority of women who were victimized by war opt for reconciliation rather than vengeance. Third, the inclusion of women in peacemaking will remedy their chronic absence in peace processes, thereby conforming to United Nations Security Council Resolution 1325 of October 2000. That resolution urged member states to increase women's representation at all decision-making levels in national, regional, and international institutions and mechanisms for the prevention, management, and resolution of conflicts.

The link between the personal experiences of women and their political activism is not uncommon. Instances of such activities direct attention to the ability of bereaved and other victimized women to transform their agony into political action and should empower women who suffered the consequences of war and its aftermath to organize political movements dedicated to conflict resolution and peace building. Examples of such activism include the large number of women widowed

1. *Jerusalem Post,* June 10, 2003, 1; Joint Palestinian-Israeli Public Opinion Poll, Apr. 3–11, 2003, Palestinian Center for Policy and Survey Research in Ramallah and the Harry S. Truman Research Institute for the Advancement of Peace at the Hebrew University, Jerusalem, and PSR Survey Research unit: Public Opinion Poll no. 7, Apr. 3–7, 2003.

as a result of the September 11 attack on the United States and their organized attempt to influence the way the World Trade Center will be memorialized. Other examples include Sarah Brady, the wife of President Ronald Reagan's White House press secretary who suffered a severe brain injury in the 1981 assassination attempt on the president. Sarah Brady became chair of Handgun Control, a Washington-based organization advocating government regulation on the manufacturing, importation, sale, transfer, and civilian possession of handguns. As a strong advocate of gun-control legislation promoting a national waiting period, the former press secretary's wife was influential in the passage of the 1994 Brady Law, requiring a five-day waiting period before purchasing a licensed handgun.

Still another example is New York congresswoman Carolyn McCarthy, who in 1996 was elected while never before running for office. She pronounced her candidacy after her husband had been murdered and her son severely injured during the 1993 Long Island Railroad massacre, strongly urging the end of gun violence. Other women who lost their children in traffic accidents caused by drunk drivers established Mothers Against Drunk Driving in an effort to find solutions to drunk driving. And mothers who lost their children to AIDS are attempting to influence health care legislation in the United States. But unlike these activists, women in societies that are plagued by war face social pressures and are thus often reluctant to transform their experience into political activism. Pressures include a siege mentality or a widespread admiration for the military, both resulting from prolonged conflicts and security concerns. Frequently in such societies, as the Israeli example shows, women are caught between their obligation to the state and their duty to themselves, accepting as primary the role of men in the political-security spheres, while tolerating the restrictive and traditional female functions reserved to them (Yishai 1997).

The subject of women and war has captivated a growing number of feminist theorists and other social scientists since the early 1980s. Some scholars surveyed the role of women warriors, the exploitation of women workers in wartime, the changing role of women in the military, or the role of women in resistant and revolutionary movements.[2] Others studied the role of women as peacemakers, often dissociating them from war and bloodshed, connecting instead womanhood with pacifism and motherhood with antiwar activism.[3] But the theme of women's be-

---

2. For some examples, see Blacksmith 1992; Braybo 1989; Cock 1993; Fraser 1988; Maxwell 1990; Norman 1990; Peterson and Runyan 1993; Rittner and Roth 1993; Stiehem 1989; Verger 1991; Vickers 1993; Walker 1985; Young 1992.

3. See Alonso 1993; Bouchier 1984; Macdonald 1988; Pierson 1988; Ruether 1983; Sharoni 1995.

reavement and other anguish brought upon them by conflict, and the conceivable role this particular group of women can play in peacemaking, has for the most part been neglected among researchers. This oversight reflects neither the sacrifice these women have made for their nations nor their potential leverage in their societies.

The link between feminism and peace has long been established: it began in the late nineteenth and early twentieth centuries, when the first feminist peace movements sprang up in the United States and Europe. Initially, the connection between the two concepts centered on the conventional belief that a relationship existed between women's nurturing nature and world peace—a correlation that continued well into the 1980s and beyond.[4] The fact that some women also led nations to war for thousands of years, that they have often willingly supported their countries' war efforts or proudly sent their sons to the battlefield, has been omitted from this linkage.[5]

Therefore, women's tenderness may not explain their yearning for peace. Instead, we must find other explanations for the emergence of feminist peace protest movements the world over. What explains, for example, the women's movements opposing nuclear armament in Europe in the early 1980s or the ongoing protests of the mothers and grandmothers of those individuals who disappeared in Argentina in the 1970s and 1980s? Likewise, what explains the emergence of Mothers Against Silence, Women in Black, or Four Mothers in Israel in the 1980s and 1990s? What explains the demonstrations that Serb mothers and wives staged in 1999 in the midst of war, demanding that their sons and husbands be released from military duty in Kosovo, or their Russian counterparts who demanded the end of war in Chechnya? Evidently, it is not their nurturing nature that motivates women to seek peace but their rejection of their social conditioning, on the one hand, and. on the other, their demand for accountability and justice.

More precisely, it was not women's compassion that linked them to peace movements but efforts to associate peace with their own human and political rights. These efforts began as early as the 1880s: because existing concepts of civil rights at that time were directly connected to one's ability to bear arms in war, women, who

4. See *Jerusalem Post*, June 10, 2003, 1; Joint Palestinian-Israeli Public Opinion Poll, Apr. 3–11, 2003, Palestinian Center for Policy and Survey Research in Ramallah and the Harry S. Truman Research Institute for the Advancement of Peace at the Hebrew University, Jerusalem.

5. Some feminist researchers attribute women's acquiescence to their country's war efforts to their relative political powerlessness. See Nancy Scheper-Huges, "Maternal Thinking and the Politics of War," in Lorentzen and Turpin 1988.

were traditionally deprived of that provision, were stripped of basic civil rights, including citizenship and suffrage. These exclusions were subsequently extended to the restriction of women from positions of power in the political hierarchy of the state. In time, women began to associate peace with the cessation of violence against them, with their inclusion in a growing middle class, and with the right of the masses to live a fearless life. Peace also became connected to the ability of women to enter into the public sphere, a less prejudiced division of labor between men and women during wartime and its aftermath, and the eradication of poverty among woman and children resulting from the loss of their husbands and fathers in war (Alonso 1993; Bouchier 1984, 19–25). Subsequently, kindled by feminist movements a decade or so earlier and aware of their social, political, and economic subordination, in the 1970s women began to reject their subservient role in society. Instead, they requested their inclusion in "high politics"—a cold war term describing politics relating to military-security issues and other matters of vital national interest, usually reserved for men. Women began to associate peace with their own right to live a fearless life and their right to raise families and see their children grow, survive, and flourish.[6] At the same time, women began to associate justice with accountability, demanding that policy makers and military strategists accept responsibility for their decisions, be liable for deeds that affect women and their families, and draw the right conclusions for the future.

Researchers may object to the assertion that bereaved women seek peace in lieu of vengeance. However, as the results of my Israeli and Arab interviews reveal, a considerable number of these women do prefer reconciliation, not only because conflict is a source of suffering but also because conflict prolongs their exclusion from the national decision-making process. Furthermore, the pursuit of peaceful means versus violent means for the purpose of achieving change is not only true about women. Indeed, political disfranchisement often motivates these pursuits of peaceful means by men. The nonviolent methods pursued by men like Mahatma Gandhi, Martin Luther King, Jr., and Desmond Tutu are powerful examples supporting this assertion.

A recent example of the desire of bereaved women to build peace comes from Israeli war widows. Making a conscious decision to use their bereavement as a platform from which their voices can be heard, a group of fifty-five war widows organ-

6. In this context, that peace is a basic human right and that governments are fundamentally obligated to preserve, promote, and implement that right was stated in UN Resolution 39/11 of Nov. 12, 1984.

ized in April 2002 for the first time since the formation of peace movements in Israel, calling for the end of bloodshed (*Haaretz,* Apr. 8, 2000). This example, as well as other patterns shown in the Israeli-Arab case below, supports many of the assertions stated above.

In 1995–96, and using the Arab-Israeli conflict as a case study, I conducted interviews with thirty Israeli Jewish women and eight Palestinian Arab women, the latter with the help of a Palestinian assistant. The purpose of my interviews was to examine whether women directly affected by conflict and war believe they have a special role to play as peacemakers.[7] This chapter describes the research and my findings.

Israeli and Palestinian Women in Peace and War

Israeli women began to resist war, however subtly, after the costly Egyptian and Syrian surprise attacks in the 1973 Yom Kippur War. Their outcry resulted in the establishment of a government-appointed commission of inquiry—the Agranat Commission—whose task was to examine the events leading to the war, including an unprecedented investigation of the conduct of the Israeli military on the eve of that war. A decade later, women organized the first feminist-oriented peace protest movement, Mothers Against Silence, which soon developed into Parents Against Silence. Initially, the movement sprang up in the aftermath of the 1982 invasion of Lebanon—the first Arab-Israeli war to be regarded as unjust by a considerable number of Israelis. Such perception, coupled with a large number of casualties, triggered the protest of mothers who objected to their sons' participation in that war, demanding Israel's withdrawal from Lebanon. The movement was dissolved with the partial Israeli Defense Forces retreat in 1985. But in 1997, with mounting casualties in Israel's remaining security zone in southern Lebanon, a similar yet smaller group named Four Mothers sprang up, advocating a unilateral withdrawal from the area. The best-known activist in that group was Orna Shimoni, a bereaved mother who had lost her son in Lebanon. Short of forming a new movement, in 1998, together with Lella Parnass, another bereaved mother because of the Lebanon scenario, Shimoni staged a well-publicized protest in front of the Israeli president residence in Jerusalem, demanding to move the Lebanon issue to the top the national priorities' list. By the end of that year, after a monthlong sit-down strike, the two mothers met with then prime minister Benjamin Netanyahu and a number of

7. The research was supported by a Fulbright-Hays Scholarship.

his cabinet members to voice their demands. Their activism became the first peace protest staged exclusively by bereaved women.

Along with her coactivists, Shimoni was widely recognized in Israel as one of the forces influencing Prime Minister Ehud Barak's decision to unilaterally withdraw the Israeli forces from Lebanon, a move that was completed without casualties in May 2000 and verified by the United Nations in June of that year. Such recognition stood in stark contrast to the ridicule and criticism Shimoni and her friends endured from the media, army officers, and government and other officials during months of activism.

Building on Shimoni's example, in July 2000, a group of bereaved Israeli parents set up the Peace Tent for Bereaved Families in Tel Aviv to express support for peace talks between Israel and the Palestinian Authority that were taking place in Camp David under the leadership of President Clinton. Five months later—using Barak's forced decision to call for new elections two months into the al-Aqsa intifada[8]—the group that by then included bereaved Palestinians parents as well assumed the official name of the Parents Circle/Bereaved Families Forum. Its activities expanded after the rise of Ariel Sharon to power in 2001 following the escalation of violence. Noticeably, at the time when mounting violence silenced the peace camp, the Parents Circle became increasingly vocal and a well-known group in Israel and the Palestinian territories.

Earlier all-female peace groups sprang up after the breakout of the 1987 intifada.[9] Alongside other female peace movements, Women in Black—the best-known Israeli feminist protest group—was organized, calling for the end of Israel's occupation of Palestinian land and the opening of a dialogue with the Palestine Liberation Organization (PLO) branded by Israel as a terrorist organization with whom contacts were prohibited. Faced with scorn, and convinced that their unorthodox ideas would be rejected, this group and other lesser-known female peace movements stopped much of their activities following the 1993 Oslo peace agreement. After the eruption of the al-Aqsa intifada in the fall of 2000, Women in Black

8. The al-Aqsa intifada refers to the second Palestinian uprising in the West Bank and Gaza, following the controversial visit of Ariel Sharon to Temple Mount/Haram al-Sharif in Jerusalem on Sept. 28, 2000.

9. The 1987 intifada was a violent popular uprising that began in the Gaza Strip on Dec. 9, 1987. It was ignited by the deaths of four Palestinians the day before in a crash involving a car driven by an Israeli.

has regrouped, staging vigils in cities where they had long disappeared. At the same time, women from all the feminist peace movements have joined hands to work together, primarily under the umbrella of the Coalition of Women for a Just Peace. Apparently, none of these groups was as influential as was Shimoni's on a government's decision on any military-security issue.

As for Palestinian women, because the conditions under which they exist are entirely different from the circumstances of their Israeli counterparts, their primary activities have concentrated on opposition to the Israeli occupation rather than building peace. Under the watchful eyes of Israelis and Palestinians alike, women assembled at meetings, established committees, and organized hunger strikes in order to protest the Israeli occupation. While becoming major producers of means to sustain their communities, they were also active in clandestine movements, often resulting in daily torture and humiliation (Young 1992).

Yet the outbreak of the first intifada provided Palestinian women the opportunity to interact with Israeli female peace activists, form dialogue groups, stage joint demonstrations, and work collaboratively on different projects. The Gulf War in 1990–91 interrupted such joint efforts, and attempts to restore ties between the two groups had not been successful (Sharoni 1995, chap. 8). Perhaps ironically, following the signing of the Oslo accords in 1993, Palestinian female peace activists once again became reluctant to collaborate with their Israeli counterparts because of their own disillusionment with these agreements. Instead, they turned toward building and protecting their own democracy. This latter trend became even more prevalent after the establishment of the Palestinian Authority in 1995.

The violent upheavals caused by the al-Aqsa intifada, the excessive use of force by the Israeli military, and an apparent radicalization on both sides seem to have destroyed any chance for collaborative peace efforts. Moreover, the pride some Palestinian mothers expressed in their suicide-bomber sons and their stated willingness to raise children to become martyrs stunned many Israeli peace activists. Nonetheless, at the time of this writing, as the number of Israeli and Palestinian casualties rose daily, female peace activists from both sides were cautiously resuming old contacts. Interestingly, even when optimism about the prospect of peace had decreased in both societies, polls indicated that a peaceful solution was still desirable by a majority of Israelis and many Palestinians.

The questions remain: Do bereaved or aggrieved women feel victimized by war? If they do, what has prevented them from becoming activists? If they view themselves as potential peacemakers, why haven't they organized to mobilize domestic support for peace at a crucial junction of Middle East history, when Israelis and

Palestinians were grappling with a delicate process of peacemaking or when the peace process was breaking apart, turning war imminent?

Research Strategy

Because Israel is a small country with a bloody history, it was not difficult to locate women directly affected by conflict and war. As the interviewer, I made no special recruiting arrangements prior to travel to Israel other than to contact a small number of women. I recruited women for the interviews through networking with friends, screening old newspapers, and talking with citizens such as taxi drivers or transit passengers. Drafting women was not an easy process. Women with recent loss were not contacted. Many women who were approached declined to be interviewed. For privacy concerns, the least-productive method of recruitment was using military and civilian organizations. Very few women who had agreed to meet changed their minds and refused to participate.

I prepared a questionnaire of twenty questions for the interviews. I interviewed all subjects face-to-face, most (with the exception of four) at the home of the subject. Other than focusing the interviews on the prepared questions, my role was passive and unbiased. An average interview lasted two hours. All of the Israeli women agreed to be recorded; only two preferred to use fictitious names.

A gap in the study is the involvement of Bedouin women, many of whom are war widows and bereaved mothers.[10] Like the Druze and Circassian Muslims, and unlike Israeli Arabs of Palestinian descent, the Bedouin are recruited into the Israeli army, suffering a relatively large number of casualties. One assumption as to the lack of interest from these bereaved women is that they are fearful of participating because it will lead to their being viewed as traitors.

My intention to show the Palestinian side through interviews was much more difficult than for the Israeli side. A major obstacle was the mutual fear and suspicion that existed in Israel and the territories resulting from a wave of terrorist attacks in Israel and the reply military countermeasures. In the summer of 1995, through a

---

10. For the unfamiliar reader, the Bedouin people are Sunni Muslims, who unlike other Arab groups that moved northward during the spread of the Islamic empire in the seventh century A.D. remained nomads, living mostly in the Arabian Desert and adhering to the simple way of life of their Semitic ancestors. In Israel the Bedouin constitute a small minority among a larger group of Muslim and some Christian Arabs who remained in the country after the establishment of the state in 1948.

professor of sociology at Birzeit University in Ramallah,[11] whom I had met with the help of colleagues, I met my assistant, a thirty-one-year-old Palestinian woman. She agreed to interview ten Palestinian women from the West Bank and possibly Gaza. Though I originally intended to accompany my assistant on the interviews, my presence had the potential to bias the results or prevent cooperation from these women or both. My assistant used the same questionnaire and was supplied with the same recorder.

Because of travel restrictions, family concerns, and fears for personal safety, it took three years for my assistant to provide me with the transcripts of the eight completed interviews. According to my assistant, she conducted the interviews herself, traveling to the homes of the women she interviewed. She did not interview the last two women from Gaza because she was unable to travel there from Ramallah owing to repeated closures. The interviews were conducted in Arabic and translated into English at Birzeit University. None of the women agreed to be recorded. Each interview lasted approximately one hour and a half. The transcripts do not reveal any unusual bias, given living conditions under Israeli control.

Before describing the data I gathered, a cautionary note is warranted: I should point out to the reader that this undertaking is not presumed to be scientific. First, my respondents do not represent a cross section of the Israeli or Palestinian population. Instead, they embody rather distinct, relatively small groups with a very specific experience. Second, within this very group I reached a small number of individuals, fewer of whom agreed to be interviewed. Furthermore, my respondents were not divided into particular age or ethnic groups, religious-secular backgrounds, levels of education, or political affiliation. Nonetheless, these women represent a segment of society that needs to be heard in the Middle East and elsewhere. The women whose stories I tell represent a group that is composed of individuals who paid the heaviest price for their leaders' military-security and political policies but were least influential in the decision-making process.

Of the thirty Israeli women interviewed, the youngest was twenty-eight years old and the oldest eighty-eight. Fifteen were widows—three from the 1967 Six-Day War, six from the 1973 Yom Kippur War; two Druze were widowed in the aftermath of the Lebanon war; and four others were widowed during the intifada.

Four women were bereaved mothers, one of whom lost her son in the 1982

11. Because of prevailing conditions in Ramallah at the time of this writing, I opted not to reveal the name of this professor.

Lebanon war; two lost their sons during Hezbollah attacks in southern Lebanon in the early 1990s; one lost her son to Hamas terrorism in the post-Oslo period.

Three were bereaved sisters. One lost her brother in the 1948 War of Independence, but she was also the widow of an underground Jewish fighter who died in a British jail prior to Israel's independence. The other lost her brother in the 1970 war of attrition, while her father subsequently committed suicide on his son's grave. The third lost her brother during a 1973 attack on PLO bases in Lebanon in retaliation for the 1972 terrorist attack in Munich, where eleven Israeli Olympic athletes were murdered.

Two women were orphans. One lost her father in the 1948 War of Independence, but she also lost her brother in the 1973 Yom Kippur War. At the time of her interview she was seeking an official exemption from combat military service for her eighteen-year-old son who was solicited by a number of elite combat units. The second lost her father in the 1973 Yom Kippur War.

One woman was the widow of a war-disabled veteran, blinded in the 1948 War of Independence. Another was a disabled female veteran, seriously injured in a Syrian attack in 1970 during the war of attrition. Still another was the mother of a soldier who has been missing in action since the 1982 Lebanon war; one other was the mother of a war-disabled veteran, seriously injured in a Hezbollah attack in Lebanon in the aftermath of that war. Two bereaved mothers were active in peace movements, but their activity began before the incident of loss.

The Findings

Based on their personal experiences, most of the respondents believed that women suffer the consequence of war in a different way than men do. Widows, for example, contended that Israeli society sets much more stringent standards of behavior for them compared to widowers. Others explained the different behavior of men and women in the contrasting roles of the two sexes in national war efforts: Men are usually engaged in war planning and in actual fighting, having no time, chance, or natural inclination to worry about life back home. Females, on the other hand, are left in the rear to carry on all civilian responsibilities in addition to worrying about their loved ones in the front. Almost all of the respondents maintained that women are emotionally stronger than men are.

Most interviewees thought that the number of Israeli women involved in decision making on military and security issues was not only disturbingly low but that their participation could change the essence of such decisions. Most were also convinced that their role in Israel's national and existential struggles was no different from the role of the male members of their society, even if such a role assumed a different pattern than it did for men. More women maintained that their sacrifices resulting from war had no special meaning than those women who thought that such sacrifices were particularly meaningful because of their sense of patriotism or because of the national honor accorded to them. Although many challenged the very notion of the need to sacrifice human life for any idea, including statehood, the women who were victimized in the 1948 War of Independence and the 1967 Six-Day War did not question their losses. That finding was hardly surprising since most Israelis perceive both wars as wars of survival.

Because of their unique agonizing experience, these women tend to view ordinary daily occurrences as trivial, often resulting in their own isolation, real or perceived. Usually, the degree of seclusion corresponds to the level of bereavement. Thus, whereas most women believed that they were an integral part of the Israeli society even when constituting a very distinct group, bereaved mothers felt especially secluded. Noticeably, women who had never met one another used identical metaphors to describe their isolation.

Whereas only three of the thirty women interviewed were politically active, all described themselves as politically aware. Generally, ideological identification remained rather consistent, with most women adhering to the same political views they had held prior to the incident of loss or injury, and supporting the same policies. The few who had changed their views were equally divided among women who had shifted from left to right and vice versa, as a result of their personal experiences. On the main, ideological affiliation remained constant even after the national trauma resulting from the murder of Prime Minister Yitzhak Rabin in November 1995: more than merely adhering to their previous ideas, most women felt stronger about them. One should expect, however, that the current violence caused many to switch their moderate ideas to more radical ones. Such shifts would reverse again once the level of violence drops to an acceptable level, confidence-building measures are taken by both sides, and the peace process resumes.

Almost all of the women interviewed thought that women with similar experiences were capable of influencing public opinion on issues of war and peace. Yet some of the women who believed they had potential influence to shape public opinion on these issues were unable to correlate between such influence and their ability to affect the Arab-Israeli peace process or the essence of an eventual peace treaty. Still, nearly two-thirds concluded that women affected by war have a special role to play as peacemakers in the conflict in which their societies were involved and that they were able to influence the peace process. The source of their potential influence was their unique experience and their beliefs that women generally desire peace more than men do and that they are more result oriented than men. But when asked whether they were able to influence the political process itself, or the type of peace that will ultimately result from that process, only about one-fourth of the interviewees were confident that they could do so. The rest were nearly evenly divided among those who were uncertain about the ability of women to do so and those who were convinced that they were unable to influence the type of an envisaged peace.

The same two-thirds who embraced their role as peacemakers also thought that shared memories of past violence could inspire reconciliation among Arabs and Jews and that bereaved women on both sides of the conflict could transform their grief into political power. Only a third believed that such memories could impede reconciliation, an equal number maintaining that personal memories or experience were, or should be, politically relevant.

Those interviewees who rejected their potential role as peacemakers also repudiated the idea that women on either side were able to transform their personal experiences into political influence. But even these women recognized their capacity to communicate, organize, mobilize, and recruit others, not to mention their ability to influence election results. Only a few women complained about the absence of Israeli women at the negotiating table.

Among the eight Palestinian women interviewed, the youngest was twenty-four years old; the oldest was in her early forties. Three were from the Ramallah area in the West Bank, three others were from Hebron, and two were from Jabalia refugee camp in the Gaza Strip. Five were widowed between 1987 and 1993 in the first intifada, and three lost their husbands in the 1994 Hebron massacre.[12] None, however, offered details about the circumstances surrounding their husband's death, except to say that he died in the intifada or in the hands of the Israelis. Understandably, all were much more cautious and reserved than the Israelis.

Their answers confirm the fact that their primary concern is the end of the Israeli occupation, the most burdensome aspect of which is the existence of Jewish settlements in the midst of Palestinian territory. (One should expect that the presence of the Israeli military in towns that have been under Palestinian control, clo-

---

12. A fanatic Jewish settler who entered the Tomb of the Patriarchs killing twenty-nine Muslim worshipers and injuring a score of others carried out the Hebron massacre.

sures, and the harsh conditions caused by the present situation are equally burdensome.) And since the occupation is the single most important obstacle to peace, peace activities involving mutual trust can begin, according to them, only after the occupation comes to an end.

Like their Israeli counterparts, they believed that women suffer from war in a different way than do men because of prevailing social norms and familial responsibilities and because of the different roles men and women have in wartime. They too thought that women are stronger than men and that their role in the national struggle of their people was equal, if different, to the role of any men in their family, and they felt an integral part of their society. All but one claimed to be politically aware; one woman was a longtime member of the Hebron Women's Association for Peace.

Seven of the eight women believed that not enough Palestinian women were involved in politics. Six of them emphasized the lack of experience or the absence of a high level of education and social traditions and customs as forces that hold women back. Three women believed that these restraints have prevented them from transforming their own grief into political action, while three others maintained that they could eventually transform their grief into political activity but not under the prevailing conditions in the territories. Only two women thought that solidarity among women can presently reinforce their participation in the political life of their society.

Five women agreed that bereaved women have a role to play in conflict resolution, while three rejected that notion. Of these three, one did so because she did not trust women's judgment; one other thought women were too emotional; the third claimed she did not understand politics enough to explain her opinion. Three women believed that mutual experience of past violence could create a bridge between women from both camps, while three others thought that past memories of violence could breed only hatred. As members of the same gender, four women felt sympathetic toward their Israeli counterparts who suffered similar losses, but they could not identify or express solidarity with them; two in fact blamed Israel for the conflict.

Unlike many Israeli women who questioned the need for the sacrifice of human lives even for the sake of the state, the Palestinian women approved of such sacrifices in the name of their national struggle, viewing it as martyrdom. Thus, all but one referred to her husband as a martyr, his eternal glory translating into honor and respect in her society. As a rule, they did not criticize the Palestinian Authority for their suffering but put 100 percent blame on the Israeli military.

In sum, Israeli women affected by war feel that they have equally shared the national and existential burdens of the state. Yet society has treated them unequally, undermining their capacity as policy makers. Hypothetically, their special status in a society afflicted by conflict and war enables them to translate their personal experiences into political power, influencing public opinion and playing a meaningful role in the political process. But because of prevailing social norms, in the end, they would be unable to utilize their power in a manner that could significantly influence the peace process and the type of the emerging peace. This paradoxical sense of helplessness can partly explain why, as a group, they have not mobilized to support—or oppose—the peace process, even though most women believed that their own experiences and the experiences of their Arab counterparts could be utilized politically. Perhaps more than any other reason, bereaved and aggrieved women have not mobilized politically because of their emotional exhaustion and their daily struggles to protect what is left of their shattered families.

Palestinian women also feel that they have equally shared the national and existential burdens of their society. But rather than blaming society for treating them unequally, they relate their inability to assume power to the lack of experience or insufficient education in addition to existing norms and traditions, and to the Israeli occupation. Presumably, their special status could enable them too to translate their personal experience into political power, but they cannot do so under the conditions of occupation.

Conclusions and Recommendations

The subject of this chapter has been the potential empowerment of women who suffered the consequences of conflict and war through becoming peace builders. As mentioned earlier, this work rests on a few assumptions: First, because of their status, these women are able to influence public opinion on peace and security matters. Second, the majority of women victimized by war opt for reconciliation rather than vengeance. Third, peacemaking is tied more to political disfranchisement rather than to an inherent "peace-loving" quality in women.

That these women are able to influence policy became evident in Israel, when the government of Ehud Barak unilaterally withdrew Israel's military forces from South Lebanon in the spring of 2000. That many such women opt for nonviolent means to solve conflicts has become apparent not only from my interviews but also from the recent example of the newly organized group of Israeli war widows who are publicly calling for the end of bloodshed.

Although bereaved women constitute a small number of peace activists, there is now a movement, Parents Circle/Bereaved Families Forum, created by bereaved Israeli and Palestinian families. They spoke loudest in March 2002, when in front of the UN headquarters in New York they staged a demonstration with more than two thousand mock coffins covered with Israeli and Palestinian flags, representing the number of casualties both sides suffered as a result of the then current situation in Israel and the Palestinian Authority. Many of the women interviewed who supported their government's peace efforts stated they were not involved in peace movements because they had never considered the subject. However, since the study, I discovered that some of the interviewed women have become active in peace movements. Apparently, raising the level of consciousness of bereaved women can motivate at least some of these women to engage in peace building. Additional rewards come with the discovery of their own leadership and recruitment skills. As shown, in the United States and the West there are good examples of seemingly ordinary women who became activists after suffering loss. Sarah Brady and Carolyn McCarthy are only two examples. Unquestionably, the inclusion of women in peacemaking will remedy their chronic absence in peace processes, especially in deep-rooted conflicts.

Finally, the assertion that peacemaking is tied more to political disfranchisement rather than to an inherent "peace-loving" quality in women is historically evident. Powerful women such as Queen Boudica, Indira Gandhi, Golda Meir, and Margaret Thatcher unhesitatingly led their nations in war, while disfranchised men like Mahatma Gandhi, Martin Luther King Jr., and Desmond Tutu set powerful examples supporting nonviolence as methods used to achieve change.

There are several steps others can take in order to motivate bereaved women to engage as peacemakers or to become like Sarah Brady or Carolyn McCarthy. First, people must try to spread the information they obtain from peace-building works, possibly by organizing small or large community lectures. Fellow researchers should expand studies into other conflict or former conflict areas, such as Northern Ireland, Bosnia, and Kosovo as well as other areas in eastern and central Europe, Africa, or Central America. Many women in such conflict areas became brave enough to talk about their ordeals as rape and other war victims. With encouragement from the political, information, and academic communities, these women's courage can be expanded into political activism.

19 Peace-Building and Reconstruction with Women

Reflections on Afghanistan, Iraq, and Palestine

VALENTINE M. MOGHADAM

VIOLENCE AGAINST WOMEN is multifaceted and occurs in different contexts. From domestic violence to "date rape," from assaults on the streets to war crimes, violence is often sexualized and occurs at times of "peace" as well as during armed conflict. All too often, armed conflict exacerbates violence against women. Rapes may occur on a large scale, men may institute controls over the women of their community, and women may suffer at the hands of husbands or male kin who feel humiliated or emasculated by occupying powers. Conditions are worsened when states lack the capacity or the will to protect the human rights of citizens, and especially the human rights of women.

It is almost a banality to note that armed conflict destroys resources and lives and stalls socioeconomic development, but it is worth repeating some of the details here. Afghanistan and Iraq have seen more than twenty-five years of conflict, starting roughly the same time, and both countries have experienced invasions and occupation by foreign troops.[1] They also are beset by ethnic, communal, and sectarian

1. The armed uprising against the government of the Democratic Republic of Afghanistan began in the latter part of 1978 and saw the military support of the United States and Pakistan in the summer of 1979, six months before the intervention of the Soviet army at the request of the Kabul government. The civil conflict raged until 1992, when the left-wing government was overthrown. It resumed when erstwhile partners of the Islamic Mujahideen alliance waged war against each other (1992–94) and the Taliban emerged to fight the Mujahideen (1994–96). Afghanistan was invaded by U.S. troops, and the Taliban removed from power, in October 2001. Iraq was at war with Iran from 1980 to 1988, and with Kuwait, Saudi Arabia, and the United States in 1990–91. It was invaded and occupied by U.S. and U.K. troops in April 2003, and at this writing (October 2006), conflict and insecurity were pervasive.

divisions. Palestine has been in conflict since at least the early 1970s, when its armed struggle for national recognition took shape. The first intifada (uprising) of the late 1980s paved the way to a peace process and the establishment of the Palestine Authority, but the outbreak of the second intifada in 2001 led to more fighting and many deaths on both sides. In addition to the infrastructural damage caused by punitive Israeli military action, a consequence of the second intifada has been a collapsed economy and exceedingly high unemployment. The rebuilding of damaged infrastructure will be a major requirement.

This situation is even more true in Afghanistan, where hardly any of the elements of a modern economy were in place prior to "reconstruction" following the ouster of the Taliban in late 2001. In a country that is predominantly rural and underdeveloped, with a majority of its population illiterate, economic development is the major requirement—along with nation-building, state formation, and the building of civil society. Iraq is a more economically and socially developed country than Afghanistan, but major infrastructure was destroyed, and health and literacy seriously damaged, as a result of the punitive sanctions of the 1990s as well as during the Iran-Iraq War in the 1980s and the military invasion of 2003. Iraq suffers from very high male unemployment, which followed the war and the restructuring of its economy by the occupying power, the United States.

Armed conflict has dire effects on all citizens, but women face specific risks. Afghanistan, Iraq, and Palestine all have weak state systems (although Iraq had a strong and centralized state prior to the U.S.-U.K. invasion of March 2003) and armed opposition groups, as well as serious problems with human security, human rights, and women's participation. An advantage that Palestine has over the other two countries is a relatively stronger civil society. However, the conflict with Israel and nonresolution of the national question have hardened identities and strengthened patriarchal tendencies, leading to the imposition of social controls on Palestinian women in the refugee camps and villages and the inability of the Palestine Authority to implement a women's rights agenda.

Violence against women is common in all three cases. In Afghanistan's highly patriarchal society, women have been long subjected to violence by husbands and male kin. "Honor killings" occur with some frequency in certain Iraqi and Palestinian communities. As feminist scholarship has shown, constructions of masculinity and femininity have tended to "normalize" and "naturalize" violence against women. Moreover, wars, and especially occupations by foreign powers, are accompanied by crises of masculinity that lead to restrictions on women's mobility and in-

creases in violence against women.[2] In all three countries, women are caught between weak states, occupying powers, armed opposition movements, and patriarchal gender arrangements. Politics have been masculine and male dominated, with
women largely excluded from political decision making.

In October 2000, the landmark UN Security Council Resolution (SCR) 1325
was adopted.[3] It reaffirms the important role of women in the prevention and resolution of conflicts and the need to implement fully international humanitarian and
human rights laws that protect the rights of women and girls during and after conflicts. However, despite the adoption of this important resolution, we continue to
see the sidelining of both women actors and gender issues in many contemporary
conflicts, peacekeeping initiatives, and reconstruction efforts.[4] In Israel and Palestine, Afghanistan, and Iraq, a culture of "hegemonic masculinity" prevails among
the major political actors, be they the occupiers, the resistance, or the state.

In such a context, what are the prospects for women's empowerment? How to
reconstruct—or, in the case of Afghanistan, construct—political and economic systems while also ensuring human security and human rights, especially for women?
These problems are among the questions addressed in this chapter, which also examines the gender dynamics of peace-building and reconstruction more broadly. In
the sections that follow, I begin by examining the cases of Afghanistan, Iraq, and
Palestine, after which I offer a conceptual framing of the issues that draws attention
to the role of the state, legal frames, women's organizations, and transnational links.
I end with some reflections on lessons learned from the three cases and some recommendations for the integration of a gender analysis, and of women themselves,
in processes of peace-building and reconstruction.

Afghanistan

Afghanistan was once considered a model of postconflict reconstruction, yet
women could hardly be said to be enjoying security, participation, and rights. Re-

---

2. See Breines, Connell, and Eide, 2000; Enloe 1990.

3. See http://www.un.org/docs/scres/2000/sc2000/htm.

4. The study *Women, Peace and Security: Study Submitted by the Secretary-General Pursuant to Security Council Resolution 1325 (2000)* (United Nations 2002) acknowledged that much remained to be
done in the realization of the resolution, while also drawing attention to the importance of women's
informal peace networking.

ports by various international agencies have cited harassment, violence, illiteracy, poverty, and extreme repression as features of everyday life for many Afghan women. These circumstances are the result of the persistence of patriarchal gender relations and the absence of a strong, centralized state with the capacity or will to implement a wide-ranging program for women's rights.

Afghanistan's 2004 constitution mandates compulsory education up to grade nine, but the majority of girls remain out of school. International agencies active within the country have confirmed attacks against schools, mostly girls' schools. Statistics are difficult to obtain and are not reliable, but in 2004, the literacy rate was reported to be 14 percent for women and 43 percent for men. Although girls represented 34 percent of children enrolled in primary schools, in ten of the country's provinces, fewer than one in four girls aged seven to twelve attended primary school. Secondary school enrollments remained extremely low, especially for girls; only 9 percent of girls attending primary school continued to secondary school. The country's Supreme Court barred married women from attending high school—in a country where girls as young as ten are married off, often to far older men. Afghan girls and women still learn to read and write in secret classrooms—girls because of attacks on schools or because their fathers will not send them to a state school, women because the government prohibits married women from attending school.[5]

Patriarchal practices, attitudes, and policies prevail. Approximately 57 percent of girls are married before the age of sixteen, according to a study by the Ministry of Women's Affairs and Afghan women's nongovernmental organizations (NGOs) (http://www.hrw.org/campaigns/afghanistan/facts.htm). Under Afghan law, the legal age for marriage is sixteen, but courts often refuse to act in the case of forced marriage (Amnesty International 2004a, 2004b). Health statistics remain dire for citizens as a whole, but UNICEF figures show that women also suffer very high rates of maternal mortality. In a culture where a woman without a *sarparast* (male household head) is often shunned, widows face many prejudices. Under the Taliban, widows were denied employment opportunities, and many had to resort to begging to provide for their families. In 2004 it was estimated that as many as 30 percent of households were headed by women; in Kabul alone there were some fifty thousand widows. Few institutions or policies are in place to assist widows' integration and independence. As one expert has put it, "Bakeries have been built, but there are no sus-

5. Sources of the data in this chapter are UNICEF, UNIFEM, UNESCO, Amnesty International, and Human Rights Watch. See the Works Cited for details.

tainable jobs or careers."[6] Despite the existence of many "gender specialists" and some two thousand NGOs, mainly set up in Kabul by expatriate Afghans, new social problems have emerged. Street children, especially boys, abound, and there has been a growth of prostitution.

Women experience considerable violence in the country. Son preference is still strong, and mothers can be abused by husbands and in-laws for not producing sons (UNIFEM 2004). Girls and women in many parts of the country are prosecuted for *zina* crimes such as adultery, running away from home, and premarital sex. Self-immolations appear to be on the rise in Afghanistan and are tied to forced marriage; the typical victim is fourteen to twenty years old and is trying to escape a marriage arranged by her father ("Self-Immolations" 2002). Under such conditions, it is not surprising that the vast majority of women continue to wear the all-encompassing burka. Veiling is determined not only by custom and tradition but also by social pressure within the family and fear of harassment in the street. Patriarchy and violence are played out on women's bodies in other ways, too, especially in the provinces: there have been reports of retaliatory rapes of Pashtun women in northern Afghanistan by non-Pashtun men.[7]

The country remains in chaos, torn apart by warlords. Human rights groups have repeatedly called for demobilization, disarmament, and reintegration to halt warlord abuses. Agriculture is largely geared toward poppy cultivation for opium exports, feeding addictions in neighboring Iran and Pakistan. The resurgence of the Taliban has resulted in attacks and killings of international staff as well as locals. Because of the continued lack of security, Medicins sans Frontières and other aid groups pulled out of Afghanistan in 2004.

What is behind the persistence of violence, patriarchy, and insecurity in post-Taliban Afghanistan? A tribal social structure, warlordism, and state compromises are key factors. The contemporary Afghan state seems to be the result of social and ideological compromise between modernists and traditionalists, feminists and fundamentalists, and Islamists and Muslims with more moderate religious views. As a result, the state cannot take a definitively pro-woman stance. Indeed, the govern-

6. Maliha Zulfacar, in a presentation on Afghanistan at the AMEWS special session "Gender and Conflicts in the Middle East," annual meetings of the Middle East Studies Association, Nov. 22, 2004, San Francisco. Dr. Zulfacar also mentioned the kidnapping of girls and organ trafficking. There is also the well-known problem of narcotics production and smuggling.

7. See the UNIFEM report on Afghanistan (UNIFEM 2005a).

ment of Hamid Karzai has accommodated extremely conservative political tendencies. For example, the government rejected a bill of rights prepared by a group of Afghan women ("New Afghan Constitution" 2004, 4). Earlier, Karzai had acquiesced to clerical demands that Dr. Sima Samar be removed from her post as minister of women's affairs. Activist and independent-minded women like Sima Samar continue to be labeled blasphemous, Westernized, and alienated from their own culture and religion.[8]

In early 2004, Afghanistan's traditional parliament, the Loya Jirga, adopted the country's first post-Taliban constitution. The majority of the 502 delegates (including 95 women) approved a presidential system, paving the way for democratic elections later that year. The new Afghan Constitution stipulates equality between women and men and reserves for women 25 percent of the seats in the lower house of Parliament and 17 percent in the upper house. Compliance with the Convention on the Elimination of All Forms of Discrimination against Women (CEDAW), which Afghanistan ratified in March 2003 without reservations, is mandated in Article 7 of the constitution. Yet the very first article of the constitution states that Afghanistan is an "Islamic republic"; Islam is declared to be the official religion of the state, and Article 3 of the constitution expressly bars any law "contrary to the beliefs and provisions of the sacred religion of Islam." Such legal anomalies and inconsistencies mean that many questions of legal interpretation—such as those considerations pertaining to women's status in the family or the right of a Muslim to change his or her religion—will have to be taken up at the Supreme Court.

In 2006, the court was still headed by the extremely conservative judge Fazul Hadi Shinwari. Originally appointed by former president Burhanuddin Rabbani, a conservative chief of the Northern Alliance, Justice Shinwari was later reconfirmed by President Karzai under the transitional administration in June 2002. The chief justice is in principle the guardian of the rights enshrined in the constitution, but Shinwari quickly attempted to ban women from singing and dancing in public. In November 2004, the Supreme Court issued a ban on cable television channels, particularly condemning films from India showing scantily clad women singing and

8. Sima Samar, in comments made at the conference "Women Defending Peace," organized by the Suzanne Mubarak Women's Peace Initiative, in cooperation with the government of Switzerland and the ILO, Geneva, Nov. 22–24, 2004; cited in the Dec. 9, 2004, report by Ingeborg Breines of the UNESCO liaison office in Geneva.

dancing in musicals. Shinwari suggested that women should cover their bodies entirely, exposing only their faces and hands, and he decreed that a woman cannot travel for more than three days without a *mahram* (a husband or a male relative she cannot legally marry). He also stated that adulterers should be stoned to death. During the campaign for the presidential elections in October 2004, Shinwari attempted to have presidential candidate Latif Pedram removed from the ballot for proposing that women and men should have equal rights in marriage and divorce.

In the transitional administration, Shinwari appointed scores of judges at all levels, all of whom were men. Article 118 of the constitution calls for judges with "a higher education in law or Islamic jurisprudence" and "sufficient expertise and experience in the judicial system of Afghanistan." Shinwari's appointments on the Supreme Court—which in 2004 had a reported 137 members and possibly more, a number that exceeded the 9 justice positions authorized by the constitution—were largely men with extreme views regarding the subordinate position of women. Such are the contradictions in the legal frameworks and decision-making bodies of the "post-Taliban" Afghan state.

Despite serious obstacles, or perhaps because of them, women's organizations continue to work with each other, transnationally, and with global feminist groups to bring pressure to bear on the Karzai government, to raise funding for women's projects, and to make women's rights a reality and not merely a formality. Groups such as RAWA, the Afghan Women's Network, the Afghan Women's Council, and, abroad, WAPHA and Negar work with international groups such as Women for Afghan Women, the Feminist Majority, and Equality Now. Another positive factor is that there is much support from international organizations.[9] For example, UNIFEM has worked with the Ministry of Women's Affairs, building a network of women's centers to provide women with health and psychosocial services, education, and income generation. It also has assisted in the establishment of a CEDAW task force. Women candidates in the September 2005 elections received much international encouragement, and the Afghan authorities were criticized when one candidate, Malalai Joya, was mistreated after critical remarks she made concerning the presence of warlords. But the assassination in September 2006 of Safia Ama Jan, a provincial director of the Ministry of Women's Affairs and fervent supporter of girls' education, underscored the dangers faced by women leaders.

9. See the Web site of the Afghan Women's Network, http://www.afghanwomensnetwork.org/.

Iraq

The record of women's rights in prewar Iraq was a mixed one, beginning with gains as a result of the Baathist ideology of Arab socialism and progress in the 1960s and 1970s but setbacks following the Gulf Wars, the sanctions, and Saddam Hussein's attempt to curry favor with tribes and religious forces by assuming an Islamic mantle and reinstating patriarchal family practices.[10] But after the invasion of 2003 and the escalation of conflict, women's human security or human rights could not be guaranteed, as neither the post-Saddam Coalition Provisional Authority (CPA) nor the U.S. military was able, or perhaps even willing, to protect women in their everyday lives. As one observer noted, "After a year of 'liberation' at the hands of the U.S. military, most Iraqi women find that they are worse off on every count" (Susskind 2004). Another stated that the CPA initially was "astonishingly insensitive" regarding women's human security and their human rights.[11] Reports showed that many more women were appearing in public in *hijab,* for fear of harassment or worse. It was an ironic but tragic consequence of the U.S. invasion and occupation that Iraq was experiencing a breakdown in public order, with reports of increases in domestic violence, honor killings, kidnapping, and rapes. What appeared to be deliberate assassinations of prominent women, including those women who do not observe *hijab,* were on the increase.[12] As one observer noted, "Women attribute the rise in violence to social disintegration triggered by the overthrow of the Saddam Hussein regime; the rise of Islamism; ongoing fighting between U.S. and Iraqi forces" (Susskind 2004). One prominent Iraqi woman said that "terrorism does not discriminate among people; parents now pay for armed guards to accompany their children to school." She emphasized that "Islamists, Baathists, foreign fighters, neighboring countries, and the U.S. army" all were responsible for the deteriorating security situation.[13]

10. Comments by Professor Naba al-Barak and Mrs. Mahdieh, Sept. 6, 9, 2004, Helsinki (seminar "Family, Society, and the Empowerment of Women: North African Women Meeting Finnish Women," Sept. 6–10, 2004, Helsinki). Mrs. Mahdieh and Professor al-Barak were in Helsinki at the invitation of the Finnish Women's Union. They had been part of the thousand-person commission that chose the Iraqi interim parliament. They described how the war with Iran changed the legal status of women. From 1981 to 2003, no woman could travel abroad without a *mahram* (husband or close male kin).

11. See, for example, Sandler 2003.

12. In March 2005, a well-known pharmacist, unveiled, was assassinated by Islamists. See "Iraq" 2005.

13. Mrs. Mahdieh, Sept. 9, 2004, Helsinki.

The veracity of the repeated refrain "without *himaya* for women, there can be no place for democracy to grow in Iraq" (Sandler 2003) was confirmed after the first post-Saddam elections took place in February 2005. Apart from fears that a majority Shiite government might institute Islamic law, the overall environment of heightened insecurity continued to pose many difficulties for women and girls. Although a quota system was established to guarantee a 25 percent share of women in the country's parliament, the legal framework for women's rights had serious limitations. There remained provisions in the Iraqi Penal Code allowing a man to escape punishment for abduction by marrying the victim and allowing for significantly reduced sentences for so-called honor killings.[14] Can Iraq undertake reconstruction and democracy-building under such conditions, when overall security is lacking and women experience fear and new forms of violence?

The continuing violence and lack of security put a brake on reconstruction, too. The World Bank noted in 2003 that "Iraq's overall reconstruction needs today are vast and are a result of nearly 20 years of neglect and degradation of the country's infrastructure, environment and social services" ("UN/World Bank" 2003). Two years later, the situation was even worse as a result of war and sabotage. A UNESCO survey documented the shortage of schools and a prevalence (more than 50 percent) of double-shift schools; many schools, moreover, were in poor physical condition. The gross enrollment ratio for girls at the secondary school level was just 31 percent in 2003; for boys it was 49 percent (UNESCO 2004, 3–4).

Ideally, a strong state should back women's rights and include it at all levels of programming and policy making. American promises to "liberate" Iraq and Iraqi women have been realized only to the extent that many more NGOs, trade unions, and women's groups have been allowed to organize and operate independently—although under conditions of frightening insecurity because of the wanton violence of the insurgency. Unlike Afghanistan, Iraq has a relatively large and well-educated middle class, with many strong and highly educated women, some of them in or around the government, others working independently. For this reason, when the Iraqi Governing Council tried to return family affairs to religious courts through the notorious Resolution 137 in early 2004, large numbers of Iraqi women mobilized opposition inside and outside the country. As related by the Iraqi activist Manal Omar, a letter of protest was sent to the U.S. and U.K. representatives, Paul Bremer and Sir Jeremy Greenstock, and Judge Zakia Hakki from the Ministry of Jus-

---

14. These are Articles 398 and 427. See *Human Rights Watch*, 15, no. 7 (July 2003). http://hrw.org/reports/2003/iraq0703/l.htm.

tice wrote a brief on concerns over Resolution 137.[15] Internationally, numerous petitions were signed and letters sent to Ambassadors Bremer and Greenstock. The result was that the resolution was withdrawn. It was an important victory for Iraqi
women leaders, and they went on to demand greater representation in government
bodies. Later, six women were appointed to the cabinet of Prime Minister Iyad
Allawi.[16]

Iraqi women have found a new space for themselves in their country's public
sphere and in the transnational public sphere. The Iraqi Women's Network comprises a number of women's groups, some with ties outside the country (for example, the transnational feminist network Women for Women International, founded,
coincidentally, by an Iraqi woman), and involves expatriates as well as long-term
residents. Iraqi women's groups include Ala Talabani's Women for a Free Iraq (formerly the Kurdish Women's Union) and the Iraqi Women's High Council; the Organization for Women's Freedom in Iraq, led by Yanar Mohammad, who works with
the U.S.-based advocacy group MADRE; among others.[17] Groups of Iraqi women
have traveled to the United States for meetings organized by the U.S. government,
Women Waging Peace, the Council on Foreign Relations, the Woodrow Wilson
Center, and others.[18] They have called for abolishing laws impeding women's employment, ensuring the appointment of qualified women judges throughout Iraq,
and hiring women for reconstruction tasks. In a series of meetings in Helsinki, Fin-
land, two Iraqi women advocates discussed the government's new NGO policy, the
family law, and the constitution. They described the 1959 family law as "fairly liberal" though "not perfect," and expressed the hope that the new constitution would
state that Islam is *a* source of legislation, not *the* source (Naba al-Barak and Mrs.

15. Personal communication, Feb. 2005. I also drafted a letter of protest on behalf of an expatriate
Iranian feminist group.

16. Minister of Agriculture Sawsan Sherif; Minister of Environment Mishkat Aimounmen; Minister of Immigration and Refugees Pascal Isho; Minister of Labor Leila Abdul-Latif; Minister of Municipalities and Public Works Nesreen Berwari; and Minister of Women's Affairs Nermin Othman (six
out of twenty-five cabinet members).

17. Yanar Mohammad is also a member of the Worker-Communist Party, which seeks a secular,
democratic, and egalitarian Iraq.

18. The prominent women include Dr. Raja Habib Dhaher Khuzai, former member of the Interim Governing Council, later a member of the Transitional National Assembly, and an ob-gyn specialist and women's health advocate, and Judge Zakia Hakki, Iraq's first judge and in 2004–2005 an
adviser to Iraq's Ministry of Justice.

Mahdieh, Sept. 6, 9, 2004, Helsinki). Many Iraqi women advocates and their international supporters insisted that women be part of the constitutional process in Iraq. But the constitution fell victim to sectarian wrangling.

Despite the growth of women's NGOs and their collective action, the violence surrounding the women's leadership is considerable. The violence began with the assassination in 2003 of Akila Hashemi, a member of the Interim Governing Council, and has continued with targeted killings of other prominent women, unveiled women, and women who work in services associated with the occupation or government. In the absence of a strong state with the capacity and will to mobilize resources, protect its citizens, and realize the stated objectives of women's rights, Iraqi activists note the rise of honor killings and domestic violence, as well as targeted assassinations and the kidnappings, rapes, and killings of ordinary Iraqi women and girls.

The reestablishment of security is a necessary condition for Iraqi reconstruction. But any plans for reconstruction must include the mobilization of the country's human resources, including its women—who in turn must be included in decision making and planning for the rebuilding and upgrading of the country's physical and social infrastructure and its public sector and civil service. Women have a stake in the type, location, and costs of schools, hospitals, roads, housing, water, and electricity—and they must have a voice in the establishment of social and economic rights. They should be strongly involved in strategic plans for food distribution and police retraining, among other issues. They also should be involved in labor-force planning and job creation: Iraqi-owned businesses are needed, including women-owned businesses. In this regard, there is a role for Iraqi expatriates to play, along with transnational women's advocacy groups.

Iraqi reconstruction will require massive international assistance. But U.S. plans are highly controversial, as they entail the privatization of Iraqi assets and special deals for U.S. corporations. These plans have come under much criticism, from feminists, human rights activists, and others.[19] In contrast to the U.S. plans for Iraqi reconstruction, what the Iraqi women hoped that international donors and partners would provide include information sharing and guidance; invitations to international conferences; help for higher education, including new schools, books, and facilities, as well as curriculum development and teacher training; and help in establishing peace studies and women's studies curricula.[20]

19. See, for example, Klare 2003; Klein 2004.

20. Naba al-Barak, Sept. 6, 2004, Heksinki.

Palestine

The problems that Palestinian women face—early marriage and high fertility, the poverty of female-headed households, difficulties in daily life, domestic violence and sexual abuse, low political participation and representation, and absence of a legal framework for rights—originate in the persistence of patriarchal gender relations, the Israeli military occupation and nonresolution of the national problem, and the conservative nature of the main political forces. Patriarchal relations are particularly acute in the refugee camps and small towns. There, Palestinian women tend to be married young, at about nineteen, often to close cousins. The *hijab* campaign of the late 1980s (see chapter 2) led to increasing observance of veiling by Palestinian women, including students at Birzeit University (author's observations, Jan. 2005). Studies also show that the high rates of unemployment, loss of livelihood, homelessness, and the frustrations of the occupation have resulted in an increase in domestic violence. One poll showed that 86 percent of respondents said that violence against women had significantly or somewhat increased as a result of changing political, economic, and social conditions. When asked if they knew of a woman who had been assaulted by her husband, 57 percent of the respondents said yes, representing an increase of 22 points on a poll taken the previous year by the Palestinian Center for Public Opinion. According to Nahla Abdo, research on Palestinian refugee camps, particularly in Gaza, has shown that refugee women and girls bear the brunt of increased physical, mental, psychological, and sexual domestic violence, including incest rape (Stein 2003; N. Abdo 2000).

Women also face the violence of the occupation. At the close of its March 2004 deliberations, the UN's Commission on the Status of Women passed a resolution expressing concern about the "grave deterioration in the situation of Palestinian women" and calling for the resumption of the peace process. Subsequently, the special rapporteur of the UN Commission on Human Rights on violence against women visited the Palestine Authority; she said in a press release that "the atmosphere of legitimized violence as a method of conflict resolution" that now pervades the Palestine Authority has become integrated into all aspects of women's lives. Women may be "killed, targeted for arrest, detained and harassed for being related to men suspected of being linked to armed groups, and may be displaced as a result of house demolitions" (cited in UNIFEM 2005c).

Women face serious obstacles in their efforts to provide food and other basic necessities for their families. Thousands of women have lost husbands and male kin to the intifada, exile, emigration in search of work, Israeli imprisonment, or death.

Half of all refugee families are headed by women, and female-headed households have been disproportionately affected by the rise in poverty that has accompanied the second intifada and the closures and curfews (UNIFEM 2005c). In refugee camps the number of female-headed households has always been high, and in 2003, out of a total population of almost four million Palestinian refugees registered with UNRWA, between 43 and 52 percent of households are headed by women. Meanwhile, women's participation in the labor force, while remaining persistently low, has been affected by the rise in unemployment since the second intifada began. The conflict, curfews, and checkpoints have also adversely affected girls' access to schooling.[21]

Settlers have been known to be verbally abusive to Palestinian women residents of East Jerusalem, who have also experienced physical harassment by them.[22] One example of graffiti in Hebron read: "Watch out Fatima—we will rape all Arab women." Rioting settlers destroyed Palestinian-owned businesses, property, farmland, and crops (for example, olive and fruit trees), thereby destroying the livelihoods of Palestinian women and their families. Settlers also attacked Palestinian homes while women and their families were inside. The Israeli human rights organization B'Tselem has collected personal testimonies describing such attacks. All of these events have compounded the difficulties Palestinian women already face in meeting their family and household responsibilities and have increased their dependence on assistance. What is more, births attended by skilled health workers decreased from 97.4 percent before the escalation of violence in 2000 to 67 percent in 2002. Home deliveries increased from 3 percent to 30 percent in the same period (UNIFEM 2005c).

It is perhaps because of all the violence, frustration, and humiliation Palestinians have faced that an unprecedented and certainly unexpected development has occurred: the participation of a number of women in suicide bombings since the second intifada began. The Palestinian national movement has produced at least one well-known guerrilla fighter (Leila Khaled, who was a People's Liberation Front of Palestine militant in the 1970s), but the image of armed militancy was invariably a masculine one. Although Palestinian women have been strongly nationalist even when engaged in peace-building initiatives, violent action seemed to have been outside the scope of their activities until relatively recently.

Palestinian women's political participation has been consistent and often sig-

21. Rema Hammami, personal communication, Feb. 22, 2005, East Jerusalem.

22. For testimonials, see http://www.wclac.org/stories/shield.html.

nificant, though usually unacknowledged. The national movement has produced outstanding diplomat-activists such as Hanan Ashrawi (the first female spokesperson for the Palestine Liberation Organization, instrumental in the Madrid peace process, though not in the secret Oslo talks), Leila Shahid (ambassador to the European Union), and Zahira Kamal (a former activist with the Democratic Front who helped found the women's movement in the 1970s). But women have not been included in formal power structures to any significant extent.[23] The Palestine Authority has not demonstrated any strong support for women's rights. Throughout the Arafat era, clientelism and patronage were often criteria for political appointments, and women have occupied fewer than 10 percent of leadership positions. A grassroots feminist push for quotas resulted in about a 17 percent female representation in the municipal elections of 2004, after which each local council began to reserve two seats for women.[24] In 2005 a campaign was under way for 20 percent representation in the Palestine Legislative Council, supported by the then minister of women's affairs, Zahira Kamal.[25]

Though not fully involved in decision making, the women's sector is active and strong, engaged in advocacy and research. Some notable organizations include the Women's Center for Legal Aid and Counseling (WCLAC), the Palestinian Working Women Society, the Jerusalem Center for Women, and the Bisan Center. Most are part of the umbrella organization the General Union of Palestinian Women. Palestinian feminist scholars reside at the Institute of Women's Studies at Birzeit University, the Women's Studies Center, and the Women's Studies program at al-Quds

23. An exception was the policy of the Democratic Front for the Liberation of Palestine (DFLP), a Marxist group that made women's rights a central plank of its program and recruited many women. This move led to its designation, by both its supporters and its detractors, as *jebheh-e mar'a* (the women's front) (see Hasso 1998). A DFLP offspring is Zahira Kamal, who was the minister for women's affairs from 2003 until January 2006.

24. Each municipality elects nine to fifteen councilors. Khadija Habashneh, deputy minister for women's affairs, in a conversation with the author in Ramallah, Ministry of Women's Affairs, Feb. 20, 2005.

25. Ms. Kamal was the sole woman in the cabinet of Prime Minister Ahmed Qurei. In discussions with the author (Jan. 21, 2005, Ramallah), she noted difficulties in implementing her mandate of gender mainstreaming across the ministries, although she did cite the development of a gender statistical database by the Ministry of Planning as a positive sign. Ms. Kamal left government after the January 2006 elections brought the Islamist party Hamas to power, and she accepted an invitation to lead the newly formed Palestinian Women's Research and Documentation Center, a joint project of UNESCO and the Ministry of Women's Affairs.

University. Scholars and activists alike maintain regional and international links, working with the Tunis-based Arab women's research center CAWTAR, the Arab Women's Forum, the UN agency for the Arab countries ESCWA, and a number of transnational feminist networks. UNIFEM supports the work of WCLAC, especially regarding violence against women, and funded two reports on the status of Palestinian women: "Impact of Armed Conflict on Palestinian Women" and "Evaluating the Status of Palestinian Women in Light of the Beijing Platform for Action."

Despite the achievements of Palestinian elite women, and the serious problems that women face generally, many of the "peace" agreements have made no mention of women: the Oslo agreement, the Cairo agreement, the Wye River Memorandum, and the Quartet-backed road map. Yet the record of Palestinian-Israeli interaction across the years exemplifies the importance of bridge-building among women and the illogic of ignoring women in negotiations and postconflict political developments. Palestinian and Israeli women have met and talked and negotiated in informal settings for years, and the Jerusalem Link—the main partners of which are Bat Shalom and the Jerusalem Center for Women—was set up to bring together progressive Israeli and Palestinian women's groups in a more formal network of communication. In October 2003, two Israeli women, but no Palestinian women, participated in the negotiation of the independently initiated (nonstate) Geneva Accord. Despite their marginalization from official peacemaking processes, women's peace-building has taken place in local homes and churches, in European cities, and in symbolic places like the Notre Dame Center on the border of Israeli and Palestinian Jerusalem. In February and March 2002, Jewish and Palestinian Israeli women from Bat Shalom together observed Land Day, focusing on Palestinian women's points of view. Israeli women belonging to MachsomWatch (Checkpoint Watch) maintain a daily presence at numerous Israeli Defense Force checkpoints throughout the West Bank, monitoring and recording the behavior of soldiers and police to prevent the abuse of Palestinians. MachsomWatch, which admits only women, works through nonviolent, nonaggressive confrontation to challenge the power of the security establishment and to demand accountability. It publishes a weekly report in order to bring to public attention the human rights abuses and humiliation that Palestinians suffer (UNIFEM 2005c).

Since SCR 1325 was adopted, Palestinian and Israeli women have studied it with a view toward making it a reality in the "peace process." In 2002, Terry Greenblatt, director of Bat Shalom, and Maha Abu-Dayyeh Shamas, WCLAC executive director and representative of Equality Now, met with members of the Security Council to discuss ways of increasing women's participation in peace and security. On March 8,

2003, women from Jerusalem Link met with national and international representatives in Ramallah, East Jerusalem, West Jerusalem, and Tel Aviv. The Jerusalem Link and Equality Now held negotiations with UN Secretary-General Kofi Annan's office to develop a mechanism for implementation of SCR 1325 in relation to the Palestinian-Israeli conflict.[26] In early February 2005, the Ad Hoc Coalition of Palestinian and Israeli Women wrote a letter to Condoleeza Rice during her mission to the Middle East, pointing out that women have been at the forefront of peace-building and that "women are the majority stakeholders in this enterprise, with a proven expertise in reconciliation and rapprochement, yet not a single Israeli woman, and only one Palestinian woman [Hanan Ashrawi], has held an official role at any Middle East peace summit. This is not only in violation of UN Security Resolution 1325 . . . but a squandering of formidable skill, talent, and experience that both nations can ill afford."[27]

Amneh Badran (2003) of the Jerusalem Coalition of Women has aptly referred to "the political turmoil we live in, the patriarchal social realities, the deteriorated economic situation, [and] the backward educational system." She has called for "active and responsible participation from the international community towards implementing international legality, ending the Israeli military occupation in all its forms, and then embarking on a process of radical democratization of political life, economy and culture so that women and men can fulfill their power to act as citizens."

Peace-Building, Reconstruction, and Gender Justice

What do the three cases presented here offer by way of lessons of a wider relevance regarding the gender dynamics of conflict, peace-building, and reconstruction? And how may feminist frameworks and insights contribute to the success of peace and reconstruction processes in Afghanistan, Iraq, Palestine, and elsewhere?

A gender perspective puts the spotlight on the social relations that exist between women and men and on the laws and actions of states. It places women at the center of analysis because of the fact that across history and cultures, women have been denied equality, autonomy, and power. Women as a group have experienced diverse forms of violence from men as a group, because women have lacked power and be-

26. See http://www.wluml.org.

27. I am grateful to Pamela Pelletreau of Search for Common Ground for bringing this matter to my attention, in a conversation in East Jerusalem, Jan. 21, 2005, and via an e-mail message.

cause states or communities have failed to protect them or have in fact punished them. Gender analysis also demonstrates that conflict, peace-building, and reconstruction processes may reflect and reinforce forms of masculinity and femininity.

The women's movement of the second wave drew attention to domestic violence, sexual harassment, and rape,[28] but it was not until the 1990s that violence against women and the problem of wartime rape acquired global prominence and action. Armed conflicts in Yugoslavia and Rwanda showed that women, like men, are victims of military onslaughts and terrorist actions; they lose life and limb and join the ranks of refugees or internally displaced persons. Unlike men, however, they also are the special victims of sexual violence, especially rape. Events in Afghanistan under both the Mujahideen (from 1992 to 1996) and the Taliban (from 1996 to 2001) demonstrated that women could experience punitive action over appearance, dress, and access to public space. During Algeria's civil conflict of the 1990s, Islamist militants not only bullied and harassed but also raped and murdered women and girls—and this ten years after the government had tried to placate the growing fundamentalist movement by instituting a patriarchal family law (Bennoune 1995).

All too often, women—their legal status, social positions, and bodies—have been pawns during conflicts or in postconflict agreements. States have been known to make compromises or accommodations at the expense of women's integrity, autonomy, and rights (Kandiyoti 1991).

What do we know about gender and conflict? We know that women's subordinate roles in peacetime render them vulnerable in wartime. Conflicts can be anticipated—so can the fact that women will be violated. Survivors of wartime trauma face inadequate services.[29] International outcries rarely succeed in bringing perpetrators to justice. The message is that women's lives matter less. Sexualized violence is implicated in armed violence, but it also exists during so-called times of peace—hence the need to recognize the gender dynamics of peace as well as conflict. Johann Galtung's well-known maxim "the absence of war does not mean peace" is complemented by Cynthia Enloe's feminist definition of peace as "women's achievement of control over their lives" (1988, 538).

For women, peace does not mean only the formal end of war and its concomitants, such as the demobilization, disarmament, and reintegration of armed com-

---

28. See especially Susan Brownmiller's classic book *Against Our Will: Men, Women, and Rape* (1975).

29. One response was the formation of Medica Mondiale, founded after the Bosnian conflict to treat women victims of sexual violence. See http://www.medicamondiale.org.

batants. It also means the enjoyment of human security and human rights, including the right not to be beaten at home or assaulted on the streets. Given this fact, it must be stated that many so-called peace processes have been at best flawed and at worse failures. The UN-sponsored peace in Afghanistan in the early 1990s did nothing to bring about stability and security, especially for women, who had to contend with marauding Mujahideen warlords initially and subsequently with the strangely medieval Taliban. The Israeli-Palestinian peace process of the early 1990s was regarded by its detractors as favoring the Israelis, but it was also accompanied by a growing Islamist movement that earlier had put pressure on the women in its communities to veil. These examples and many others show that women's human security and human rights, along with the attenuation of inequalities generally, are rarely considered in so-called peace processes.

Ending gender and other social inequalities and bringing about human security, including women's security, lies at the heart of feminist analyses of peace-building. Indeed, a significant feminist contribution to analyses of international relations, as Ann Tickner has noted, "is to point out how unequal social relations can make all individuals more insecure" (1992, 193). She adds, "The achievement of peace, economic justice, and ecological sustainability is inseparable from overcoming social relations of domination and subordination; genuine security requires not only the absence of war but also the elimination of unjust social relations" (128).

The concept of human security has been defined in different ways, but some aspects are personal security, water and food security, rights to health care and political participation, and economic security. There is thus a connection between human security and human rights and links among security, rights, and participation. That is, achieving peace and security for women can be guaranteed within a broader sociopolitical and economic project that rests on participation and redistribution of resources. Reconstruction should therefore be viewed not only in terms of the repair or building of physical and social infrastructure but also in terms of the establishment of participatory and egalitarian social and gender relations. In this regard, women have a special role to play, because they have experienced inequality, because they have a stake in reconstruction that is woman friendly, and because of their roles in bridge-building and peacemaking.

Women's role in peace movements is well known, and "maternalist politics" has a long history. Women peace-builders often have deployed the discourse of motherhood and emphasized feminine values of nurturing and care in their efforts to build bridges, mediate, or encourage reconciliation. Whether we are referring to the Women's International League for Peace and Freedom at the beginning of the twentieth century or Women Strike for Peace in midcentury or organizations such as Israel's Four Mothers Movement, the Saturday Mothers of Turkey, and the Mothers and Grandmothers of the Plaza de Mayo in Argentina in the late twentieth century, or Code Pink in the new century, we see that women activists often draw on motherhood, maternity, and femininity as resources and discursive strategies.[30] An example comes from the Palestinian activist Zahira Kamal. At a rally of the Coalition of Women for a Just Peace, she declared: "I am bonded to women. I believe in their power. Women are grounded in their awareness of the sanctity of all human beings, the equal value of each human being, and a commitment to justice, applied equally through adherence to law. I believe we can work together for ending the occupation and its related measures, and we can live in peace together."[31]

Maternalist politics constitutes one model of women's activism, seen largely in peace, antimilitarist, and human rights movements. But there is another model as well: that of women in armed struggles, liberation movements, and revolutions.[32] Whether these two models of women vis-à-vis peace and conflict are completely contradictory or simply two dimensions of women's lives, experiences, and collective action is a difficult question. Feminists rely on women to lead the way in peace, conflict resolution, and human rights, while also accepting that women will be active participants in armed struggles and resistance movements.[33]

Peace-building requires justice, including gender justice. A situation of longstanding injustice and deep tensions—whether within a society or between countries—is not a situation of peace. In other words, the "peace process" between

30. See Azmon 1997; Berkovitch 1999; Bouvard 1994; Ruddick 1980; Strange 1990. It is true also of MADRE, a New York–based women's human rights organization that since 1993 has worked in partnership with women's community-based groups in conflict areas worldwide.

31. Kamal, general director of the Ministry for Gender Planning and Development of the Palestine Authority, in a statement on May 30, 2003, distributed by the Coalition of Women for a Just Peace; translated from the Arabic by Ruth Roded.

32. Women have taken up arms in many liberation or resistance movements. Notable examples are the women partisans of the Spanish civil war of 1936–39, the Soviet Union and Yugoslavia during World War II, Vietnam during the war of liberation against the French in the 1950s and the Americans in the 1960s and early 1970s, and the liberation movements of Central America in the 1970s and 1980s. Although many feminists and leftists have hailed the women of those movements as heroines and role models, the participation of women in the Tamil Tigers of Sri Lanka is more controversial because of the use of suicide bombings and similar tactics. The same holds true for the small number of Palestinian women who have carried out "martyrdom operations."

33. See Kampwirth 2002; Shayne 2004.

Israel-Palestine in the 1990s was not a just peace at all, but rather a war, or at the very least hegemonic politics, by other means. And a cease-fire or a brokered "peace" in which essential issues of security, justice, and redress have not been addressed should not be called peace at all. A just peace is more than a cease-fire and demobilization. Its sustainability depends on the achievement of social and economic justice, human security, democratization, participation, and equality. Furthermore, it entails gender justice. As one advocate stated, "Women survivors of armed conflicts and advocates for women's rights during and after these conflicts recognize that meaningful justice must protect the fundamental human rights of all people and that there cannot be meaningful reconciliation without gender justice" (McKay 2000, 561).

Gender justice has at least three components. One is the participation of women in peace-building, reconstruction, and decision making. Another is the establishment of laws and institutions for the realization of women's human rights. A third pertains to redress for sexualized or other forms of violence against women during conflict or war. A major international achievement was the designation of rape as a war crime when carried out in the context of armed conflict. All too often, however, the perpetrators of sexualized violence are not brought to justice—thus denying gender justice to women.[34] The continuing struggle in Argentina of the Grandmothers of the Plaza de Mayo against "impunity" via the blanket amnesty is a prime example of the need to link peace and conflict resolution to justice (Arditti 1999).

Positive developments, however, should be noted. Tribunals in The Hague on human rights violations in the former Yugoslavia and on the genocide in Rwanda, as well as the Special Court for Sierra Leone, constitute one model of justice. South Africa's Truth and Reconciliation Commission (1996–2001) is another model of linking peace to justice. In Morocco's Justice and Reconciliation Commission, people have testified on television about the abuses and torture that they experienced in the 1970s and 1980s. There were limitations to this new exercise in truth-telling, as

34. Feminists and other democrats in Algeria, as well as Afghan women's groups such as RAWA, have insisted on trials for those individuals who perpetuated sexualized violence. In Afghanistan, however, Mujahideen-Northern Alliance commanders responsible for rape and sexual slavery were given government posts after the overthrow of the Taliban. It is notable, if dismaying, that Algerian president Bouteflika's call for a general amnesty would exonerate even the worst of the GIA terrorists of the 1990s who are currently in prison and that the commission he has formed includes not one woman. See Ouazani 2005.

the government refused to put people on trial for past sins, or even name names. But it has been especially moving to witness the testimonies of the former women prisoners (Slyomovics 2005).

Such tribunals may be needed in the cases of Afghanistan and Algeria (as well as in Iraq, when the time comes), certainly to redress the violence visited on women, but also to educate the public and raise its awareness of women's rights and of what constitutes violations of human rights and women's rights.

Women must be involved in formal processes of peace-building and reconstruction for at least five reasons. The first and most basic reason is that women constitute half, and in some cases a majority, of any population. Without their participation, there can be no claim of equity and representation. Second, because women are often the special victims of armed conflict, their experiences, perspectives, and aspirations need to be incorporated into negotiations, mediation, and peace-building processes. For the same reason, women experts and leaders must be involved in processes of demilitarization, demobilization, and reintegration of fighters. Women experience not only sexualized violence but also bereavement and the loss of family members, resources, and livelihood. Sanctions may lead to the feminization of poverty, while widowhood increases the number of female-headed households living in dire conditions. The gender-specific experiences and outcomes of conflict need to be considered and addressed in peace-building and postconflict reconstruction. Third, women often play a key role in bridge building and peace-making at the local level, a role that should be acknowledged as well as translated into higher-level participation and representation. Indeed, the important role played by women at the community level can serve as a model of mediation and reconciliation at the national level. Fourth, women are major stakeholders and actors in the reconstruction or building of infrastructure, the state, and civil society. They have a direct stake in strategies for social development, the allocation of financial and human resources across economic sectors, the adoption of progressive legal frameworks, and the flourishing of associational life. Without their participation, half the population is automatically disfranchised, postconflict reconstruction remains an exclusively masculine endeavor, and rights-based development is compromised. Fifth, exclusion and marginalization of women is part of the logic of authoritarian, patriarchal state systems. This is why including women is so important—*it helps to change the nature of the state.*

Conflict is traumatic, but it sometimes can lead to major social transformations that could favor women's political participation. In at least three examples, South Africa, Namibia, and Rwanda, the postconflict democratic transitions have led to high rates of women's political participation and to the integration of women and gender issues into government planning. This pattern is not, however, universal. Why?

Research has shown that how women fare in a postconflict situation depends on a number of factors, both internal and external. Internal factors include: (1) preexisting gender relations and women's legal status and social positions before the conflict; (2) the extent of women's mobilizations before and during the conflict, including the number and type of women's organizations and other institutions; (3) the ideology, values, and norms of the ruling group; and (4) the state's capacity and will to mobilize resource endowments for rights-based reconstruction and development.[35] The salience of these factors has been well illustrated by the cases of Afghanistan, Iraq, and Palestine. In an era of globalization, however, we can expect external factors to play an important part. In particular, transnational feminist monitoring and advocacy can make a difference in terms of laws, policies, and resources available for women's participation and rights (Moghadam 2005).

Strong transnational links may ensure global solidarities and collective action toward the promotion of women's participation, rights, and empowerment in the postconflict situation. Links to, or an active role within, global feminism could prevent the isolation or marginalization of "the woman question" and lead to vigorous and effective campaigns to protect or build women's empowerment. The state, economic resources, and legal frameworks matter enormously to women, but transnational solidarity can influence national-level decisions and raise international awareness of women's conditions and needs in various national contexts. Transnational feminist networks can affect national-level processes through advocacy, lobbying of donors to increase allocations to women's units and institutions, and campaigns to compel the postconflict governments to prioritize women's empowerment.

In defending the interests of women in postconflict reconstruction processes, global feminism can play an important role by exposing and criticizing corrupt or oppressive measures taken by neighboring countries or the big powers. An example would be the planned privatization of the Iraqi economy and the lucrative contracts given to American corporations such as Halliburton and Bechtel. The question that feminist organizations, especially the ones in the United States, need to ask is the following: apart from enriching U.S. corporations, how will these economic plans result in women's participation and rights—in their empowerment?

35. These insights are drawn from the literature on gender and revolution, including Moghadam 1997, Kampwirth 2002, and Shayne 2004.

Reconstruction with Women: Concluding Thoughts

The three case studies have allowed us to make generalizations, draw conclusions, and offer recommendations, but specificities should be noted. For example, in Afghanistan, compulsory and quality schooling for girls right through grade twelve will be absolutely necessary if the country is to make the transition from patriarchy to modernity and build its human resources as well as women's capabilities. As Maliha Zulfacar has noted, some laws may have changed, but "old customs die hard."[36]

The expansion of girls' education—which has always been contested by the country's traditional and patriarchal social forces—must be at the center of a rights-based development strategy in Afghanistan. In Iraq, the legal reforms and quotas for political participation that have been established are important, but women leaders must be equally involved in issues of security, constitution-building, reconstruction, and development. In Palestine, SCR 1325 must be fully implemented, and more than lip service must be paid to women's contributions to Palestinian society. Proactive policies such as quotas and affirmative action must redress women's long-standing marginalization from decision making, and international agencies and negotiators must bring Palestinian women to the table.

In all three countries women must be integrated into all levels—from the cabinet to the local police force, if women's perspectives, needs, and rights are to be recognized and addressed. Special efforts should be taken at the community level to involve women as teachers, social workers, managers, and decision makers. Government and international donors alike should emphasize capacity-building of women's organizations, women's studies centers, and women's resource centers—these resources are, after all, key institutions of a democratic civil society. In all three countries, establishing conditions for security, well-being, and justice will require costly, long-term investments on the part of donor countries. But the investments will be well worth the costs.

The importance of "gender mainstreaming" in the state sector is tied to the goals of capacity-building and institution-building for women, and ensuring the integration of women's perspectives across government agencies, including such key ministries as finance and justice. What it requires is the establishment of "women and development" or gender units that are involved in decision making and are given adequate staffing and budgets. The success of gender mainstreaming depends on the (re)building of the "national machinery for women" through re-

---

36. AMEWS panel on gender and conflict, MESA conference, Nov. 2004, San Francisco.

sources allocated to the ministry of women's affairs and to other state agencies dedicated to women's participation and empowerment. The women's ministry can work with women's civil society organizations to develop a strategy for women's empowerment at micro (family), meso (community and organizational) and macro (national and state) levels.

Without idealizing women, one may plausibly postulate that an enhanced role for women in reconstruction could minimize corruption and cronyism—if only because women's absence from economic and political domains of power has prevented their involvement in clientelism. In addition, such a role would likely increase attention and allocations toward social policies to alleviate poverty, provide welfare, and promote social development. And since women have a stake in a welfare state that is also women friendly, they are likely to assist in the (re)construction of strong social institutions such as social service organizations; health facilities; schools, universities, and training institutes; and nurseries.

Another important area for women in reconstruction pertains to the cultural domain. Here, again, the global feminist movement can be of much assistance, through support for media campaigns in favor of women's participation and rights, promoting women's media, gender awareness and sensitivity in the mainstream and government-controlled media, and women's involvement in cultural institutions such as the ministries of culture, education, religious affairs, and communications. Through such involvement, women would play a key role in the transition from a culture of violence to a culture of peace, human rights, and women's empowerment.

APPENDIX

WORKS CITED

INDEX

Appendix | *Measuring Women's Empowerment*
in the Middle East, North Africa, and South Asia

VALENTINE M. MOGHADAM *and* LUCIE SENFTOVA

THE DATA IN THE TABLE that follows group the countries alphabetically by region, in order to facilitate intraregional and cross-regional comparisons. The data are from a variety of international sources, mainly UN yearbooks, but empty cells are found all too often. (Note that in the tables, the symbol—indicates data not available or country not listed.) Although the table provides only a limited picture of women's socioeconomic and political participation and rights, some patterns and trends may be discerned.

• There remains an adverse sex ratio (that is, a larger male than female population) in most countries in the regions. The worst cases are Afghanistan and India. Elsewhere, the sex ratio is more or less balanced, or in women's favor, as in Israel, Morocco, and Tunisia.

• Birthrates to teenage girls are high in South Asia and in Palestine. Fertility rates are high in Afghanistan, Palestine, and Iraq.

• In Tunisia, women are marrying later and having fewer children. This trend may be observed in Iran, too.

• Women's bodily integrity and health are seriously compromised in countries with large rural or poor populations: Iraq, Egypt, and Morocco in the Middle East and North Africa, and Afghanistan, India, and Nepal in South Asia.

• Literacy and educational attainment are rising everywhere, and the old gender gaps are narrowing rapidly. The highest secondary school and tertiary enrollments are in Israel, but high rates are also found in Jordan and Lebanon.

• Women's economic participation is not sufficiently high in the regions, and the gender gap in estimated income is quite wide. Women have rights to paid maternity leaves, but in most countries relatively few women are entitled to them, as they are not situated in the formal labor force.

• Political participation and decision making also are limited, especially in government structures. We know that women are increasingly forming their own organizations, but the quantitative information is not available. Other areas of participation and rights, such as the domain of culture, lack data.

• All countries under consideration have signed on to the major international conventions and declarations on women's rights and human rights. Yet the problem of implementation remains.

Table A.1

Measuring Women's Civil, Political, Socioeconomic, and Cultural Participation and Rights

1. Sociodemographic Indicators

Country	Life Expectancy at Birth (years, female/male), ca. 2005	Sex Ratio (thousands, female/male), 2005	Average Female Age at First Marriage, All Women, 2000	Adolescent Marriage (% of female in age group 15–19 ever married), 2000	Number of Births to 1,000 Women (ages 15–19), ca. 2005	Total Fertility Rate (births per women), ca. 2005
Iran	72.6 F / 69.5 M	34,266 F / 35,250 M	22	22	20	2.08
Iraq	61.5 F / 58.4 M	14,221 F / 14,587 M	22	18	40	4.54
Israel	82.1 F / 78.0 M	3,398 F / 3,327 M	23	6	15	2.76
Jordan	73.5 F / 70.4 M	2,739 F / 2,964 M	22	8	26	3.33
Kuwait	79.8 F / 75.5 M	1,075 F / 1,612 M	23	11	24	2.32
Lebanon	74.7 F / 70.3 M	1,824 F / 1,753 M	—	—	26	2.26
Palestine	74.4 F / 71.3 M	1,819 F / 1,883 M	—	—	85	5.28
Turkey	71.5 F / 66.9 M	36,314 F / 36,878 M	24	13	41	2.39
Egypt	72.7 F / 68.2 M	36,913 F / 37,120 M	19	14	42	3.14

Country	Life Expectancy at Birth (years, female/male), ca. 2005	Sex Ratio (thousands, female/male), 2005	Average Female Age at First Marriage, All Women, 2000	Adolescent Marriage (% of female in age group 15–19 ever married), 2000	Number of Births to 1,000 Women (ages 15–19), ca. 2005	Total Fertility Rate (births per women), ca. 2005
Morocco	72.5 F 68.1 M	15,833 F 15,646 M	20	10	24	2.67
Tunisia	75.8 F 71.6 M	5,013 F 5,090 M	25	4	7	1.93
Afghanistan	47.1 F 46.6 M	14,459 F 15,404 M	—	53	123	7.27
India	65.7 F 62.4 M	537,593 F 565,778 M	20	38	72	2.92
Nepal	62.9 F 62.0 M	13,687 F 13,446 M	16	43	113	3.50

Source: UNFPA State of World Population 2005; The World's Women 2000 and its updated online version as of Oct. 11, 2005; Population Reference Bureau: The World's Youth 2000.

(continued on next page)

2. Bodily Integrity and Health

Country	Maternal Mortality (per 100,000 live births), ca. 2005	Child Mortality Rate under 5 (per 1,000 live births, female/ male), 2005	Contraceptive Prevalence (% of married women using contraception, any method), 2005	Female Genital Mutilation Prevalence (%)	People HIV Infected (% female among adults), 2003–2004	Sexual Abuse of Women (% of total population), 1995	Prevalence of Physical Violence Against Women by an Intimate Partner (%)
Iran	76	35 F 36 M	74	—	12	—	—
Iraq	250	110 F 119 M	—	—	—	—	—
Israel	17	6 F 6 M	—	—	—	—	—
Jordan	41	23 F 25 M	56	—	—	—	—
Kuwait	5	12 F 12 M	52	—	—	—	—
Lebanon	150	19 F 29 M	63	—	—	—	—
Palestine	100	20 F 25 M	51	—	—	—	—
Turkey	70	40 F 51 M	64	—	—	—	58 (2000)
Egypt	84	35 F 43 M	60	97 (1995)	13	1.8 (Cairo, 1991)	34 (1995)

Country	Maternal Mortality (per 100,000 live births), ca. 2005	Child Mortality Rate under 5 (per 1,000 live births, female/male), 2005	Contraceptive Prevalence (% of married women using contraception, any method), 2005	Female Genital Mutilation Prevalence (%)	People HIV Infected (% female among adults), 2003–2004	Sexual Abuse of Women (% of total population), 1995	Prevalence of Physical Violence Against Women by an Intimate Partner (%)
Morocco	220	34 F / 49 M	63	—	—	—	—
Tunisia	120	22 F / 25 M	60	—	—	1.5 (Tunis, 1991)	—
Afghanistan	1,900	247 F / 242 M	5	—	—	—	—
India	540	95 F / 90 M	48	—	37	3.5 (Mumbai) / 1.7 (New Delhi, 1995)	—
Nepal	740	83 F / 78 M	39	—	27	—	—

(continued on next page)

Source: UNFPA State of World Population 2005; World Health Organization, May 2001; Human Development Report 2005; Population Reference Bureau: 2005 Women of Our World; World Bank's GenderStats.

3. Literacy and Educational Attainment

Country	Youth Literacy Rates (% ages 15–24, female/male), 2000–2004	Estimated Adult Literacy Rates (% ages 15 and over, female/male), 2000–2004	School Life Expectancy (expected number of years of formal schooling (female/male), 2001	Net Secondary School Enrollment (% female/male), 2001	Tertiary Enrollment Rates, Gross Enrollment Ratio (%, female/male), 2001
Iran	91.3 F / 96.2 M	70.4 F / 83.5 M	10.9 F / 12.0 M	68 F / 74 M (1995)	20.4 F / 20.2 M
Iraq	29.1 F / 59.3 M	—	7.6 F / 10.4 M	26.0 F / 39.7 M	9.8 F / 18.2 M
Israel	99.4 F / 99.6 M	93.4 F / 97.3 M	16.2 F / 14.8 M	89.4 F / 88.5 M	67.1 F / 48.7 M
Jordan	99.5 F / 99.3 M	85.9 F / 95.5 M	12.7 F / 12.5 M	81.4 F / 79.3 M	31.3 F / 30.7 M
Kuwait	93.9 F / 92.2 M	81.0 F / 84.7 M	—	79.3 F / 75.2 M	—
Lebanon	93.0 F / 97.2 M	80.3 F / 92.1 M	13.3 F / 12.8 M	71 F / 62 M (1995)	47.6 F / 41.8 M
Palestine	—	—	12.9 F / 12.2 M	83.2 F / 78.3 M	30.2 F / 30.9 M
Turkey	93.2 F / 97.8 M	78.5 F / 94.4 M	9.8 F / 11.6 M	41 F / 58 M (1995)	20.9 F / 28.5 M
Egypt	66.9 F / 79.0 M	43.6 F / 67.2 M	—	78.5 F / 83.1 M	—
Morocco	61.3 F / 77.4 M	38.3 F / 63.3 M	8.4 F / 9.9 M	28.3 F / 34.0 M	9.2 F / 11.4 M

Country	Youth Literacy Rates (% ages 15–24, female/male), 2000–2004	Estimated Adult Literacy Rates (% ages 15 and over, female/male), 2000–2004	School Life Expectancy (expected number of years of formal schooling (female/male), 2001	Net Secondary School Enrollment (% female/male), 2001	Tertiary Enrollment Rates, Gross Enrollment Ratio (%, female/male), 2001
Tunisia	90.6 F 97.9 M	63.1 F 83.1 M	13.4 F 13.4 M	69.1 F 66.7 M	21.4 F 22.0 M
Afghanistan	—	—	—	7 F 20 M (1995)	—
India	64.8 F 79.7 M	45.4 F 68.4 M	7.9 F 10.0 M	—	9.3 F 13.4 M
Nepal	46.0 F 78.1 M	26.4 F 61.6 M	8.5 F 10.5 M	—	2.3 F 8.2 M

Source: UNESCO EFA Global Monitoring Report 2003–2004 and 2005; World Bank GenderStats.

(continued on next page)

4. Economic Participation and Rights

Country	Labor Force Participation Rate (% female/male, ages 15+)	Female Share of Paid Labor Force	Unemployment rate (% female/male)	Estimated Earned Income (PPP US$, female/male), 2003	Female Professional and Technical Workers (as % of total)[a]	Length, Amount and Source of Paid Maternity Leave, 2004
Iran	11 F / 75 M (1996)	12.6 (1996)	4.1 F	3,094 F / 8.2 M (2002)	33	90 days, 67%, social security
Iraq	9 F / 77 M (1997)	—	—	—	10,856 M	62 days, 100%, social security
Israel	49 F / 60 M (2003)	48.7 (2003)	11.3 F / 10.2 M (2003)	14,159 F / 25,969 M	54	12 weeks, 100% up to a ceiling, social security
Jordan	12 F / 64 M (2000)	—	20.7 F / 11.8 M (2000)	2,004 F / 6,491 M	—	10 weeks, 100%, employer
Kuwait	30 F / 53 M (1998)	—	1.7 F / 1.0 M (2002)	8,448 F / 24,204 M	—	70 days, 100%, employer
Lebanon	—	—	—	2,430 F / 7,789 M	—	7 weeks, 100%, employer/social security
Palestine	10 F / 66 M (2002)	—	18.6 F / 26.9 M (2003)	—	34	—
Turkey	27 F / 70 M (2003)	19.0 (1999)	9.9 F / 10.9 M (2002) Persons aged 15 and over	4,276 F / 9,286 M	30	16 weeks, 67% for 12 weeks, social security
Egypt	20 F / 69 M (2001)	17.7 (1995)	22.7 F / 5.1 M (2000)	1,614 F / 6,203 M	31	90 days, 100%, employer

Country	Labor Force Participation Rate (% female/male, ages 15+)	Female Share of Paid Labor Force	Unemployment rate (% female/male)	Estimated Earned Income (PPP US$, female/male), 2003	Female Professional and Technical Workers (as % of total)[a]	Length, Amount and Source of Paid Maternity Leave, 2004
Morocco	27 F 77 M (2003)	—	24.2 F 16.6 M (2002) Urban	2,299 F 5,699 M	—	14 weeks, 100%, social security
Tunisia	18 F 52 M (2003)	—	—	3,840 F 10,420 M	—	30 days, 67%, social security
Afghanistan	—	—	—	—	—	90 days, 100%, employer
India	34 F 80 M (1991)	18.4 (2003)	4.3 F 4.3 M (2000)	1,569 F 4,130 M	—	12 weeks, 100%, social security or employer
Nepal	60 F 82 M (2001)	—	—	949 F 1,868 M	—	52 days, 100%, employer

(continued on next page)

Source: The World's Women 2000 and its updated online version as of Oct. 11, 2005; ILO Labousta database and ILO's Yearbook of Labour Statistics 2003; Human Development Report 2005.

Note: In some cases the ILO and World's Women data do not agree on labor-force participation (for instance, Kuwait and Tunisia). We have listed the data that are most recent, whether from the ILO or the World's Women (updated 2005 version).

[a] According to Human Development Report 2005, data refer to the most recent year available during the period 1992–2003.

5. Political Participation and Rights

Country	Seats in Parliament in Single or Lower Chamber (% female), 2005	Female Legislators, Senior Officials, and Managers (as % of total)[a]	Seats in Government at Ministerial Level (% female), 1998[b]	Seats in Government at Subministerial Level (% female), 1998[b]
Iran	4	13	0	1
Iraq	—	—	0	0
Israel	15	29	0	9
Jordan	6	—	2	0
Kuwait	0[c]	—	0	7
Lebanon	2	12	0	0
Palestine	—	12	—	—
Turkey	4	6	5	17
Egypt	3	9	6	4
Morocco	11	—	0	8
Tunisia	23	—	3	10
Afghanistan	—	—	—[d]	—
India	8	—		—[e]
Nepal	6	—	3	0

Source: The World's Women 2000 and its updated online version as of Oct. 11, 2005; Human Development Report 2005.

[a] According to Human Development Report 2005, data refer to the most recent year available during the period 1992–2003.

[b] This indicator is not available in the World's Women 2005 version.

[c] On May 16, 2005, Parliament voted a law granting women the right to vote and stand for election.

[d] 1994: 3 percent.

[e] 1994: 7 percent.

6. Ratification of International Legal Frames for Women's Rights

Country	CEDAW, ratified 1979[a]; Optional Protocol, ratified 1999[a]	BPFA, adopted 1995[b]	ICESCR, ratified 1966	ICCPR, ratified 1966	UNESCO Convention,[1] ratified 1960	UNESCO Convention,[2] ratified 1984	ILO Convention,[3] ratified 1958	ILO Convention,[4] ratified 1951	ILO Convention,[5] ratified 1948
Iran	— / —	adopted[c]	1976	1976	accepted 1968	—	1964	1972	—
Iraq	1986 / —	adopted[c]	1976	1976	ratified 1977	—	1959	1963	—
Israel	1991 / —	adopted[c]	1992	1992	ratified 1961	ratified 1991	1959	1965	1957
Jordan	1992 / —	adopted[c]	1976	1976	accepted 1976	acceded 1991	1963	1966	—
Kuwait	1994 / —	adopted[c]	1996	1996	accepted 1963	acceded 1996	1966	—	1961
Lebanon	1997 / —	adopted[c]	1976	1976	ratified 1964	acceded 2000	1977	1977	—
Palestine		adopted[c]							
Turkey	1986 / 2003	adopted	2003	2003	—	ratified 1988	1967	1967	1993
Egypt	1981 / —	adopted[c]	1982	1982	accepted 1962	acceded 1986	1960	1960	1957
Morocco	1993 / —	adopted[c]	1979	1979	accepted 1968	ratified 1993	1963	1979	—

(continued on next page)

Country	CEDAW, ratified 1979; Optional Protocol, ratified 1999[a]	BPFA, adopted 1995[b]	ICESCR, ratified 1966	ICCPR, ratified 1966	UNESCO Convention,[1] ratified 1960	UNESCO Convention,[2] ratified 1984	ILO Convention,[3] ratified 1958	ILO Convention,[4] ratified 1951	ILO Convention,[5] ratified 1948
Tunisia	1985 / —	adopted[c]	1976	1976	ratified 1969	ratified 1988	1959	1968	1957
Afghanistan	2003 / —	adopted	1983	1983	—	ratified 1987	1969	1969	—
India	1993 / —	adopted[c]	1979	1979	—	signed 1997	1960	1958	—
Nepal	1991 / 2001	adopted[c]	1991	1991	—	acceded 1991	1974	1976	—

Source: UNHCHR International Human Rights Instruments; UNHCHR Status of Ratifications of the Principal International Human Rights Treaties; The Convention on the Elimination of All Forms of Discrimination against Women (CEDAW); Report of the Fourth World Conference on Women.

Note: —— indicates no signature or ratification.

a Ratified with or without reservations.

b Beijing Platform for Action, adopted with or without reservations and interpretive statements.

c Made general or interpretative statements or expressed reservations.

1 Discrimination in Education.

2 Torture and Other Cruel, Inhuman, or Degrading Treatment or Punishment.

3 Discrimination in Employment/Occupation.

4 Equal Remuneration for Men and Women for Equal Work.

5 Freedom of Association and Right to Organize.

Works Cited

Abdo, Leila. 1985. "Iman Khalifeh Receives 'Right to Livelihood Alternative Nobel Prize for Peace.' " *Alumni Bulletin* (Beirut Univ. College): 15–16.

Abdo, Nahla. 1994. "Nationalism and Feminism: Palestinian Women and the Intifada—No Going Back?" In *Gender and National Identity,* edited by Valentine M. Moghadam. London: Zed Books.

———. 1999. "Gender and Politics under the Palestinian Authority." *Journal of Palestine Studies* 28, no. 2 (Winter).

———. 2000. "Engendering Compensation: Making Refugee Women Count!" Prepared for the Expert and Advisory Services Fund, International Development Research Center, Ottawa (Mar.).

Abu-Ajaj, S., and J. Ben-David. 1988. "Traditional Education among the Bedouin of the Negev." In *Reshimot Benoseh Habeduim,* edited by J. Ben-David. Sdeh Boker, Israel: Ben-Gurion Univ.; in Hebrew.

Abu Amr, Ziad. 1994. "Palestinian Political Parties: Between Democracy and Pluralism." In *Whither Palestine?* edited by J. Ben-David, 34–35. Washington, D.C.: Center for Policy Analysis on Palestine.

———. 1997. "The Palestinian Legislative Council: A Critical Assessment." *Journal of Palestine Studies* 26, no. 4 (Summer).

Abu Jaber, Kamel. 1969. "The Legislative in the Hashemite Kingdom of Jordan: A Study in Political Development." *Muslim World* 59, no. 3–4 (July-Oct.): 220–50.

Abu-Lughod, L. 1986. *Honor and Poetry in the Bedouin Society.* Berkeley and Los Angeles: Univ. of California Press.

———, ed. 1998. *Remaking Women: Feminism and Modernity in the Middle East.* Princeton: Princeton Univ. Press.

Abu-Rabia, A. 1993. "Educational Anthropology in Bedouin Society." *Practicing Anthropology* 15, no. 2: 21–25.

———. 2001. *A Bedouin Century: Educational Development among the Negev Tribes in the 20th Century.* New York: Beghanhn Books.

Abu-Saad, I. 1991. "Towards an Understanding of Minority Education in Israel: The Case of the Bedouin Arabs of the Negev." *Comparative Education* 27, no. 2: 235–42.

————. 1995. "Bedouin Arabs' Education in the Context of Radical Social Change: What Is the Future?" *Compare* 25, no. 2: 149–61.

————. 1996. "Provision of Public Educational Services and Access to Higher Education among the Negev Bedouin Arabs in Israel." *Journal of Education Policy* 11, no. 5: 527–41.

————. 1997. "The Education of Israel's Negev Bedouin: Background and Prospects." *Israel Studies* 2, no. 2: 21–39.

————. 1998. "Minority Higher Education in an Ethnic Periphery: The Bedouin Arabs." In *Ethnic Frontiers and Peripheries: Landscapes of Development and Inequality in Israel,* edited by A. Meir and Y. Oren, 269–86. Boulder: Westview Press.

————. 2001. "Education as a Tool for Control vs. Development among Indigenous Peoples: The Case of Bedouin Arabs in Israel." *HAGAR-International Social Science Review* 2, no. 2: 241–61.

Adnan, Etel. 1977. *Sitt Marie Rose.* Paris: Des Femmes.

————. 1982. *Sitt Marie-Rose.* Sausalito, Calif.: Post-Apollo Press.

Afshar, H. 1985. "The Position of Women in an Iranian Village." In *Women, Work, and Ideology in the Third World,* edited by H. Afshar. London: Tavistock.

————. 1997. "Women's Studies in the Middle East: Some Problems and Prospects." In *Arab Regional Women's Studies Workshop,* edited by C. Nelson and S. Altork, 17–28. Cairo: American Univ. in Cairo Press.

Agarwal, Bina, ed. 1988. *Structures of Patriarchy.* London: Zed Books.

Ahmed, L. 1982. "Western Ethnocentrism and the Perception of the Harem." *Feminist Studies* 8, no. 3.

Allan, S., and P. Gilbert. 1997. "Psychopathology and Submissive Behaviour." *British Journal of Clinical Psychology* 36: 467–88.

Al-Multqa al-Insani Li-Hoqoq al-Mara'a [The Human Forum for Women's Rights]. 1997. *Ri'ayyat wa-ta'heel al-nazilat al-mawqofat idariyan hifathan 'alla hayatihun* [The care and rehabilitation of those under administrative detention to protect their lives]. Workshop Proceedings, Ministry of Social Development and Public Security Department, Amman, Jordan.

Alonso, Harriet Hyman. 1993. *Peace as a Women's Issue.* Syracuse: Syracuse Univ. Press.

Al-Urdun al-Jadid Research Center. 1997. *Al-mar'ah al-Urdunniyyah wa qanun al intikhabat* [Jordanian woman and the election law]. Amman, Jordan: Al-Urdun al-Jadid Research Center.

Alvarez, Sonia E. 2000. "Translating the Global: Effects of Transnational Organizing on Local Feminist Discourses and Practices in Latin America." *Meridians* 1: 29–67.

Amawi, Abla. 1992. "Democracy Dilemmas in Jordan." *Middle East Report,* no. 174 (Jan.-Feb.): 26–29.

————. 1994. "The 1993 Elections in Jordan." *Arab Studies Quarterly* 16, no. 3 (Summer).

———. 1996a. "Poverty and Vulnerability in Jordan." *Jordanies* (Centre d'Études et de Recherches sur le Moyen-Orient Contemporain [CERMOC], Amman), no. 1, 6.

———. 1996b. "Women's Education in Jordan." In *Arab Women: Between Defiance and Constraint,* edited by Suha Sabbagh. New York: Olive Branch Press.

———. 2000. "Gender and Citizenship in Jordan." In *Gender and Citizenship in the Middle East,* edited by Suad Joseph, 158–84. Syracuse: Syracuse Univ. Press.

———. 2001. *Against All Odds: Jordanian Women, Elections and Political Empowerment.* Jordan: Konrad Adenauer Stiftung and al-Kutba Center for Human Development.

Amnesty International. 2004a. "Afghanistan: Women Failed by Progress in Afghanistan." http://www.amnestyusa.org/countries/afghanistan/document.do?id=703DEEA7977D 0E8F80256F3A00631972.

———. 2004b. "Unfulfilled Promises to the Women of Afghanistan." *Interact: A Bulletin about Women's Human Rights* (Winter).

———. 2005. "Afghanistan: Women Still under Attack—a Systematic Failure to Protect." http://www.amnestyusa.org/countries/afghanistan/document.do?id=8BFA552432877 9D88025700B00425BF9.

Amr, Hady. 1996. "Electoral Systems and Democracy." *Middle East Report* 201 (Fall): 19–22.

Anderson, John. 2001. "Iranians' Film Struggles." *Newsday,* Apr. 1.

An-Naim, Abdullahi. 2002. *Islamic Family Law in a Changing World: A Global Resource Book.* London: Zed Books.

Antonelli, Alessandra. 1998. "Women's Parliament Sparks Gender War." *Palestine Report* 4, no. 39 (Mar. 20).

Antonius, Soraya. 1983. "Fighting on Two Fronts: Conversations with Palestinian Women." In *Third World, Second Sex,* edited by Miranda Davies. London: Zed Press.

el-Aoufi, N., ed. 1992. *La société civile au Maroc.* Casablanca: Smer.

Arditti, Rita. 1999. *Searching for Life: The Grandmothers of the Plaza de Mayo and the Disappeared Children of Argentina.* Berkeley and Los Angeles: Univ. of California Press.

Arishie, Mohssen. 1998. "War over Virginity." *Egyptian Gazette,* Oct. 27.

Associated Press. 2003. "Jordanian Parliament Rejects Women's Rights Bills as Anti-Islamic." Aug. 4.

Association Tunisienne des Femmes Démocrates [ATFD]. 1999. "Dix ans d'expérience: Quelles lectures? Quel devenir?" Tunis, unpublished report from ATFD's Tenth Anniversary Forum, Apr. 9–11.

———. 2001. "Rapport aux décideurs: Les violences à l'encontre des femmes." Tunis, unpublished report.

Augustin, Ebba, ed. 1993. *Palestinian Women: Identity and Experience.* London: Zed Books.

Awwad, Tawfiq. 1972. *Tawaheen Beirut.* Beirut: Dar al-Adab.

———. 1976. *Death in Beirut.* London: Heinemann.

Azmaz, A. 1984. *Migration and Reintegration in Rural Turkey: The Role of Women Left Behind.* Göttingen, Germany: Heredot GmbH.

Azmon, Yael. 1997. "War, Mothers and a Girl with Braids: Involvement of Mothers' Peace Movements in the National Discourse in Israel." *Israel Social Science Research* 12, no. 1: 109–28.

Badran, Amneh. 2003. "Recovering from Violent Conflict: Gender and Post-conflict Reconstruction in Palestine." Paper presented at the conference "Clash or Consensus? Gender and Human Security in a Globalized World." SAIS, Washington, D.C. (Oct. 8–9). Organized by the Women's Learning Partnership. http://www.learningpartnership.org/news/events/2003/clashorconsensus.

Bahçeli, Devlet. 1988. *MHP and Women.* Ankara: MHP Media and Propaganda Section Publication.

Barakat, Halim. 1969. *'Awdat alta'ir ilal bahr.* Beirut: Al'Mu'assassat al-'Arabiya.

———. 1977. *Le vaisseau reprend le large.* Sherbrooke, Quebec: Naaman.

———. 1983. *Days of Dust.* Washington, D.C.: Three Continents Press.

———. 1993. *The Arab World: Society, Culture and State.* Berkeley and Los Angeles: Univ. of California Press.

Barron, Andrea. 2002. "The Palestinian Women's Movement: Agent of Democracy in a Future State?" *Critique* 11, no. 1 (Spring).

Bar-Tzvi, S. 1991. *Jurisdiction among the Bedouins of the Negev.* Jerusalem: Ministry of Defense; in Hebrew.

Basu, Amrita, ed. 1995. *The Challenge of Local Feminisms: Women's Movements in Global Perspective.* Boulder: Westview Press.

Belarbi, Aicha. 1989. "Mouvement de femmes au Maroc." *Annuaire de l'Afrique du Nord* 27: 455–65.

———. 1995. "Women's Movement and the Democratic Transition." In *Femmes et société civile au Maghreb,* 5–25. Publication Universitaire du Maghreb; in Arabic.

———. 1997. "Femmes et société civile: Réflexions sur le cas du Maroc." In *Droits de citoyenneté des femmes au Maghreb,* 249–72. Casablanca: Editions le Fennec.

Beller-Hann, I. 1993. "Women, Religion and Beliefs in Northeast Turkey." In *Proceedings of the Colloqium on Popular Customs and the Monotheistic Religions in the Middle East and North Africa,* edited by A. Fodor and A. Shivtiel, 258–82. Budapest: Eötvos Loránd Univ.

Belloumi, Ahmed. 1994. "La criminalité en Tunisie de 1970 à 1989: Essai d'explication." In *Les déterminismes socio-culturels de la pauvreté en Tunisie.* Tunis: CERES.

Ben-David, J. 1982. *Report of the Processes of the Spontaneous Settlements Development in the Negev.* Jerusalem: Israeli National Council for Research and Development; in Hebrew.

———. 2000. *Report of the Cultural and Environmental Factors Determining Bedouin Dropout of School System.* Jerusalem: Ministry of Education.

Bennoune, Karima. 1995. "Between Betrayal and Betrayal: Fundamentalism, Family Law and Feminist Struggle in Algeria." *Arab Studies Quarterly* 51 (Spring).

Berg, B. L. 1995. *Qualitative Research Methods for Social Sciences.* Boston: Allyn and Bacon.

Berik, G. 1987. "From 'Enemy of the Spoon' to 'Factory': Women's Labor in the Carpet Weaving Industry in Rural Turkey." Paper presented at Middle East Studies Association meetings, New Orleans, Nov. 22–26.

Berkovitch, Nitza. 1999. *From Motherhood to Citizenship: Women's Rights and International Organizations.* Baltimore: Johns Hopkins Univ. Press.

Berkovitch, Nitza, and Valentine M. Moghadam. 1999. "Middle East Politics and Women's Collective Action: Challenging the Status Quo." *Social Politics* (Fall): 273–91.

Bhabha, H. 1994. *The Location of Culture.* London and New York: Routledge.

Bianchi, Robert. 1984. *Interest Groups and Political Development in Turkey.* Princeton: Princeton Univ. Press.

Blackorby, J., and L. J. Kortering. 1992. "High School Dropout and Students Identified with Behavioral Disorders." *Behavioral Disorders* 18, no. 1: 24–32.

Blacksmith, E. A. 1992. *Women in the Military.* New York: H. W. Wilson.

el-Bokhari. n.d. *Les traditions islamiques.* Notes by Houdas and W. Marçais. Vol. 5. Paris: Ed. Ernest Leroux.

Boserup, E. 1970. *Women's Role in Economic Development.* New York: St. Martin's Press.
————. 1977. "Preface." *Signs* 3, no. 1: xi-xiii.

Bouchier, David. 1984. *The Feminist Challenge.* London: Macmillan.

Boulatta, Terry. 2001. "The Role and Achievements of Women's NGOs in Palestinian Civil Society: Lobbying and Actions." PASSIA Seminar, Apr. 26. http://www.passia.org.

Bouvard, Marguerite Guzman. 1994. *Revolutionizing Motherhood: The Mothers of the Plaza de Mayo.* Wilmington, Del.: Scholarly Resources.

Brand, Laurie. 1998. *Women, the State and Political Liberalization: Middle Eastern and North African Experiences.* New York: Columbia Univ. Press.

Braybo, Gail. 1989. *Women Workers in the First World War.* New York: Routledge.

Breines, Ingeborg, Robert Connell, and Ingrid Eide, eds. 2000. *Male Roles, Masculinities and Violence: A Culture of Peace Perspective.* Paris: UNESCO.

Brenoff, Ann. 1998. "Interview with Zahira Kamal." *Los Angeles Times,* Nov. 29.

Brown, G. W., and T. O. Harris. 1978. *The Social Origins of Depression: A Study of Psychiatric Disorders in Women.* New York: Free Press.

Brown, Wendy. 1995. *States of Injury: Power and Freedom in Late Modernity.* Princeton: Princeton Univ. Press.

Browning, J. 1985. *Ataturk's Legacy to the Women of Turkey.* Durham, N.C.: Centre for Middle Eastern and Islamic Studies.

Brownmiller, Susan. 1975. *Against Our Will: Men, Women, and Rape.* New York: Ballantine.

Brynen, Rex. 1998. "From Occupation to Uncertainty: Palestine." In *Political Liberalization and Democratization in the Arab World,* edited by Bahgat Korany, Rex Brynen, and Paul Noble, vol. 2. Boulder: Lynne Rienner Publishers.

Büyük Birlik Partisi. 1998. *Büyük Birlik Partisi Programmi.* Ankara: Takav Matbaacilik.

Cabral, Meena, and Jill Astbury. 2000. *Women's Mental Health: An Evidence Based Review.* Geneva: World Health Organization. Available online at http://www.who.int/ mental_health.org.

Caldwell, John. 1982. *Theory of Fertility Decline.* London: Academic Press.

Central Bureau of Statistics. 1999. *Statistical Abstract of Israel.* Jerusalem: Center for Statistical Office; in Hebrew.

Chambers, Robert. 2005. *Ideas for Development.* London: Earthscan.

Charrad, Mounira M. 1990. "State and Gender in the Maghreb." *Middle East Report* (Mar.-Apr.): 19–24.

———. 2001. *States and Women's Rights: The Making of Postcolonial Tunisia, Algeria and Morocco.* Berkeley and Los Angeles: Univ. of California Press.

Chattopadhyay, A. 2005. "Women and Entrepreneurship." *Yojana* (New Delhi) 28, no. 49.

Chedid, Andrée. 1985. *La maison sans racines.* Paris: Flammarion.

———. 1989. *Return to Beirut.* London: Serpent's Tail.

el-Cheikh, Hanan. 1980a. *Hikayat Zahra.* Beirut: Al-Nahar.

———. 1980b. *Histoire de Zahra.* Paris: Lattès.

———. 1986. *The Story of Zahra.* London: Readers International, Quartet Books.

Chekir, Hafidha. 1995. "Quelques reflexions autour du forum des ONG de la quatrième conférence mondiale des femmes." Unpublished paper.

———. 1998a. "Le cadre juridique de la vie associative en Tunisie." Unpublished paper.

———. 1998b. "Le role du droit dans la promotion du statut des femmes: L'exemple Tunisien." Ph.D. diss., Université de Tunis III.

Cock, Jacklyn. 1993. *Women and War in South Africa.* Cleveland: Pilgrim Press.

Cohn, Martin Gregg. 1997. "Playing Iran's Censorship Game." *Toronto Star,* May 24.

Colabrese, R. L., and J. Poe. 1990. "Alienation: An Explanation of High School Dropout Rates among African-American and Latino Students." *Educational Research Quarterly* 14, no. 4: 22–26.

Collectif 95 Égalité Maghreb. 1995a. *Maghreb Women "with All Reserve."* Stuttgart: Friedrich Ebert Stiftung.

———. 1995b. *One Hundred Measures and Provisions for a Maghrebian Egalitarian Codification of the Personal Statute and Family Law.* Stuttgart: Friedrich Ebert Stiftung.

———. 1995c. *Women in the Maghreb: Change and Resistance.* Stuttgart: Friedrich Ebert Stiftung.

———. 1998. *Violations flagrantes des droits et violences à l'égard des femmes au Maghreb: Rapport annuel, 1996–97.* Salé, Morocco: Impression al-Harf al-Mo'tadil.

Connell, Dan. 1995. "For Palestinian Women, Arafat's Pals-Only Rule Won't Do." *Christian Science Monitor,* Mar. 27.

Connell, R. W. 1985. "Masculinity, Violence and War." In *War/Masculinity,* edited by Paul Patton and Ross Poole. Sydney: Intervention.

———. 1987. *Gender and Power.* Palo Alto, Calif.: Stanford Univ. Press.

———. 1995. *Masculinities.* Berkeley and Los Angeles: Univ. of California Press.

Cooke, Miriam. 1988. *War's Other Voices: Women Writers on the Lebanese Civil War, 1975–82.* Cambridge: Cambridge Univ. Press.

Corm, Georges. 1986. *Géopolitique du conflit libanais.* Paris: La Découverte.

Crittenden, Ann. 1991. "Nations Are Like Children." *Nation,* Feb. 4, 119–23.

Cunningham, Robert B., and Yasin K. Sarayrah. 1993. *Wasta: The Hidden Force in Middle Eastern Society.* Westport, Conn.: Praeger.

Dabashi, Hamid. 2001. *Close Up: Iranian Cinema, Past, Present, and Future.* London: Verso Books.

Dajani, Souad. 1994. "Between National and Social Liberation: The Palestinian Women's Movement in the Israeli Occupied West Bank and Gaza Strip." In *Women and the Israeli Occupation,* edited by Tamar Mayer, 33–61. London: Routledge.

Dal, Yousri. 2000. *Malamah ash-shakhsiyya min khilal tahlil jara'im ash-sharaf fi Tunis wa alaqatuha bi haqq al-insan f-il ferdana.* DEA in Clinical Psychology, under the direction of Professor Lilia Labidi, Faculté des Sciences Humaines et Sociales de Tunis.

Daoud, Zakya. 1993. *Féminisme et Politique au Maghreb.* Casablanca: Editions Eddif.

Davis, Susan Schaeffer. 1983. *Patience and Power: Women's Lives in a Moroccan Village.* New York: Schenkman.

Deneoux, G., and L. Gateau. 1995. "L'essor des associations au Maroc: À la recherche de la citoyenneté." *Monde Arabe: Maghreb/Machrek,* no. 150: 19–39.

DHS+. 2003. "About DHS+ Surveys and Research." http://www.measuredhs.com.

Draft Basic Law for the National Authority in the Transitional Period. 1996. Jerusalem: Jerusalem Media and Communication Centre (Feb.).

Duaibis, Salwa. 1999. "Palestinian Women Acknowledged." *Sabeel CornerStone* 14.

Duclos, Louis Jean. 1998. "November 1997 Parliamentary Elections, Special Issue: The 1997 Parliamentary Elections." *Jordanies* (Centre d'Études et de Recherches sur le Moyen-Orient Contemporain [CERMOC], Amman), no. 5–6 (June-Dec.): 210–232.

Dupree, Nancy H. 1984. "Revolutionary Rhetoric and Afghan Women." In *Revolutions and Rebellions in Afghanistan: Anthropological Perspectives,* edited by N. Shahrani and R. Canfield. Berkeley and Los Angeles: Univ. of California Press.

Eickelman, Dale F. 1989. *The Middle East: An Anthropological Approach.* 2nd ed. New York: Prentice-Hall.

———, and Jon W. Anderson, eds. 1999. *New Media in the Muslim World: The Emerging Public Sphere.* Bloomington: Indiana Univ. Press.

Emrys, P. L. 1990. "The Status of Women." In *The Bedouin of Cyrenaica,* edited by J. Goody and E. Marx, 243–78. New York: Cambridge Univ. Press.

Enloe, Cynthia. 1988. *Does Khaki Become You? The Militarisation of Women's Lives.* London: Pandora Press.

———. 1990. *Bananas, Beaches and Bases: Making Feminist Sense of International Politics.* Berkeley and Los Angeles: Univ. of California Press.

Ertürk, Y. 1987. "The Impact of National Integration on Rural Households in Southeastern Turkey." *Journal of Human Sciences* 6, no. 1: 81–97.

Essadani, Ezet. 1999a. "Al-I'dam l-il Mughtasib hetta law tazawwaja dhahiyatahou." Interview with the imam of el-Azhar. *Al-Ahram,* May 8.

———. 1999b. "Al-mughtasiba ma zalat bikran shar'an." Interview with the mufti of the Republic of Egypt, Dr. Nasr Ferid Wassel, N.F. *Al-Ahram,* May 22.

Essbai, Ikbal. 1998. "Al-ightisab hetta al-zawaj." *Rose el-Youssef,* Dec. 14.

Fadhl, S., and Ibrahim, F. 1999. "Zawaj 'al-mughtasib' min dhaHiyatihi . . . baatel." *Al-Jamhoouriya,* Feb. 20.

Fakhfakh, Françoise. 1973. "Deux types d'immigration: Le déterminisme migratoire: Carnoy, cité populaire." *Revue Tunisienne des Sciences Sociales,* no. 32/35: 166–67.

Falk, John H., and Lynn D. Dierking. 2000. *Learning from Museums: Visitor Experiences and the Making of Meaning.* Walnut Creek, Calif.: Alta Mira Press/AASLH.

Faramarzi, Scheherezade. 1997. "Iranian Films Winning Awards Despite Strict Islamic Rules." *Ottowa Citizen,* Nov. 6.

Farrar, Adam. 1985. "War, Machining Male Desire." In *War/Masculinity,* edited by Paul Patton and Ross Poole. Sydney: Intervention.

Fejjal, Ali. 1987. "Industrie et industrialisation à Fès." *Revue de Geographie Marocaine,* n.s., 11, no. 2: 55–70.

Feldman, E. J. 1981. *A Practical Guide to the Conduct of Field Research in the Social Sciences.* Boulder: Westview Press.

Finlay, B. 1989. *The Women of Azua: Work and Family in the Rural Dominican Republic.* New York; Westport, Conn.; and London: Praeger.

Fitzpatrick, K. M., and W. C. Yoel. 1992. "Policy, School Structure and Socio-demographics: Effects on Statewide High School Dropout Rates." *Sociology of Education* 65, no. 1: 76–93.

Fleischmann, Ellen L. 1995. "Jerusalem Women's Organizations During the British Mandate, 1920s–1930s." Jerusalem: PASSIA. http://www.passia.org/jerusalem/publications.

———. 1996. "Selective Memory, Gender and Nationalism: Palestinian Women Leaders of the Mandate Period." *History Workshop Journal* 47 (1999): 141–58.

Forum for Women, Law, and Development. 1999. *Shadow Report on Initial Report of Government of Nepal on CEDAW: Briefing of Initial Report and Concluding Comments (Response* to the Nepalese Government's Report on the Convention on the Elimination of All Forms of Discrimination Against Women). Kathmandu: Forum for Women, Law, and Development.

Fraser, Antonia. 1988. The Warrior Queens. New York: Vintage.

Frodon, Jean Michel. 2001. "The Universal Iranian." SAIS Review 21, no. 2 (Summer-Fall): 217–24.

Gendzier, Irene. 1982. Foreword to The Hidden Face of Eve: Women in the Arab World, by Nawal el-Saadawi. Translated by Sharif Hetata. Boston: Beacon Press.

General Union of Palestinian Women, Jerusalem-Palestine. 1998. "Declaration of Principles on Palestinian Women's Rights, Third Draft." In Palestinian Women of Gaza and the West Bank, edited by Suha Sabbagh, 251–54. Bloomington: Indiana Univ. Press.

Gerner, Deborah J. 1990. "Evolution of the Palestinian Uprising." International Journal of Group Tensions 20, no. 3 (Fall): 233–65.

———. 1991. "Palestinians, Israelis, and the Intifada: The Third Year and Beyond." Arab Studies Quarterly 13, no. 3–4 (Summer-Fall): 19–60.

Ghazali, Ahmed. 1989. "Contribution à l'analyse du phenomene associatif au Maroc." Annuaire de l'Afrique du Nord 28: 243–60.

Giacaman, Rita. 1989. "Palestinian Women in the Uprising: From the Followers to Leaders." Journal of Refugee Studies 2, no. 1.

———, and Penny Johnson. 2001. "Searching for Strategies: The Palestinian Women's Movement in the New Era." In Women and Power in the Middle East, edited by Suad Joseph and Susan Slyomovics. Philadelphia: Univ. of Pennsylvania Press.

Gibb, H. A. R., and J. H. Kramers. 1953. Shorter Encyclopedia of Islam. Ithaca: Cornell Univ. Press.

Giele, Janet Z. 1977. "Introduction: The Status of Women in Comparative Perspective." In Women: Roles and Status in Eight Countries, edited by Janet Z. Giele and Audrey C. Smock, 3–31. New York: John Wiley.

———. 1992. "Promise and Disappointment of the Modern Era: Equality for Women." In Women's Work and Women's Lives: The Continuing Struggle Worldwide, edited by H. Kahne and J. Giele. Boulder: Westview Press.

Gilligan, Carole. 1982. In a Different Voice: Psychological Theory and Women's Development. Cambridge: Harvard Univ. Press.

Gilman, Sarah E. 2000. "Feminist Organizing in Tunisia: Resisting Appropriation while Maintaining Autonomy." Master's thesis, Univ. of Oregon.

Glendon, Mary Ann. 1977. State, Law and Family: Family Law in Transition in the United States and Western Europe. Cambridge: Harvard Univ. Press.

———. 1989. The Transformation of Family Law. Chicago: Univ. of Chicago Press.

Gluck, Sherna Berger. 1995. "Palestinian Women: Gender Politics and Nationalism." Journal of Palestine Studies 24, no. 3 (Spring): 5–15.

Government of Afghanistan. 1345/1966. *Afghanistan Almanac.* Kabul: Ministry of Information and Culture Press.

———. 1355/1976. *Rasmi Jarida* [Official Gazette]. Kabul: Government Press.

———. 1369/1990a. *Afghanistan Almanac.* Kabul: Government Press.

———. 1369/1990b. *Salnama-i-Kabul* [Kabul Almanac]. Kabul: Government Press.

Government of India. 2001. *National Policy for the Empowerment of Women, 2001.* New Delhi: Department of Women and Child Development, Human Resource Development Ministry.

———. 2002. *Approach Paper of Tenth Five Year Plan, 2002–07.* New Delhi: Planning Commission.

———. 2003. *Employment Review, January-March 2001.* New Delhi: Ministry of Labor, Directorate General of Employment and Training, Employment Market Information Programme.

———. 2004a. *Census of India, 2001: Primary Census Abstract—Total Population.* New Delhi: India, Registrar General and Census Commissioner.

———. 2004b. *Employment Review (2003–04).* New Delhi: Ministry of Labour.

———. 2004c. *Selected Educational Statistics, 2000–2004.* New Delhi: Department of Education, Human Resource Development Ministry.

Government of Jordan. 1954/1987. "Jordanian Nationality Law, No. 6 for 1954." *Official Gazette,* no. 1171 (Feb. 15): 106; and its amendment, "No. 22 for 1987," *Official Gazette* (Amman), no. 3496 (Sept. 1): 1632.

———. 1959. "The Civil Retirement Law, No. 34 for 1959." *Official Gazette* (Amman).

———. 1960. "Penal Code No. 16 for 1960, Article 98." *Official Gazette* (Amman).

———. 1976. "Temporary Personal Status Law (PSL), Provisional Law No. 61 of 1976." *Official Gazette* (Amman).

———. 1983. "The Civil Health Insurance Ordinance, No. 10 for 1983." *Official Gazette* (Amman).

———. 1997. *Department of Statistics: The 1997 Household Expenditure and Income Survey.* Amman, Jordan: Department of Statistics.

Govinda, R., ed. 2004. *India Education Report.* New Delhi: Oxford Univ. Press.

Grabar, Oleg. 1995. "Toward an Aesthetic of Persian Painting." In *The Art of Interpreting,* edited by Susan C. Scott, 129–39. Philadelphia: Pennsylvania Univ. Press.

Gubser, Peter. 1983. *Jordan: Crossroads of Middle Eastern Events.* Boulder: Westview Press.

Guettel, Charnie. 1989. *Marxism and Feminism.* Toronto: Hunter Rose.

Gündüz-Hoşgör, Ayşe. 2001. "Convergence Between Theoretical Perspectives in Women-Gender and Development Literature Regarding Women's Economic Status in the Middle East." *METU Studies in Development* 28, no. 1–2.

Haddad, Tahar. 1978. *Notre femme, la législation islamique et la société.* Tunis: Maison Tunisienne d'Édition.

Halliday, Fred. 1998. "The Communist Regime in Afghanistan, 1978–1992: Institutions and Conflicts." *Europe-Asia Studies* (Dec.).

Hamdan. Dina. 2000. "Government Accused of Shirking Responsibilities before UN High Commissioner for Human Rights." *Jordan Times,* Mar. 11.

Hamdi, Abdelaziz. 1998. "Az-zawaj al-mughtasib min al-mughtasiba, lan ya fihi min al-iqab . . ." *Rose el-Youssef,* Dec. 7.

Hammami, Rema. 1990. "Women, the Hijab, and the Intifada." *Middle East Report* 164–65 (May-Aug.): 24–28.

———, and Penny Johnson. 1999. "Equality with a Difference: Gender and Citizenship in Transitional Palestine." *Social Politics* (Fall): 314–43.

Hanssen-Bauer, Jon, Jon Pedersen, and Age A. Tiltnes, eds. 1998. *Jordanian Society: Living Conditions in the Hashemite Kingdom of Jordan.* Oslo: FAFO Institute for Applied Social Science.

Hardoy, Jorge E. 1986. *The Popular Sum of Knowledge and the Museum.* Paris: ICOM.

Hasso, Frances. 1998. "The 'Women's Front': Nationalism, Feminism, and Modernity in Palestine." *Gender and Society* 12, no. 4 (Aug.): 441–65.

Hegland, Mary Elaine. 1999. "Gender and Religion in the Middle East and South Asia: Women's Voices Rising." In *A Social History of Women and Gender in the Modern Middle East,* edited by Margaret L. Meriwether and Judith E. Tucker. Boulder: Westview Press.

Hein, George, and Mary Alexander. 1998. *Museums: Places of Learning.* Washington, D.C.: AAM.

Helie-Lucas, M. 1993. "Women's Struggle and Strategies in the Rise of Fundamentalism in the Muslim World: From Entryism to Internationalism." In *Women in the Middle East,* edited by Haleh Afshar, 206–42. London: Macmillan Press.

Hijab, Nadia. 1988. *Womanpower: The Arab Debate on Women at Work.* New York: Cambridge Univ. Press.

Hiltermann, Joost. 1990. "Trade Unions and Women's Committees: Sustaining Movement, Creating Space." *Middle East Report* 164–65 (May-Aug.).

———. 1991. *Behind the Intifada: Labor and Women's Movements in the Occupied Territories.* Princeton: Princeton Univ. Press.

Hoch-Smith, Judith, and Anita Spring. 1978. *Women in Ritual and Symbolic Roles.* New York: Plenum Press.

Horowitz, R. T. 1992. "Dropout Mertonian or Reproduction Scheme?" *Adolescence* 27, no. 106: 451–59.

Hos, R., and A. Kenan. 1997. *Report of Personal and Community Aspects Related to the Educational Enrollment of Bedouin Girls.* Jerusalem: Ministry of Education; in Hebrew.

el-Hosael, A. 1997. *Education and Demography in Rabat.* Rabat Municipality, Morocco: Unit for Strategy Planning; in Arabic.

Hourani, Hani. 1997. "Jordan's Parliamentary Elections, 1997: A Reading of the Elections for the 13th." Jordanian Parliament draft paper. Amman, Jordan: Al-Urdun al-Jadid Research Center.

Human Rights Watch. 1997. "Political Communiqué of the Groups for National Reform and the Boycott of the 1997 Parliamentary Elections." *Middle East* 9, no. 12 (E) (Oct.): 18.

———. 2005. "Campaigning against Fear: Women's Participation in Afghanistan's 2005 Elections." http://www.hrw.org/backgrounder/wrd/afghanistan0805/index.htm.

"IAS Officers Worth 50 Lakhs in Marriage Market." 1987. *Indian Post.* July 15.

Ibrahim, Saad Eddin. 1998. "Liberalization and Democratization in the Arab World: An Overview." In *Political Liberalization and Democratization in the Arab World,* edited by Bahgat Korany, Rex Brynen, and Paul Noble, vol. 2. Boulder: Lynne Rienner Publishers.

Ilcan, S. 1994. "Peasant Struggles and Social Change: Migration, Households and Gender in Rural Turkish Society." *International Migration Review* 28: 554–79.

"Iraq: Focus on Threats Against Progressive Women." 2005. *IRIN* (Mar. 21).

Iyer, Shyamala M. 1985. "Their Daughters Were Gold." *Times of India,* Aug. 4.

Jack, Dana C. 1991. *Silencing the Self: Women and Depression.* Cambridge: Harvard Univ. Press.

———. 1999. *Behind the Mask: Destruction and Creativity in Women's Aggression.* Cambridge: Harvard Univ. Press.

Jack, D. C., and D. Dill. 1992. "Silencing the Self Scale: Schemas of Intimacy Associated with Depression in Women." *Psychology of Women Quarterly* 16: 97–106.

Jacoby, Tami Amanda. 1999. "Feminism, Nationalism, and Difference: Reflections on the Palestinian Women's Movement." *Women's Studies International Forum* 22, no. 5.

Jad, Islah. 1990. "From Salons to the Popular Committees: Palestinian Women, 1919–1989." In *Intifada: Palestine at the Crossroads,* edited by Jamal R. Nassar and Roger Heacock. New York: Praeger.

Jain, S. C. 1996. *Law of Marriage and Divorce.* 4th ed. New Delhi: Universal Law Publishing.

Jankari, Rachid. 2002. "ONG et Internet: Le fossé "associatif Marocain." http://webzinecnd.mpep.gov.ma/article.php3?id_article=56.

Jayawardena, Kumari. 1986. *Feminism and Nationalism in the Third World.* London: Zed Press.

Joekes, Susan. 1987. *Women in the World Economy: An INSTRAW Study.* New York: Oxford: Oxford Univ. Press.

Jordan Times. 1997a. Aug. 4.

Jordan Times. 1997b. Oct. 15.

Jordan Times. 1997c. Nov. 12.

Joseph, Suad, ed. 2000. *Gender and Citizenship in the Middle East.* Syracuse: Syracuse Univ. Press.

Jureidini, Paul A., and R. D. McLaurin. 1984. *Jordan: The Impact of Social Change on the Role of the Tribes.* The Washington Papers, vol. 12, no. 108. New York: Praeger.

Kabeer, Naila. 1994. "Women's Labour in the Bangladesh Garment Industry: Choices and Constraints." In *Muslim Women's Choices: Religious Belief and Social Reality,* edited by Camilia Fawzi el-Solh and Judy Mabro. Oxford: Berg.

————. 2001. "Resources, Agency, Achievements: Reflections on the Measurement of Women's Empowerment." In *Discussing Women's Empowerment—Theory and Practice,* edited by B. Sevefjord et al. Stockholm: SIDA.

Kalaycioglu, Ersin. 1983. *Karsilastirmali Siyasal Katilma: Siyasal Eylemin Kokenleri Üzerine Bir Inceleme* [Comparative Political Participation: An Analysis on the Roots of a Political Action]. Istanbul: Istanbul Univ. Publication.

Kamal, Zahira. 1998. "The Development of the Palestinian Women's Movement in the Occupied Territories: Twenty Years after the Israeli Occupation." In *Palestinian Women of Gaza and the West Bank,* edited by Suha Sabbagh, 78–88. Bloomington: Indiana Univ. Press.

Kamalakannan, K. 2005. "The Role of Financial Institutions in Development of Women Entrepreneurs." *Kurukshetra* (New Delhi) 53, no. 6.

Kampwirth, Karen. 2002. *Women and Guerrilla Movements: Nicaragua, El Salvador, Chiapas, Cuba.* University Park: Pennsylvania State Univ. Press.

Kandiyoti, D. 1977. "Sex Roles and Social Change: A Comparative Appraisal of Turkey's Women." In *Women and National Development,* edited by Wellesley Editorial Committee. Chicago: Univ. of Chicago Press.

————. 1984. "Rural Transformation in Turkey and Its Implications for Women's Status." In *Women on the Move: Contemporary Changes in Family and Society.* Paris: UNESCO.

————. 1988. "Bargaining with Patriarchy." *Gender and Society* 2, no. 3 (Sept.): 274–90.

————. 1992. "Islam and Patriarchy: A Comparative Perspective." In *Shifting Boundaries: Women and Gender in Middle Eastern History,* edited by N. R. Keddie and B. Baron. New Haven: Yale Univ. Press.

————, ed. 1991. *Women, Islam and the State.* London: Macmillan.

Kaplan, Flora E. S., ed. 1994. *Museums and the Making of "Ourselves": The Role of Objects in National Identity.* London: Leicester Univ. Press.

Karl, Marilee. 1995. *Women and Empowerment: Participation in Decision Making.* London: Zed Books.

Katz, Y. 1998. *Report of the Investigating Committee on the Bedouin Education System in the Negev.* Jerusalem: Ministry of Education.

Kawar, Amal. 1996. *Daughters of Palestine: Leading Women of the Palestinian National Movement.* Albany: State Univ. of New York Press.

Kawar, Mary. 2000. *Gender, Employment and the Life Course: The Case of Working Daughters.* Amman, Jordan: Konrad Adenauer Stiftung and Community Centers Association.

Kazami, Ali Rached. 1990. *Islam et réparation du préjudice moral.* Geneva: Librairie Droz.

Keck, Margaret, and Kathryn Sikkink. 1998. *Activists Beyond Borders: Advocacy Networks in International Politics.* Ithaca: Cornell Univ. Press.

Kessel, Jerrold. 1993. "Palestinian Women Reject Back-Seat Role." *The Guardian* (London), Dec. 6.

Khanna, S. S. 2001. *Entrepreneurial Development.* New Delhi: S. Chand.

Khoury, Elias. 1977. *Al-jabal al-saghir.* Beirut: Mu'assassat al-Abhath.

———. 1987. *La petite montagne.* Paris: Arléa.

———. 1990. *The Small Mountain.* Minneapolis: Univ. of Minnesota Press.

King, Ursula. 1993. *Women and Spirituality: Voices of Protest and Promise.* University Park: Pennsylvania State Univ. Press.

Klare, Michael. 2003. "It's the Oil, Stupid." *Nation,* May 12.

Klein, Naomi. 2004. "The Multibillion Dollar Robbery the U.S. Calls Reconstruction." *The Guardian* (London), June 24.

Kleinman, A., and B. Good. 1986. *Culture and Depression.* Berkeley and Los Angeles: Univ. of California Press.

Klinov, R. 1996. "Changes in School Enrollment Patterns in Israel: A Comparison Between Two Disadvantaged Groups." *Economics of Education Review* 15, no. 3: 289–301.

Kobtani, Abdelraouf Hassen. 1999. "Al-madda 291, uqubat . . . wa jara'im al-ightisab." *Al-Jamhoouriya,* Mar. 2.

Kressel, G. M. 1992. *Descent Through Males.* Mediterranean Language and Culture Monograph Series. Wiesbaden, Germany: O. Harrassowitz.

———. 1993. "Shame and Gender." *Anthropological Quarterly* 65, no. 1: 34–46.

Kuttab, Daoud. 1999. "From the Female Perspective." *Jerusalem Post,* Mar. 11.

Kuttab, Eileen S. 1993. "Palestinian Women in the Intifada: Fighting on Two Fronts." *Arab Studies Quarterly* 15, no. 2 (Spring): 69–85.

———. 1997. "The Women Studies Program in Palestine: Between Criticism and New Vision." In *Muslim Women and the Politics of Participation: Implementing the Beijing Platform,* edited by Mahnaz Afkhami and Erika Friedl, 94–100. Syracuse: Syracuse Univ. Press.

Labidi, Lilia. 1991. *L'intelligentsia féminine face à la Guerre du Golfe en Tunisie.* Tunis: Institut de Recherches Appliquées.

Laghmani, Slim. 1996. "La Loi Organique No. 92 du 2 avril 1992 complétant la Loi No. 59–154 du 7 novembre 1959 relative aux associations." Unpublished paper.

Lapierre, Jean-William. 1981. "Femmes: Une oppression millénaire." *Alternatives Non-violentes: Femmes et Violences* 40 (Spring).

Layachi, Azzedine. 1995. *Civil Society and Democratization in Morocco.* Cairo: Dar al-Ameen.

Layne, Linda. 1987. "Tribesmen as Citizens: 'Primordial Ties' and Democracy in Rural Jordan." In *Elections in the Middle East: Implications of Recent Trends,* edited by Linda Layne. Boulder: Westview Press.

Lewis, P. 1993. "Journals for an Emerging Women's Movement: The Thamania Mars Collective." In *Alternative Media: Linking the Global and Local,* edited by P. Lewis. Reports and Papers in Mass Communication, no. 107. Paris: UNESCO.

Lockman, Zachary, and Joel Beinin, eds. 1989. *Intifada: The Palestinian Uprising Against Israeli Occupation.* Boston: South End Press.

Lorentzen, Lois Ann, and Jennifer Turpin, eds. 1988. *The Women and War Reader.* New York: New York Univ. Press.

Macdonald, Sharon. 1988. "Drawing the Lines—Gender, Peace and War: An Introduction." In *Images of Women in Peace and War,* edited by Sharon Macdonald, Pat Holden, and Shirley Ardener. Madison: Univ. of Wisconsin Press.

Mackie, M. 1991. *Gender Relations in Canada.* Toronto: Butterworths.

Majdi, Salama. 1998. "Khawfan min al-fadhia." *El-Wafd,* Dec. 12.

Makarem, May. 1988. "Avec la non-violence Laure Moghaïzel, l'autre visage du Liban." *L'Orient-Le Jour* (Beirut) (Mar. 16): 4.

al-Makkawi, Hanaa, and Khouloud al-Gamal. 1998. "La virginité à tout prix." *El-Ahram Hebdo,* Nov. 11–17.

Malakh, Mouna, and Ahmed Ayoub. 1998. "Ahl shara mukhtalifun wa al-ittiba' muwafiqun wa al-uquba wasalat illa al-adam." *El-Moussaouer* (Nov. 12).

Malhas, 'Abd al-Raheem. 1997. Editorial. *Al-Ra'y,* Sept. 11.

Malt, Carol. 2002a. *The Free Woman.* Pensacola, Fla.: Ethos Publishing.

———. 2002b. *Museums of Jordan: A Directory.* Pensacola, Fla.: Ethos Publishing.

———. 2005. *Women's Voices in Middle East Museums: Case Studies in Jordan.* Syracuse: Syracuse Univ. Press.

Massel, Gregory. 1972. *The Surrogate Proletariat: Muslim Women and the Revolutionary Strategies in Central Asia, 1919–1929.* Princeton: Princeton Univ. Press.

Matn-i-Awalin Canfrans-i-Sartasari-i-Zanan-i-Afghanistan [The Manual of the First All Women's Conference]. 1980. Kabul: Government Press.

Maxwell, Margaret. 1990. *Narodniki Women.* New York: Paragon.

Mayer, Tamar. 1994. "Heightened Palestinian Nationalism: Military Occupation, Repression, Difference and Gender." In *Women and the Israeli Occupation,* edited by Tamar Mayer. London: Routledge.

McKay, Susan. 2000. "Gender Justice and Reconciliation." *Women's Studies International Forum* 23, no. 5: 561–70.

Meir, A. 1986. "Pastoral Nomads and the Dialectics of Development and Modernization: Delivering Public Educational Services to the Israeli Negev Bedouin." *Environment and Planning: Society and Space* 4, no. 2: 85–95.

———. 1997. *As Nomadism Ends: The Israeli Bedouin of the Negev.* Boulder: Westview Press.

Meir, A., and D. Barnea. 1986. *Development of the Bedouin Educational System in the Negev.* Jerusalem: Ministry of Education; in Hebrew.

———. 1988. "Space Aspects and Structural Changes in the Bedouin Educational System in the Negev." In *Reshimot Benoseh Habedouim*, edited by A. Orion and Y. Eini. Sdeh Boker, Israel: Ben-Gurion Univ.; in Hebrew.

Melitz, A. 1995. *Changes in the Bedouin Educational System in the Negev.* Jerusalem: Ministry of Education; in Hebrew.

Mir-Hosseini, Ziba. 2001. "Iranian Cinema: Art, Society and the State." *Middle East Report* 219 (Summer).

Moghadam, Valentine M. 1992. "Development and Women's Emancipation: Is There a Connection?" *Development and Change* 23, no. 4: 215–55.

———. 1997. "Gender and Revolutions." In *Theorizing Revolutions,* edited by John Foran, 137–65. New York and London: Routledge.

———. 1998. *Women, Work and Economic Reform in the Middle East and North Africa.* Boulder: Lynne Rienner Publishers.

———. 2002. "Patriarchy, the Taleban, and the Politics of Public Space in Afghanistan." *Women's Studies International Forum* 25, no. 1: 19–31.

———. 2003. *Modernizing Women: Gender and Social Change in the Middle East.* 2nd ed. Boulder: Lynne Rienner Publishers.

———. 2005. *Globalizing Women: Transnational Feminist Networks.* Baltimore: Johns Hopkins Univ. Press.

———, ed. 1994. *Identity Politics and Women: Cultural Reassertions and Feminisms in International Perspective.* Boulder: Westview Press.

———, and Lucie Senftova. 2005. "Measuring Women's Empowerment: Participation and Rights in Civil, Political, Social, Economic, and Cultural Domains." *International Social Science Journal,* no. 184 (June), special issue on "Beijing + 10."

Moghissi, Haideh. 1994. *Populism and Feminism in Iran: Women's Struggle in a Male-Defined Revolutionary Movement.* New York: St. Martin's Press.

Molavi, Afshin. 2000. "A Tale of Two Women." *SAIS Review* 20, no. 2 (Summer-Fall): 217–21.

Molyneux, Maxine. 1985. "Mobilization Without Emancipation?" *Feminist Studies* 11, no. 2.

Moruzzi, Norma. 2001. "Notes from the Field." *Feminist Studies* 27, no. 1 (Spring): 89–100.

Murphy, Emma C. 1999. *Economic and Political Change in Tunisia: From Bourguiba to Ben Ali.* London: Macmillan.

Nafadi, Mahmoud. 1999. "Al-mughtasib fi sijn . . . badalan min al-kusha." *Al-Jamhooriya,* Feb. 18.

Naficy, Hamid. 1994. "Veiled Vision/Powerful Presences: Women in Post-revolutionary Iranian Cinema." In *In the Eye of the Storm: Women in Post-revolutionary Iran,* edited by Mahnaz Afkhami and Erika Friedl. Syracuse: Syracuse Univ. Press.

———. 2001. *An Accented Cinema: Exilic and Diasporic Filmmaking.* Princeton: Princeton Univ. Press.

Naik, S. 2003. "The Need for Developing Women Entrepreneurs." *Yojana* 47, no. 7.

Narayan, Y., S. N. Sahu, and L. Lakshmi. 2005. "Political Empowerment of Women." *Indian Journal of Public Administration* (Indian Institute of Public Administration, New Delhi): 35–36.

Narli, Nilufer, and Yasar Nari. 1999. "Türkiye'de hemseri derneklerinin siyasete katilmasi ve demokratiklesme sürecine etkileri: Bursa örnegi" [The political participation of hemsehri associations and democratization in Turkey: The case of Bursa]. *Yeni Türkiye* (Ankara), year 5, 1, no. 29 (Eylul-Ekim [Sept.-Oct.]): 176–84.

Nash, June, and Maria Fernandez-Kelly, eds. 1983. *Women, Men and the International Division of Labor.* Albany: State Univ. of New York Press.

Nassar, Jamal R., and Roger Heacock, eds. 1990. *Intifada: Palestine at the Crossroads.* New York: Praeger.

Nawid, Senzil. 1993. "Comparing the Regimes of Amanullah and the Afghan Marxists (1978–92)." *Critique* (Spring).

———. 1999. *Religious Response to Social Change in Afghanistan: King Aman-Allah and the Afghan Ulama, 1919–1929.* Costa Mesa, Calif.: Mazda Publishers.

Nelofer. 1981. *Women's International Democratic Movement in the Present Stage.* Kabul, Afghanistan: Government Printing Press.

Nelson, Cynthia, and Soraya Altorki. 1998. *Arab Regional Women's Studies Workshop.* Cairo: American Univ. in Cairo Press.

Nepal Human Development Report. 1998. Kathmandu: Nepal South Asia Centre.

Nepal National Planning Commission, His Majesty's Government of Nepal, and UNICEF, Nepal. 1996. *Children and Women of Nepal: A Situational Analysis.* Kathmandu, Nepal: UNICEF.

"New Afghan Constitution Illustrates Progress, Hurdles." 2004. *Centerpoint: Woodrow Wilson International Center for Scholars Newsletter,* Apr.

Norman, Elizabeth. 1990. *Women at War.* Philadelphia: Univ. of Pennsylvania Press.

Nyrop, Richard F., ed. 1994. *Jordan: A Country Study.* Washington, D.C.: American Univ., Foreign Area Studies Division.

Ong, Aiwa. 1987. *Spirits of Resistance and Capitalist Discipline: Factory Women in Malaysia.* Albany: State Univ. of New York Press.

———. 1991. "The Gender and Labor Politics of Postmodernity." *Annual Review of Anthropology* 20: 279–309.

Ouazani, Cherif. 2005. "La paix ou la justice?" *Jeune Afrique: L'Intelligent* (Paris), no. 2306 (Mar. 20–26): 66–67.

Oumrane, Nadia. 1999. "La dernière répudiation du siècle." *Réalités* 692: 32–33.

Patel, V., R. Araya, M. de Lima, A. Ludermir, and C. Todd. 1999. "Women, Poverty and Common Mental Disorders in Four Restructuring Societies." *Social Science and Medicine* 49: 1461–71.

Peerzada, S. A., and P. Prande. 2005. "Empowerment of Women: A Study." *Kurukshetra* (New Delhi) 54, no. 1.

Peteet, Julie. 1991. *Gender in Crisis: Women and the Palestinian Resistance Movement.* New York: Columbia Univ. Press.

Peterson, V. Spike, and Anne Sisson Runyan. 1993. *Global Gender Issues.* Boulder: Westview Press.

Piccinelli, M., and F. G. Homen. 1997. *Gender Differences in the Epidemiology of Affective Disorders and Schizophrenia.* Geneva: World Health Organization.

Pierson, Ruth Roach. 1988. "Did Your Mother Wear Army Boots? Feminist Theory and Women's Relation to War, Peace and Revolution." In *Images of Women in Peace and War,* edited by Sharon Macdonald, Pat Holden, and Shirley Ardener. Madison: Univ. of Wisconsin Press.

Polity-Charara. 1983. "Women and Politics in Lebanon." In *Third World, Second Sex,* edited by Miranda Davies. London: Zed Books.

Portes, A. 1980. "Convergencies Between Conflicting Theoretical Perspectives in National Development." In *Sociological Theory and Research,* edited by Herbert Blalock. New York: Free Press.

Prasad, R. R. 2002. "Participation and Empowerment: Rhetorics and Realities." *Kurukshetra* (New Delhi) 50, no. 7.

"Princess Sarvath Highlights Islam's Role in Women's Emancipation." 1998. *Jordan Times,* Oct. 29–30, 1998, 5.

Quinn, Naomi. 1977. "Anthropological Studies on Women's Status." *Annual Review of Anthropology* (Palo Alto, Calif.) 6.

Rachidi, Ilhem. 2003. "After Struggle, New Equality for Moroccan Women." *Christian Science Monitor,* Oct. 24.

Ranchod-Nïlsson, Sita, and Mary Ann Tétreault, eds. 2000. *Women, States, and Nationalism: At Home in the Nation?* Boulder: Lynne Rienner Publishers.

Randall, Vicky. 1987. *Women and Politics: An International Perspective.* 2nd ed. Chicago: Chicago Univ. Press.

Rathgeber, E. 1990. "WID, WAD, GAD: Trends in Research and Practice." *Journal of Developing Areas* 24: 489–502.

Ray, Raka. 1999. *Fields of Protest: Women's Movements in India.* Minneapolis: Univ. of Minnesota Press.

Reardon, Betty. 1985. *Sexism and the War System.* New York: Teachers College Press, Columbia Univ.

République Tunisienne. 1992. *Recueil des textes relatifs à l'organisation politique et aux libertés publiques.* 2nd ed. Tunis: Imprimerie Officielle de la République Tunisienne.

———. 1999. *La Code du Statut Personnelle.* 1966. Reprint. Tunis: Imprimerie Officielle de la République Tunisienne.

Rittner, Carol, and John K. Roth, eds. 1993. *Different Voices.* New York: Paragon.

Royaum du Maroc. 1995a. *D.P.C.I. au service de l'investisseur.* Rabat, Morocco: Ministry of Commerce, Industry, and Crafts.

———. 1995b. *1995 Guide de l'investisseur.* Fez, Morocco: Delegation du Commerce et de l'Industrie.

———. 1997. *Etude portant sur l'élaboration de la strategie d'action de la promotion de la femme au Maroc.* Rabat, Morocco: Ministry of Employment and Social Affairs.

Rubenberg, Cheryl. 2001. *Palestinian Women: Patriarchy and Resistance in the West Bank.* Boulder: Lynne Rienner Publishers.

Rubin, Barnett. 1995. *The Fragmentation of Afghanistan.* New Haven: Yale Univ. Press.

Ruddick, Sara. 1980. "Maternal Thinking." *Feminist Studies* 6 (Summer): 342–67.

Ruether, Rosemary Radford. 1983. "Feminism and Peace." *Christian Century* 100, no. 25 (Aug.): 771–76.

Rumberger, R. W. 1983. "Dropping Out of High School: The Influence of Race, Sex and Family Background." *American Educational Research Journal* 20, no. 2: 199–220.

———. 1987. "High School Dropouts: A Review of Issues and Evidence." *Review of Educational Research* 57, no. 2: 101–22.

el-Saadawi, Nawal. 1982. *The Hidden Face of Eve: Women in the Arab World.* Translated by Sharif Hetata. Boston: Beacon Press.

———. 1997. *The Nawal el-Saadawi Reader.* London and New York: Zed Books.

SAATHI. 1997. *A Situational Analysis of Violence Against Women and Girls in Nepal.* Kathmandu: SAATHI.

Sabbagh, Suha, ed. 1998. *Palestinian Women of Gaza and the West Bank.* Bloomington: Indiana Univ. Press.

Safa, Helen. 1983. "Women, Production, and Reproduction in Industrial Capitalism: A Comparison of Brazilian and U.S. Factory Workers." In *Women, Men and the International Division of Labor,* edited by June Nash and Maria Fernandez-Kelly. Albany: State Univ. of New York Press.

———. 1988. *The Myth of the Male Breadwinner: Women and Industrialization in the Caribbean.* Boulder: Westview Press.

Saffioti, Heleith. 1978. *Women in Class Society.* New York: Monthly Review Press.

Salaff, Janet. 1995. *Working Daughters of Hong Kong: Filial Piety or Power in the Family?* New York: Columbia Univ. Press.

Sandler, Lauren. 2003. "Veiled and Worried in Baghdad." *New York Times,* Sept. 16.

Sangroula, Geeta. 2001. "Law and Existing Reality of Nepalese Women." In *Gender and Democracy in Nepal,* edited by L. K. Manandhar and K. B. Bhattachan. Kathmandu, Nepal: Central Department of Home Science, Tribhuvan Univ.

Saoud, Dalal. 2002. "Palestinian Women: Resistance Is Priority." United Press International, Sept. 25.

Scheindlin, Dahlia. 1998. "Palestinian Women's Model Parliament." *Women's International Net (WIN) Magazine* 11 (July). Reprinted in *Middle East Review of International Affairs Journal* 2, no. 3 (Sept. 1998).

Schiff, Ze'ev, and Ehud Ya'ari. 1990. *Intifada: The Palestinian Uprising—Israel's Third Front.* Translated by Ina Friedman. 1989. Reprint. New York: Simon and Schuster.

"Self-Immolations on the Rise in Afghanistan." 2002. *Los Angeles Times,* Nov. 18. Posted on RAWA Web site http://www.rawa.fancymarketing.net/immolation.htm.

Sharabi, Hisham. 1975. *Muqaddamat li-dirast 'al mujtama' al-'Arabi* [An introduction to the study of Arab society]. Jerusalem: Manshurat Salahad Din.

———. 1988. *Neopatriarchy: A Theory of Distorted Change in Arab Society.* Oxford: Oxford Univ. Press.

———. 1990. *Theory, Politics and the Arab World: Critical Responses.* London and New York: Routledge.

Sharoni, Simona. 1995. *Gender and the Israeli-Palestinian Conflict: The Politics of Women's Resistance.* Syracuse: Syracuse Univ. Press.

Shayne, Julie D. 2004. *The Revolution Question: Feminisms in El Salvador, Chile, and Cuba.* New Brunswick: Rutgers Univ. Press.

SIS [State Institute of Statistics]. 1994. *Statistical Indicators, 1923–1992.* Ankara: SIS Press.

Skalli, Loubna H. 1999. "Women's Press in a Transitional Society, Morocco: Strategies for the Counter-production of Knowledge." Paper presented at the Second Biennial Feminism(s) and Rhetoric(s) Conference, "Challenging Rhetoric(s): Cross-disciplinary Sites of Feminist Discourse." Minneapolis, Univ. of Minnesota, Oct. 7–9.

———. 2000. *Articulating the Local and the Global: A Case Study in Moroccan Women's Magazines.* Ph.D. diss., Pennsylvania State Univ.

Slyomovics, Susan. 2005. "Morocco's Justice and Reconciliation Commission." *Middle East Report Online* (Apr. 4). http://www.merip.org/mero/mero.html.

Smits, Jeroen, and Ayse Gündüz-Hosgör. 2003. "Linguistic Capital: Language as a Socio-economic Resource among Kurdish and Arabic Women in Turkey." *Ethnic and Racial Studies* 26.

Sperberg, E. D., and S. D. Stabb. 1998. "Depression in Women as Related to Anger and Mutuality in Relationships." *Psychology of Women Quarterly* 22: 223–38.

Sreberny-Mohammadi, A., and Ali Mohammadi. 1994. *Small Media, Big Revolution: Communication, Culture and the Iranian Revolution.* Minneapolis: Univ. of Minnesota Press.

Standing, Guy. 1989. "Global Feminization Through Flexible Labor." *World Development* 17, no. 7: 1077–95.

Stark, E., and A. Flitcraft. 1991. "Spouse Abuse." In *Violence in America: A Public Health Approach,* edited by M. Rosenberg and M. Fenley. New York: Oxford Univ. Press.

Stein, Dorothy. 2003. "The Lives of Palestinian Women." *Off Our Backs* (Washington, D.C.) (Mar.-Apr.): 13–15.

Stephan, Wafa. 1984. "Women and War in Lebanon." *Al-Raïda* (Beirut Univ. College), no. 30.

Stiehem, Judith Hicks. 1989. *Arms and the Enlisted Woman.* Philadelphia: Temple Univ. Press.

Stites, Richard. 1978. *The Women's Liberation Movement in Russia: Feminism, Nihilism, and Bolshevism, 1860–1930.* Princeton: Princeton Univ. Press.

Strange, Carolyn. 1990. "Mothers on the March: Maternalism in Women's Protest for Peace in North America and Western Europe, 1900–1985." In *Women and Social Protest,* edited by Guida West and Rhoda Blumberg, 209–24. New York: Oxford Univ. Press.

Subrahmanyam, K. S. 2002. "Empowerment of Women and Marginalized Groups in Panchayats." *Kurukshetra* (New Delhi) 50, no. 7.

Susskind, Yael. 2004. "One Year Later: Women's Human Rights in 'Liberated' Iraq." *MADRE* (international women's human rights organization), articles (Spring). http://www .madre.org/articles/me/womensrights/html.

Talhami, Ghada. 1990. "Women under Occupation: The Great Transformation." In *Images and Reality: Palestinian Women under Occupation and in the Diaspora,* edited by Suha Sabbagh and Ghada Talhami. Washington, D.C.: Institute for Arab Women's Studies.

Tan, M. 1981. "Atatürk' çü Düsünüs ve Karma Egitim." In *Proceedings of the International Conference on Atatürk.* Paper no. 61, vol. 3. Bogaziçi Univ., Nov. 9–13, Bebek. Istanbul: Bogaziçi Üniversitesi Matbaasi.

Tanweer, M. Halim. 2000. *Tarikh wa ruznama-nigari: Afghanistan* [History and Journalism: Afghanistan]. Peshawar, Pakistan: Nasharat-i-Islami-i-Sabur.

Taplin, R. 1989. *Economic Development and the Role of Women.* Avebury, England: Aldershot.

Tapper, Richard. 2002. *The New Iranian Cinema: Politics, Representation and Identity.* London: I. B. Taurus.

TDHS. 1999. *Demographic and Health Survey, 1998, Turkey.* Ankara: Hacettepe Univ. Institute of Population Studies and MEASURE DHS+ Macro International Inc. Press.

Tickner, J. Ann. 1992. *Gender in International Relations: Feminist Perspectives on Achieving Global Security.* New York: Columbia Univ. Press.

Tucker, Judith. 1993. *Arab Women: Old Boundaries, New Frontiers.* Bloomington: Indiana Univ. Press.

———. 1999. "Women in the Middle East and North Africa: The Nineteenth and Twentieth Centuries." In *Women in the Middle East and North Africa,* edited by Guity Nashat and Judith E. Tucker. Bloomington: Indiana Univ. Press.

Tunaligil, B. G. 1980. "Tarimsal Mekanizasyonda Isgücü Yönünde Kadin." In *Uluslararasi Tarimsal Mekanizasyon ve Enerji Sempozyumu.* Ankara: Ankara Üniversitesi Basimevi.

"Turban Dosyasi." 2003. *Milliyet,* May 27–29.

Türkiye Ekonomik ve Toplumsal Tarih Vakfi. 1996. *Sivil toplum kuruluslari rehberi* [Civil society guide]. Istanbul: Turkey Economic and Social Foundation.

Uday, D. 1991. "Determinants of Educational Performance in India: Role of Home and Family." *International Review of Education* 37, no. 2: 245–65.

UNESCO. 2004. *Iraq: Education in Transition—Needs and Challenges.* Paris: UNESCO.

UNICEF. 2006. "At a Glance: Afghanistan Statistics." http://www.unicef.org/infobycountry/afghanistan_statistics.html.

UNIFEM. 2004. *Afghanistan: Women in the News.* No. 35 (July 10–15). Kabul, Afghanistan: UNIFEM.

———. 2005a. "Women, War, Peace: Gender Profile—Afghanistan." http://www.womenwarpeace.org/afghanistan/afghanistan.htm.

———. 2005b. "Women, War, Peace: Gender Profile—Iraq." http://www.womenwarpeace.org/iraq/iraq.htm.

———. 2005c. "Women, War, Peace: Gender Profile—Occupied Palestinian Territory." http://www.womenwarpeace.org/opt/opt.htm.

United Nations. 1996. *The Beijing Declaration and Platform for Action.* New York: United Nations.

———. 2002. *Women, Peace and Security: Study Submitted by the Secretary-General Pursuant to Security Council Resolution 1325 (2000).* New York: United Nations.

"UN/World Bank Present Iraq Reconstruction Needs to Core Group." 2003. *DevNews Media Center* (World Bank Group, online).

van Ommeren, M., J. deJong, B. Sharma, I. Komproe, S. Thapa, R. Makaju, and E. Cardena. 2001. "Psychiatric Disorders among Tortured Bhutanese Refugees." *Archives of General Psychiatry* 58, no. 5: 475–82.

van Ommeren, M., B. Sharma, S. Thapa, R. Makaju, D. Prasain, R. Bhattarai, and J. de Jong. 1999. "Preparing Instruments for Transcultural Research: Use of the Translation Monitoring Form with Nepali-Speaking Bhutanese Refugees." *Transcultural Psychiatry* 36: 285–301.

Verger, Marrianne. 1991. *On Silver Wings.* New York: Ballantine.

Veri Arastirma, A. S. 2000. *Kadinin sosyal hayata katilimi ve siyasal mobilizasyonu* [Women's participation in political life and their mobilization]. No. 17. Ankara: Kadinin Sosyal Hayatini Arastirma ve Inceleme Dernegi Yayinlari.

Vickers, Jeanne. 1993. *Women and War.* London: Zed Books.

Walker, Keith. 1985. *A Piece of My Heart.* New York: Ballantine.

Ward, Katherine B. 1984. *Women in the World System: Its Impact on Status and Fertility.* New York: Praeger.

Weizman, S., and R. Freidman. 1994. "Dropping Out of School: Conceptual Approach for Literature Review." *Magamot* (Jerusalem) 37, no. 2: 174–89; in Hebrew.

Wing, Adrien Katherine. 1994. "Palestinian Women: Their Future Legal Rights." *Arab Studies Quarterly* 16, no. 1 (Winter).

Wolf, Diane. 1992. *Factory Daughters: Gender, Household Dynamics, and Rural Industrialization in Java*. Berkeley and Los Angeles: Univ. of California Press.

World Bank. 1996. *The World Bank's Participation Sourcebook, 1996*. Washington, D.C.: World Bank.

World Health Organization. 1997. *Composite International Diagnostic Interview (Core Version 2.1)*. Geneva: World Health Organization.

Yadav, S. S. 2005. "Institutional Finance to Small-Scale Industries." *Kurukshetra* (New Delhi) 53, no. 6: 22.

Yishai, Yael. 1997. *Between the Flag and the Banner*. Albany: State Univ. of New York Press.

Younes, Mohamed. 1998. "Al-mashru al-muqtarah laisa fi-hi ghishun wa yashtarat dhawabit li man'at tadlis." *Al-Ahram*, Nov. 27.

Young, Elise G. 1992. *Keepers of History*. New York: Teachers College Press, Columbia Univ.

"Young, Gifted, Dressed in Black." 2001. *Irish Times*, Mar. 17.

Youssouf, Ahmed Hassen. 1999. "Ta'liq . . . 'ala 'uqubat jarima al-ightisab." *Al-Jamhoouriya*, Feb. 5.

Ziai, Fati. 1997. "Personal Status Codes and Women's Rights in the Maghreb." In *Muslim Women and the Politics of Participation: Implementing the Beijing Platform*, edited by Mahnaz Afkhami and Erica Friedl, 72–82. Syracuse: Syracuse Univ. Press.

Zirari, Najia, and Naima Ouakrim. 1998. "Les associations feminines au Maroc." In *Action associatif au Maroc*, 1:51–62. Rabat: El-Maarif el-Jadida (Publication of Espace Associatif).

Index

Page number in italics denotes either a table or a map.

women's rights: in Afghanistan, 332; Decree
No. 7 on, 62, 63, 66, 69; "handed down" in
Tunisia, 97–98; in Iraq, 334, 335; Islam and,
95; in Jordan, 50; in the Middle East, North
Africa and South Asia, 360–61, 363–64;
in Morocco, 171–72; Palestine's Basic
Law and, 29–31; peace and, 315, 315n. 6;
in postconflict situations, 348; Tunisia's
women's organizations on, 111; in Turkey,
95, 184–85, 201
women's role: in Afghanistan, 70; changes with
aging, 175–76, 175n. 8; as daughters, 173,
176; domestic, 187; factory labor and, 173,
179, 179n. 10; in the household, 161; in
Islamic rituals, 176–77, 176n. 9; Islamist
movement on, 42, 77; Islamist parties on,
84; in Jordan, 49–50, 51; as married women,
174, 175; in Morocco, 170, 175; in peace
movements, 312–16, 323, 325–26, 344–46;
in political parties, 75; in reconstruction,
347, 349–50, 349–50; in reproduction, 161,
178; in Turkey, 75, 187; in war, 313–14,
314n. 5, 321. *See also* gender roles
Women's Studies Center (WSC), 35
Women's Studies Committee (Bisan Center),
27–28

Women Strike for Peace, 345
work. *See* domestic work; employment
workforce. *See* labor force
working conditions, 165–69, 167n. 6, 222–24
World Bank, 140, 162–63, 164
World Conference on Human Rights (UN,
1993), 107
World Health Organization, 243, 257
World Health Report (WHO, 1998), 257
*World's Women, 1995: Trends and Statistics,
The,* 3
World Trade Center attacks, 313

Yazicioglu, Muhsin, 83
Yessayan, Norma, 225
Yom Kippur War (1973), 316
Yugoslavia, 343

Za'im, 295
Zayyaden, Fowzia, 224
Zeid, Fahrelnissa, 224
zina crimes, 331
Zionist settlements, 20
Zulfacar, Maliha, 349